This Side of Philosophy

SUNY SERIES
LITERATURE...IN THEORY

SERIES EDITORS

David E. Johnson, *Comparative Literature, University at Buffalo*
Scott Michaelsen, *English, Michigan State University*

SERIES ADVISORY BOARD

Nahum Dimitri Chandler, *African American Studies, University of California, Irvine*
Rebecca Comay, *Philosophy and Comparative Literature, University of Toronto*
Marc Crépon, *Philosophy, École Normale Supérieure, Paris*
Jonathan Culler, *Comparative Literature, Cornell University*
Johanna Drucker, *Design Media Arts and Information Studies, University of California, Los Angeles*
Christopher Fynsk, *Modern Thought, Aberdeen University*
Rodolphe Gasché, *Comparative Literature, University at Buffalo*
Martin Hägglund, *Comparative Literature, Yale University*
Carol Jacobs, *German and Comparative Literature, Yale University*
Peggy Kamuf, *French and Comparative Literature, University of Southern California*
David Marriott, *History of Consciousness, University of California, Santa Cruz*
Steven Miller, *English, University at Buffalo*
Alberto Moreiras, *Hispanic Studies, Texas A&M University*
Patrick O'Donnell, *English, Michigan State University*
Pablo Oyarzun, *Teoría del Arte, Universidad de Chile*
Scott Cutler Shershow, *English, University of California, Davis*
Henry Sussman, *German and Comparative Literature, Yale University*
Samuel Weber, *Comparative Literature, Northwestern University*
Ewa Ziarek, *Comparative Literature, University at Buffalo*

This Side of Philosophy

Literature and Thinking in Twentieth-Century Spanish Letters

Stephen Gingerich

Published by State University of New York Press, Albany

© 2023 State University of New York

All rights reserved

Printed in the United States of America

No part of this book may be used or reproduced in any manner whatsoever without written permission. No part of this book may be stored in a retrieval system or transmitted in any form or by any means including electronic, electrostatic, magnetic tape, mechanical, photocopying, recording, or otherwise without the prior permission in writing of the publisher.

For information, contact State University of New York Press, Albany, NY
www.sunypress.edu

Library of Congress Cataloging-in-Publication Data

Name: Gingerich, Stephen, author.
Title: This side of philosophy : literature and thinking in twentieth-century Spanish letters / Stephen Gingerich.
Description: Albany : State University of New York Press, [2023] | Series: SUNY series, literature . . . in theory | Includes bibliographical references and index.
Identifiers: LCCN 2022026188 | ISBN 9781438492216 (hardcover : alk. paper) | ISBN 9781438492223 (ebook) | ISBN 9781438492209 (pbk. : alk. paper)
Subjects: LCSH: Unamuno, Miguel de, 1864–1936—Philosophy. | Ortega y Gasset, José, 1883–1955—Philosophy. | Machado, Antonio, 1875–1939—Philosophy. | Zambrano, María—Philosophy. | Philosophy in literature. | Literature—Philosophy. | Spain—Intellectual life—20th century. | LCGFT: Literary criticism.
Classification: LCC PQ6639.N3 Z676 2023 | DDC 860.9/006—dc23/eng/20220830
LC record available at https://lccn.loc.gov/2022026188

10 9 8 7 6 5 4 3 2 1

For

Elizabeth Roche, who has been with me every step of the way

and

Bruce Kurland (1938–2013), who was not able to be

Contents

Preface: Life (before) Philosophy — ix

Acknowledgments — xvii

Chapter 1 Closer Than You Think: Spain and Philosophy — 1

Chapter 2 Relating Philosophy and Literature: Greeks and Romantics, *Dichten-Denken*, and *le Poématique* — 53

Chapter 3 Unamuno's Twins: Feeling Philosophy and Philosophical Aesthesis — 91

Chapter 4 Josué Ortiga y Gazette and Reason's Living Narrative — 137

Chapter 5 Antonio Machado, Writing Ephemeral Passages — 167

Chapter 6 "Inconstant Clarity": The Antagonism of Philosophy and Poetry in María Zambrano — 215

Epilogue: Philosophy after Life — 257

Notes — 267

Bibliography — 313

Index — 337

Preface

Life (before) Philosophy

This is a preface to a book about three enthusiastic writers of prefaces and one who, it seems, undertook to compose them only for new editions of work she had published long before. For his part, Miguel de Unamuno was capable of appending many to his novels through the years, and in them he or a proxy welcomed, threatened, explained, and even "made believe." José Ortega y Gasset often attached "Advertencias" (Warnings) at the beginning of his books, letting the reader know the ways in which they were not really books but, rather, relatively incomplete and nevertheless coherent collections of occasional texts and lectures. Antonio Machado's prologues challenge his readers to discern the philosophical ambitions in poems that often dwell on his own personal experiences and surroundings. María Zambrano's prologues provide no more direct, programmatic guidelines to interpretation than her books offer, highlighting the extent to which they manifest a writing life that has moved on and will keep on the move. No such daring in this modest work of scholarship. Because the first two chapters serve, in different ways, introductory functions, I will be brief and conventional.

This Side of Philosophy weaves together three general themes whose urgency and interconnectedness I try to establish at the beginning of chapter 1. First, it treats the relationship of literature and philosophy by examining in detail a series of Spanish writers whose work is commonly interpreted as a particular, more or less unique configuration of this relation. In short, it is said that Spain's best philosophy is literary, its canon—from *Don Quixote* to the series of writers discussed in this book—joining philosophical thought with literature in a variety of ways. A narrative account of the emergence of this trend from debates in the nineteenth century, occupies much of chapter

1, where I begin to discuss my main protagonists: the novelist Unamuno, who also wrote essays and what appear to be philosophical treatises; the poet Machado, who created a series of fictional "poet-philosophers," complete with biographies, poems, and philosophical works represented by titles and extensive summaries; two very literary philosophers, Ortega y Gasset and Zambrano, with unique styles of writing, including autobiographical aspects and, in Ortega's case, fictional voices. As a prolegomenon to my more extensive assessments of the relation of literature and philosophy in their oeuvres, chapter 2 offers an overview of the contemporary academic field that has formed around this relation, along with detailed interpretations of four key moments: ancient Greece, Romanticism, Heidegger, and Derrida. By devoting independent discussions to these touchstones in the relation between literature and philosophy, I intend to provide a compelling assessment of the relevance of Unamuno, Ortega, Machado, and Zambrano beyond the borders of Iberian studies and the Hispanic world.

Second, I discuss the polemic about the exclusion of Spain from the philosophical canon and the consequent impression that Spanish thought does not measure up to philosophical standards. Such a problem occupies the writers and scholars I discuss in chapter 1, and in chapter 2 I confirm the marginal position of Spain even in the field that concentrates on the relation between philosophy and literature. One response—legible both in the primary authors I examine and in the scholars who study them—has been to argue that Hispanic traditions of thought and writing have always been more closely tied to individual lives and cultures than to the epistemic and ontological discourses that orient mainstream philosophy. That is, it is said that Spanish philosophy's literary character has rendered it *Lebensphilosophie*, before and after the heyday of that term in late nineteenth century Germany. The first two chapters document and discuss this exclusion and the particular impact it had in a major current of Spanish writing, the emergence of a tradition in which the relation between literature and philosophy took a central role as the formulation of a "feeling philosophy and philosophical aesthesis" (Unamuno), a fundamentally aesthetic philosophy (Ortega), a "poetic thinking" (Machado), and a "poetic reason" (Zambrano).

Third, I examine the conventional characterization of this sequence of writers, a portrayal that is often extended to Spain or a Spanish tradition in general. By reference to handbooks of Spanish philosophy and works of scholarship on the preeminent figures, I document the conviction that Spanish "thinkers" reconfigure the traditional relation of literature and philosophy, providing access to something more primordial or more fundamental than what philosophy alone aims at and achieves. "This side" of philosophical knowledge or activity, previous to or behind scientific truth, rational argumentation, and things themselves, we can experience the sources of life, a locus of vitality associated with religion, love of others, appreciation for our mortal existence, and creativity. Furthermore, this "typically Spanish" mode of thinking depends on exposition in literary genres and poetic language, where engagement with idiom and emotion combine with communicative and argumentative functions of language to achieve ends that still might deserve to be called *philosophical*. It has had no shortage of recognition at home and abroad, in the original language and in translation, but often with a lingering doubt about its philosophical bona fides.

As my discussions show, I am not alone in hoping for something like redemption for the Hispanic perspective, and I would also agree with the many colleagues who envision disciplinary revitalizations coming via a reassessment of the relation between philosophy and literature, together with an expansion of the traditional notions of "Hispanic" to embrace formerly excluded subjects, peoples, and heritages. This book ventures a step in that direction by providing new interpretations of a series of texts and writers well known in the Hispanic world but somewhat unfamiliar outside of it, especially Machado's prose and most of Zambrano's work, of which relatively little has been translated into English. No other study has given these four writers equal weight in an assessment of their inquiries into the potentialities of a literary philosophy or a genuinely philosophical literature. All four figures are treated as part of a history of ideas in José Luis Abellán's and Manuel Garrido's encyclopedic volumes, which I discuss in chapter 1. Abellán, Pedro Cerezo Galán, and Antonio Sánchez Barbudo have all produced separate book-length studies of three or four of these figures, including extensive discussions of the connection between the main figure and the others. A handful of prominent scholars have contributed articles and books to understand several of them together and in isolation; Roberta Johnson, Francisco Larubia-Prados, Janet Pérez, and Ana Bundgård have especially stood out for work that establishes coherence between them. I have learned much from these scholars and have tried to acknowledge how they point in the direction of my own contribution to these individual subfields and the relation of literature and philosophy.

It may be foolhardy to address a book to readers from such diverse spheres of study, thought, and life experience. Throughout this discussion I refer to indications that some philosophers mistrust literary scholars and writers, who not only have some antagonism between them, but sometimes look upon the philosophers with suspicion, if not scorn. Novelists and poets, readers and scholars of Unamuno and Machado might take an interest in my observations and interpretations of novels, poems, and statements on poetics, even as they follow the discussions of philosophical themes and propositions, polemics and inquiries. If these discussions don't appeal to philosophers, Ortega and Zambrano's claims on that discipline might hold their attention. Given a persistent tension within philosophical institutions between Hispanist and generalist philosophy (discussed in chapter 2), I might hope to interest some philosophers with discussions of Plato, Schlegel, Hegel, Heidegger, Derrida, and others, with a commitment to reading primary texts and engaging traditions of interpretation of classics of "philosophical Hispanism." That philosophers and literati might lose interest as the focus of my discussions shifts from one topic or mode of discourse to the other is a risk I will have to run. In a book that takes as its primary topic the relation between philosophy and literature, that risk is both a theme and a reality.

Chapter 1 provides initial discussions of Unamuno, Ortega, Machado, and Zambrano. They are not summaries of later chapters. Rather, they set out to acknowledge the canonical and common interpretations of the relationship between literature and philosophy in the oeuvres. By close attention to texts, they also begin the process of loosening the grip of that representation, which, to my mind, often hypostatizes the relation of literature and philosophy, simplifying it, but, more importantly, reducing its potential to evoke the vital element that so interested these writers. Chapter 2's account of the relation of literature and philosophy demonstrates the extent to which Greek thinkers connect philosophy to the living, feeling human. Hispanists may also be surprised to find discussion of "poetic reason" and "poetic thinking" in the secondary literature on Romanticism and Heidegger. Finally, Derrida's notions of "some poem" (du poème) and "the poematic" will cast light on Machado's reflections on the temporal mechanisms of verse and the precarious poeticity of all thoughtful discourse. Chapter 3 interprets an episode in Unamuno's writing life that seems to set a unique configuration, the time of gestation and composition of *Niebla* (*Mist*) and *Del sentimiento trágico de la vida* (*On the Tragic Sense of Life*). This path leads from some of his statements on writing as an expression of Unamuno's singular existence to the lengths he goes to in order to imbue both novel and philosophical treatise with what he considers the essential characteristics of life.

Chapter 4 focusses on the most widely celebrated Spanish philosopher, the one most unambiguously accepted into the international philosophical community. In an interpretation spanning a wide range of Ortega y Gasset's work, I follow him in seeking a consistent and comprehensive representation of his signature doctrine. I belong to a readership that is skeptical of Ortega's revolutionary claims to have definitively overcome a philosophical tradition that neglects the individual life of the "philosophizing philosopher." Nonetheless, the followers of Ortega seem to me to have failed to provide an adequate account of the mechanisms by which Ortega persuades readers of his own status, of what a person would have to accept in order to subscribe to his doctrine of ratiovitalism. Chapter 5 follows through Antonio Machado's oeuvre the claim to produce something like a living philosophical thought using literary resources. While announced in some ways in earlier poems and prefaces to his best known work—the volumes of poetry *Soledades* and *Campos de Castilla* (*Fields of Castile*)—this project mainly concerns "Cancioneros apócrifos" (Apocryphal songbooks) in which he created the characters Abel Martín and Juan de Mairena, and the series of articles he published as *Juan de Mairena*. In chapter 6, I approach María Zambrano's work by following the motif of the relation between philosophy and literature from the 1930s to some of her final writings in the late 1980s. As in my chapters on Unamuno and Ortega, I begin with some prefatory observations about reading Zambrano, following her more or less explicit prescriptions for making sense of her writing, and even for letting precise meaning escape or lie dormant. I trace the relation in more metaphysical texts like *Filosofía y poesía* and *El hombre y lo divino* (Man and the divine), before considering its appearance in the form of reflections on poetry in general and in the person of her friend, the poet Emilio Prados.

A final word about the dialogue I attempt to create between these Spanish writers and the philosophical canon. I do not perform some of the most familiar gestures that connect literature and philosophy: comparing ideas of one and another or finding theories that serve as lenses to clarify some relevant issues. Instead, after chapter 2's panoramic view of the field, my interpretation shows the philosophical prestige of the notion of life and related figures of tension and movement, so that their appearance in Spanish letters does not seem idiosyncratic or lead us exclusively to more intuitive, perhaps more familiar, figures of an organic, chemical, or personal nature. The philosophical digressions in chapters 3–6, in addition to an important one in chapter 1, sometimes have this function: by seeing a problem in a canonical philosopher, we are perhaps more likely to give credence to an interpretation that finds it in the marginal, Spanish writer. These philosophical discussions also serve other functions, and, in general, highlight the heterogeneity in the relation between literature and philosophy. For example, in chapter 3, I show that, contrary to what Unamuno says, emotion, autobiography, and death have never been simply external to philosophy. In chapter 5, I elaborate on the theoretical implications and destabilizing effects of heteronymity, the displacement or erasure of the proper name. And in the chapter on Zambrano, I relate her mythopoetic narrative of poetry and philosophy to Nietzsche's and Rousseau's genealogies in order to hypothesize about her implicit methodological principles.

While the first two chapters gather together figures and motives into a coherent whole, chapters 3–6 place a greater emphasis on the uniqueness of each separate figure. I recognize the value of historical and sociological accounts of trends in intellectual history. Although my approach makes use of research with emphasis on concrete history—institutional histories, history of ideas, biographies, and public records—my approach focusses on the texts as sites of literature and philosophy's encounter, interaction, and transformation. Unamuno, Ortega, Machado, and Zambrano were concerned about philosophy and scholarship reducing the heterogeneity of real objects of experience. I share this concern at the same time that I try to work out both the ways in which it might be true and the ways in which they might overstate the case. In my interpretations I am sensitive to differences between these writers, between different phases of their work, and between distinct layers of meaning that might be found in the same works, even in the same words, elements that sometimes harmonize and sometimes clash. My readings also vary in degree of magnification and manner of approach, as they focus on expositions of ideas, narrative structures, poetic condensation and indirection, even on punctuation, pronunciation, the grammar behind phrases, and the spaces between words. While some of chapters 3–6 are devoted to making connections between the main authors and the philosophers discussed in chapter 2, I devote an epilogical chapter 7 to drawing some general conclusions about this series of thinkers and the three general themes mentioned above.

A final word on references to primary sources. I've made the effort to provide references to available English language versions of texts. Like other scholars in Iberian studies, I work primarily with Spanish originals; references to both versions, if possible, are indicated parenthetically. In the text, I cite in the original titles first, and provide an English translation afterwards in the first mention. If there is an English translation available, this is indicated by my using the punctuation for publications (italics or quotation marks), otherwise the translation of the title is mine. In cases of titles or phrases made up of cognates, I have omitted English translations in order to avoid insulting the intelligence of my readers. Subsequent references to books and articles only available in the original Spanish will be in Spanish, although I refer to translated works with the English title. I follow the same practice in cases when I work from French, German, Italian, Latin, or Greek, although I sometimes work directly from English translations and, in that case, cite only the translation throughout. If there is no translation available, the English versions are my own. I prefer to cite specific works instead of general titles like *Complete Works*, so that readers can get a sense of the sources as discursive units that can be easily consulted in their own rights.

One of the reasons prefaces inspire such circumspection is the fear that the guidance for the reading of the following pages will preclude the need to continue reading. As we will see, Unamuno's many prologues plant questions that might draw a reader back after reading the work proper, but that also anticipate the affront to discursive conventions that he produces by playing with the border between the fictional characters' actions and worlds, on one side, and our apparently real discussion of them, on the other. The passage from Machado's or Zambrano's prefaces to the texts they introduce is rarely a simple one, requiring similar efforts of interpretation to those demanded by the multifarious texts that follow. For all its philosophical and critical allegiances, this book should not be assumed to be essentially different, at least regarding its relationship to literary and philosophical work. Just as a prologue is not intended to replace the book, the interpretations in this book do not intend to render redundant the reading of the texts. Instead, consider them invitations to read and reread, to translate and retranslate, to confirm and to dispute points about literature and philosophy and a trend in Spanish letters.

Acknowledgments

This first book of mine has brought home to me the travail faced and overcome by all writers of books, even of those that I do not especially admire. You would not be reading this volume if not for the family, friends, students, and colleagues who helped and encouraged me over the years. The project grew out of an essay on María Zambrano that I wrote for a 2008 special issue of *CR: The New Centennial Review*, "Paying Attention to Rodolphe Gasché." In "Europe's Frenzy," I introduced a reading of Zambrano's notions of Europe and Spain with brief discussions of Unamuno and Ortega. That was the beginning of this book's more patient consideration of Spanish intellectuals' claims to possess a predilection for literary philosophy and philosophical literature. I thank David Johnson for the invitation to contribute to that volume and Rodolphe Gasché for the model of thinking and writing that inspired it.

Over the next decade, I had the opportunity to share my work at conferences and symposia where I received valuable feedback: the Mid-America Conference on Hispanic Literature; the Kentucky Foreign Language Conference; the American Literary Translators Association; and the Mediterranean Studies Association Conference. I thank the students and faculty of the Comparative Literature Department at the University at Buffalo for the invitation to speak on Unamuno in the "Just Theory" speaker series. Some of the ideas in chapter 4 reiterate elements of my contribution to "Literature and the Secret of the World," a symposium organized by David Johnson at the University at Buffalo. Like "Europe's Frenzy," "Ortega: Secrecy and the World" was published in *CR* and contains a few ideas and observations that reappear in this book's chapters on Zambrano and Ortega. The interpretations in this book form part of a larger analysis and are certainly better for what I learned by presenting and publishing the earlier work.

I am grateful to those friends who read parts of my manuscript and provided helpful comments, and also to those with whom I was able to discuss my vision of the whole project. Others provided me, in one way or another, with the right words or deeds at the right time. For the time they spent reading and giving feedback, I thank my wife, Elizabeth Roche; my parents, David and Judy Gingerich; Cheryl Lester, Brian Cope, Ryan Pinchot, Tama Engelking, and David Johnson. I am grateful to Rebecca Colesworthy for her patience and encouragement and to SUNY Press's anonymous readers for their roles in refining my ideas and shaping the manuscript into this version. While my way of approaching research and writing owes very much to people and experiences at the University at Buffalo, I could not have made a life as a teacher and scholar of Hispanic Studies without the guidance and examples of Spanish faculty from the University of Kansas: Andrew Debicki, Michael Doudoroff, Mary Jane Kelley, Jonathan Mayhew, Robert Spires, Vicky Unruh, and George Woodyard. From Bob, among so many other things, I learned the value of having a secret office (referred to by a friend and colleague at Cleveland State as my *baticueva*), an idea my daughters especially relish. I am grateful to my fellow Gingeroches—Elizabeth, Helen, Lillian, and Olive—for having had the wisdom to understand, by analogy with their own creations, when I was busy or preoccupied with this project. I do hope the end product earns not only appreciation for years of work and reflection but some admiration, too. I am grateful for many (but not enough) happy hours discussing with Bruce Kurland the challenge of making things that are both ambitious and personal, informed and inspired. I regret not getting a chance to show him—whether to celebrate or lament it—that I do have one quality he considered a necessary but not sufficient condition of great work: obsessiveness.

Chapter 1

Closer Than You Think

Spain and Philosophy

"Spanish Thought," Living on the Margins of Philosophy

At the outset of his 1995 history of Spanish philosophy, the French Hispanist Alain Guy quotes his countryman Victor Delbos's low opinion of thinking south of the Pyrenees, expressed in the early decades of the twentieth century: "If we want to get to know philosophy in its entirety, it is necessary to possess every single language, with the exception of Spanish."[1] Though unmatched in his severity, Delbos was not alone in considering the Hispanic world devoid of interest for the historian of philosophy and unpromising for contemporary and future thinking. Ivo Hollhüber quotes a fellow German scholar who claims that Spanish philosophy is "insignificant" (ohne Bedeutung).[2] Like Guy, Hollhüber expresses a hope that a collection of profiles of Spanish thinkers might remedy the low esteem in which colleagues in the mainstream of the discipline hold the Hispanic tradition, taking a broad view to include "thinkers" who might be considered "literary."[3] Guy refers to Spanish thinkers who agree with Delbos, notably the novelist, critic, and professor Juan Valera, whose 1873 "De la filosofía española" (On Spanish philosophy) noted the clear superiority of German and French philosophy.[4] But contemporary Spanish scholars have also expressed doubts about Spain's philosophical relevance. Toward the end of a career that included books on José Ortega y Gasset and the editorship of *Revista de Occidente*—Ortega's vehicle for integrating Spanish thinking into the Western intellectual scene, and vice versa—Paulino Garagorri considers Spain's place in European philosophy "ambiguous."[5] "The mediocrity of Spanish philosophy during the modern age," he says, "is perfectly apparent [un hecho palmario]," although he grants exceptions for Miguel de Unamuno and Ortega on the basis of "literary quality."[6] The author of the prologue to *Pensadores españoles universales* (Universal Spanish thinkers)—a 2014 collection of profiles of ten Spanish thinkers, much in the style of Guy and Hollhüber—strikes a somewhat defensive tone in his first sentence: "Some poorly informed individuals insist that Spain, in contrast to Germany or France, has never produced great thinkers."[7] He goes on to repeat a conventional history, that in the eighteenth and nineteenth centuries Spain lacked much philosophical activity at all, until a period when "literary movements included thinkers among their members."[8]

What is behind this dismissal of Spanish philosophy and its prompting of defenders and promoters? Moreover, why the tendency to appeal to literature's involvement in Spanish thinking? In *Les Philosophes espagnoles d'hier et aujourd'hui* (Spanish philosophers of yesterday and today), Guy avoids explicit evaluation, asserting that "psychological, historical, and social factors" have marginalized Spanish thinkers. The list of characteristics he offers provides some hints about the causes of widespread neglect. Alongside a reminder of Spain's Catholic heritage, Guy reiterates the cliché about two Spains, an anarchist one, and an authoritarian one whose perpetual struggle occupies philosophers.[9] Following the Spanish scholar Joaquín Carreras y Artau, he calls the analysis of this conflict a "nationalist prejudice" and adds to it a "literary prejudice" that assumes that Spain's philosophy is typically subordinate to its literature.[10] In his 2010 *Other Voices: Readings in Spanish Philosophy*, John Welch complains of the "cultural lopsidedness" that mars histories of philosophy and agrees with A.R. Caponigri that social and political forces have conspired against the prestige of Spanish culture, in favor of the French and Germans.[11] An educated Westerner ought to know "Spanish speculative thought" in addition to "Spanish culture in all its forms and dimensions," says Caponigri, before calling for "reintegration of Spanish culture with the culture of the West."[12] Welch and Caponigri are not alone in thinking Spain has been marginalized in histories of European culture, in general, and particularly in accounts of science and thought. But while the inclusion of literary figures might appear a recourse to fill out a meager archive, it has also been argued that Spain's intense commitment to literature or poetry accounts for its exclusion from philosophy's canon and conventional history. In other words, the historical course of philosophy has led it away from Spain and away from literature. As philosophy learns to take literature seriously again, it should find a new appreciation for the Spanish tradition, where the close relationship between intuition, invention, and thought has maintained a central role.

Such, at least, is the hope of the advocates for "Spanish" "philosophy": that writers whose work has remained at the margins of philosophical debates should move beyond specialized discussions of their literary genres or historical milieux to participate in broader dialogues about thought and ideas. While this first chapter provides a portrait of the relationship between literature and philosophy in twentieth-century Spanish letters, subsequent chapters focus on the ways its major figures' works put that relationship into play in unique and powerful ways. The broadest purpose of *This Side of Philosophy* is to assess the contention that Spanish philosophy is by nature literary, and perhaps at its best when most literary, and for this very reason has been excluded from conventional histories of philosophy. In the works that deal with this topic, it is often taken for granted that literature and philosophy coexist in an unproblematic way, as two modes of discourse or forms of human intellectual production that can be more or less adopted and taken up at will. Another task of this book is to integrate this Spanish tendency into a debate that has occupied philosophers throughout Western history, beginning with the ancient Greeks. Because literature seems opposed to philosophy, Spanish writers and scholars came to believe that literature offers philosophical resources that *other* philosophers—especially those in the more prestigious national traditions—deliberately rejected. For this trend in Spanish philosophy, the integration of literary elements into philosophical inquiry and exposition, promised to confront philosophy with its shortcomings, and even managed to overcome them, resulting, to put it simply, in either an end of philosophy or a renovation, renewal, or rebirth of a genuine thinking, designated as a literary or poetical philosophy. In short, this episode in Spanish philosophy aims at a *this side*, by being more philosophical than philosophy, seeking to achieve a new interiority, a new or renewed concept of the human, or perhaps a space of encounter in which the human is constituted.

Before returning to the topic of scholarly discussions about Spanish philosophy, I would like to dwell for a moment on the relationship between the adjective and the noun. It is not my intention to deny the legitimacy of a national or cultural, let's say *communal*, designation or categorization of philosophy, but to call attention to the restrictions and conceptual tension that such a perspective creates. I limit my scope to four intellectual figures who wrote in the language conventionally called "Spanish" and who identified themselves with the country of their birth, even through their periods of study abroad and the experience of exile, which all four had in one way or another. Their shared interests and familiarity with each others' work produces a kind of unity, stronger than the one their common Spanish identity might impose. However, they all attribute some of the traits of their thought to a Spanish character at the same time that they clearly intend to intervene in that identity, to define, communicate, and even alter it.[13] While that might seem a worthy topic in itself, I have chosen to devote my research to the philosophical claims, and that means, in a sense, to the effort to accede to a mode of speech beyond what might be exhaustively determined by culture or ethnicity.

In the next chapter, we will look at the origins of philosophy and its effort at self-definition in relation to poetry and narrative, but for the moment I would like to recall Hegel's vision of philosophy's uniqueness, what he refers to as the "difference of philosophy" in his *Lectures on the History of Philosophy*.[14] Throughout his introductions to these lectures, Hegel grapples with the historical variety of his subject, a multiplicity determined by the span of millennia and the diverse people among whom philosophy has been practiced. For Hegel, not only do the cultural determinants fail to invalidate the universality of philosophy; in addition, the world spirit develops historically by producing varied manifestations of the possibilities inherent in the abstract truth that it possessed from its beginnings in ancient Greece. The concrete forms spirit takes are not only the individual thinkers and their works; those thinkers also all represent a people or nation. In his well-known organic metaphor, the people are a plant that shows its vigor through the "supreme blossom" of a philosophical system.[15] But the flower is not a mere ornament; rather, it is a sign of the fecundity that lives on in the subsequent manifestations of spirit, such as art, politics, or religion. Any particular philosophy can thus be accurately regarded as simultaneously individual, collective, and universal, but for Hegel a philosophy is only properly what it is from the point of view of universality. Therefore, Hegel's *Lectures* also attempt to establish the way in which the truth is absolute—that is, objective and subjective, unified and diverse, abstract and concrete—and he contrasts the strict concept of philosophy with religion, mythology, natural science, and popular (merely subjective) philosophies.

In spite of its universal character, using one particular communal determinant, such as "Spanish," as a principle of selection for a philosophical study would not be invalid, because all of human history has taken the form of distinct linguistic and political units. But to speak about what is philosophical about Spanish thought would require a perspective that reckons with the claim to universality. When Unamuno and Ortega seek to establish the philosophical credentials of the novel *Don Quixote*, they follow Hegel's conviction that philosophy is a people's greatest achievement, diverging from Hegel only by refusing to accept a spiritually subordinate place for a literary work, that is, by maintaining that literature can be as philosophical as philosophy. Along with Machado and Zambrano, they share a privileging of the literary, placing it at the level of philosophy or even in a place beyond. Although Hegel is often a relevant point of reference, they frequently respond to the anti-Hegelianism of Nietzsche, Kierkegaard, and Marx, and to other imposing thinkers of the tradition, among them Plato, Aristotle, Descartes, and Kant. Their dialogues with canonical philosophical figures manifest their intention to be "universally" relevant, not merely Spanish or Hispanic philosophers.

"Universality" is often used in unphilosophical ways, such as when *Don Quixote* is said to be "universal literature" because it is so widely translated, as if its international appeal could be empirically extended to the cosmos at large. At the same time, universality is sometimes assumed to be a simple impossibility, values and principles imposed hegemonically and tyrannically on cultural others by a particular interested party, such as Hegel or the West. The history of Europe certainly shows that the word and concept of an unrestricted applicability have been wielded as a weapon in the service of racism, imperialism, and sexism, to say the least. By studying the effort to define universality through the concept of Europe, Rodolphe Gasché's *Europe, or the Infinite Task* serves to elaborate the philosophical concept of universality in contrast to empirical and commonplace meanings. In Gasché's account, universality is inextricable from particular determinations—linguistic, historical, cultural—and therefore engaged in an endless process of realization. The "philosophical difference"—what Hegel describes as different from religion, science, and so on—becomes transformed into an ongoing process of extrication from individual and communal particularities, an approach to shared knowledge and practice whose terms require constant reexamination. Gasché proposes that we think of Europe not as a concept, idea, or even proper name, but rather as "a form of identity intrinsically tied to the relentless demand of having to be critically rethought, reinvented, and recast, time and again, at any given turn in history, in short, at every moment, every day."[16] He sets out from Edmund Husserl's insistence that "unlike all other cultural works, philosophy is not a movement of interest which is bound to the soil of the national tradition" (quoted 29). Instead, philosophy directs a process of transcendence of all ethnically defined customs, all "given identities" (27), in order to assume the freedom and responsibility of rational humanity. The phenomenological tradition interpreted by Gasché—Husserl, Martin Heidegger, Jan Patočka, and Jacques Derrida—continues to associate this process of transcendence with the name "Europe." Paradoxically, then, "Europe" is defined as the demand to break away from particular historical and cultural forms of human existence in order to make a claim to universality. Gasché points out—although he attributes the idea to the contemporary Japanese philosopher Tadashi Ogawa—that the "infinite task" of Europe is "nothing less than the very de-Europeanization of European life and thought" (33). Those who identify themselves as Europeans in this sense strive to step behind European identity in a quest for standards of truth that would not be limited to Europe. Paradoxically, such an extreme transcendence of cultural determinations constitutes both the particularity of this pursuit and the limitations that it seeks to overcome. Furthermore, Gasché points out that the stakes of "European" existence are those of philosophy itself, listing concepts that name possibilities of culture-neutral judgment, emerging in an idiom, at a historical moment in a cultural context: "universality, rationality, apodicticity, responsibility, and so forth" (6). In contrast to the philosophers for whom these notions serve as the guiding principles—holding that philosophy must be valid without exception, obey rational laws, be susceptible of complete certainty, and follow moral precepts—the post-Hegelian philosophers that Gasché analyzes provide different ways of opening to an inconceivable future, one that may or may not be Christian, or even European, but whose questions might go by different but still familiar names such as *democracy*, *justice*, *knowledge*, and *invention*. While they all make claims to address the status of rationality—most often conflating it with philosophy itself—Unamuno, Ortega, Machado, and Zambrano also show an interest in problems that were traditionally seen as subordinate to the more primordial problem of defining the nature of philosophical thought. Like Gasché's figures in *Europe*, the four Spanish thinkers treated here distinguish themselves by the opportunities they offer to think the relationship between idiomaticity and generality, between the philosophical demand for universality and the particularities of culture and language, as well as the idiosyncrasies of individual lives.

Gasché's discussion of universality and Europe—especially the observation that Europe seeks a "de-Europeanization" in its radical quest for universality—indicates a tension within the word "Europe" between a philosophical concept and an ethnological or ethnographic one. While some Europeans might embrace the vision of a society that welcomes the challenge of diversity and hospitality held out by the philosophical concept of *Europe*, others patently do not. As we will see when we delve deeper into the meanings of philosophy and literature in chapter 2, philosophy, too, has philosophical and nonphilosophical definitions. One of the most politically suspect projects in twentieth-century Spanish thought—a minor motif of this book—is the creation of a philosophical concept of Spain, that is, of a Spanishness that, like "European," might aspire to a universal validity and even to a (de-)Hispanization. It is worth noting, however, that within contemporary historiography of philosophy, Spain occupies a consistent place, if not a prominent one. Philosophical history has long accepted an international perspective, departing from Hegel's *History of Philosophy* to allow a looser, less hierarchical survey of its subject matter, including Indian and Chinese thinking, and other traditions that do not stem directly from the Greek origins. Some contemporary philosophical historiography concedes Spain a unique position, even within Europe. The 1998 *Routledge Encyclopedia of Philosophy* includes articles on specific philosophical movements in France, Germany, and Russia, but only offers portraits of one region (Scandinavia) and three national traditions (Italy, Poland, and Spain). The author of its article "Spain, Philosophy in," José Luis Abellán, reiterates the vision he has elaborated in his career as the foremost authority on Spanish philosophy, which we will discuss shortly.[17] The 2003 *Cambridge History of Philosophy, 1879–1945* likewise includes an article profiling "Spanish philosophy" within a section devoted to "The Diversity of Philosophy," which includes Latin America and Japan, but no other European nation.[18] While Manuel Garrido's brief article does expand on the notion of diversity even beyond the philosophical marginality of Spain by referring to Eugeni d'Ors as a "Catalan philosopher," his insistence on approaching the other three major philosophers as part of generations could be seen as a corrective gesture, emphasizing that the major figures were part of a larger national scene. Spanish philosophy is now included in the disciplinary panorama, but its presence continues to be marked by a history of disparagement in the perceived need for advocacy and rehabilitation. For example, in her 2012 review article of Garrido's recent *El legado filosófico español e hispanoamericano del siglo XX* (The Spanish and Hispanoamerican philosophical legacy in the twentieth century), Susana Nuccetelli praises the volume for its role in "fill[ing] an embarrassing gap in the philosophical literature," and she expands a disciplinary discussion about the "invisibility problem in Latin American philosophy" to include Spain.[19]

It might be argued, however, that the dismissals of Spanish philosophy with which I began this chapter are simply a thing of the past, and, indeed, my purpose is not to ask whether there *is* a Spanish philosophy, but to examine *how* a certain Spanish claim to philosophical significance traverses an inquiry into the relationship of philosophy to literature. This has not escaped the notice of historians of Spanish philosophy, but the most authoritative volumes suffer from the choice of a narrow methodological framework to justify a lack of critical distance and the author's somewhat ambivalent patriotism. In an effort to explain the title of his five-volume *Historia crítica del pensamiento español* (Critical history of Spanish thought), José Luis Abellán explains his choice to treat "thought" rather than "philosophy" on pragmatic grounds, the former word being "broader and more flexible" than the alternative.[20] A history of Spanish *philosophy*, he suggests, might be in the embarrassing position of acknowledging the broad consensus that Spain has a rather modest, if not barely existent, philosophical tradition. Surprisingly, though, Abellán adds that this history of Spanish thought does not differ essentially from literary histories, for which it can serve as a sort of supplement. For Abellán, the thought particular to Spain can be adequately understood by literary history, but this more inclusive account will add "precision" and "exactitude" to the previously available portraits of a Spanish "conception of the world" based on literature alone (15). According to the *Historia crítica*, literature has provided a worldview by virtue of being a linguistic manifestation of "national consciousness"; the absence of "the study of our philosophical tradition" has forced *literature* to take an outsized role in representing Spanish thought (15). Attempting to account for this institutional deficiency, Abellán also sees fit to confess on behalf of all Spaniards that it stems from a certain incapacity, "a flaw, by all appearances, in the constitution of our collective personality as Spaniards" (15). Abellán's readers hold in their hands the history that might overcome this lack, providing both the methodology for and the fulfillment of a history that embraces both philosophy and literature in a history of *thought*.

On the first page of the prologue to the *Historia Crítica*, we read Abellán's definition of thought, "the maximum intellectual consciousness of a people, a nation, or a man," along with the promise to justify it in his methodological introduction. It is in the first part of the work that he treats the polemic about the existence of Spanish philosophy and takes sides with the revered Spanish historian Marcelino Menéndez Pelayo for what is, like his choice of the word "thought" in the title, a patriotic and pragmatic rationale. Of the positions he surveys, Menéndez Pelayo's is the only one "with a future": it is based on history, stimulating a search for the best of Spanish accomplishments and projecting it forward for the sake of "the national culture" (49). Toward the end of the introduction, after proclaiming that the question of the existence of Spanish philosophy has been "resolved in the positive," he contends that a "crisis in metaphysics and philosophy" threatens what he calls the "validity of the discipline" (77). Here, he implicitly acknowledges that whatever Spanish philosophy there might be is inscribed in a larger context, measured by transnational, if not universal intellectual, spiritual, and cultural criteria. In Abellán's telling, the crisis of legitimacy has a linear trajectory from Auguste Comte to Heidegger, in whose wake Ortega put the problem to rest. As is well known, Comte declared the end of a metaphysical era and the apotheosis of the "positive" sciences. Comte declares the end of searches for "absolute notions, the origin and destination of the universe, and the causes of phenomena" and claims that "all men who are up to their age" devote themselves solely to natural sciences.[21] Abellán tells how Wilhelm Dilthey adopts Comte's point of view, including the renunciation of metaphysics; Heidegger invented phenomenology as a "transformation" of metaphysics, but, in Spain, Ortega and his student José Gaos were able to see that, in spite of Heidegger, the philosophical search for grounds or "first causes" was a dead end, an apparent detour from the forward march of Comte's positivist revolution. In short, for Abellán, the history of "Spanish thought" assumes the end of metaphysics as the transformation of philosophy into positive science, with literature and philosophy both forming a part of the social science that Comte called "social physics" and Dilthey dubbed "Geisteswissenschaften" or "Human sciences" (79–83).

Abellán recognizes the lack of consensus regarding the meaning of "philosophy," but he responds to this lack by installing a history of philosophy in which *Spanish* philosophy stands at the end of philosophy, authorizing the very history that it postulates. Julián Marías, too, ends his *Historia de la filosofía* (*History of Philosophy*), which aspires to represent the entirety of philosophical history, with a long chapter on Ortega's "philosophy of vital reason," suggesting that Ortega brings not just the *History of Philosophy* but the history of philosophy to a close.[22] In addition to this particular philosophical basis of his history of thought, Abellán insists that he has no choice but to believe in Spanish philosophy or to proceed as if it existed, and he claims to act to the benefit of Spain and its greater Hispanization (15–16). According to his methodological exposition, Spain has only arrived at its privileged place by wrapping up a larger, more general philosophical project. Incidentally, although Comte is the first name mentioned in Abellán's account of philosophy's denouement, the *Cours de philosophie positive* (named in French in the English edition) identifies Descartes, Kepler, and Bacon as instigators of his revolution, while noting that no Spaniards deserve to be commemorated in his movement, since "the superiority of Spain, admirable as it is, is a superiority in feeling" (469).

Abellán attaches his own historiographic project to Comte and Dilthey, insofar as he sees them as precursors of Ortega. This gesture requires dismissing as merely incidental Comte's broader, somewhat ambivalent representation of Spain and whatever philosophy it might produce. For Comte, European society was entering into a scientific or "positive" phase, rejecting all "first principles" as fictions. While he rejects what he disparages as theology and metaphysics, he maintains a definition of philosophy as a "system of conceptions" that permits the understanding of the world, while characterizing as "laws" that which mediates between the world and the human mind. His ideal, he says, would be the reduction of the world's complexity to a limited number of laws: "The ultimate perfection of the positive system would be . . . to represent all phenomena as particular aspects of a single general fact, such as gravitation, for instance" (73). In the *Cours*, we see philosophy, reason, and logic characterized again and again as a reduction, with the constant suspicion that even the richest conceptual fabric violates the uniqueness of the phenomenon it is intended to bring into the realm of understanding. Applying the model of the natural sciences to all human activity, Comte explicitly prohibits reflection on the nature of the "laws" that govern "succession and resemblance," while other philosophers define philosophy's particularity as an inquiry into the very principles that Comte excludes. Comte's delineation of the laws of human society illustrates how oppressive his "philosophy" can be in action. He declares Europe superior to the rest of the world and identifies its five constituents and their "special contribution." These are the concluding words to the *Cours*:

> France will bring a philosophical and political superiority; England, an earnest predilection for reality and utility; Germany, a natural aptitude for systematic generalization; Italy, its genius for art; and Spain, its familiar combined sense of personal dignity and universal brotherhood. By their natural cooperation, the positive philosophy will lead us on to a social condition the most conformable to human nature, in which our characteristic qualities will find their most perfect respective confirmation,

their completest mutual harmony, and the freest expansion for each and all. (306)

In spite of the cheerful tone and assurance that everyone in the world will be able to fulfill her, his, or their potential, Comte's vision clearly imposes a character upon its subjects, implying an obligation to become nothing else but what the positive philosophy has declared them to be. A "combined sense of personal dignity and universal brotherhood" grants Spaniards the distinction of representing, somehow, the relation between the individual human and the human in general, but Comte implies that Spaniards are inevitably deficient at *thinking* this relation. Their sense is "familiar" to others, who, according to their own national predilection, might actually make something of it.

That Spain's final position in the list is also a hierarchical position, is suggested in the "Second System," the *Système de politique positive* (again retaining the French name in the English edition), in which Comte contemplates the establishment of human society based on positivist principles and proposes objects for the "abstract glorification of the past" (469). There he explains that, "of the five constituents of the Western world, the Spanish type receives but scant honor; for the superiority of Spain, admirable as it is, is a superiority in *feeling*, and as such cannot be adequately appreciated when we are commemorating the development of *intellect and activity*" (469 [emphasis added]). At the same time, Comte sees fit to include in his "Positivist Library" a selection of Spanish theater, the medieval *Romancero*, and the best known works of Cervantes (477). Excluded from philosophy and action, Spain's virtues are as immediate and ephemeral as feeling, and its accomplishments are confined to literature. Abellán's history would show Comte that in the next century, Spanish thinkers will make the most of that feeling and produce a body of thought that rivals that of France, Germany, and England. Unamuno, Ortega, Machado, and Zambrano make the highest philosophical claims, often by appealing to something like a particularly Spanish "realism," all without neglecting to mention Spanish literary art, architecture, and painting. Thus, Abellán might be justified in considering *philosophy* too narrow of a focus for an assessment of what Spain contributes *to* philosophy. Nonetheless, he admits a "flaw" insofar as Spaniards had not yet been able to make the "readjustment of optics" necessary to change the operative category of philosophy in Spain to a notion of thought that would include literature alongside more conventional philosophical forms (15). Reflecting the principle of empirical science from

Aristotle to Dilthey's hermeneutic circle, he says that in the *Historia critical del pensamiento español* "methodology and history were mutually implicated," that is, that the particular history of Spanish cultural production required its own particular concepts. Hence, concluding the prologue to his introductory volume on methodology, Abellán expresses the hope that his multivolume work should help combat the contemporary ills of "depersonalization and de-Hispanization" (17–18).

In a 2000 article, Abellán confirms a sense of his own achievement while transforming the patriotic gesture of his *Historia crítica*. "Pensamiento español" attributes the dominant character of philosophical historiography to "the Germans" and claims that they reserve a privilege for "the philosophical system" (the very character Comte attributed to Germans in his *Système*).[23] Applied to Spanish philosophy and Spanish reality ("nuestra filosofía" and "nuestra realidad," he says), they "ended up demeaning, blurring, and distorting it" (acaban por desvirtuarlo, desenfocarlo, tergiversarlo) (307). Abellán declares success at resolving the question of the existence of Spanish philosophy by avowing that Spanish philosophy exists as a part of the history of *thought*, one formulated by Spaniards for Spaniards (310). Finally, he acknowledges a historic shift away from patriotic history toward an "intercultural" ethos. For Abellán, now that Spanish philosophy and thought have been correctly interpreted, this project can go forward both with a particular cultural character that can be "defended and respected" and as a model for how underappreciated traditions might find tools for raising their status using their own particular character. Abellán advocates nothing less than a complete reversal of the Black Legend's image of Spain: rather than the epitome of intolerance, Spain provides a privileged site of meditation on diversity.

Abellán's declaration of theoretical victory in discussions of Spanish philosophy only applies to the question we began with regarding the existence of Spanish philosophy. Closing that question exacts a rather steep price, that of accepting a particular brand of historical thinking, one that "coincides with José Ortega y Gasset" (309), embraces a certain end of metaphysics (an end more Comtean than Hegelian, Nietzschean, or Heideggerian), and provides a particular configuration of the relation between literature and philosophy. Compared to the positions we will review, Abellán's can be stated rather simply: literature and philosophy both express thought in a form determined by their discursive genres, inflected by the national character of the thinker. As I maintain in this book, extending the question of the relationship of literature and philosophy to other configurations permits a more expansive interpretation of the moments—texts and writers—in that history. Moreover, the very figures of that history, including Ortega, can be read as calling for a radical opening up, at the same time that they might offer a means for closing off and considering the question resolved.

The more recent *El legado filosófico español y latinoamericano del siglo XX* promises to broaden the question of Spanish thought in various ways. First, it includes Latin America together with Spain, dividing the subject into seven regional accounts. It represents a collective effort, including the perspectives of a team of researchers chosen by the editors, who also contribute overviews, specific entries, and bibliographies. It addresses directly some of the shortcomings of Abellán's work, providing a representation of Spanish scientists and theologians and making an effort to represent "reflection on woman."[24] However we judge the success of these efforts of broadening the account of Hispanic philosophy, the editors of *El legado filosófico* explicitly locate their project within the Ortegan framework that Abellán defined in his *Historia crítica*. While accepting some revisions of methodology proposed by Julián Marías, they maintain the concept of a "generation" as a principle, assuming a homogeneity of work produced within the same time period and the same country or group of countries, according to principles of "circumstances" and "the spirit of the age."[25] The result is slightly more than a new compendium of rather conventional perspectives on canonical thinkers, expanding the panorama and changing Abellán's polemical tone for a panegyric one, presenting the "legacy" as a "saga" and "epic" of Hispanic "geniuses."[26]

Neither of these historical accounts of Spanish intellectual life discuss the question raised by Delbos of the necessity of learning languages for the sake of philosophy or the likelihood that Spanish might have to fight to take a place beside other languages—Greek and Latin, German and French—for the sake of studying primary texts. If adding another language to philosophical curricula is not too tall an order, it would be worth wondering, also, the extent to which the inclusion of literary texts in a purportedly philosophical history might make particular demands on readers, whether multiple-language learners or not. In contrast to encyclopedias and histories, my studies of Unamuno, Ortega, Machado, and Zambrano engage texts in readings that find meaning in the intricacies and accidents of language, in the untranslatable elements bound up with the Castilian idiom that most of the world refers to as "Spanish," and occasionally others. I contend that these are not only resources for the expression of a universally comprehensible idea but that the ins and outs of language serve as signposts for the movement of thought, for which the particularities of idiom—not just those of ethnic character—provide a means of rupturing restrictive cultural or individual perspectives.

From the Outside In, Valera to Unamuno

After Unamuno produced an oeuvre including novels, short stories, poems, and essays, Ortega and his student Zambrano cultivated a metaphorical and rambling, "literary" style that is inseparable from their philosophical accomplishments. For his part, the poet Antonio Machado wrote poems focused on the nature of time and experience and created fictional, "apocryphal" writers to whom he attributed verses, literary criticism, and overtly philosophical texts. Because of and beyond these canonical writers, Spain possesses a distinct and coherent tradition of questioning the relation of literature and philosophy. This tradition gives rise to a conventional image that appears in many forms throughout contemporary Hispanic culture, both popular and elite: Spanish and Latin American writers blend or even fuse literature and philosophy in order to produce a hybrid discourse unique to the Hispanic world, one that overcomes the weaknesses of excessively anti-literary philosophy in the rest of Europe.[27] It is a forceful tradition, but certainly not the only or the dominant one; in fact, much Spanish literary and philosophical writing seems to be produced in indifference to this debate within it, even though it claims to address the most fundamental questions of individual and national identity, the nature of art and the humanities, and the meaning of life. Moreover, the oeuvres of the four major figures in this history also offer other themes. Unamuno's novel *Niebla* (*Mist*) alone invites discussion of feminism, Esperanto and other forms of language reform, childrearing, homosociality, and love, to name a few. If the story of the relation between literature and philosophy has not occupied center stage, it is perhaps because it still occupies a prominent and even axiomatic place in more conventional histories, where it is often taken for granted that it culminates in the effacement of the difference between the two. Most commonly, the concept of the Generation of '98 defined Unamuno's and Machado's work in terms of an effort to restore Spain's self-regard and international prestige by way of the successful melding of literature and philosophy in their work. Other writers customarily included in the Generation—Pío Baroja, Ramón del Valle Inclán, José Martínez Ruiz ("Azorín")—shared in a "concern for Spain" (preocupación por España), as the saying went, that gave rise to not only literary work in a range of genres, but to a self-determined tradition of interpretation. Over the last fifty years, scholars in Spanish literature have discussed not only the questionable legitimacy of the concept of a generation devoted to the "concern for Spain," but also its homogenizing effect on the representation of the literature of the era, with the consequent tendency to restrict the interpretation of the texts and to exclude other writers who do not fit into this canonical vision.[28] No one has yet assessed the claim by some of these figures of the philosophical preeminence of literature in a way that does not embrace the notion of a Spanish or Hispanic philosophical advantage that grows out of its commitment to literature.

Historical analyses based on the genres of the "philosophical novel" and the essay sidestep the issue by postulating that literature and philosophy are adequately defined in terms of form and content. In such a view, both literature and philosophy must distinguish themselves from everyday speech and do so by their extraordinary investment in form or content. Such a conception easily embraces texts that stand out for both their formal and thematic departure from ordinary discourse, and, for this reason, it is not especially surprising that the question of the relation simply failed to occupy many talented thinkers and writers beyond the handful on which I will focus here. As we will see, one of the most radical aspects of the question involves the extent to which (literary) experimentation with form, or the experience of form, provides access to certain kinds of (philosophical) content. In these cases, without the predominance of form, literature might not be philosophical. What is interesting, then, is how form opens up new content and, conversely, the demands of a certain kind of assertion or theme calls for formal invention. That being said, I have not set out to write a complete history of literary and philosophical figures in whom these dynamics are explored. Besides the abundance of fiction and poetry that explore philosophical ideas and engage in argumentation, apparently nonphilosophical work such as Ana María Matute's stories about children, Federico García Lorca's oneiric fantasies in verse, and Juan Ramón Jiménez's search for a "pure" poetry also speak implicitly to the relation between literature and philosophy.[29]

In his 1790 *Discurso sobre el estudio metódico de la historia literaria* (Discourse on the methodical study of literary history), Cándido María Trigueros calls for a literary history that would be, among other things, "philosophical."[30] Trigueros acknowledges that our approach to literature can be enriched by exposure to philosophy and shows that, even though Spanish philosophers have failed to become prominent figures on the international stage, philosophical thinking played an important role in Enlightenment and Romantic Spain.[31] Debate about these issues takes concrete shape in Juan Valera's good-natured discussion "De la filosofía española" (About Spanish philosophy), from 1871, before becoming a bitter feud—whose remnants can be glimpsed in Abellán's history—and setting in motion the series of engagements with the question of literature and philosophy studied in this book. Reviewing what he regards as the beginning of an effort to understand the history of Spanish philosophy, Valera remarks that Spain is "behind" ("estamos atrasados").[32] Speaking with all modesty in the first-person plural, he states that Spain has never had an important philosopher. Nonetheless, he admits that the meaning of *philosophy* is as "elastic" as the definition of *Spanish*, and he advocates for the inclusion of Jewish and Muslim thinkers born in the Iberian Peninsula in any projected history of Spanish philosophy (1561–62).

In a discussion with Ramón de Campoamor compiled and published in 1891 as *Metafísica y poesía* (Metaphysics and poetry), Valera maintains his position, even when it means failing to give credit to his friend's 1855 effort at systematic philosophy, *Personalismo*. Valera distinguishes between the philosophical discipline of metaphysics and the implicit, perhaps inarticulate foundation of all human experience. He calls the latter "spontaneous prescientific metaphysics, which is just short of being innate or congenital in our being [punto menos que innata o congenital]."[33] Valera appears to assume that a metaphysical orientation in the world cannot be racially determined, as some of his contemporaries believed, but that multiple, distinct ways of being human are indeed experienced with a level of intimacy somewhere in between nature and culture. His disagreement with Campoamor revolves around the question of whether metaphysics and poetry are the most common thing in the world or, as his interlocutor maintained, rare, and whether they are, respectively, the most or least useful products of human consciousness. For Valera, the answer depends on whether one accepts the idea of an implicit, "spontaneous" metaphysics as existing in the same way as the one elaborated in a tome such as *Personalismo*, which aspires to articulate "the general law that resolves all the particular cases."[34] For Valera, such a "metaphysical" framework for human existence would guarantee that all human activity participates to some degree in poetry and philosophy, though the "metaphysical" basis is shared in common.

In "De la filosofía española," Valera asserts that the question of whether Spanish philosophy even exists will "remain unresolved indefinitely" (1567). As long as a "speculative prescientific metaphysics" lacks explicit articulation, there is no reason to recognize its legitimacy and status alongside philosophical treatises and, in addition, no reason to privilege one above others or place some "prescientific metaphysics" in the ranks of the philosophical canon. More importantly, Valera acknowledges that the existence of Spanish philosophy depends on the stature conceded to whomever gets distinguished as a Spanish philosopher and the fact that, given the historicity of thought, we can never know once and for all whether a Spanish philosopher, past or future, will achieve the status of a Descartes, Kant, or Hobbes (1567). Consequently, while he expresses doubts about the existence of Spanish philosophy, he also maintains that the mystics St. John of the Cross and St. Teresa of Avila are probably "our most exalted and original philosophers" (1563). Henri Bergson, according to Alain Guy, will say something similar, claiming that the Spanish mystics received by revelation what philosophers try to obtain by reason.[35]

Valera believed, nonetheless, that scholarship might make it possible to detect some common threads in Spanish philosophy, and in "De la filosofía española" he proposes a search for the "speculative element" manifested in Spanish science, literature, history, medicine, or law (1562). In short, he looks for a pragmatic, scholarly representation of philosophical content as a way of acknowledging national traditions without abandoning a cultural neutrality proper to philosophy. Valera's framing of the discussion of Spanish philosophy gained intellectual prominence in the form of a vehement public debate between Marcelino Menéndez Pelayo and Manuel de la Revilla. Don Marcelino is now a household name in Spanish letters, while Revilla is perhaps best known among specialists as the provocateur that motivated Pelayo's early book *La ciencia española* (Spanish science).[36] A philosophy professor at the University of Madrid, Revilla published an article in 1876 acknowledging, five years after Valera had, the relative insignificance of Spanish philosophy, going so far as to declare that Spanish philosophy did not even exist (193).[37] The twenty-year-old Pelayo responded by enlisting his already massive encyclopedic learning (Julián Marías attributed to him "probably . . . the outer limits of the human capacity for erudition")[38] to defend the Spanish race's "particular place [lugar aparte] in the history of philosophy."[39] After providing long lists of names of Spanish philosophers, Pelayo proclaims himself a "believer in Spanish philosophy."[40] Constantino Lascaris Comneno's 1955 anthology of Pelayo's writings, entitled *Filosofía española* (Spanish philosophy), proposes that the history of philosophy should include literary figures like Pedro Calderón de la Barca, whose *La vida es sueño* (*Life Is a Dream*) is considered part of "the genre that we call symbolic, philosophical, or ideal."[41] With his comment on Spanish mystics, Valera anticipated this inclusion within Spanish philosophy of what is conventionally considered literary, although St. Teresa and St. John both participated in theological debates in addition to writing more conventionally literary texts. Calderón, too, could be said to put doctrine into literary form, namely, the epistemological skepticism and moral dogmatism of the baroque era.[42] Hence, although Pelayo's reminder that Corneille modeled *Heraclio* on *Life Is a Dream* attests to the Spaniard's originality and influence,[43] Spanish philosophy's stature does not necessarily rise by its incorporation of Calderón's play, which is still more remarkable for its poetry than its thought.

Pelayo's account of Spanish philosophy initiated a larger project of rehabilitating the image of Spanish science after centuries of disparagement by European scholars. As Víctor Navarro Brotóns and William Eamon point out in the introduction to *Más allá de la Leyenda Negra/Beyond the Black Legend*, Spanish contributions to science from the fifteenth century on had been the target of a politically motivated campaign to cast Spain as "the quintessentially anti-modern villain" in a melodrama constructed by English and French historians.[44] The dismissal of Spanish philosophy forms a part of this characterization of Spain as, in the words of one of the Black Legend's instigators, "the most ignorant nation in Europe," which came to represent, as Eamon and Navarro Brotóns explain, "the country that typified everything against which the philosophes were struggling" (27). Naturally, we understand that the "philosophes" embodied a concept of philosophy that included the natural sciences and mathematics and culminated, not in work of reflection or what Aristotle would call "first philosophy," but in the compendia of knowledge known as *encyclopédies*, of which Diderot and D'Alembert's is the best known. Referring to what is perhaps a worse effect than the neglect of Spanish intellectual life on the part of northern Europeans, Navarro Brotóns and Eames describe the pernicious effect of this provocation in Spain, dividing scientists into two camps, a "nationalist" one that devoted itself to a patriotic defense of "Spanish character" and a "liberal" one that agreed with the charge of Spain's "backwardness" and attempted to correct it with its own achievements (29). For the editors of *Beyond the Black Legend*, this dichotomy lasted well into the twentieth century, if one takes into account Ortega's characterization of an "anti-modern" Spain and Amerigo Castro's conviction that science was "alien to the Spanish way of life" (quoted 29). While Pelayo's association with nationalism seems accurate, I would take issue with this understanding of Ortega, who, like Unamuno and Zambrano, combined the two tendencies in historiography by promoting a Hispanization of Europe. For Unamuno's part, his response to the debate between Revilla and Pelayo offers a provocative but principled defense of a distinctively Spanish spiritual character on the basis of the very deficiency that the Black Legend attaches to Spain.

Both Pelayo and Valera were on Unamuno's examination committee for his appointment to a chair of Greek, and the younger man referred to Pelayo as a "great teacher"; but, as Laureano Robles points out, he considered his master a "timid thinker," one who had fallen victim to his own erudition.[45] The relation between literature and philosophy concerned Unamuno in many ways throughout his lifetime, and he addresses it most directly in formulations about philosophy and poetry, the novel, language, fiction, or literature in general in free-standing essays, prologues, and narrative exposition and dialogues in his novels. We may begin to assess this complex dynamic and its continuity with the Revilla-Pelayo polemic by taking stock of a number of texts written in the decade before the publication of the works I will study in depth later. In his article on Pelayo and Unamuno, Robles includes the text of an unpublished manuscript from the Unamuno archives called "Filosofía, lírica y poesía española" (Philosophy, lyricism, and Spanish poetry), which shows signs of being written in 1905. The long neglect to which this text has been subject might owe something to the frankly weird proposition that modern Spanish poetry suffers from its African character, with all of its warmth ("ardor" and "*calor*") coming "from outside," rather than, presumably, from inside (quoted 109). Pelayo's timidity shares in the inner frigidity of Unamuno's contemporaries, and his "catalogical arguments" (argumentos catalógicos) lacked not only the proper emotion but a more appropriate, philosophical logic. Unamuno joins Valera and Revilla in denying the existence of Spanish philosophy, saying of Pelayo and his followers, "It was much easier not to doubt [philosophy's] existence than to philosophize" (108). This sounds more like an accusation of laziness than timidity: a generation of Spanish intellectuals chose to gather the evidence that removes doubt, but did not practice the philosophical thinking that might render Spanish philosophy a genuine reality. In "Filosofía, lírica y poesía española" he expands the lack of Spanish philosophy to a broader absence of literary creation and appeals to divine intervention to address this lack, repeating throughout this manuscript some version of the words, "Lord, what are we to do?" (Señor, ¿qué le vamos a hacer?) (107–8). Unamuno apparently reserved this new step in Spanish philosophy for himself. Provoked by the possibility that the Spanish tradition had dwelled outside philosophy, Unamuno had already set about asserting the philosophical character of a tradition whose literary achievement was not in doubt. While Calderón and Francisco de Quevedo, Saint Teresa of Ávila and Saint John of the Cross, don Juan and don Quixote might be marginally philosophical, he reinterpreted them and extended their legacy as the forgotten center of philosophy. This process, in his mind, generated some of the appropriate affect, the *ardor* that would be necessary for a genuine philosophy and literature in his own place and time.

The 1904 essay/dialogue "Sobre la filosofía española" (About Spanish philosophy), like Valera and Campoamor's *Metafísica y poesía*, takes the form of a dialogue between two interlocutors, both of whom express Unamuno's thoughts in a way that undercuts an attempt to pin down his position. We find that both speakers accept Valera's conviction of the absence of contemporary Spanish philosophy and argue that philosophical treatises and literary works have equal philosophical status. One of the interlocutors proposes an interpretation of philosophy as a response to knowledge of the world: "Every people [pueblo] derives a different philosophy from the same sciences. After all, philosophy is the total vision of the universe and life seen through an ethnic temperament."[46] A certain kind of objective knowledge (Unamuno calls it "science") seems indisputable, but different communities draw different conclusions, and for this reason Unamuno's discursive voice considers it legitimate to speak of a Spanish philosophy. In contrast to the debate between Revilla and Pelayo, Unamuno's affirmation of Spanish philosophy shifts his focus from philosophers to philosophy. Spain is a nation without philosophers—this Unamuno does not question—but, as a people, Spain could not possibly lack philosophy. Nonetheless, Spain has not produced a philosophical exposition of its philosophy: "As far as our people are concerned, I don't know of anyone who has formulated its philosophy systematically" (557). This same dialogic voice goes on to claim that Spain's philosophy has indeed been revealed fragmentarily, appearing in other (literary and popular) genres plus "fleeting glimpses of isolated thinkers" (557). In another text, clearly thinking of Pelayo, he seems to specify that these "isolated thinkers" include "scholars, commentators, and explicators of philosophy, and the odd almost-philosopher" (eruditos, comentaristas y expositores de filósofos, y alguno que otro casi filósofo) (121). Unamuno distinguishes, then, between two types of philosophy: an implicit one that finds expression in a variety of ways; and the philosophy of philosophers, who explicitly attempt a "totalizing vision of the universe," unaware that this vision ultimately has an ethnic or national character. He does not question whether Spain exists as an ethnicity and thus appears to have paved the way for affirming, like Valera, that Spain has a philosophy that has not yet found its philosopher. Instead, he proposes that Spain's philosophers are its literary writers and their work: *Don Quixote*, *Life Is a Dream*, the mystics. Cervantes, Calderón, and others are the "almost-philosophers" who ought to have put Spain in philosophical history books (121–22). While his 1904 *Vida de Don Quijote y Sancho* (*Our Lord Don Quixote: The Life of Don Quixote and Sancho*) could still be perceived as an argument in favor of Cervantes's philosophical import, the following decade will see his effort to add his own name to the list of "almost-philosophers," with the philosophical novel *Mist* and the unconventional philosophical treatise *The Tragic Sense of Life*. It goes without saying that he means the "almost" as a compliment, for he will persist in the idea that the most profound philosophers do not go full philosophy.

In a well-known 1906 letter to the Uruguayan poet Juan Zorrilla de San Martín, Unamuno declares his taste for "poetic philosophy or philosophical poetry," distinguishing poetry that offers a "mixture of poetry and philosophy," differing essentially from "others in which poetry and philosophy melt [se funden] into one, like in a chemical compound."[47] Such a proclamation might be held up as a description of Unamuno's larger poetics, and, indeed, a powerful vein of Unamuno criticism characterizes the relationship between literature and philosophy as such a "fusion" or "union."[48] I would like to emphasize, however, that Unamuno's own words point to how problematic such an amalgamation would be. Although Unamuno will later experiment with neologisms that might adequately capture the relation that is established in a single locution, here he speaks of a philosophy that takes on a poetic character and poetry with philosophical attributes. He goes on to say, "I only feel philosophy in a poetic way and poetry in a philosophical way."[49] Such statements attribute their own particularities to literature and philosophy, a difference that, as I insist throughout this book, must maintain itself during the various efforts at approximation to the other. In *Our Lord Don Quixote*, too, from roughly the same time, the narrator speaks of the possibility of a vision of life that would unite opposites with this ambivalent figure: "something in which both join and are confused [algo en que ambas se aúnan y confunden], where head and heart are melded, where Don Quixote and Sancho become as one [algo en que se funden corazón y cabeza, y en que se hacen uno]."[50] Later he repeats, "Fused into one—or better, Sancho quixotized before Quixote is sanchofied" (fundidos en uno, o mejor, quijotizado Sancho antes que sanchizado Don Quijote).[51] Here, too, one notes the desire for an erasure of difference while in practice the result is a dynamic relationship of approximation and transformation that stops somewhere short of the obliteration of difference.

In the 1905 essay "Sobre la erudición y la crítica" (On erudition and criticism), Unamuno calls philosophers and poets "twin sisters": they both spring from the same unifying vision; easily mistaken for one another, they are practically the same.[52] This metaphor of a living double seems to have guided Unamuno's work on companion pieces in the first decade of the new millennium. *Mist* presents the demise of a human life when confronted with its creator. For its part, the treatise *The Tragic Sense of Life* repeats the basic argument of implicit and explicit philosophy and attempts to carry out a critique of the philosophical tradition in order to forge a genuine philosophy whose literary form would be adequate to its metaphysical primordiality. But Unamuno was not satisfied with a simple dichotomy of literature and philosophy embodied in two distinct units, nor with the related idea of a theory expounded directly in a treatise and dramatized in fiction. Behind the two works stands a common aim, disturbing the reader's complacent existence, including facile ideas about works of thought and of aesthetic intention. In the novel, his characters theorize about literature and life, and in the treatise he aligns his discourse with literature by declaring its spontaneity and idiosyncrasy. I will argue in chapter 3 that Unamuno demonstrates, sometimes against his own declarations, that one can only intertwine elements that are different; when philosophy and literature become too close, Unamuno turns to the contrary task of driving them apart again.

"This Side": More Philosophical Than Philosophy

Whether by the creation of a literary philosophy or a philosophical literature, Unamuno inaugurates a series of Spanish intellectual figures who attempt to bring philosophical discourse closer than previous philosophers did to the center of the thinking human being. Before providing an initial characterization of Ortega, Machado, and Zambrano, let us pause to observe how Unamuno first articulates this task as a passage *this side* of metaphysics. The first chapter of *Mist* follows narrative conventions in introducing a protagonist, Augusto Pérez, and providing a conflict to orient the reader around a unified plot: a young bachelor applies himself to courting a young woman and overcoming her resistance to marrying him. Early in the novel Augusto's friend Victor warns him that he proceeds blindly, since he will lack knowledge of "the soul of woman" until he marries; all that bachelors know, compared to married men, is "metaphysics, pure and simple," Victor says. Recalling the origin of the term in Aristotle—where it is "beyond the *Physics*," that is, subsequent to the study of nature—he adds that what Augusto knows is "beyond physics and beyond nature."⁵³ "Am I in the realm of metaphysics?" Augusto replies, immediately proposing, to the contrary, "I am not beyond physics but this side of it" (no estoy más allá de la física sino más acá) (S 251; E 188 [revised]). For Augusto, "this side of metaphysics" refers to his own innocence with regard to women, a lack of experience he has decided to address with psychological experimentation (in Spanish, a single word, *experimentar*, means both *to experiment* and *to experience*). Augusto's point of departure "this side of metaphysics" appears to him to be without prejudice, determined by nothing else but his being in the world. He asserts that he has not yet gone beyond, outside of himself and into nature, and by taking advantage of these near homophonic phrases, he suggests that he remains in an emphatic interiority, not yet having gone forth from out of himself. Victor argues briefly that this side differs not from that side, that behind is the same as beyond, that closeness is distance, reducing Augusto to a state of confusion (S 251–52; E 189). I should like to retain this figure, even giving it a place of privilege in my narrative of literature and philosophy in Spanish letters. As we will see in our studies of four major figures (the last of whom, María Zambrano, will repeat this figure literally), the search for an account of the unprejudiced human in contact with otherness leads to an investment in discursive gestures and strategies that they explicitly link to literature. From Unamuno on, a tradition of writers associate the old philosophy with a superfluous intermediacy that Spanish literati have been adept at discarding, circumventing, or simply refusing to insert between the raw self and the richness of the world. Hence the claim to being on the near side, closer than philosophy to the real issue, often evoked as life or the human.

Within Unamuno's novel, the question of what the "this side" of Augusto's world is initially receives a somewhat facile answer. After Victor and Augusto's conversation (and before the latter's first trip to Eugenia's house), Unamuno makes an appearance, indicated by italics and by the narrative voice's reference to itself as the author indicated on the book cover: "*While Augusto and Victor were carrying on this 'nivolistic' conversation, I, the author of the* nivola, *that you have in hand and are reading, dear reader, smiled to myself enigmatically as I watched my 'nivolistic' characters pleading my case and justifying my method*" (E 189–90; S 252). This initial moment of contact between the world of the protagonist and that of Unamuno does not refer us back to the writer, his ethnic milieu, or God, but, rather, conjures the position of a pristine self-consciousness, this side of metaphysics. As we can see from the two philosophical references contained in the conversation between Augusto and Victor, metaphysics has also been formulated as not only a beyond but a kind of *behind* or *closeness* to self, an interiority that coincides with the self itself, as it were. While a look at these two references to the "meta" of metaphysics takes us away from Unamuno, they will help us appraise his philosophical claims and his legacy without overstating the uniqueness or force of their literary character.

Reading Aristotle, we might be struck by the extent to which, as Victor would say, "this side [más acá] of the natural is the same as beyond it [más allá]" (S 251; E 188 [revised]). Aristotle himself did not give the name "metaphysics" to the text that goes by that name; rather, we owe the coinage of the term "metaphysics" to the editor who assembled Aristotle's explorations of "first philosophy" and placed them "after the *Physics*," that is, after the treatises on nature.[54] In the first book of the *Metaphysics*, Aristotle summarizes previous thinkers and acknowledges their accomplishments: in accordance with his conception of philosophy or "wisdom" (*sophia*), they have all searched for first causes or "principles" (*archai* and *aitiai*; 982a).[55] However, the principles his predecessors have mentioned have all found a place in Aristotle's earlier discussions of nature (988a). He thus concludes that "although in one sense they have all been stated before, in another they have not been stated at all" (993a). The principles that govern the natural world have indeed been investigated before Aristotle's inquiry in the *Metaphysics*, not just in the extraneous ordering of his own work, but by Empedocles, Pythagoras, Parmenides, and others. Aristotle claims to be the first to inquire into the principial nature of those originary principles. Without specifically naming it *metaphysics*, Aristotle identifies first philosophy as the inquiry into the most general principles, which he refers to as those that belong to "the science which is desirable in itself and in the interest of knowledge" (tōn epistēmōn de tēn autēs heneken kai tou eidenai charin aireten) (982a). As the "more controlling science" (282b), as the most difficult, rarest, and most distant from the senses, this inquiry is last in chronological order but first in rank, the source from which the other principles flow.[56] First philosophy is this side of "physics," of the knowledge of nature and the physical. One cannot, in a sense, speak of the latter without already—"in another sense"—saying something about what precedes it.

In *Fundamental Concepts of Metaphysics*, Heidegger explains an ambivalence that appears in Aristotle because the search for principles of *physis* requires also an inquiry into the "nature" of those principles. Heidegger characterizes the two kinds of inquiry in the text of the *Metaphysics* as, first, research into the relationships among beings (including, for example, the relationship of "physical" to "technical" beings, that which is of its own accord and that which is brought into being by the initiative of humans) and, second, a question about being as such, which can be represented as the relationship between that which is (*das Seiende*, in German) and Being, referred to in German by the nominal infinitive "to be" (*das Sein*).[57] Heidegger points out that the technical meaning—"metaphysics" as the book after the *Physics*—comes to be understood in terms of *"turning away* from one matter toward another [matter]," and from nature (*physis*) to "beings in general and toward that being which properly is."[58] This change from *meta* as *post* to *meta* as *trans* further obscures the orientation of Aristotle's inquiry, a "first" philosophy that would ask about being as such, contributing to the covering up of the problem of being in Aristotle and taking a decisive step toward modern metaphysics. Incidentally, Heidegger acknowledges "the Spanish Jesuit" from Salamanca, Francisco Suárez, as the thinker whose "acumen and independence of questioning" brought about this decisive development in the history of philosophy.[59] In book 6 of the *Metaphysics*, Aristotle proposes *ousia* as the most primordial of principles, recognizing that " 'primary' has several meanings; but nevertheless substance is primary in all senses, both in definition and in knowledge and in time [pantōs hē ousia prōton, kai logōi kai gnōsei kai khronōi]"(1028a). Before all else, there is *ousia*, this first cause or principle of principles. Aristotle also discusses a "cause that is not caused," which gets interpreted historically as the highest being, God; consequently what is *before* sense experience gets cast also, if not predominantly, as a *beyond* of sense experience, that is, as the suprasensible. For Heidegger, Aristotle's *Metaphysics* identifies a question about and an experience of a primordial realm that the subsequent philosophy will obscure, as it directs its attention to relations among beings rather than to Being as such. As Unamuno and his characters insist, such an inquiry requires a certain turning inward without cutting oneself off in an absolute difference from the world.

The characters of *Mist* return more than once to the *cogito* as Augusto struggles with questions about his mode of existence, grasping for certainty about his own existence and freedom. Eventually, as we will see later, Victor will propose an overcoming of Descartes, which critics have deemed one of Unamuno's philosophical achievements.[60] A reader of Descartes might well note in his texts an effort to delve into the enabling structures of the thinking subject, in addition to appeals to innocence from philosophical knowledge. The dialogue from *Mist* alludes to Descartes when Victor reminds Augusto, "You think, therefore you are" (E 189; S 252). For the Descartes of the *Principles of Philosophy*, metaphysics is defined as a treatment of "principles" *this side* of the sciences of nature. He credits Aristotle with identifying the "principles of philosophy" that are the key to "a perfect knowledge of all the things that man is capable of knowing" and persists in dividing them into "immaterial or Metaphysical things" and "corporeal or Physical things."[61] Philosophy includes, then, all the sciences, but when it comes to discovering the first things, he says, "those who have learned *the least* about everything which has hitherto been called Philosophy are *the most capable* of learning true Philosophy" (183 [emphasis added]). Descartes suspects that while Aristotle "propounded [the principles] to be true and certain . . . it is unlikely that he ever judged them to be so" (182). As if in response to a fear that his own judgment should be questioned, Descartes testifies to it in three major "metaphysical" works, which seek to provide a foundation for inquiry in various scientific fields, as the roots provide the foundation for the tree. The first step in the establishment of roots, says Descartes in the *Discourse on the Method*, is to discard all principles and set in their place only "what presented itself to [his] mind so clearly and so distinctly that [he] had no occasion to doubt it."[62]

Of the chapter of the *Discourse* that presents his "first meditation," the one to which Augusto refers, Descartes warns it might be "too metaphysical and uncommon for everyone's taste" (126). For Descartes, Aristotle would have had to start from the principle that Descartes articulates, in order to "judge" correctly that his own principles were "true and certain." Descartes thinks of the ways in which his senses and reasoning have deceived him and arrives at this earliest principle:

> Considering that the very thoughts we have while awake may also occur while we sleep without any of them being at that time true, I resolved to pretend that all the things that had ever entered my mind were no more true than the illusions of my dreams. But immediately I noticed that while I was trying thus to think everything false, it was necessary that I, who was

thinking this, was something. And observing that this truth "*I am thinking, therefore I exist*" was so firm and sure that all the most extravagant suppositions of the skeptics were incapable of shaking it, I decided that I could accept it without scruple as the first principle of the philosophy I was seeking. (127)

The main point of this "truth" is not to reassure us of our own existence but of the solid foundations of subsequent knowledge acquired by this self-assured ego. Victor's evocation of it stops at a primordial affirmation of the existence of the thinking subject as *res cogitans*, a thinking thing. In addition, while it is true that reassurance for the subject of its own existence sufficed, in practice, for Descartes to develop a secure picture of the physical world—one that would, in turn, provide ground for his own experiments in optics, acoustics, and human anatomy—the cogito may not be said to provide a solid foundation, once and for all, for science. Rather, as Jacques Derrida points out in his discussion of the relationship of the cogito to madness and dreams, it "is only valid during the instant of intuition, the instant of thought being attentive to itself, at the point, the sharpest point, of the instant."[63] In Descartes, as in *Mist*, the passage "this side" does not lead to security and certainty but, at best, momentary reassurance and a reminder of the quickening effect of a movement that represents itself, as a taking up of a more self-present position. Descartes states quite directly here the role of imagination in weighing possible truths, and one can observe a fragmentation of the thinker into a figure that performs that observation and one that draws conclusions. For his part, Unamuno dismisses the narrative and personal character of Descartes's thought and deals only with the proposition "I think therefore I am." He believes such a position would be antithetical to pure philosophy and insists that we consider Descartes a one-dimensional, archetypally "philosophical" figure.[64]

As Aristotle's and Descartes's texts already suggest, and counter to the common representation of a dominant and domineering philosophical tradition, the claim to being more philosophical than philosophy is not unique to the Spanish figures who take up the relation between literature and philosophy. My point is not to dwell on the shortcomings of Unamuno's philosophical readings but to show how interpretive decisions made in those readings underestimate the tradition and consequently overstate the originality of some aspects of Unamuno's thought. At the same time, Unamuno's gestures bind him to a larger European tradition; while assessments of his philosophical import often merely echo Unamuno's claims to enact a radical confrontation with philosophy, the texts permit a different story to be told, perhaps less radical, but maybe more compelling.

In *Mist*, Victor's dismissive accusation of mere "metaphysics" recalls, more than anything, Auguste Comte's ambitious positivist project. Historical accounts of philosophy in Spain have insisted that positivism was one of the dominant trends in nineteenth-century Hispanic philosophical institutions.[65] Unamuno does not stage a debate between positivism and the more speculative philosophical inquiries of Aristotle and Descartes; however, greater precision regarding Comte's conception of philosophy and his declaration of the end of all beyonds and behinds can offer a better understanding of Unamuno's way of thinking and distinguish it from Abellán's willful historiographic methodology. The beginning of Comte's *Cours de philosophie positive* proposes a history of humanity, "the progressive course of the human mind, regarded as a whole," with the corresponding claim that "no conception can be understood otherwise than through its history" (71). Comte defines philosophy as a collection of "general systems of conceptions on the aggregate of phenomena" and divides human history into three "theoretical conditions," the theological, the metaphysical, and the positive (71). That is, the world consists of a collection of perceptible objects whose behavior can be grasped by an array of related notions; the multiplicity of philosophies depends on variations in the "systems of conceptions" that mediate between the world and the human mind. For Comte, theological and metaphysical philosophies posit "fictions" *behind* the facts of perception, the former "supernatural beings" and the latter "abstract forces, veritable entities, inherent in all beings and capable of producing all phenomena" (72). Aristotle's and Descartes's first principles, along with the conceptual fabric in which they are woven with other concepts, are mere contrivances that, for Comte, distract the mind from reality. Positivism ceases to look *behind* things; instead, the mind looks at things themselves and "applies itself to the study of [the laws of phenomena], that is, their invariable relations of succession and resemblance" (72). For Comte, neither the *laws* nor the *beings* he mentions qualify as either *behind* or *beyond* phenomena; they are not first causes or principles, but a posteriori descriptive propositions that orient our relationship to the world and confer mastery. Modeled on the natural sciences, which in fact make up five of the six divisions of the "system of positive philosophy," Comte's philosophy represents the whole of human knowledge and society as a set of predictive rules derived from observations taking place without an intensive reflection on conceptual or methodological foundations. This is more or less what Unamuno declares in his one mention of Comte in *On the Tragic Sense of Life*: positivism seems brilliant in its claim to supersede a theological and then a metaphysical "age," but it "is nothing but metaphysics whenever it leaves off negating and affirms anything" (E 158 [revised]; S 111). For Unamuno, positivism's positing of predictive laws still produces units of the same, fantastical nature as theology and metaphysics (E 157–58; S 111).

While Victor warns against the metaphysical point of view—that is, a perspective that lacks direct observation of laws governing women's behavior—Augusto commits himself to a search for the principles of nature that would precede any kind of determination of the particular being called "woman." Like Aristotle and Descartes, Unamuno—through Augusto—will lay claim to the discovery of a definitive truth that relates to the philosophical tradition but exceeds it and, for the first time, completes it by getting closer than ever to bare existence. In spite of this lineage, Unamuno will insist that his philosophical discovery is literature. More precisely, he considers his own originality to be the self-conscious embrace of the fantastical nature of all discourses of the beyond: religion, theology, metaphysics, and philosophy. *Mist* and *The Tragic Sense of Life* inaugurate a Spanish intellectual tradition that embraces the fictionalizing that Comte pretends to overcome, inventing human characters, cultivating figurative language, telling stories, and constructing a persona of the writer from which any philosophical doctrine or vision should not be detached. In this way, the literary and philosophical achievements are always intertwined in writing that reaches back behind human experience.

Ortega, the Philosophical-Literary Life

Unamuno's oeuvre consists of counterposed twins, literary and philosophical discourses that push and pull at each other for the sake of an evocation of individual souls, the writer's, a reader's, and even a fictional character's. In Ortega we find occasional statements about the relation of literature to philosophy, mainly the assertion that both are types of "spiritual production" of humanity, finding their unity in a dialectical movement back to a common origin. The question may be approached in different ways, due to the many ways in which literature and philosophy interact in his work, beginning, at least, with their more or less conventional meanings. Their intertwining shows most vividly in the consistency of Ortega's mature voice, which does not modulate as dramatically as Unamuno's but projects itself in a recognizable style, combining conventionally literary and philosophical elements. Ortega offers stories and descriptions, often using rhetorical figures and surprising expository strategies rather than argumentation and extensive thematic reflections, and his discourse often addresses or bears on literary, artistic, or cultural issues. But Ortega's writing never lacks a connection to philosophy, striving to provide a unified and consistent "doctrine" that would ground his interpretations and conclusions and provide a complete and inclusive account of the world. While the connections between his explanations and his ideas are not always direct or clear, Ortega insists that the authority of his speech rests on his own embodiment of life's historical unfolding at the moment of thinking and speaking. This postulate of a vital force that informs concrete individual lives and, from there, communal experience and historical events, develops over the course of his life, taking shape in well-known conceptions of generations, and of vital or historical reason. Chapter 4 will elaborate the sometimes surprising traits of this trajectory from "Adán en el Paraíso" (Adam in Paradise) through the *Meditaciones del Quijote* (*Meditations on Quixote*) and *El tema de nuestro tiempo* (*The Modern Theme*), to *¿Qué es la filosofía* (*What Is Philosophy?*).

It is commonplace for commentary on Ortega to frame his work by means of a unification of literature and philosophy. On the simplest terms, this might follow upon what I've already mentioned, placing the two activities together in the person of José Ortega y Gasset and explaining the necessity of their synthesis within that of the self-conscious human being.[66] If literature and philosophy are determined exhaustively as the activity of an individual human in history, their unity appears to be a forgone conclusion, but the way in which they relate does not go without saying. One frequently reads that the critical consensus holds to an erasure of difference. Juan José Lanz identifies two scholarly approaches to Ortega that seem very much in agreement with each other. One examines his perspectives on literature, interested in what he says about many texts and topics. The second group "[studies] the fusion of literature and philosophy and [underlines] the literary essence of his philosophical thought."[67] Echoing the principal critic in the latter trend, José Luis Molinuevo, Lanz insists that literature is "the very entrails of philosophical thought."[68] Indeed, for Molinuevo, it is the investment in something called "literature" that permits Ortega to make of life both a theme and the ultimate ground of a new metaphysics. The earliest of first principles, life requires a speech adequate to its peculiarity and, for Molinuevo, literature serves that function for Ortega, "[integrating] text and life in the autobiographical narrativity of historical reason."[69] As in Molinuevo's account, Julián Marías concurs that literature "vivifies" philosophy, especially in the new form Ortega gives philosophy as one "literary genre" among others.[70] Other critics, too, describe this moment in the history of philosophy as a movement back to the earliest, most primordial level of thought. In *La voluntad de aventura* (The will to adventure), Pedro Cerezo Galán concludes his chapter titled "The Level of Ortega's Radicality" by stating that, "faced with the beyond [más allá] of metaphysics, Ortega's work always dwells this side of it [más acá de ella], in its roots in the 'world of life.'"[71] When Javier San Martín speaks of the "anteriority" and "origineity" preceding the difference between literature and philosophy, he is speaking not only of the "autobiographical" character they assume but of a notion of life this side of the subject that writes his own life.[72]

But what might it mean to fuse literature and philosophy? If philosophy can now—in Ortega and Spanish thinking and beyond—be considered literature, and not just one half of Unamuno's pairing of literary philosophy and philosophical literature, what does this mean for literature? As one of the forms that produce concretions of vital reason, literature rises to the status of philosophy as an equal, offspring of what Ortega calls the parent, the time when the text was born.[73] As a writer-philosopher, Ortega sets out to determine the proper character of his time, to be, and to describe what would count as existence "at the level of his time" (a la altura del tiempo). Jorge Luis Borges protested Ortega's arrogating to philosophy the right to dictate, prescribe, and even proscribe directions for the pursuit of literary art.[74] In spite of Lanz's characterization of Ortega scholarship, I am not alone in questioning Ortega's right to this authority, or the revolutionary and definitive character of his philosophy. In his comprehensive biography, Jordi Gracia tells the "story of a frustration," noting that Ortega never produced a magnum opus, instead turning out a series of editorially contrived publications to present his "compulsive and explosive writing."[75] In his writing Ortega often invoked a moment of fruition in which the solution of over two millennia of philosophical investigations appeared to him as his own inner experience, but, Gracia says, the work that would adequately articulate and express this "new and radical philosophy" "lived [only] in his imagination."[76] Such a conclusion would not necessarily constitute a reproach, since, for many readers, the autobiographical character of philosophy required an incomplete work to go with an incomplete life, and life in general as open-ended. Thus José Ferrater Mora speaks of Ortega's "open system" and reminds us that, for Ortega, all books turn out to be "falsifications" because of their illegitimate closure.[77] Cerezo generally grants Ortega's most exorbitant claims about his philosophical achievements' potential to open a new historical era or to announce the inauguration of an incipient one, but he also notes an unresolved inner tension in the work, an "intimate discomfort" (desazón íntima) that Ortega tried to cover up.[78] Reading Ortega, one cannot miss the frequent recourse to a rhetoric of certainty and plenitude in order to assert a moment of epiphany or revelation of full truth. But one can already see in Ortega's earliest publications how that vein of his text coexists with another in which the elements that might appear fused or synthesized—among them literature and philosophy—are placed in a necessary and fruitful tension.

As often happens in Ortega, a question he poses turns out to require a series of preliminary discussions that go to the heart of his philosophy, and these preparatory or propaedeutic matters constitute the keystones of his status as a thinker. They are also the postulates about which one might reasonably demand more discussion, if the very standards of reason and discourse weren't already among the stakes of his thought. For the moment, suffice it to say that Ortega always asserts that more discussion could settle these preliminary matters, at least for those capable of hearing his explanations; they are, in effect, not axioms to be assumed but theorems capable of proof. Although "Adán" has much to offer, *Meditations on Quixote* can count as the beginning of Ortega's work as a philosopher, rather than as a mere journalist or professor.[79] Here he declares himself to be writing essays, drawing a literary-philosophical distinction that he will maintain for the next decade: "The *Meditations* . . . are driven by philosophical desires. . . . The essay is science minus the explicit proof. For a writer there is a question of intellectual honor in not writing something that *can* be proven without first *possessing* the proof" (S 20; E 40 [revised]). He goes on to say that he has the "proof" but has omitted it in order to convey the "intimate heat" of his thoughts (S 20; E 40). In fact, Ortega will never really make this "rigid mechanics of proof" public, counting on his readers to appropriate the material through their own living experience, referred to here as a feeling of veracity, or at least to place trust in him. From the *Meditations* forward, Ortega will occupy himself with sketching out the nature of this possible intersubjective agreement: how ideas are generated, how they are channeled through literary genres and obey historical laws governing generations, and so on. I would like to suspend judgement on the truth of this structure of temporal unfolding of human activity, in order to gain, from the texts, some clarity regarding what Ortega would have us accept. In *Meditations on*

Quixote, Ortega already casts suspicion on those who question his intentions and conclusions. He doubts that those who are too beholden to what he calls "learning" and "idealism," those who—not being sufficiently Spanish—are indifferent to Spain's fate, and those of us who are simply too old, will be able to join him in the new "continent" that he has opened up.[80] Nonetheless, we read on, for this is the possibility of both assessing and assuming, let alone resuming Ortega's thought on behalf of Spain or humanity.

Ortega published the *Meditations on Quixote* shortly after the appearance of *On the Tragic Sense of Life*, and in its effort to provide an account of first principles, it bears some resemblance to Unamuno's major treatise, in addition to taking up the question of Spanish philosophy that had occupied Unamuno, Valera, and others. Like Unamuno, Ortega expresses dismay at the state of his homeland, and he does so in terms of national or ethnic character, some of the terms of which even seem borrowed from Antonio Machado's already well-known poems in *Campos de Castilla* (*Fields of Castile*). He speaks, for example, of a Spanish tendency towards resentment, *rencor*, of a general attitude of hatred toward the world (S 13–15; E 33–34). Ortega expresses his intention in apparently religious terms, speaking of the effort to provide Spain with "salvation" and of his own position as a Spanish philosopher "in partibus infidelium," that is, representing philosophy in a nonphilosophical land, analogous to Christian evangelists in the lands of "infidels" (S 11; E 31). Indeed, he offers love to the hateful Spanish in the *philos* of a philosophy that will teach them to embrace the uniqueness of things, to know better in order to love better, and to reawaken this potential in other Spaniards (S 13–15; E 34). Like in Unamuno, then, philosophy is not primarily a matter of doctrine but an attunement to existence that can be found in cultural practices and literary texts as well as in philosophical treatises: "A poetic style carries along with it a philosophy and a morality, a science and a politics," he says (S 75; E 107 [revised]). Style not only conveys these theoretical and practical discourses but gathers them together in a unified form, both a product of philosophy and itself a philosophical intervention that plays a role in the evolution of human intellect within the historical logic of "life." In fact, a conventional work of philosophy could be a deficient means of expressing this primordial, implicit philosophy, and compelling a greater harmony with it, since it is one literary genre among others. "Every era brings along with it a radical interpretation of man" and hence "prefers a particular genre," insists Ortega (S 79; E 113). For Ortega, the "meditation" is the genre that appears in the time of philosophy's transformation into "vital reason," a transition that may even lead to the disappearance of the label "philosophy."⁸¹ What Ortega calls *Don Quixote*'s "poetic style" provides guidance for Ortega's thought, keeping it focused on Spain and its relationship to Europe (S 75; E 107).

Meditations on Quixote presents itself, then, as a kind of remedy to a Spanish ailment, which would work by forming its own vision in conjunction with the well-known, widely celebrated novel's. Ortega must explain how *Don Quixote* operates in order to determine anew the way it is read, provide a new text that responds to this new mode of reading, and predict what this reorientation will achieve. Although philosophy forms a part of a list of discourses possessing and functioning according to "poetic style," philosophy also means, occasionally, the task that gives rise to their comanifestation in writing. Philosophy looks for a "hidden unity" and finds it as "pure synthesis" (S 18–19; E 38–19 [revised]). In this passage, the fruits of philosophical labor appear in "maximal illumination" (S 19; E 39 [revised]). In later passages, speaking of the process of interpretation, Ortega speaks of "intensifying" (potenciar), suggesting that the object of philosophical discourse requires intervention and supplementation in order to reach the full, pure meaning he had already attributed to it. In this process, "the work completes itself, completing its reading" (la obra se completa completando su lectura) (S 29; E 50 [revised]). According to Ortega's description, the reader finds something that requires completion, that offers the means for the reader to achieve that thing's own completion, a process that, he implies, will result in the sensation of plenitude in the reader. Such a process, however, poses the problem again and again, with new readers and new interpretive encounters, making incompletion every bit as essential as full meaning. One finds this ambivalence again later in a description of meditation as "keeping the spirit at full tension [sostenerse el ánimo a toda tension], in a painful and integral effort" (S 47; E 74).

Ortega's characterization of Spain as a "borderline culture" also puts into question the sense that it could be a readily occupied space of stable identity, with a well-defined capacity for unique insight. Ortega suggests that he intends to provide such ethnic characterizations in his lengthy discussion of Mediterranean and Germanic peoples, inspired by the "faith" that seized him in his readings of Menéndez Pelayo (S 47; E 74 [revised]). These two categories line up with other dichotomies to define European culture's range of activity: superficiality and depth, clear vision and clear reasoning, sensuality and intelligibility, and so on, and within this framework Ortega addresses Spain's marginal status within the canon of philosophy. Briefly put, Ortega associates the description of traditional philosophy—as opposed to his new philosophy of style and "pure synthesis"—with Germanic culture. For Ortega, although all of Europe was Germanicized, Italy, France, and Spain only incompletely lost their Mediterranean character (S 47–50; E 75–78). Uniquely, for Ortega, Spain's Germanic character was so incomplete that it never produced philosophers of the stature of Descartes or Leibniz, Galileo or Bruno (S 51; E 78). Spanish philosophers, he says, practiced an activity for which they were simply unsuited: "Our *Latin* thinkers are characterized by an apparent gentility, under which lies—when not grotesque combinations of concepts—a radical imprecision, a defect of mental elegance, that clumsiness of movement that an organism suffers when it moves in an element that is not its own" (S 53; E 81). For reasons Ortega does not address, Spain was not able to go full Germanic, and this deficiency resulted in both second-rate philosophy and preeminent literature, starting with Cervantes's "incomparable power of vision [potencia de visualidad]" (S 55; E 83). Goethe serves as a model for Ortega, because he is a Germanic spirit who approached the Mediterranean, and Ortega offers himself as the revolutionary Spaniard who will redefine philosophy not by fully embracing his own Mediterranean culture but remaining true to it while approaching Germanic culture. By dwelling in the borderland between the two, he will claim a new perspective. Granted, he will speak of "an attempt to make peace among my inner men" and of "integration" (S 67, 69; E 98, 100). He suggests he is an organic hybrid of two distinct elements when he says, invoking his patronyms, that he knows who his parents are (S 67; E 97). We will see in chapter 4 exactly what he might associate with *Ortega* and *Gasset*, as well as his given name, *José*. The border, however, is no more an unequivocal site of reconciliation than children constitute a harmonic coalescence of two parents. Moreover, Ortega will conclude the "Preliminary Meditation" by describing Spain as *both* "contradiction" (S 73; E 105) and "plenitude" (S 75; E 107). Such a gesture suggests that something like antagonism might have a more primordial status than the conciliatory terms generally preferred in interpretations of Ortega, and the struggle this textual inconsistency implies seems more consequential than the common evocation of resolution and integrity to describe his view of philosophy.

We need not make too much of the strange fact that the *Meditations* end at their own professed commencement, after two prefatory chapters ("To the Reader," "Preliminary Meditation") and a "First Meditation," which, moreover, was written four years earlier than the "preliminary" one that precedes it.[82] The "First Meditation" (which is numerically second and subtitled "Treatise on the Novel") continues the elaboration of a long series of binary oppositions: myth and novel, fantasy and reality, imagination and reality, form and content, and so on. To the extent that literature and philosophy fit in this list, their relation, too, turns out to be rather more complex than we might be led to expect, requiring a sustained look at how the terms are transformed and put into action in order to articulate how Ortega y Gasset stands for life, whether in a literature, a philosophy, or something that might demand a novel name and an unprecedented use of language. As we will see, Ortega y Gasset indeed puts his name on the line in a proposal that projects a transformation of thought, reality, and meaningful human existence.

Machado, the Figure of the Poet-Philosopher

While Ortega faced criticism because of the literary qualities of his philosophical work, Machado has been accused of letting his poetry be ruined by his commitments to philosophical thinking and writing. His renown grew steadily through his youth and was solidified in 1912 with his second book of poems, *Fields of Castile*. It already included a section called "Proverbios y cantares" (Proverbs and songs), dedicated to sententious poetry that clearly manifested a certain philosophical sphere within his poetic aspirations.[83] The complaint of letting himself go to philosophy, expressed most famously by Dámaso Alonso in a 1962 essay, arose after decades of earnest study and reflection on Machado's part.[84] His 1917 prologues to *Fields of Castile* and to his first book, *Soledades* (*Solitudes*), began a series of prose works of a theoretical bent, and the 1926 "De un cancionero apócrifo" (From an apocryphal songbook) veers from the conventional by introducing a fictitious "poet-philosopher" named Abel Martín, complete with sample poems and glosses of both poem collections and philosophical treatises.[85] In the late 1920s and 1930s, Machado's primary creative activity consisted of the elaboration of similar characters, producing thirty-two apocryphal writers, according to one count, but concentrating primarily on Juan de Mairena, who is described as a student of Abel Martín in the "Cancionero apócrifo" devoted to him, included in the *Poesías completas* in 1928.[86] Eventually, Mairena becomes the figure through which Machado stakes his greatest philosophical claim with the volume *Juan de Mairena*, a collection of miscellaneous texts discussing poetry, philosophy, pedagogy, Spain, and more.[87] Efforts to capture Machado's ideas on poetry and philosophy commonly take Martín and Mairena as Machado's spokesmen, although this does not mean that no account is taken of the device of pseudonymity or heteronymity, which I will discuss in chapter 5. One can also find coherent theoretical propositions in other texts signed directly by Machado, such as his draft for an inaugural lecture to the Spanish Royal Academy and various prefatory statements for anthologies. As Machado's attention shifted toward statements about poetry, his production of poetry in the conventional sense—of poems—indeed decreased. However, he clearly maintained an interest in poetry as theme and as the formal character of his works. Perhaps "literature" is a better word, since he created complex fictitious characters and attributed to them the thought that became his priority.

Machado read Unamuno and Ortega and took from them many of his cues in philosophy. Although he was eight years older than Ortega, he seems to come of age as a thinker later and was, in any case, the younger philosopher's student and admirer. Unlike Unamuno, whose philosophical essays and treatises make some claim to setting out directly the author's point of view, Machado could be said to speak predominantly by indirection, philosophizing through his heteronyms, often elaborating them as commentary on his own poetry or the writings of others. This indirection is at least doubled when, as often happens, a fictitious writer (Juan de Mairena) describes the poetic or philosophical work of another fictitious writer (Abel Martín). José Martínez Hernández echoes commonplace ideas on Spanish philosophy when he considers Machado one of the "masters" of a Spanish tradition of thought that has been unjustly neglected within the European one.[88] In addition, there is enough thematic coherence for Machado to have been pronounced "one of the great poet-metaphysicians of all times."[89] While one commonly reads of a "fusion between philosophy and poetry," of symbiosis or of a simultaneity uncapturable by the written words, it has also been said that the hyphen in "poet-philosopher" shows a "crack" or "disturbance" in the relationship between philosophy and poetry.[90] This tension between the two sides of Machado's intellectual activity generates some of the vital force inherent in each. Like Unamuno, then, Machado is credited with creating texts that confer life upon fictional characters, who join a community upon which they might have a revitalizing effect. The critical disagreement, then, seems to concern whether the potentialities of literature depend on the identity of thought and poetic creation or their fertile differentiation. Chapter 5 takes a closer look at the different scholarly efforts to characterize the relationship between poet and philosopher before examining how Machado's writings propose figures of wholeness and complementarity at the same time that the motif of heterogeneity represents a more dissonant and indeterminate relationship between philosophy and literature.

Machado attributes to the poem and to the activity of writing poetry an ability to overcome the shortcomings of the entire history of metaphysics, recovering for philosophy an ability to give an account of otherness and temporality. The future would come to us in a form determined not entirely by rational calculation or its surfeit, but with poetry playing a part in elite and popular culture, forming a new attitude and manner of thinking that would address Europe's crisis of reason and Spain's marginalization. As Nicolás Fernández-Medina elaborates in *The Poetics of Otherness*, Machado developed ideas about the necessary place of the "Other" in the constitution of the self, in such a way that human others might not be "objectified" or reduced to an ideologically restricted notion of personhood.[91] Xon de Ros extends this concern for the otherness of other human beings—which she also studies in terms of gender and linguistic diversity—to an environmental concern in line with ecopoetics.[92] Machado's response to this problem, starting in the 1917 prologue to *Fields of Castile*, involved poetizing philosophy, addressing, especially, the relationship to otherness and temporality not only in poems but in texts that approach poetry while taking on the specifically literary power of invention by speaking through fictional voices. Thus Machado's philosophical achievement is bound up with particular potentialities of literature.

We can get an initial sense of some of the issues and tensions involved and their continuity with Unamuno and Ortega by turning to a passage from *Juan de Mairena*. The second section of chapter 14 begins with three lines of verse, lines that Mairena attributes to "a poet for whom the world was beginning to take on a new magic" (S 145; E 31). This poet happens to be—as Fernández Ferrer points out in a footnote to his edition—Antonio Machado, in whose name the poem had also been published (S 145n2). The narrative voice, attributed to Juan de Mairena here, explains that the "new magic" corresponds to "a whole metaphysic that is, in its own way, a new system of poetics" (S 145; E 31). One can see how the melding of poetry and philosophy could be inferred from this, that when Machado produces poems with an implicit poetics, a metaphysics goes along with them. Juan de Mairena says as much in the "Cancionero apócrifo" devoted to him: "Every poet . . . presupposes [supone] a metaphysics; maybe every poem should have its own—implicit—one—never an explicit one, of course."[93] The novelty in *Juan de Mairena* consists of the integration of otherness within the verses quoted by Mairena: "¡Esta gran placentería / de ruiseñores que cantan! / Ninguna voz es la mía" (this great delight / of nightingales singing! . . . / Not one of their voices is my own) (S 145; E 31 [revised]). Like some moments in *Mist*, Machado's fictional character undertakes a commentary on the real poet's work, noting the celebration of otherness, of the pleasure of encountering what is not the poet's own voice, nor even a stand-in for it. The next sentences propose two types of thought, one of which is exemplified here: "For the world is innately pristine [lo nuevo por excelencia]: everything that the poet invents he discovers in every moment [lo que el poeta inventa, descubre a cada momento], although—contrary to what many think—he does not always discover himself" (S 145; E 31 [revised]). When the poet evokes birdsong in verse, and the feeling associated with it, he participates in a tradition that gives him words and produces the expectation in the reader of fulfilment of a form whose existence extends into the past and the future. In Spanish, the operative tradition is the octosyllabic tercet with a rhyme in the first and last line. His choice of a word for "delight" would also evoke the sense of the birth of the new, a new other, with the infrequent "placentería." The idea could easily have been conveyed with the more common word "placer," but in the poem it prepares a rhyme with "mía." It also recalls the *placenta*, a powerful figure for the living connection between self and other, generated by a self that will nurture the other in its separateness. In standard English, unfortunately, one cannot yet say "placentery," and "pleasantry" implies a degree of formality and superficiality foreign to the verses and Mairena's interpretation of them. Here we have the exposition of thought—the connection of pleasurable song and ontogenesis—combined with a temporal experience that Machado associates with poetry. In this passage, the main character of *Juan de Mairena* associates these verses with "poetic thinking" (pensamiento poético), contrasting it with "logical or mathematical thinking":

> Poetic thought [El pensamiento poético], which wants to be creative, does not produce equations but essential, irreducible differences; only in contact with what is other, a real or apparent other, can it be fruitful. Poetic thought, which is essentially heterogenizing [heterogeneizador], exists in opposition to logical or mathematical thought, which is homogenizing thought [pensamiento homogeneizador], in the end a thinking of nothingness [pensar de la nada]. (S 145; E 31 [revised])

As a thought that "heterogenizes," this new kind of thinking would take note of otherness and make essential distinctions. He does not dwell on it explicitly here, but we might note that the nightingale's song, while not that of the poet, is still a song, and as such could still be considered an anthropomorphization of otherness. Machado's verse announces, together with Mairena's commentary, an intention within a conventional sign system, but does not go beyond declaration. It is perhaps for this reason that the next text in *Juan de Mairena* to take up the notion of poetic thinking, in chapter 25, after providing a long list of "rules" and "objectives," confesses its own precarious nature: "Our logic aspires to being a poetic, *heterogenizing* thinking, one that *invents* or discovers the real [pensar poético, *heterogeneizante, inventor* o descubridor de lo real]. That our objective might be more or less unrealizable, does not reduce its dignity" (S 207–8). As we will see at length in chapter 5, poetic thinking depends for its realization on a general reorientation of language and life, one that Machado and his characters devote themselves to imagining and preparing, but do not actually claim to accomplish.

Preparation for this "new logical form"—as Abel Martín calls it in his apocryphal songbook—seems very different from its existence and availability as something, a method or program, that could be appropriated and put into practice. Machado's verse and prose, which includes, after all, strategically composed critical commentary, intervenes in the way we read, whether in an everyday manner or in the specialized way of critics. The general thrust is to raise the prestige of poetry, but this goes along with a defense of philosophy. It can often seem in the scholarly discussions that philosophy must be brought down as poetry is brought up, but, as we will see in a brief look at the early German Romantics in chapter 2, the more status philosophy maintains, the greater an honor it is for poetry to provide philosophy with the possibility for completion. Of the four figures studied in *This Side of Philosophy*, Machado is the one that most often insists on the accomplishments of the philosophical tradition and most clearly describes the difference of poetry and philosophy as a necessary facet of his vision.[94]

Zambrano, "Reason and Poetic Reason"

In an essay on Antonio Machado's volume, *La guerra* (The war), María Zambrano explicitly connects her own writing and thought with his, suggesting that Machado pursued a path of "poetic reason" in his own reflections on "poetic thought."⁹⁵ Zambrano scholars have explored how she not only takes up central problems in Machado's work but repeats motifs of Unamuno's and Ortega's. Goretti Ramírez places Zambrano's thought in the center of an isoceles triangle whose angles are the three older Spanish figures, and one of the most comprehensive monographs on Zambrano, Ana Bundgård's *Más allá de la filosofía* (Beyond philosophy), dwells at length on her debts and responses to these predecessors, anchoring her exposition in "poetic reason as a hermeneutic method."⁹⁶ Although Bundgård's title locates Zambrano's thought "beyond metaphysics," her commentary occasionally acknowledges that it would be situated before philosophy, in a space of unprecedented interiority better described as "más acá." At one point, Bundgård identifies her own titular phrase, "más allá" with "more inside" (más adentro) (30), and she explains how Zambrano "yearns to create a new modality of thinking that would be simultaneously action and an intellection of a deep reality anterior to judgment" (49). Indeed, these are Zambrano's aims when she discusses philosophy's others: religion, dream, literature, and Spain. Zambrano indeed weaves together some of her predecessors' interests in her own affirmation of a sense of vitality they associate with creative activity and consider under threat from philosophy. An analysis of her recurring story of the relationship of poetry and philosophy provides some clarity about a difficult and sometimes perplexing corpus but also challenges some of the central convictions of Zambrano studies and scholarship in Hispanic philosophy, in general.

The daughter of a distinguished activist for popular education, María Zambrano grew up in an intellectual atmosphere dominated by Unamuno, Ortega, and Machado and wrote her first books while participating in the cultural initiatives of the Second Spanish Republic. However, her canonization in Spanish letters only began after the death of Ortega, coinciding with the long transition from a Francoist to a democratic Spain. Alain Guy included a paragraph-long introduction and a selection from a recent publication in *Les Philosophes espagnoles d'aujourd'hui* in 1955.⁹⁷ If Abellán's profile of her—subtitled "La razón poética en marcha" (Poetic reason in action)—escaped notice in his 1966 *Filósofos españoles en América*, the same year saw the prominent postwar intellectual José Luis L. Aranguren decry the neglect of her work.⁹⁸ While Aranguren undertook a brief review of two recently published books centered on dreams, Zambrano's major work had been available in Latin American editions for years: *Pensamiento y poesía en la vida española* (Thought and poetry in Spanish life) and *Filosofía y poesía* from 1939, 1940's *La agonía de Europa* (Europe's agony), and *El hombre y lo divino* (Man and the divine), the book that many consider her most important, published in 1955. Her work had appeared in such prestigious journals as *Revista de Occidente*, *Orígenes*, and *Taller*. She received a Prince of Asturias Prize in Communication and Humanities for her work as a philosopher, in 1981, the inaugural year for this national honor, while the prize in Letters went to a poet. For Juan Fernando Ortega Muñoz, the real beginning of recognition can be traced to the appearance of the first collection of essays he edited, *María Zambrano o la metafísica recuperada*, in 1982, while the effort led by Jesús Moreno Sanz to secure her physical return to Spain makes 1984 an important milestone.[99] Throughout the 1980s, new editions with panoramic scholarly introductions bore witness to and stimulated interest in Zambrano, culminating in the creation of the Fundación María Zambrano in 1987 and her receipt of the Cervantes Prize in 1989. A cultural fixture established just after Franco's death, the Cervantes Prize had been awarded to writers from Latin America and Spain of the stature of Jorge Luis Borges and Octavio Paz. The choice of Zambrano as the fourteenth recipient marked not only the first time a woman had been honored by the state's Ministry of Culture, but the first and only time a philosopher has obtained the distinction, if one insists on keeping the title from the likes of Borges, Paz, and Francisco Ayala.[100] Since then, many special journal issues, monographs, and critical anthologies have been devoted to Zambrano's work, and an ongoing edition of complete works brought out its first volume in 2010.[101] A review of a recent collection of work in English on Zambrano declares that she has attained a "high profile" in Italy, France, and Mexico—where she spent some of her nearly forty years outside of Spain—and only recently began to attract attention in the "Anglophone world."[102] Time will tell whether her work becomes as available and familiar to readers the world over as Unamuno, Machado, and Ortega, whose work is widely translated and appears in panoramic studies and anthologies of world writing and thought. Specialists largely bank on Zambrano's entrée to the canon occurring through the theme of "poetic reason," her "main contribution to twentieth century philosophy."[103]

Before an initial discussion of the story of the relation between literature and philosophy, it is worth taking stock of the unique character of Zambrano's writing and the anxiety it provokes in scholars approaching her work. Like Unamuno, Ortega, and Machado, Zambrano made claims to producing a text that approximates or appropriates life. For her, as for many of her readers, the vitality of her discourse, its spontaneity and incarnation of the temporal character of thinking, is precisely what renders it poetic.

Thus, for example, Francis Lough describes the adequation of expressive form to the content.[104] More specifically, Janet Pérez explains that Zambrano creates an "emotional logical nexus" corresponding to her thought, in texts that "express philosophical ideas through literature."[105] With Bundgård, Pérez contrasts Zambrano with Ortega, whose "clarity" and logical discursiveness they somewhat overstate, although they rightly recognize a principle in the woman philosopher of following her instincts while taking up their shared discipline's traditional themes.[106] Ros and Daniela Omlar explicitly associate this "sentient thought" with a resistance to a "masculine paradigm" belonging to the philosophical tradition, joining Bundgård and others in detecting a "fluid vision."[107] Nonetheless, some descriptions of Zambrano's oeuvre depict this amorphous spontaneity as a potential flaw. Bundgård says her subject "prefers to ignore" the texts upon which her characterizations of philosophical periods and movements are based, as well as the entire nineteenth-century tradition of thinking about "creation" (465). Her description of Zambrano's "diffuse and dispersed" writing is repeated in other scholars. In the introduction to volume 1 of the *Obras completas* (Complete works), Jesús Moreno Sanz will recognize that *Filosofía y poesía* was "finished hurriedly, excessively schematic in many of its passages, and with not always sufficiently argued leaps between philosophy, poetry, and above all mysticism."[108] These leaps, for the editors of *The Cultural Legacy of María Zambrano*, align her with the contemporary, "interdisciplinary" trends in theoretical humanistic studies.[109] In other words, though they might be deficient from the point of view of conventional criticism, beholden to the same standards as philosophy, Zambrano's texts can also be praised for surpassing not only formal but thematic deficiencies of philosophy and for thereby pointing to a new realm of thinking. Ramírez's sensitive and inspired characterizations of Zambrano's oeuvre seem to do the best at accounting for the problem of Zambrano's style of writing. She describes the work as "serpentine and protean, discontinuous . . . polycentric, polyphonic, polyrhythmic" (23). If there are no clear, unequivocal definitions, even of such central terms as "philosophy" and "rationalism," Ramírez casts this as one of the operating principles: "There are never . . . fixed and univocal definitions in her work: everything is in a *perpetuum movile*, as if Maria Zambrano were writing herself and erasing herself at the same time" (74).

Little surprise, then, that scholars feel compelled to dwell on the principles of their own approaches to Zambrano, to implicitly reject readings that they might judge too rational or insufficiently sympathetic to the (poetic) thinker herself. At one extreme, witness Abellán's declaration of "empathy" or Mercedes Gómez Blesa's avowal that she writes "from the complicity of sharing an identical territory (with Zambrano), from which to launch oneself into the task of thinking."[110] Bundgård declares that she will adhere to Ortega's method and offer only "partial conclusions" in order to avoid the "homogenizing" effect of excessive generalization; moreover, she will declare that, like Zambrano, she only stands at the threshold of philosophy without crossing over into its interior (*Más allá*, 463). In *El logos oscuro*, Jesús Moreno Sanz describes a "kaleidoscopic" method that will offer many glimpses of Zambrano and elaborate the interconnections between her thought and a great variety of Western and Eastern thinkers. However, the most important thought to take into account, he asserts, is his own, as he experiences the "dangers, adventures, and felicities" implied in his subject matter.[111] Scholars of Zambrano often accept their subject's association of science and philosophy with a reductive and aggressive attitude, and consequently wish to avoid committing further transgressions against life and poetry, to the extent they are able. Ramírez notes, then, the predominance of a "poetic" approach to Zambrano; the alternative that Ramírez accepts involves accepting responsibility for the affiliation with the very disciplines and discourses that Zambrano interrogates as the price of joining dialogue about the apparent conflict of a poetic and a philosophical disposition (20–23).

In practice, those avowedly poetic approaches still offer the analyses, arguments, and propositions belonging to philosophical and literary critical discourse. Several of them speak of "reconstructing" implicit hierarchies of concepts and dialogues with sources that Zambrano "prefers" not to carry out. Yet disconnection from the philosophical sources seems, in fact, to serve as an enabling factor in her work, for Zambrano. In her essay on her teacher Ortega, she tells of making the decision to divest herself of her class notes, claiming that it would result in her only retaining "the essential."[112] Unless we dare to commit the same scholarly improprieties, we have to find another approach than "poetic reason," but this does not necessarily mean that we reject or disdain Zambrano's central insights. Reading her texts, we must distinguish between dispensing with the norms and procedures, standards and protocols according to which literature and philosophy get interpreted, and, as an alternative, modulating or inflecting them as needed to carry out the work of documentation, dialogue, and interpretation.

While sometimes presented as a means of abandoning the old, blameworthy rationality, "poetic reason" is also proposed as a more comprehensive discourse that would provide a corrective to the restrictive and abusive tendencies of its substantive term by the intervention of the adjectival term. Paradoxically, "poetic reason" is, in Zambrano's words, "broader" than reason alone, a problem sometimes addressed by specifying the bad reason as "philosophical," "idealist," or even "rationalist." One wonders why the term "rational poetry" is never considered and why another term coined by critics, such as "ratio-poetic thinking," did not take hold. It is indeed strange that "poetic reason" should be positioned as the keystone to Zambrano's thought. Like Bundgård and Moreno Sanz in the first and most authoritative panoramic studies, several anthologies have deployed the phrase "poetic reason" as a privileged term around which to gather Zambrano's goals and methods—*María Zambrano: la razón poética o la filosofía, Claves de la razón poética, María Zambrano 1904–1991: de la razón civil a la razón poética*—and recent studies in English insist on the centrality of this term to appreciate her original style of thinking: Beatriz Caballero Rodríguez's *Maria Zambrano: A Life of Poetic Reason and Political Commitment* and Karolina Enquist Källgren's book, *Maria Zambrano's Ontology of Exile: Expressive Subjectivity*, in which she declares her intention of providing the most "thorough interpretation of the poetic reason."[113] At the same time, scholars recognize that such a choice of a central concept presents problems. Bundgård and Enquist Källgren recognize that the concept so named is not "directly" treated or expounded in Zambrano, and nevertheless set out to give it a definite character, a method, and a content.[114] Once again, there is no single text that develops "poetic reason" at length; we are left generalizing from a few scattered statements and drawing connections from many similar expressions: "poetic knowledge," "the new reason," "poetic thinking," "initiatory" or "mediatory" thinking, "narrative thinking," and so on. Diametrically opposed to that dearth of direct treatment, every word Zambrano uttered can be considered an instance of poetic reason.

In chapter 6, I will address the theme of "poetic reason" on the basis of the leitmotiv of the relationship between literature and philosophy. The common understanding of this relationship, as in the work of her predecessors, fails to adequately take stock of its complexity, preferring to fix it in the clichés and imprecision that weaken interpretations of Unamuno, Ortega, and Machado. An early and influential article on Zambrano by poet José Ángel Valente speaks of "the violation of the borders between literature—or poetry in the broadest sense of the word—and philosophy," a rupture that will result in the "nullification" (anulación) of their difference.[115] In "Filosofía y poesía," José Ignacio Eguizábal describes Zambrano's "project of unification of philosophy and literature," and in a passage of the first volume of her *Obras completas*, Moreno Sanz identifies as the "center" of her entire oeuvre the "yearning, realized in her work, for fusion of philosophy and poetry."[116] There are also signs of confusion in some of the more precise and methodical interpretive projects. The editors of *Filosofía y poesía* for the *Obras completas* join Moreno Sanz in reaffirming the notion of "unification" and even "communion," but also call the relationship a "game" and acknowledge that philosophy and literature "keep their own shape, properly speaking."[117] Although Bundgård speaks of a "Zambranian synthesis of philosophy and poetry" and the search for a "reconciliation" (218), she also describes a "pulling in two directions" (doble tirón)—a phrase used in *Agonía*—and concludes that Zambrano's efforts at merging philosophy and poetry were "frustrated" by "insurmountable contradictions" that were never resolved (215–16). Francisco Larubia-Prado makes a persuasive case for viewing the relationship in terms of an organic structure in accordance with Romantic poetics, resulting in what he calls "authentic communication without violence."[118] However, his precise description of Zambrano's text sounds anything like nonviolence, combining her two protagonists in "a double and simultaneous analytic-synthetic movement," which continually takes them apart and puts them back together.[119] Tatiana Gajić's treatment of Zambrano in her fascinating study of democracy in Spain, *Paradoxes of Stasis*, observes how her discussion of Antigone and the subject of exile depict their suffering under "the weight of an insoluble contradiction."[120] These motifs, then, connect to Gajić's principal theme of stasis by referring us to the "irreducible tension between the human and the divine, philosophy and religion, history and politics," a situation that totalitarian regimes simultaneously strive to resolve and fail to recognize.[121] It is surprising, then, when Gajić later begins to echo the common theme of Zambrano studies that this "irreducible tension" must give way to new concepts of politics and society that would eradicate the violence of this aporetic condition.[122] We could trace the common theme of nonviolence to Moreno Sanz's repeated characterization of Zambrano's goal as a "non-polemical reason" that would be "non-sacrificial, non-violent, non-instrumental."[123] While chapter 6 attempts to dislodge this interpretation (made official in Moreno Sanz's *Obras completas* project) by close attention to Zambrano's texts, we can get an initial sense of my assertion by returning to the first text by Zambrano that I mentioned, "*La guerra* de Antonio Machado."

At the beginning, Zambrano declares all history "ultimately poetry, creation, total fulfillment" (186). With the statement of this premise, one can already see that she considers philosophy an instance of universal principles, rather than the discourse on those principles themselves. Throughout *Los intelectuales en la drama de España*, where this essay appeared along with other writings from the late 1930s, Zambrano depicts Spain as an exceptional place, on the margins of Europe, where the principles that governed the latter's formation are most intensely manifested and put to the test. This question frames her reading of Machado, whose work in general, and *La guerra* in particular, embody, for Zambrano, the exemplary Spanish poet speaking to the Spanish people in a moment of upheaval (194). Here she chooses to speak of the part of Machado's work that most approximates her own diagnosis of the present moment, in that she views the civil war of his title as a crisis regarding the relationship of poetry and philosophy. Rather than getting this from her poet, initially, she speaks as though Machado's importance formed a part of Spain's general role in the playing out of the perennial conflict between poetry and philosophy. Like Unamuno and Ortega, she also conceives of her own role as clarifying Spain's peculiarity with respect to European culture before intervening in this culture on behalf of Spain, thereby speaking through metonymic displacement for Europe and humanity at large.

Zambrano's reading of Machado starts with the complaint that he "submits poetry to reason, saying that it carries it implicit within itself [que la lleva implícita]" (190). Machado's fictional Juan de Mairena does state fairly unambiguously that poems manifest a prior metaphysics, a certain logic or logos this side of the poetry. But Zambrano will still persist in calling the vital historical basis for human existence "reason" in the form of a "new," "poetic reason" that might even exist alongside the old one. In the text where she first uses the term "poetic reason"—the epilogue to an anthology of Chilean poets, published during the civil war—she says, "We need, now more than ever, to exercise reason and poetic reason [el ejercicio de la razón y de la razón poética]," distinguishing between the methodical work of the "intellect" and an instantaneous knowledge attributed to poets.[124] In her gloss of Machado, she speaks of a unity of philosophy and poetry, but a unity of persistently different elements. Her echoes of Machado's language should be noted in this description: "This is not the first time in the world that this happens: that thought and poetry, philosophy and poetry should love each other and require each other in contraposition [que se amen y requieran en contraposición]" (190). As we have seen, Machado sees love's particularity in its need for the other to retain an otherness. For those who consider respect for the other to be a formula for perpetual peace and harmony, I note that granting others their otherness requires accepting even unpleasant, incomprehensible differences, including animosity. Zambrano describes conflict as something that could be only periodically remedied: "Perhaps for some, [the relationship of loving contraposition would be] consolation for those moments in which they reject each other and go about in discord" (190). It sounds like Zambrano is applying a personal experience: lovers do not always get along, perhaps inevitably disengage and retreat, only to be called back together by some factor that seems irrational.

Zambrano continues by quoting and glossing passages from *Juan de Mairena* and the apocryphal songbook of Abel Martín, concluding with formulations that appear much simpler than the foregoing exposition: "Poetry and reason complete each other," she says, but poetry remains the deeper of the two in that it seems to govern the relationship of reciprocal love. Even in the form of "poetic reason," the adjective dominates the noun. She describes it as an outgrowth "of the deep root of love," in the hard-to-translate phrase, given its own complete paragraph in the text: "Razón poética, de honda raíz de amor" (193). Poetry is one side of the philosophy-poetry relation, but it also governs that relation, since, for Zambrano as for commonplace ideas of poetry, love belongs more properly to poetry than to philosophy. One could assert that the two elements of "poetic reason" correspond to and reconfigure the two lexical components of philosophy, the *philos* and the *sophia*, love and wisdom.[125] Quoting Abel Martín on heterogeneity, Zambrano identifies "poetic reason" with "poetic thinking"; by apposition, she defines it as "this reason of reintegrative love of the rich substance of the world" (193). While it may be reassuring to hear that they are the same, we are also committed to looking at them as *heterai*, as distinct accounts of a "world" composed of differences.

The secondary literature on "poetic reason" tends to emphasize similarities and identities, both between poetry and philosophy and between the various precursors—mostly Spanish—for a new relation between the two, often speaking as though "fusion" were not an obliteration of difference and therefore of the relation. In addition, scholars often describe this new rationality primarily in terms of what it is not. "Poetic reason" is not violent and reductive, not dismissive of the senses, intuition, inspiration, nor disdainful of the things to which the latter bear witness: God or the divine, the inarticulate wisdom of the body, ethnic community, creative activity, the unexpected. By inference from its difference from merely rational reason, it doesn't limit itself to logic (such as inference), to the scientific method based on experiment and precise observation, evidence, and the formulation and testing of hypotheses. Also, we can extrapolate that it affirms everything that "philosophical reason" might claim to negate. The question remains how to distinguish between what one can do with philosophical reason and what one can do with poetic reasons. Abstract philosophical questions clearly leave room for something like what "poetry" names—for intuition and feeling one's way into and out of a problem—and for integrating it into the humanities and social sciences. But, for reasons we will see in the next chapter, "philosophy" has also traditionally contained the natural sciences and, by extension, medicine and engineering. If it exists—without the quotes that bracket it off merely as a motif in the thought of Zambrano and her admirers—does poetic reason have a role in fighting pandemics or building earthquake-proof buildings and sturdy viaducts? What would we call the discourse that inquires into the relationship between poetic reason and a nonpoetic reason, and how poetic would that seemingly more inclusive questioning be? Or rather, in what way would it be *poetic*? Could one legitimately speak of it without poetic speech? And how would we discern that an instance of speech is poetic, or not?

One traditional answer to these questions is that the broadest type of questioning is already called *philosophy*. Zambrano's lengthy indictment of philosophy repeatedly characterizes it as an activity that has almost always limited its range by self-imposed demands for certainty, finality, and precision to the exclusion of all that fails to meet its standard. It seems intuitive that one could infuse philosophy's rationality with poetry in order to "broaden" it. By taking a sustained look at how poetry and philosophy interrelate and the multifarious ways in which Zambrano speaks of their relation, we can be in a better position to assess the limitation and promise of a newly poetized rational orientation toward intellectual activity and the world where it happens.

A Literary Path toward Philosophy

In his 1902 novel *Camino de la perfección* (*The Road to Perfection*), Pío Baroja puts a northern European character in dialogue with one of his characteristically contemplative protagonists. "You Spaniards," he says, "have resolved all the metaphysical and moral problems that seem to preoccupy us people of the North. . . . You have resolved them by denying their existence [negándolos]; that's the only way to resolve them."[126] Baroja's character assumes the still commonplace impression that the problems that concern Spaniards are distinct from those of their neighbors to the north, whose countrymen occupy the philosophical canon and maintain strong philosophical institutions. It would not have escaped Baroja's attention that this minor character expresses a paradox: neglecting to resolve a problem indeed provides a sort of resolution, the peace of mind one sometimes attributes to children or noble savages. *The Road to Perfection* goes on to develop the protagonist, the aptly named Fernando Ossorio, whose last name's proximity to *osario* (ossuary) serves as a reminder of a physical existence attached to the thinking psyche. The title connects Ossorio's tale to the Spanish tradition with its allusion to Saint Teresa of Ávila. While Menéndez Pelayo and others attempted to raise the prestige of the Spaniards who did apply themselves to "metaphysical and moral problems," Baroja joined a larger effort to overcome the perceived prejudice against Spain that Ossorio's Swiss friend expresses, both abroad and in Spaniards' self-perception. As we have already begun to see, if we remove or transgress common disciplinary boundaries, the category of Spanish letters includes thinkers who lay claim to philosophical relevance, in particular, to approaching the vital sources of knowledge and meaning. Having been closer to life throughout history, Spain's writers suggest, its literature has also been closer than it has seemed to philosophical thinking.

The next chapter examines four significant moments in the relationship between literature and philosophy: ancient Greece, Romanticism, Heidegger, and Derrida. Others might have been included, especially Nietzsche and Kierkegaard, whose importance for all but Ortega seems indisputable. For better or for worse, one of the strongest impressions such an overview can give is of the shortcomings of the interpretations one finds in Unamuno, Ortega, Machado, and Zambrano and the scholarly traditions of their interpretation. Unamuno and Machado, not professional philosophers, may sometimes quote from sources, but they maintain fairly rigid and often not very generous ideas about philosophical predecessors. Ortega and Zambrano, the professionals, are surprisingly similar. Although Ortega devoted lengthy works to Leibniz, Kant, Hegel, and other canonical philosophers, he typically claims to expound an essential kernel while dispensing with methodical rigor or close attention to primary source materials, relying on his own sense of the philosopher's role in history's ratio-vital unfolding. Zambrano, too, concerns herself primarily with individual thinkers and their texts as representatives of historical periods whose particularities and inner tensions she largely ignores. Although I occasionally attempt to provide a more complex picture of the tradition, I do so in order to show that philosophical figures are more complex and more interesting, more conflicted and in a sense more alive than they appear to be in the interpretations offered in the primary texts that I focus on here. Rather than an effort to discredit Unamuno, Ortega, Machado, and Zambrano, one of the effects their work can have is to elicit a rereading of the specifics of the philosophical canon that they so insistently disparage as a whole. In general, I intend to work out their positive accomplishments, and how the limitations in reading philosophy and an antagonism toward a sometimes narrowly defined, homogeneously conceived "philosophy" drives an attempt to restore the role of thought and creativity in individual and communal life. Their exploration of literature's power—of figurative language, of fiction, of the disruptive capacity of narrative temporality and voice—may have been performed often in the name of "Spain," but what each achieves does not seem exclusively Spanish in conception or in its relevance.

Baroja's Fernando Ossorio points to another aspect that predominates in this study. Clearly, he contrasts a well-known northern philosophical heritage with an impoverished or even nonexistent one in Spain. Yet another paradox: northern superiority in philosophy comes from failing to "resolve" problems, for "the only way to resolve them" consists in a denial of their existence. Philosophy lives by irresolution, by turning things over, subjecting solutions to questioning, seeking confrontation or revision in an endless task of thinking. Baroja can lead us to ask whether literature represents an effort to deny the legitimacy of philosophical inquiry or a neglected resource that is, perhaps, uniquely cultivated in Spain. If literature offers promise, we should not be too quick to attribute to it a solution or resolution to what has occupied and preoccupied the so-called philosophical cultures. As an other to philosophy, its role might be better described as a means of drawing philosophy out and into relations, where the singularities of heterogeneous thinkers and texts we regard as philosophical can be taken into account. Such an understanding of the relationship of literature and philosophy in Spanish letters will benefit from a consideration of that relation in the Western tradition.

Chapter 2

Relating Philosophy and Literature
Greeks and Romantics, *Dichten-Denken*, and *le Poématique*

"Philosophy and Literature," and Their Relations

Socrates's announcement in the *Politeia* (*Republic*) that poetry and philosophy have engaged, already in his time, in an "ancient quarrel" itself provokes passionate disagreements. Perhaps that is the secret to its longevity. Broadly speaking, one could even organize the approach to the question of the relation between literature and philosophy around the notion of conflict, distinguishing, first of all, between those who consider the quarrel resolved or a prelude to reconciliation and those who regard it as a fruitful tension between essentially different elements. Hans Feger describes the difference between Anglo-American and continental thinking on the issue as, respectively, a "leveling out of the difference" and a "displacement," before devoting the *Handbuch Literatur und Philosophie* to fleshing out only the continental perspective.[1] The recent *Palgrave Handbook of Philosophy and Literature* sets out to represent a variety of approaches to what is, for its editors, a fully constituted interdisciplinary field, "philosophy and literature," insisting on the peaceful coexistence of different interests and activities.[2] By contrast, several studies insist that a polemical, antagonistic relationship (whether it is between discourses, human activities, or disciplines is one persistent bone of contention) offers not just an accurate representation, but a productive one, one that has spurred literature and philosophy to ever greater development in a history of interaction. In *The Ancient Quarrel Continued: The Troubled Marriage of Philosophy and Literature*, Louis Mackey describes the "dialectical interdependency" and "duplicitous distinction" that separate and join the two.³ The principle of strife requires that the diverse essays in Mackey's book should let the "quarrel" play out as a way of letting philosophy and literature be themselves in their relationship to each other. In a similar way, Raymond Barfield's *The Ancient Quarrel between Philosophy and Poetry* presents Plato's figure of speech as an "image," invented in an effort to provide a self-image of philosophy by representing its "interaction" with poetry.⁴ In a gesture that resembles Hans Blumenberg's history of theory as the repeated encounter of Thales of Miletus with the Thracian maid, Barfield holds that "the so-called ancient quarrel is itself neither poetry nor philosophy."⁵ Moreover, it cannot appear as such but must manifest itself indirectly in various modalities of literary philosophy or philosophical literature, providing enough unity to form the guiding thread of Barfield's selected readings in the history of the relationship, from the ancient Greeks to Mikhail Bakhtin. In *The Cambridge Introduction to Literature and Philosophy*, Anthony Cascardi gives equal attention to Anglo-American and continental philosophers, and presents the relationship as a diplomatic disputation. Although he at one point refers to them as "twins," suggesting a relationship based on common origins and near identity, he recognizes that "divergent orientations and interests have sparked fierce battles," of which he intends to give an account.⁶ He ultimately calls for "mutual acknowledgement" (3) and a respectful "negotiation" (183) to provide development both in common and in difference: "philosophy has always been part literature, and literature always partly philosophical," and "to erase all their differences would be to deprive ourselves of whatever light they can shed on each other from positions that are always partly strange to one other" (187). For Cascardi, the quarrel might become a well-meaning disagreement between respectful interlocutors, although the irreducible strangeness would always threaten to revert to conflict.

After all, even when the claim is made that a peace has been reached, arguments and protests to the contrary remain possible. One could always argue—as Zambrano might have said about Ortega—that resolutions of literature and philosophy's quarrel take place on philosophy's terms. In earlier work, Cascardi invokes Spanish characterizations of philosophy as a tyrannical interlocutor. His introduction to *Literature and the Question of Philosophy* speculates about photography as an "extreme form of writing" that offers "an image of what literature might be were it to clear free of those constraints that 'philosophy' imposes on it."⁷ In "Between Philosophy and Literature," Cascardi explains that Unamuno's and Ortega's blending of literature and philosophy into an in-between discourse moderates philosophy's despotic tendencies, creating "a model for philosophical change" out of the encounter with literary works.[8] In the prologue to *Literature against Philosophy*, Mark Edmundson justifies his defense of literature against the excesses of theory by asserting that philosophy has mostly won the "ancient quarrel," in the form of theoretical literary criticism.[9] For Edmundson, the philosophical attack on literature has employed "dismissal, subordination, tendentious celebration, costly defense" (10), and philosophy's aggression highlights the need for a criticism that would seek, instead, genuine "exchange" (4) rather than subordination in the form of "discipline" (2). While these examples do not outline any particular method, they highlight the difficulty of identifying what exactly is at issue when one speaks of the relationship between philosophy and literature, a difficulty that itself gives rise to disagreements beyond the one about the potential for reconciliation between the two. Certainly, as Barfield's approach acknowledges, Plato spoke on behalf of a particular notion of philosophy, and he attacked and embraced only certain aspects of certain poets. When the relationship is taken up in Romanticism (whose meaning is also disputed), modes of exposition and the nature of language represent an expansion of the category of the literary, putting it in a complex relation to philosophy that is presented in systematic essays and treatises. In order to inquire into the relationship between literature and philosophy—including whether it deserves to be called a "quarrel"—we would be tempted to fix the meanings of the terms. How else would we study their relation? A loose, inclusive definition, however, could either be a questionable means of evasion or a wise recognition of heterogeneity within the fields, even of the threatening force of singularity within them. Literature, after all, can be understood as loosely as referring to any text, and as strictly as linguistic works that conform to a specific set of formal, thematic, and historical criteria. Philosophy, too, has strict definitions—usually involving criteria related to the truth of propositions and standards of argumentation—but in everyday speech it can be applied to anything an individual or collective might happen to think, explicitly or only implicitly. One can hardly begin to inquire regarding the relation without already taking up a certain practice of writing that could be described as both literary and philosophical, as a particular configuration of relations to literature and philosophy as it shifts from description to interpretation, speculation to narration.

That being said, Socrates's quarrel takes an identifiable shape that, together with transformations over the centuries, contributed to the debate regarding Spanish thought. Moreover, the way the relation is understood contributes in a larger sense to the experience and understanding of the humanities, including the practice of Hispanism and cultural, literary, and philosophical studies, in general. Indeed the relation between philosophy and literature serves as a proxy for other central philosophical questions, such as the relation between idea and form, between reason and passion or the senses, between conceptual and figural language, or between generality and particularity.[10] Some of the critical voices proclaiming or seeking to establish peaceful interaction between literature and philosophy hope to restore literature's particularity and, with it, a relevance to everyday life that philosophical approaches might seem to diminish. Others assert that philosophical encounters with literature make philosophy more responsive and more relevant.[11] For the editors of the provocatively titled *Beyond the Ancient Quarrel*, it is the practice of a philosophically informed literary criticism that takes us to a new sphere of respectful dialogue after millennia of squabbling.[12]

Since the opening to theory that has characterized the last half-century of Hispanic studies, scholars have a general feeling of approximation between philosophy and literature, although a debate continues whether the quarrel might be resolved in a series of figures, such as the "philosopher-poet" or "poetic reason"—which might themselves represent a confrontation in the seemingly innocuous form of a single locution—or whether literature and philosophy themselves get transformed into new hybrid structures or a kind of interdisciplinary practice in which fields respect difference and collaborate freely and openly. For the moment, I merely note that an assertion of resolution, ironically, takes place within a controversy that, since it involves others, it lacks the power to end. I am more interested in fleshing out the issues than in taking a position, although it certainly appears that peace could obscure the very differences that we may want to respect. Some notion of productive conflict not only accounts for certain textual exchanges involving philosophy and literature but, also, for the character of the debate about the relation of literature and philosophy. It is not only the case that, as Cascardi says, "to erase all [the] differences [between literature and philosophy] would be to deprive ourselves of whatever light they can shed on each other from positions that are always partly strange to one another."[13] In addition, as Mackey stresses, the difference must be "played out" in readings of their relation in concrete textual instances.[14] It is not enough to say that they are the same or different, or that they exist in harmony or dissonance. One must delve into the meanings of these predicates and put their signifying activity on display.

While the relation between philosophy and literature constitutes a distinct motif in Spanish intellectual life of the last 150 years, it is not unique to Spain, nor does its particular engagement with the relation figure prominently in recent scholarly discussions of literature and philosophy. Although they do not hesitate to invite scholarship that would complement their own, Mackey, Barfield, and Feger do not mention a single Hispanic thinker in their books, nor do most other authors and editors of studies of "philosophy and literature." The *Palgrave Handbook*, with a list of contributors from an impressive variety of countries, explicitly acknowledges that its "survey of the field" is limited to what is "most known to an English-speaking audience."[15] Its two Hispanist contributors—Marsha Collins and Isabel Jaén Portillo—discuss *Don Quixote* and issues in early modern Spain, respectively,[16] suggesting that English-speakers have not appreciably altered their conception of Spanish letters in the last fifty years.[17] As a prominent Hispanist and comparatist, Cascardi has made important scholarly contributions to his fields, yet his comprehensive *Introduction to Literature and Philosophy* reinforces the impression that Hispanic thinkers occupy, at best, the margins of this debate. The characterization of the relation as one between twins echoes Unamuno, and brief mention is made of Ortega and Jorge Luis Borges.[18] However, his *Introduction* maintains a canon in which none of the contemporary Spanish writers I examine in this book has managed to join Sophocles, Voltaire, Dostoyevsky, Wordsworth, Henry James, Nietzsche, and so on. This disconnection between Hispanism and the field of "philosophy and literature" mirrors two other disconnections that I began to discuss in chapter 1.

In spite of an acceptance of theory in Hispanic studies, the field retains a tendency to regard philosophy as a source of ideas about humanity and the world, rather than any of the more open-ended characterizations that philosophers give their activity. As an example, take Gilles Deleuze and Félix Guattari, in *What Is Philosophy?*, which also has much to say about the relationship of literature and philosophy.[19] They describe the task to which they have devoted their lives as the creation of a "plane of concepts" whose interaction attains a life of its own (28). The "plague of philosophy," for Deleuze and Guattari, consists in the widespread practice of employing concepts without "returning them to life" by creatively reiterating their relationships to other concepts (28). For these contemporary thinkers, philosophy does not produce ideas for open-ended reflection, nor concepts for practical application, but "events," moments that reveal the grounds of our world, "space, time, matter, thought, and possibility" (33). Philosophy does indeed produce ideas, and a restrictive conception of philosophy can operate in literary and philosophical studies as tools to accurately interpret and represent texts and authors. In such cases, it is sometimes called "doxography," the representation of points of view, and it can produce rich and nuanced analyses, to which subsequent scholars are indebted. As Richard Rorty and Jorge Gracia point out, histories of philosophy cannot do without the task of representing points of view, but philosophy demands that points of view be subjected to some kind of evaluation that would assess their truth-value.[20] Such a commitment to philosophical thinking indeed appears in critical studies of Unamuno, Ortega, Machado, and Zambrano, expanding the role of criticism from the historical representation assigned to it by a traditional disciplinary definition as a *Geisteswissenschaft*. Yet philosophers might fairly charge that praise for Hispanic writers' originality or superiority in philosophical terms fails to reach a threshold for consideration as a, strictly speaking, philosophical discussion. In the same way that discussions in the field of "philosophy and literature" maintain their distance from most Hispanic thinkers and writers, Hispanist critics who discuss philosophy often restrict it to the philosophemes that enable their own scholarship.[21]

Because Hispanists often operate with a restricted notion of philosophy indebted to the history of ideas, their disconnection from non-Hispanic philosophy in Spain and elsewhere should come as no surprise. Gerardo Bolado's "Luces y sombras de la última historiografía filosófica en España" (Lights and shadows of the latest philosophical historiography in Spain) provides an overview of histories of philosophy in general and histories of Spanish thought in particular published in Spain since the 1970s, and he observes a "gap" opened by the latter's "doxographical tendency" and the widespread decision to follow a methodology of "history of ideas."[22] Designating itself as "philosophical Hispanism," scholarship in Spanish thought, especially in the work of Alain Guy and José Luis Abellán, aimed at achieving "universal projection of our culture" (617). Meanwhile, other Spanish philosophers produced a wide variety of historical accounts of "general history of philosophy," including intensive metaphilosophical discussions that involved, among other things, textual hermeneutics, Heideggerian epochs, Lyotard's notion of grand narratives, and innovative structures of rupture and discontinuity (603–15). An avid participant in the Asociación de Hispanistas Filosóficos pioneered by Guy and Abellán, Bolado strenuously insists that this "schism" should be mended by "returning the philosophical production of Spanish authors to their place in the general history of philosophy" (620).[23] Notably, this charge involves both an adjustment of the perspective of Hispanists and an appeal to greater inclusiveness on the part of philosophers not focused on the Hispanic tradition.

In this chapter, I examine four touchstones in the relations of philosophy and literature. They all figure prominently in conventional accounts of the "quarrel," but have been selected, just as importantly, for the role they play in the discussion of literature and philosophy in the primary texts and traditions of interpretation of the four canonical figures I study in chapters 3–6. The Greek beginning presents literature as a kind of making—*technē* or *poiēsis*—with the potential for philosophical truth, the element that provides principles for all knowledge and action. Romanticism proposes a reversal of the implicit hierarchy, envisioning, in the wake of Kant's analysis of the genius, a moment of insightful, primordial creation that would even include the philosophical presentation of first principles. Heidegger's interest in poetry should not be mistaken for a renewal or reiteration of either the Greek or Romantic moments but, rather, casts thinking and poetic activity—*Denken* and *Dichten*—as modalities of Being's coming to words, thereby constituting worlds. Finally, Derrida harnesses the potentiality of literature's investment in materiality and invention to account for the possibility and impossibility of philosophical universality. In what follows, I do not intend to debate the interpretations of these particular figures that one finds in primary and secondary texts treated in later chapters, or, by extension, the labels with which they have been embraced or dismissed (idealism, phenomenology, ontology, existentialism, post-structuralism, postmodernism, deconstruction, etc.). By providing extensive accounts of touchstones and looking for points of connection and tension as well as differences, distortions, and dissonance with familiar philosophical figures, I contribute to this disciplinary rapprochement, whether friendly or antagonistic.

Literature and the Wisdom-Loving Greeks

In *Keywords*, Raymond Williams claims that "philosophy" maintains its original meaning, "love of wisdom," understood to be "study and knowledge of things and their causes."[24] As is often the case, clarity is deceptive. We have already seen how Descartes and Kant question the connection between philosophical expertise and the most fundamental conditions of knowledge. It may be that, among those who pursue knowledge, the wise distinguish themselves by the limits they place on knowledge and their commitment to principles whose origins and authority lie somewhere inaccessible to a consciousness defined exclusively by knowledge. Just such a situation is already described in Plato's dialogues, where the term *philosophy* begins its long trajectory. Literature, meanwhile, has its root in Latin, in reference to the phonetic alphabet and the discourses that it allows us to archive. In ancient Greek philosophy, what we think of as literature includes both myth and poetry, oral traditions that sometimes attach to precisely fixed texts and sometimes take the form of loosely narrative traditions. In the final book of the *Republic*, Socrates mentions an "ancient quarrel between philosophy and poets" (hoti palaia men tis diaphora philosophiai ti kai poiētikēi) (607b), suggesting a stable identity for philosophy (philosophia) juxtaposed to a plurality of adversaries, the poet (poiētikēi) representing poetry, or perhaps creative activity in general.[25] In a note for this passage, the editors at the Perseus website see fit to inform us that "it still goes on in modern times." However, Plato (through the voice of Socrates) defines *philosophia* in a way that might institute a canon of eminent philosophers, begins the controversy about just who deserves to be called a *philosopher* or *poet*, and proposes how they might qualify for that status.[26] Looking at some of the relevant textual moments in ancient philosophy gives us a chance to observe conventional ideas about the philosophical tradition's relation to literature and begin to contend with some of the issues that interest Spanish thinkers of the twentieth century.

In *Phaedrus*, philosophy receives a precise definition in relation to both poetry and writing in general. After defining rhetoric as good speech-making, Socrates proposes examining the relationship of rhetoric to writing. He defines writing as a mere recollection of speech, since it recalls the reality of a speaker, but does not speak for itself. Because of its distance from the soul who speaks in it, writing always deserves reproach, says Socrates; it fails to accomplish one of the requirements of good speech, that it reveal truth and compel the hearer toward the truth, because it cannot adapt to the particularities of an interlocutor's soul. It cannot hear protests or detect confusion and adapt its presentation, and hence it gives merely the "appearance of wisdom" (275a). Nevertheless, Socrates also describes good speech as a kind of correspondence between what is said and writing in the soul: "Only what is said for the sake of understanding and learning, what is truly written in the soul concerning what is just, noble, and good, can be clear, perfect, and worth serious attention" (278a–b; 554). The writing on the soul still points to a characteristic of writing that Socrates denounces: its ability to remain silent, waiting for a reiteration or actualization of its content.[27] In any case, Socrates will also compare the writing on the soul to a message that must be delivered to all who speak, that is, he says, to speech makers, law givers, and poets. In *Phaedrus,* the message concerns, first of all, the right to be called *philosopher*: "If any one of you has composed these things with a knowledge of the truth . . . then you must be called by a name derived not from these writings but rather from those things that you are seriously pursuing" (278d). In short, any composers of texts intended for instruction about justice, beauty, or goodness, has the right to be called *philosopher.* Socrates says, switching from the second to the third person: "To call him wise, Phaedrus, seems to me too much, and proper only for a god. To call him wisdom's lover—a philosopher—or something similar would fit him better and be more seemly" (278d; 555). I follow the Perseus archive and the *Complete Works* in translating *he philosophon* literally before also transposing it into English. A "composer" of speeches, laws, or poetry deserves to be called *philosopher* because such composition is an act of love or friendship (*philos*) toward wisdom (*sophia*). The philosopher ought to be, says Socrates, too modest to claim to possess wisdom. But in spite of the concern for an inner truth, written on the soul, the true mark of a philosopher is the effort to spread a truth that is conceived broadly in moral, political, and theoretical terms. *Phaedrus* indicates, without further elaboration, a tension between philosophical attitude of an individual philosopher and the universality of philosophical knowledge, the knowledge possessed and passed on by philosophy.

Elsewhere, Socrates coins parallel constructions, all associated with the philosopher: friend of knowledge or learning (*philomathei*), of power (*philarchoi*), of honor (*philotimoi*) (see *Phaedo,* 82b–c). He even designates friends of poetry *philopoiētai* (*Republic,* 607d), but *philosophia* and *philologia* (see *Thaetetus,* 146a) seem to be among the few concepts of this sort to have taken root in modern European languages. As love of wisdom, philosophy entails possessing truth and bearing witness to it, and, as the passage from the *Phaedrus* suggests, it takes no account of the mode of conveyance of truth. A poet might be a philosopher, as well as an orator or a teacher; qualification as philosopher depends only on content, on what is said, rather than how it is said. But this indifference does not extend to written discourse; rather, Socrates stipulates that, as love of wisdom, philosophy must include the denunciation of writing. In the ellipsis of the above quote, he adds: not only must you possess the truth, but also, "if you can defend your writing when you are challenged, and if you can yourself make the argument that your writing is of little worth, then you must be called by a name not derived from these writings" (278c). To be called an orator or poet when one loves the truth is a dishonor, at least as long as one is alive. For the defense of one's writings and argumentation are only possible while one is alive and present when they are delivered. It may not be excessive to say, then, that a philosopher must be alive, and that, when absent from the scene of communication, he becomes a mere orator, lawgiver, or poet. Furthermore, and perhaps as a hedge against death, true speech must always include, no matter what else it speaks of, a denunciation of writing. Remaining true to *inner writing* requires the censure of writing as an empirical object or experience. Socrates's prayer, near the close of *Phaedrus*, is "O dear Pan and other gods of this place, grant that I may be beautiful inside," relating the truth of inner writing to beauty (279c), and hence, potentially at least, to the Kantian and romantic apotheosis of the aesthetic.

The "ancient quarrel" mentioned in the *Republic* might be clarified as the tension between the philosopher's exclusive concern with truth and poet's inordinate concern with the material and form of speech, manifested in the acquiescence to or even celebration of written language. In the *Republic*, Socrates makes a point of distinguishing poets from lovers of poetry, who may speak philosophically about poetry, but must therefore do it in prose, literally "speech without meter" (aneu metrou logon) (607d). Metrical speech calls attention to the sensual aspects of language, and could be said to represent metonymically all figurative language as a kind of careful, *measured* speech. In the framing story of *Phaedrus*, in anticipation of the obligatory philosophical denunciation of writing, Plato dramatizes the susceptibility of all speech to being written down: Phaedrus has surreptitiously copied out a speech by Lysias and hidden it in his cloak, where he holds it in his left hand, planning to deliver it to an unsuspecting listener as if it were his own (227a–230e). Because of this possibility of language, even the coinage of a powerful signifier like *philosophia* can be wielded in a way that jeopardizes the truth. One can pose as a philosopher, reading out words whose meaning one hasn't grasped and merely imitating a love for wisdom. For Socrates, the only guarantee of being a philosopher is the possibility of spontaneous exposition of the writing on one's soul and, implicitly, an ability to respond intuitively and without inhibitions to challenges. This requires that the philosopher should live, be present, and participate in dialogue with a shared idiom. If we recall Socrates's reverence for poets throughout the dialogues, the "ancient quarrel" seems to point to an incompatibility between, on the one hand, the fact that a literary discourse is intended to be repeated word-for-word, and, on the other hand, philosophy's devotion to truth enacted by way of impromptu reiteration and maximal communication between interlocutors. The *Republic*'s discussion of the quarrel appears after a long discussion in book 3 of specific passages that poets are not able to defend, demonstrating that the problem with language is in fact a problem with quotation, to which all language is susceptible. In book 10, he famously declares that an ideal city (the *polis* that the *Politeia* sets out to describe) would exclude poets as long as poetry cannot provide an account of its ability to stimulate justice and virtue (607c). Socrates therefore requires that poetry be subjected to the conditions of his notion of philosophy.[28] At the limit, Socrates suggests that only a living human being can love wisdom, something that does not appear to be the case with *philomathei*, *philopoiētai*, and so on. The philosopher, of all human figures, represents the possible virtue of human life in its *actuality* but not in hindsight. Even Socrates, though he might have been a philosopher, ought not be properly called one any longer, according to his own assertions.

In Plato, another important factor that distinguishes poetry and philosophy is the notion of *logon didonai*, the giving of an account. In the *Republic*, Socrates says it is not enough to possess truth; one must also "exact an account of the essence of each thing," "[render] an account to himself and others" in order to "possess full reason and intelligence about the matter" (534b). After the foregoing discussion, it should not worry us that such a person is not called "philosopher" but *dialectician* (*he dialektikon*). The dialectician is the person engaged in philosophical dialogue. Likewise, in *Theaetetus*, Socrates distinguishes true judgment from "true judgment with an account," only the latter making a person "perfect in knowledge," because not only does he possess the truth but he knows that and how he possesses it (202c). In sum, Plato's philosophers not only possess the truth, written on their souls, but love it in such a way that they are obliged to give account of it, wary of the danger to which they thus expose it by speech and writing. Part of the modernist experimentation with literature involved the intensification of theoretical reflection within novels and theater, which had previously been defined by mimetic elements: character, plot, setting. From the beginning, though, literature's lack of the obligation of giving an account determined both its strength and its weakness as a theoretical discourse. Poets may speak of the true and the good, and what they say may even be right, but they have no obligation to append the principles to discourse, or to explicitly distinguish their own truth from falsehoods. Although Spanish thinkers will embrace the attribution of the philosophical character to poetic writers, this insistence on explicit grounding will be attacked for excessive reliance on rationality and adjusted to include autobiographical or openly confessional accounting.

In the *Metaphysics*, Aristotle acknowledges the roots of *philosophia* and displays how it begins its long trajectory toward science, how its *philos* gets obscured in the concern for *sophia*. "All wisdom follows knowledge" (to eidenai mallon akolouthosan ten sophian pasi), he says, as he lays out a hierarchy of human accomplishment that places knowledge in a privileged position (981a). "All humans reach out for knowledge of things" (pantes anthrōpoi tou eidenai oregontai physei) according to the famous first words of the *Metaphysics* (980a). The beginning of philosophy is the wonder humans feel at sense experience, the "obvious perplexities" around them (982b). Aristotle tells how some were inclined to render the primary causes of natural phenomena as myths, and others accepted those accounts to satisfy their sense of wonder. For this reason, Aristotle says, "even a lover of myth [philomuthos] is in a way a lover of wisdom [philosophos], for a myth is made up of wonders [ho gar muthos sugkeitai ek thaumasion]" (982b; 7).[29] But Aristotle proposes a progression in knowledge, from experience of concrete things to the ability to create according to natural laws, and, finally, to knowing what those laws are. Furthermore, the most philosophical of knowledge is the most general, the one with the most comprehensive "governing" function: "The more controlling science is wiser than the subservient" (982b; 6). Hence, the greatest wisdom is knowledge of "first principles and basic reasons, since it is by and through them that any given subject becomes intelligible" (982b; 7). Whereas mythical "logic" is aimed at a principle that precedes myth in logical order, the object of first philosophy is earlier than myth in that it is able to know the principles upon which even myth must rest.

For Aristotle, then, philosophy can embrace a wide range of knowledge and experience, within which the more ancient discourse of myth would have a place. As in Plato, being a poet does not disqualify one from being a philosopher, even if the latter was the most wisdom-loving pursuit, and poetry's greatest achievement would be to attain philosophical excellence in addition to possessing merit sui generis. As Barfield points out, one of the major differences between Plato and Aristotle concerns the "ancient quarrel," which, while articulated for the first time in Plato, was practically resolved in Aristotle.[30] The difference hinges on their different treatments of mimesis. According to the standard interpretation of the *Republic*, Socrates justifies his expulsion of the poets as a response to their intense commitment to imitation (*mimesis*), at least until such a time as poetry (or its defenders, the *philopoiētai*) (607d) could give an account that would exonerate the poets. Unlike lovers of wisdom, who strive to know things themselves and, through them, eternal ideas, poets strive to produce imitations, not only of ideas but of things in the world (see *Republic*, 595–607). Since they are, according to Socrates, imitators of imitations, they revel in distance to truth, gladly incite all manner of emotions, and parade a vast repertoire of moral shortcomings, obsessively detailed by Socrates in book 3 of the *Republic*.

Aristotle's understanding of mimesis is more abstract and institutes what is still a powerful way of understanding art and literature, one that seems so natural that it often goes unnoticed and unquestioned: the perfect correspondence of form and content. In the extant parts of the *Poetics*, Aristotle, first of all, clarifies that his object of study not only includes writing with certain linguistic forms but extends to all discourse that imitates (1447). Furthermore, the poet does not imitate things—as Socrates seems to say—but "actions": "imitators imitate actions [epei de mimountai hoi mimoumenoi prattontas], with agents who imitate what is happening" (1448a). *Prattontas* is related to *praxis*, the deeds of humans, who also form a part of the created scenario that accomplishes the presentation, or imitation, of an event. Hence, as a standard translation has it, "poetry," in the form of tragic drama, captures life: "Tragedy is essentially an imitation not of persons but of action and life [epei de praxeos esti mimesis], of happiness and misery" (1450a). At this point the description of tragedy serves to describe all poetry: it takes abstract ideas such as happiness and misery, life and knowledge, and puts them on display by means of concrete, created elements. Literature is this kind of work: it renders ideas perceptible, provides a sensuous presentation of the nonsensuous.

Aristotle goes further to elevate the status of literature within a realm governed by philosophy. First of all, it provides theoretical benefits to humanity, not only lessons regarding how virtues and vices might look, and in this, Aristotle says, it is "more philosophical" than history (1451b). Furthermore, in the form of tragedy, it performs a therapeutic act, providing a practical, medical benefit by producing catharsis in the viewer. Aristotle does not give an explanation or description in the *Poetics*, though the word refers to a "purgation" of precise emotions, "pity and fear" (1453a), whose excessive accumulation threatens the health of an individual. These feelings are purged when they are effectively aroused by the tragic poet, and, having appeared in imitation, may be released. Aristotle does not simply oppose dangerous emotions—as Plato does—but proposes that literature might help deal with them. Without catharsis, humans become overwhelmed by their pity and fear, their own vulnerability to misfortune and the aggression of ruthless individuals. By experiencing pity and fear through a mimetic transference, our pity and fear may be reduced to manageable levels in order to allow them to reconcile us with the uncertainty of our fates.

It may remain true that for Aristotle "bards tell many a lie" (*Metaphysics*, 282b), but their engagement with the emotional life of human beings provides an important service. While philosophy describes the effect of tragedy, it itself does not and cannot perform the purgative effect. If the quarrel resolves here, it should be no surprise that this can be no definitive end to it, since philosophy concedes a purpose to poetry that acknowledges the necessity of an irreducible emotional charge in life. The place of *pathos*—like the place of the literature that controls it, or at least keeps it under control—receives its determination through a certain mastery maintained by the practitioners of philosophy.

Literature's Arrival: Romantic Reversals

For the Greeks, there is no such thing as *literature*. We are accustomed to the notion that philosophy is a genre of writing or literature, that philosophy would not exist if it weren't for the written letters, and hence the essays, aphorisms, treatises through which thought reaches our hands. Our common notion comes to us in the time of Romanticism, as we will see in a moment, although the Romantics offer more than a name for a particular textual discourse. Raymond Williams counts *literature* among our "difficult words" because of its deceptive simplicity.[31] Having emerged from the Latin word for "letter" (*litera*), the term *literature* is connected to the popularization of reading in the wake of the invention of the printing press. According to Williams, the association of "literacy" with the acquisition of learning set the stage for the evolution of its meaning from a term for all written matter to its reduction to an elite subgroup, "imaginative or creative [writing]" (152–53). Once literature's meaning is restricted to a "well-written text," Williams says, its meaning depends entirely on fickle and discontinuous social and historical determinations of quality (153). Williams gives some indicators of the historical evolution of the term, quoting, for example, the philosopher David Hume's admission that his "ruling passion" was his "love of literary fame" (152). Madame de Staël's 1800 *De la littérature* (On literature) proposes we consider literature "in its widest meaning, that is, including philosophical writings and works of the imagination—in short, everything that involves the exercise of thought in writings, the physical sciences excepted."[32] Just as the Greeks allowed poetry to be considered a genre of philosophy, philosophy can be considered a genre of literature.

The time of Romanticism also saw the emergence of a concept of literature as a particular form of thought, distinguishing itself from other types of discourse and writing. *Romanticism*, too, has many meanings that can confuse us, if we are not among those who, as Jacques Barzun regrets, simply attribute to it any meaning they like.[33] Barzun's contrast of the romantic with the classic attempts to bring the meanings into some helpful order and has the merit of identifying the main issue as the relationship between reason and its others, whether they are thought as religious faith, imagination, tradition, or anything else that reason might be said to circumscribe or serve. In the conventional representation of romanticism as an intellectual and artistic trend between the Enlightenment and the alliance of positivism and realism in the late nineteenth century, a rigid conception of reason as guide for human activity gave way to an exaltation of motives with more obscure, less communicable grounds, principles that are typically said to be emotional—residing in the individual—or national, dwelling in a common legacy embodied in language and popular culture. In this representation one can glimpse a reversal of the hierarchy inherited from the Greeks, for whom philosophy rooted in knowledge ought to be the attitude or discursive practice that sets standards and evaluates. In European culture of the Middle Ages, that philosophical role merged with the role of religion, and much debate seems to have centered on the relationship between the Greek classics and the religious texts and doctrine of the three religions.[34] In a complex process that culminated in early German Romanticism, art and literature acquire a new status, more primordial and more authoritative than philosophical knowledge.[35] For the early German Romantics, the work of art or literature guarantees the fulfillment of the philosophical project and provides principles for the pursuit of knowledge in its broadest and deepest possibilities.

While literature as *poiesis* troubled Socrates with the possibility that its creations might violate norms of truth and virtue, the Romantics focus on its display of creative force. Literature may be a site of untrue speech, but it also represents the potential for forging links between heterogeneous elements. In this sense, literature's ability to depict the limitations of heroes or the laughter of the gods—both denounced in book 3 of the *Republic* (387c, 389a)—also enables the establishment of a connection, however tenuous, between mortals and immortals, between life and law, or between object and subject. Such a connection becomes the primary concern in modern philosophy after Descartes, and Romanticism regards it not theoretically, as a structure to be discovered, but practically, as a task, something to be accomplished through creative activity. Standard histories of early German Romanticism begin with Baumgarten's notion of "sensuous knowledge" (cognitio sensitiva)[36] and point to Kant's *Kritik der Urteilskraft* (*Critique of Judgement*), where theoretical and practical reason are grounded in the experience of beauty, where the *power* of judgment puts its universality on display.[37] For Kant, the activity of the genius reveals the universality of judgments by providing examples of a universal feeling of pleasure free of the demand of providing rules. Beautiful work, created by genius, is defined by the presentation of an object that obeys rules that are unpresentable in themselves.[38] Without beautiful work, then, the constellation of theoretical knowledge and moral understanding would lack a foundation. It is Johann Gottlieb Fichte and the early German Romantics—August Wilhelm and Friedrich Schlegel, Friedrich Schelling, Novalis, and their interlocutors Hegel, Friedrich Hölderlin, Caroline Schlegel-Schelling, and Dorothea Veit-Schlegel—that home in on this Kantian event and draw out its consequences.

A brief overview can lay out some of the motifs for which the first Romantics are celebrated, and that will appear in Spanish writers of the twentieth century. First, the Romantics assert that creative work realizes the task of philosophy as they understand it. In his *System of Transcendental Idealism*, Schelling defines philosophy as the attainment of the highest possible degree of self-consciousness, a process that requires the orderliness of what he calls "system" but attains its completion only in art, including writing, which he calls "a universal organ of philosophy."[39] Novalis's conclusion about philosophy and creative work responds to Fichte's reworking of Kant's critique of pure reason from the point of departure of an "absolute subject." He takes issue with the relationship of immediate identity described by Fichte as "I=I," concerned that the self-identity of the knowing and acting subject must be preceded by a *feeling* of self, rather than a mathematical principle of equivalence expressed in an unequivocal formula. For Fichte, only poetry is capable of presenting an original self-identity, in the form of a co-revelation in which "the producer can be inferred from the product."[40] For Novalis, poetry accounts for and testifies to the origin of the subject, while for Schelling, it provides completion. For these Romantics, any and all philosophy without poetry will necessarily lack either an adequate beginning or a means of fulfillment.

Friedrich Schlegel's elaboration of a *Transcendental Philosophy* focuses on the fundamental Kantian distinction between reason and understanding, which exist in essential opposition to one another. As Andreas Michel and Assenka Oksiloff explain in their introduction to an English translation of this text, reason imposes limits to both what is known and what should be done, and understanding strives to surpass these limits.[41] They are thus "opposing activities that together form the whole of knowledge."[42] Schlegel does not describe understanding in the lecture course published as *Transcendental Philosophy*, but he characterizes it as "fantasy," a "force that 'drives' finite identities through the dissolution of rationally determined boundaries."[43] As we will see shortly, knowledge and philosophy thus require a continual, endless oscillation between established limits, exceeding them and establishing new limits. The whole of philosophy, for Schlegel, comes to resemble a literary practice, the production of this interplay between enabling conditions and transgression of those conditions. Novalis's understanding of philosophy's poetic origins likewise leads him to think of philosophy as a discourse that attempts to bind together mutually exclusive or antagonistic elements through a temporal exposition that continually shifts positions and a spatial one that remarks its incompletion. Literature shows its priority with regard to philosophy by assuming the forms of fragments, dialogues (in dramatic or epistolary forms), and the novels *Lucinde* and *Heinrich von Ofterdingen*. Because of its apparently supplementary status, *Kritik*—criticism or critique of works—also provides an approach to the literature-philosophy problem outlined here: the philosophical achievements of literature come into view while a rational discourse engages with the mystery of creation. What defines literature, then, as Walter Benjamin pointed out in his study "Der Begriff der Kunstkritik in der deutschen Romantik" ("The Concept of Criticism in German Romanticism"), is the strange attribute of its "criticizability": no work is literature until criticism has revealed the force that already resides in it.[44] This literary power, its power to start or complete philosophical inquiry, sets to work even before criticism shows it or what it is. Thus, for Benjamin, the revolutionary character of the Romantics and their relevance for his own literary-philosophical practice of writing.

Romanticism deserves to be characterized as a reversal of the hierarchy of philosophy and literature, but it hardly disparages philosophy, with its pursuit of different levels of knowledge, including, at its historical moment, the natural sciences, physics, the burgeoning social sciences, and metaphysical inquiry into first principles. Instead, it attempts to render an account of philosophy and finds that such an account cannot do without things traditionally associated with literature: creation and beauty, narrative and rhetoric, the senses and temporal succession, the heterogeneous discourses and disciplines contained in an encyclopedia. One could describe this, as Jean-Luc Nancy and Philippe Lacoue-Labarthe have, as an event that involves literature and philosophy and their relation, but that also goes beyond them. In Romanticism, according to *The Literary Absolute*, "the question of art" becomes nothing less than "the question of philosophy"[45] and the "aesthetic act" of writing counts as "the highest act of reason" (35–36). However, the Romantics "will not be a literary project and will open up a crisis not in literature but a general crisis and critique . . . for which literature or literary theory will be the privileged locus of expression" (5). This "general crisis" will affect everything, all genres of writing, life in general, the way we think and feel, read and understand the products of human activity, including literature, philosophy, and ourselves. It also, obviously, takes us beyond Romanticism to rethink how we conceive of creativity, knowledge and invention, and the relationship of knowledge to conceptual foundations, all of which are revisited in contemporary theoretical debates that include Lacoue-Labarthe and Nancy.

It would be misleading to characterize Romanticism as a fusion of literature and philosophy or an elimination of their differences. "The literary absolute" is, in Lacoue-Labarthe and Nancy's telling, "an entirely new and unforeseeable relation between aesthetics and philosophy" (29), the subjection of philosophy's ambition for absolute knowledge to the necessity of material exposition. Feger's more recent description of the early German Romantics as "poetic reason" (poetische Vernunft) emphasizes their reversal of the traditional philosophical hierarchy—which would advocate for a "reasonable poetry"—but is somewhat less insistent on its unprecedented character.[46] In his study of the emergence of a concept of Romanticism, A. O. Lovejoy insists that it does not only represent one particular genre of literature or art among others but a way of understanding all literature.[47] We could go farther and say that the Romantic insistence on pushing self-consciousness to its limits maintains that philosophy and literature always already operated under the conditions they and the authors of *The Literary Absolute* describe, that their innovation consisted of an intensified self-consciousness not just of individuals but of the philosophical project in general. Hence Friedrich Schlegel's insistence that philosophy must become "philosophy of philosophy."[48]

Rather than resulting in a melding of two traditionally antagonistic activities or attitudes, the relation of literature and philosophy proposed by the early German Romantics consists in modulating their relationships, bringing about a movement from one to the other in the space of their difference. As we will see by examining Schlegel's "Brief über die Philosophie: an Dorothea"—literally, "Letter on Philosophy: to Dorothea"—explicit engagement in relating the two is inspired by the potential for enlivening or vitalizing philosophy, increasing its connection to life or perhaps infusing it with life. Surprisingly, Schlegel proposes this by an appeal to writing and figures of motion, spontaneity, and irresolution, with which he intends to keep the relation open and vibrant. The "Letter" poses as private correspondence, taking the subtitle "To Dorothea," as Schlegel addresses his future wife directly, in a spirit of friendship. This personal character frames the entire discourse, which speaks of universal things in a written discourse with a particular moment, between two individuals. As one editor of the "Letter" points out, Schlegel wanted to carry out Kant's project of critique, but transform it into "a living critique [lebendige Kritik] of spirit."[49] Notably, Kant's *Critique of Judgement* located in the perception of beauty the power to "quicken" or "enliven [beleben] all knowledge."[50] A living critique would supply, as Kant intended, a demonstration of reason's legitimate use and its limits, but it would also, presumably, extend the liveliness of the activity of critique to the whole philosophical enterprise, to expand the reach of life to include heterogeneous voices and perspectives more characteristic of literature than philosophy.

The "Letter on Philosophy" represents an occasion for Schlegel to explain life to Dorothea, a task that, he insists from the start, only reveals to her something she already senses. Dorothea's silence deserves to be noted; certainly Friedrich's distinction between men and women imposes one man's ideas on her, and Lisa Roetzel—coeditor of *Theory in Practice*, an anthology that includes the "Letter"—is right to highlight the limits this imposes on Friedrich's perspective. The "Letter" itself inscribes this discussion within an ongoing conversation, however, and deploys a number of strategies to invite a response. Roetzel's well-chosen selections from Dorothea Veit-Schlegel's diaries show that she struggled with the possibility that the self-exteriorization of writing appeared to her to subtract from the individual self, seeming to justify the relative silence that she maintained. She worries, for example, that "one comes to the point where one is more interested in ideas than in human beings—and finally, in one's own idea above all."[51] It is true that Schlegel's writings have failed to present a human being, to the extent that he more emphatically expounds ideas. The essential human trait, he says, encompasses both an extreme interiority and a projection beyond, a linking up that he calls religion and describes as "this interiority, this motionless excitability [stille Regsamkeit] of all poetizing and striving [Dichtens und Trachtens]" (G 78; E 425 [revised]). Notably, Schlegel puts interiority in apposition to activity, creation, and purposiveness; he typically describes it with an antithesis, *still* (silent, calm or motionless) and *regsam* (active, excitable, mobile). One's inner life involves, from the start, a curious relationship to a temporal and spatial beyond where activity is carried out.

Schlegel explicitly links this essential human "disposition" (Anlage) to male and female principles and to philosophy and poetry (G 78; E 425). Roetzl's analysis of gender accurately describes that relationship as an "exchange" in which "each takes on the qualities of the other without losing its own fundamental character" and without "the collapsing of the two poles into an androgynous whole."[52] Her description of this as *Wechsel* (exchange or alternation), however, comes from the analogous relation between individual and universal and between poetry and philosophy. In order to describe the relationship of *Wechsel*, Schlegel's discourse passes from expressions of unity to affirmations of difference, making it easy for a selective reading to overstate the identity of the two. First, Schlegel describes his own life: "A certain regulated exchange between individuality and universality is the actual heartbeat of the higher life" (E 427; G 80). In the same way, moral health—the promise of life and vitality—joins "lavish abundance" and "prudent self-restraint" (E 427; G 81). It should not surprise us that these traits line up with literature and philosophy, one being the celebration of the singular and the other the controlled study of the universal. But Schlegel's expression again collapses them into a single unit, expressed even in the grammar of his sentence:

> I know you agree that philosophy and poetry is more than a means of filling the gaps that . . . remain for idle people who have some education and that it is a necessary part of life, the spirit and soul of humanity. (dass *die Philosophie und Poesie mehr sei*, als etwas, was die Lücken, die müssigen Menschen . . . auszufüllen vermag, dass *sie ein notwendiger Theil des Lebens sei*, Geist und Seele der Menschheit.) (G 82; E 429 [revised and emphasis added])

Schlegel immediately breaks this union apart, however, telling Dorothea that she must choose in her life between poetry and philosophy. Both are already inherent in human life, he says, but each individual ought to devote herself or himself to one or the other (G 82; E 429).

The next section explicitly gives an account of the alternating fusion and separation of poetry and philosophy. They are a single unit made up of two units, he says, without observing the contradiction in his own sentence: "An indivisible whole [ein unteilbares Ganz]; like Castor and Pollux, they are forever linked [ewig verbunden], though rarely together" (E 430; G 82). Unlike the two stars or two mythological twins, Schlegel says, they are "entirely melted into one" (völlig Eins und verschmolzen) (E 431; G 82). But in practice, one must still approach the two separately: "He who regards the study of humanity as his sole profession could link [verbinden] poesy and philosophy only by devoting himself completely, now to the one, now to the other" (E 431; G 84). This task of binding or connecting through a motion back and forth is contrasted by Schlegel with the "harmony" that one could achieve by devotion to one or the other (E 430–31; G 83–84). Yet Schlegel adds immediately that devotion to one is already devotion to the other. The "Letter" wanders off to a discussion of exactly which philosophers in particular Dorothea should read, the relationship of philosophy to the sciences, friendship, and Friedrich's projected *"philosophy for humanity"* (E 439; G 95). But he has established that philosophy and poetry must relate to each other in such a way that they maintain difference yet resist all efforts to separate them absolutely or to meld into a stable alloy or hybrid.

This resistance to stasis appears to conflict with the nature of writing, and it might be surprising that Schlegel extolls the virtues of the written text over spoken discourse, especially when he presents depictions of speeches in the *Gespräch über die Poesie* (*Dialogue on Poesy*), the most famous of early German Romantic theoretical texts. In contrast to Socrates's predication of love of wisdom upon the living presence of the philosopher, Friedrich says his love and friendship for Dorothea account for his choice of writing, which will possess "an indescribable magic, perhaps because of the glimmer of eternity that hovers around it [durch die Dämmerung der Ewigkeit]" (G 72; E 420). Appropriately enough, "Dämmerung" embodies a contradiction, meaning both the illumination of the dawn or the darkening of dusk, something the English "twilight" resembles. The expression seems to refer to writing's durability, evoked in the Latin proverb "verba volant, scripta manent." Eternity seems to happen in writing, but not in speech, making possible the creation of enduring texts and ideas. Friedrich writes further on, "The silent and motionless characters seem to me a more proper cloak for these most profound, most immediate expressions of mind than the sound made by lips" (die stillen Züge scheinen mir eine schicklichere Hülle für diese tiefsten unmittelbarsten Aeusserungen des Geistes als das Geräusch der Lippen) (G 72; E 420 [revised]). He thus recognizes the antithesis that writing always presents and affirms the value of a phenomenon that holds two extremes in a tense relationship. Letters are motionless, while the spirit is in constant motion. To the extent that the spirit is also a sort of eternal life, letters' "twilight of eternity" represents their fallenness into temporality. They provide a persistent indication of the ephemeral producer, whose absence the text remarks in a way that speech did not make as apparent until the means of sound recording was invented.

Romanticism thus does not only exalt literary texts, or literary texts of a particular quality or character. The praise for letters includes certain philosophical texts as well as literary ones, in a conventional sense, in a quest for an intensification of a life of spirit within or behind them. At the same time, the Romantics show, in performative and declarative modes that seem more closely aligned with the literary, that philosophy and literature deserve equal prestige as they continue to displace each other by continually surpassing each other.

Taking Back Philosophy and Poetry: Heideggerian *Denken* and *Dichten*

Ancient Greek philosophy and Romanticism share a concern with removing the obstacles to truth and virtue, something that they express by attempting to provide an adequate articulation of what is and what should be. The Romantics maintain a conviction that the highest matters of thought deserve their superior status because of their association with life, and that the discourse that gives an account of life must live, doing so in the collaboration of several thinkers in conversation or in deliberately incomplete, open-ended literary forms. Heidegger differs from these predecessors by a shift in overall concern. While he seems to represent simply another position with regard to thinking, knowledge, and philosophical praxis, with a particular set of ideas and operative concepts, we need to remember from the start that Heidegger set out to transform his discipline and the nonspecialist understanding of it. The canonical concepts that purport to capture what happens in philosophy, what philosophers do, are subjected in Heidegger's oeuvre to interrogation and transformation: ideas, concepts, themes, methods, propositions, and arguments are not merely replaced with a new concept of the concept, nor merely supplanted by words that overcome the deficiencies of the old ones (word, path, modes of being, etc.). Already in early texts about Wilhelm Dilthey and Karl Jaspers, Heidegger affirms an inherited concern about the reduction of the complexity of life.[53] As Thomas Sheehan observes in his work on the early Heidegger, he worried about how the theoretical point of view of modern science "[drained the world] of all life, meaning and history."[54] While Heidegger will eventually limit his references to the problem of "life" in his philosophical texts, he remains engaged with the problem of restriction carried out in inquiries into the whole of beings, especially when he regards that whole not as the aggregate totality of all beings but as the opening up of a primordial realm in which all possible beings can manifest themselves as phenomena.

Whatever the limitations of Heidegger's perspective, he deserves recognition for his effort to diagnose obscure structural constraints that have accompanied the rise of science and technology and that have to do with the prestige of a particular determination of rationality in thought. As Sheehan explains, the theoretical perspective that, for Heidegger, "[leaves] lived experience behind," regards all other approaches to beings as simply "irrational."[55] Like Freud, Marx, and Nietzsche, Heidegger analyzes how rational discourses follow structures more primordial than what normally goes by the name of *reason*, rather than directing human life in conformity with an unequivocal logic. The Heideggerian description of the dynamic that opens worlds of meaning seeks to account for the structural possibilities of theoretical matrixes, such as semantics and culture, rather than constituting a theory as such. His structural accounting most famously began with the worldwide sensation of *Being and Time*, which brought him "immediate fame" in 1927, but took a surprising turn in the 1930s with interpretations of the "thinking poet" Hölderlin and the "poetic thinker" Nietzsche.[56] During this time he begins to develop what Rodolphe Gasché, in *Europe, or the Infinite Task*, calls a "mythology" centered on Heidegger's own "story about the nuptials of the world and the sky, the gathering of the inhabitants of the world and those of the heavens, of heaven and earth," aspects of which appear in the well-known essays "The Origin of the Work of Art" and "The Question Concerning Technology" (146). *Dichten* and *Denken* become key terms in an inquiry into the primordial opening that logically preceded the determination of concepts that commonly describe modern humanity: the subject, politics, culture, and so on. In German, *Dichten* refers most commonly to the activity of a poet (*Dichter* or *Dichterin*), producing poems

(*Gedichte*) or poetry (*Dichtung*). But Heidegger will often contrast it with *Poesie*, a cognate to English and Spanish terms, and develop the specialized meanings of *das Dichten* that we will see in a moment. *Denken*, the nominal infinitive we normally translate as *thinking*, also has a very precise meaning that, for Heidegger, degenerates in the common conceptions of thought as cogitation or philosophical speculation.

A perspective on Heidegger that picks out a few motifs in isolation, as Juan de Mairena does when he highlights anguish and "das Man" (speciously translated into Spanish as "the man in the street"), threatens to trivialize these themes to the extent that they serve in *Being and Time* primarily to elaborate a structural aspect of the primordial opening.[57] In a similar way, to consider Heidegger one philosopher among others, presenting what Ortega calls "an analysis of life" that expounds an "integral system of intellectual attitudes," goes behind philosophy only as far as the subject and its historical milieu, satisfied with designating these constitutive elements and with the explanation that a different man in different circumstances will produce a different philosophy.[58] *Being and Time* aims at a description of the structural possibilities of what Ortega calls the "I" that "philosophizes," explicitly connecting this from the outset to Plato's and Aristotles's descriptions of first principles.[59] Ortega's and Machado's perspectives on Heidegger are often echoed in criticism and, though often laudatory, indicate that they will not engage with Heidegger's unique claims on philosophy as a whole, and, beyond them, the entire ecology of thought with which he engages. This is all the more surprising in this case in that the primary authors and critics I discuss share with Heidegger a desire to a radical openness to the richness of experience.

Heidegger's interest in *Dichten* and *Denken* and the relation between them emerges in the work of the 1930s and 1940s, notably in his lectures on Hölderlin, Nietzsche, and the pre-Socratics. In his account of the emergence of *Dichten* as a motif, Krzysztof Ziarek notes Heidegger's discussion of "'dichtende' Rede" in *Being and Time*.[60] While Ziarek distinguishes between two meanings of *Dichtung*, the normal conflation of *Dichtung* and *Poesie* constitutes a third, everyday meaning that emanates from the more determinate meanings. First, Heidegger speaks of "das Dichterische," the poetic, in "The Origin of the Work of Art," as the opening up of a world. Heidegger articulates such an opening in different ways across his oeuvre: it is the disclosure of truth in *Being and Time*, *Ereignis* in *Contributions to Philosophy* and other late work, and *Geschick* in "The Question Concerning Technology" and "The Age of the World Picture." Sheehan describes it as the prestructuring of the world, the laying out of a horizon of possibilities prior to the particular possibilities that belong to different shapes that metaphysics has taken.[61] If metaphysics restricts our possibilities of understanding and acting in the world, a step back to phenomena *before* metaphysics is the chance of opening another orientation toward things, individual people, and community. As Ziarek puts it, *Dichtung* is in this first sense "more primordial than poetry and thinking as the happening of truth" (26). While in "The Origin of the Work of Art" that opening is held open by the work of art, in which it can be glimpsed *as* opening, other texts make it clear that human modes of being called *Dichten* and *Denken* also have this capacity because they are charged with manifesting the truth, which in Heidegger's description as *aletheia* is a hiding that shows itself in its withdrawal into hiding. *Dichtung* and *Denken* do not speak the truth, as it were, but give a chance to sense truth's opening of a world. Both attend to this primordial event and respond in language. The first sense of *Dichten*, then, "das Dichterische," appears in a second sense of *Dichten*, which Ziarek aptly calls the "after-saying" (26). *Dichten* and *Denken*, as secondary phenomena, share a "neighborhood" and achieve their own particular mode of speech in which the nearness of the other remains an integral part of its activity. Thus the privilege conferred on Hölderlin and Nietzsche: as Heidegger stresses in the *Introduction to Philosophy*, the rendering of thinking *poetic* and of poetry *thoughtful* does not eliminate difference but allows each to be more emphatically itself in an event he calls *Aus-einander-setzung*, contestation or, literally, setting-apart-from one another.[62] Not everything that goes by the name of *Dichtung* achieves this reaching behind speech into the opening of a world. Heidegger reserves the word *Poesie* for verse with a less primordial meaning, discourse that pleases or merely offers ideas for the reader's consideration but that does not aspire to echo, in an after-saying, the originary event.

Heidegger's curious "Aus der Erfahrung des Denkens" offers a succinct articulation of these concerns, and unlike most other texts, it ties Heidegger's thinking to his own personal life and a concrete environment. In the volume *Poetry Language Thought*, editor and translator Albert Hofstadter calls this piece "The Thinker as Poet," a renaming that suggests that the thinker steps into a different role than the usual one.[63] The printing in short lines resembles stanzas more than the German edition, which isolates sentences but does not strive for uniform line lengths. The author of "Aus der Erfahrung des Denkens" is a thinker approaching poetry, in form, and speaking in the nearness of two modes of speech, but the piece also maintains certain distinctions while thematizing their togetherness. For one thing, the opening stanzas, which feature uniform verses with rhyme, advise the reader to "go . . . your single way" (Geh . . . deinen einen Weg entlang), recalling Heidegger's frequent assertion that thinkers devote themselves to a single thought. Speaking "as poet" or "out of the experience of thinking" does not mean abandoning that unique thought. The text emphatically divides into two modes of speech, through eleven sections, each of which features a description of a scene from the surroundings of Heidegger's cabin near Todtnauberg (on the left page in German and with a left-aligned paragraph in English) and a quasi-philosophical discourse (on the right hand page in German and centered on the page in English).[64] The descriptive passages focus on images and sounds one can associate with the Black Forest: light, sky, sun, flowers, cattle (and their bells), trees, a mountain stream, snow. The initial, pensive sentences convey the principles that Heidegger has already discussed in his work: "As soon as we have the thing before / our eyes, and in our hearts an ear / for the word, thinking prospers" (E 5; G 77). A disclosure of a realm of being must precede human experience, of which disclosive thinking can be a mode. Such an opening is called "Being's poem" (angefangenes Gedicht des Seyns) (E 4; G 76). The bulk of the meditative passages concern the dangers posed to thinking, to which we will return. At the end, however, Heidegger distinguishes between the two "stems" of this primordial *Dichten*, the two activities that grow directly out of it: "singing" (Singen) and "thinking" (E 13; G 85). The second type of *Dichten*, then, called "singing" here, is related to thinking in that both hearken back to a more primordial *Dichten*.

Heidegger's description of the three "dangers [that] threaten thinking" distinguish the inquiry into the originary disclosive opening of Being or truth, on the one hand, from philosophy in its classical definition, on the other. The first danger is "the singing poet"; while, he says, its relationship to thinking is "wholesome" (heilsam), that is, it promotes healing, Heidegger does not elaborate immediately on what makes it dangerous (G 80; E 8). He will later warn of the "utopianism of the half-poetic intellect," suggesting that a mix of a restricted kind of thinking and poetry renders discourse irrelevant, a nonplace in contrast to the "topology of Being" that the "thinking poetry" (dichtendes Denken) might provide (E 12; G 84). As Heidegger will warn in many other texts, a poetry that is not essential by being thoughtful obstructs the view of the essential in "genuine *Dichten*."[65] As *Dichten* is obstructed by *Poesie*, *Denken* is hampered by *Philosophie*. "Aus der Erfahrung" speaks of the "bad and muddled danger of philosophizing" (schlechte, und darum wirre Gefahr des Philosophieren) (E 8; G 80) and insists that thinking should distinguish itself by "[stepping] back out of philosophy into the thinking of Being" (G 82; E 10). Such thinking itself poses a third danger, which occupies Heidegger little in "Aus der Erfahrung," but could be quickly described as the tragic nature of thinking as thinking of Being.[66]

Heidegger's "Aus der Erfahrung des Denkens" thus confronts us with a series of incongruities: the title; a discourse bifurcated into description and meditation; the contrast between a verse prologue and epilogue and a series of propositional sentences; and an explicit description of the hazards of the very kinds of speech the text deploys. Timothy Clark describes the tendentious interpretations of Heidegger that cast him as a romantic personage who lets his natural surroundings and the wisdom of his community speak through him. Subsequently, he proposes an approach to Heidegger that takes the tensions and dangers described by Heidegger seriously, associating thinking with "unanchoring certainties" such as facile categorizations and assimilation of the thinker to inherited notions.[67] For Clark, the stubborn meaninglessness of the natural-physical world does not comfort, but, rather, challenges assumptions about human life. Heidegger's *Introduction to Metaphysics* discusses Sophocles's *Antigone,* contrasting "poetic-thoughtful projection" with "eyes that merely describe and ascertain something present at hand."[68] While Heidegger characterizes thinkers as those who face "the most extreme limits and the most abrupt abysses," poets are the ones who open abysses in the first place.[69] Therefore, thinking looks to poets as others whose difference provides the occasion for their engagement with the originary opening of self and other. Ziarek is right to describe as "poetic thinking," then, the activity that invokes the most noble and difficult, throwing into relief the ethical dimension of Heidegger's thought.[70]

In the criticism about Unamuno, Machado, Ortega, and Zambrano, Heidegger's work is predominantly characterized as an effort to envision harmony and conviviality between literature and philosophy, if not their identity.[71] Heidegger is also often an important figure for us to question the tendency to characterize philosophy as the subordination of life to reason or as the tyranny of cold-hearted logic. Heidegger's work does not lack the impulse to find comfortable resolution to the troubling nature of the relation of literature to philosophy. In his most direct discussion of *Dichten* and *Denken,* the *Introduction to Philosophy: Thinking and Poetizing,* Heidegger explains the privilege of Nietzsche and Hölderlin in his work. It is no exaggeration to say that only a handful of thinkers and poets are worth serving as the occasion of reflection. In the *Introduction*, he develops a conception of philosophy as "genuine thinking," within which all human beings stand, and which is implicit in everything we do.[72] As such, for Heidegger, we also all exist within a certain poetic opening. Nonetheless, among us dwell *Denker* and *Dichter*, humans who think or who poetize "in a distinguished sense" (2). In the time of the end of metaphysics, Heidegger says, the preeminent thinkers and poets think while poetizing and poetize while thinking, and one may recognize them according to a kind of harmony or even redundancy: "The decisive [massgebenden] thinkers and the decisive poets themselves provide the standard [Mass] according to which we grasp and assess [ermessen] the essence and necessity of thinking and poetizing" (44–45). For Heidegger, Nietzsche and Hölderlin seem to be the only figures who meet this standard, although a handful of others (Rilke and Trakl stand out) follow Hölderlin's example. Heidegger does recognize the problem of this circularity in some of the notes to the *Introduction*, suggesting that his readings presuppose a reception or hearing that he cannot teach, that is beyond conveying to others (50). What else could he refer to here except a certain comfortable coincidence between the canon and his personal preferences, between the institutions of learning and research and his own tastes? He also notes that the approach to the relation between *Dichtung* and *Denken* through the thoughtful poet and the poetizing thinker must take place "from the side of thinking" (50). While "Aus der Erfahrung" appears to be an attempt to approach from the side of poetizing, Heidegger also seems to recognize the irremediable otherness of poetic speech, even when its thoughtful traits might be brought into dialogue. Rather than dismiss this as a weakness of Heidegger's thinking of poetry, I would like to retain it, too, for its resemblance to certain claims of untranslatability and singularity made by Spanish thinkers.

Invention (in Principle) Impossible: Literature and Derrida

Chronologically, Jacques Derrida's work coincides only with Zambrano, the last of the series of Spanish thinkers I study in detail in this book, and, to my knowledge, he did not write about any of them. His suggestion that he should be considered a *marrano* is his most direct connection to something like a Hispanic tradition, in the conventional sense.[73] Derrida is a worthwhile reference point, however, for his continuation and expansion of Heidegger's rapprochement of literature and philosophy. Ziarek's and

Clark's provocative readings of Heidegger, in fact, are largely propelled by Derrida's inflection of phenomenology, which in Heidegger was already a turn from "what shows itself in itself" to what "announces" itself by refusing to show itself.[74] Derrida explains Heidegger's sense that poetry is a mode of receiving and responding to otherness and expands the range of those encounters with otherness. His thinking—to give a conventional name to the activity his published corpus transcribes—includes not just readings of a few poets and painters but a wide range of art and creative writing, heterogeneous and seemingly trivial moments in canonical philosophical texts, so-called real lives—including his own and others'—and real events. Derrida is considered a standard-setter for thinking, though far from the only one, and his presence in Hispanic studies would be enough to justify a place of honor in this assessment of the relation of literature and philosophy in a particular strand of the intellectual life of Spain. In addition, certain recurrent motifs of his thought illuminate the work of authors on which I focus. In this discussion, I will treat Derrida's unique concept of literature, the way he relates philosophy and literature, and some of the stakes of his approach to these issues.

Like Heideggerian *Dichtung*, *literature* in Derrida can mean several things, and those meanings can be difficult to distinguish in the different iterations of the word. Following J. Hillis Miller's "Derrida and Literature," we can separate out two primary meanings that are closely related, the "institutional" and the "infrastructural." The first, less revolutionary sense, plays an important role in contemporary education and scholarship, and certainly guided Derrida as it guides us to read particular texts with specific expectations in mind. It is what Miller calls "a complex set of conventions, rules, institutions, and historical features that are both within the text and within the understanding of the one who performs the act . . . of taking a given text as literature."[75] Derrida recognizes that the designation of certain texts as *literary* maintains a validity within sociocultural and legal contexts that can be determined and described. He also recognizes that these normative traits can be located in texts, as part of their discernable meaning. In *Of Grammatology*, speaking of the specificity of *philosophical* texts, he describes "the project of effacing itself in the face of a signified content which it transports and in general shows [enseigne]."[76] Because of this conventional trait, the philosophical text calls for what he calls a "transcendent reading," marked by the use of a particular rhetoric and argumentative structures. He notes that "literary writing," too, "has . . . lent itself to this *transcendent* reading," especially "philosophical literature" such as Rousseau's, citing both the hybrid *Social Contract* and the novel *La Nouvelle Héloïse*.[77] Literature is identifiable according to its conventions, which are, furthermore, sustained by "institutions" in a more concrete sense: writing centers and other academic programs, publishing houses, grants, prizes, archives, and so on.

Derrida will also use the second, infrastructural meaning of literature as an institution. "Infrastructure" is the name Rodolphe Gasché proposes for the nonconceptual enabling structures that Derrida devises in his texts: *différance*, the trace, the pharmakon, and so on.[78] Miller associates literature in this sense with the textual character of all meaningful utterances, including, of course, everyday speech, literature, and philosophy. He chooses "iterability" as a concept to describe this, referring us to Derrida's reading of J. L. Austin in "Signature, Event, Context." In that essay, Derrida celebrates Austin's speech act theory for its effort to recognize a kind of extralinguistic force previous to utterances.[79] But he is also struck by Austin's exclusion of literature as an abnormal, nonserious, parasitic use of language, citing a passage that describes actors on a stage and poetic speech in order to exclude them from his analysis of language.[80] Drama and poetry, in Miller's discussion, exemplify the "as if" characteristic of literature: literary writers create speech that acts *as if* they did not belong to the writer's conscious intention. "Signature, Event, Context," however, demonstrates that this characteristically "literary" use of language is internal to all speech. As the condition of its existence, any signifying act—mark, gesture, speech, writing—must be repeatable without its meaning remaining present to a subject, without signification being anchored to a particular consciousness or speaker. This "essential iterability" goes along with an "essential drift" of the signifier, guaranteeing the possibility of its functioning as a signifier but assuring also the unforeseeability and openness of its meaning, since one cannot determine in advance the contexts in which it might function. Such a characterization suggests that the "institution" of literature should *also* include within it—along with the familiar, traditional approaches to literature—a reference to this strange and potentially disruptive condition of possibility of all speech.

Miller notes a tension between the two components of the institution of literature, going so far as to say that most of the things we do with literature in university classes have nothing to do with what is uniquely literature, that is, its infrastructural aspect.[81] Indeed, the predominant modes of interpretation—whether envisioned as an interdisciplinary republic of letters or a struggle for predominance between different theoretical orientations—might be seen as opposed to its particularity, supplying knowledge and theoretical insights while literature also calls, in a sense, for the radical nonknowledge that Derrida sometimes refers to as "secrecy."[82] In order to clarify further this unique facet of literature, Miller discusses the connection to democracy, with its sanctioning of a right to free speech, including the freedom of literature. As Derrida explains in his interview with the editor of *Acts of Literature*, although all language is characterized by a certain possibility of radical freedom in its detachment from conscious intention, the invention of literature made that linguistic possibility into an institution.[83] In this sense, literature is the institution of "tout dire," an expression translated as the right to "say anything, in any way"; we could also note that "all saying" (another translation of *tout dire*) has a literary aspect, even when the political context of the speaker does not endorse free speech. Literature's freedom provides the possibility of linguistic invention beyond what the subject and cultural context can prescribe and foresee. This is key to the thinking of democracy because, historically, the *demos* has been determined in ways that exclude people who later seem like obvious members and to define power in ways that surreptitiously oppress even those who supposedly wield the power. Thinking democracy calls for the broadest possible scope of thinking, a thinking that responds to otherness, to the unforeseeable future, to what is heterogeneous to institutional discourses. For Miller, literature serves to take the measure of heterogeneity by exploring the otherness of the other, and, in particular, by its peculiarly secretive nature. Miller elaborates this claim by reference to Derrida's unrealized thesis project on "The Ideality of the Literary Object," described in "The Time of the Thesis" and the interview from *Acts of Literature*. In short, Derrida will retain the notion of a description of an ideal object *in principle*; that is, the literary object's principles can be formalized even if the principles cannot be realized, strictly speaking, in an object corresponding to them. Literature thus displays *in principle* the possibility of radical detachment from meaning, characteristic of iterability. But because the display of the principle would defy or defile the purity of such nonsignifying indifference to signification, the literary object is unrealizable. Thus Miller says, in a related text, the literary object is "possible impossible."[84] One sees here a philosophical operation—the determination of principle and ideality—reaching an insight thanks to literature but without settling comfortably into the institutional determination of the literary.

The motif of literature as infrastructure accounts for the commonplace assertion that, for Derrida, all thought, including philosophy, is literature; in order to exist even as a meaningful inner monologue—as it sometimes is described, from Plato on—let alone as a philosophical treatise, thinking must submit to the condition of literature as the condition of any signifying act. But as with Romanticism and Heidegger, one should not conclude from this that literature and philosophy become indistinguishable or that their difference falls away. After all, the first institutional meaning of literature remains active and valid still when it becomes "the institution that tends to overflow the institution."[85] Gasché has provided a clear and suggestive analysis of the relation between philosophy and literature both in the two relevant chapters of *The Tain of the Mirror* and the subsequent essay "A Relation Called 'Literary,'" placing this problem in the larger context of Derrida's work and establishing some guidelines for literary theory and criticism that would take it into account. "A Relation Called 'Literary'" builds on earlier work arguing against the categorization of Derrida's work as literature and defines the relation between literature and philosophy as one of "constitution." That is, "they begin to become what they are in their respective difference."[86] Gasché explicitly indicates that neither ever realizes what it is once and for all, but only becomes literature or philosophy as they bear a simultaneous conformity to and rupture of the institutions that bear their names. Gasché focuses on Derrida's "Before the Law," an ostensibly philosophical essay that shares a name, mediated by translation, with a well-known story by Franz Kafka. His concern here has to do with the necessity of "prejudices" (préjugés), in the application of any law. Among the "structures" that govern the institutions of literature and philosophy as they encounter each other in Derrida's essay, law is the most important. Laws determine what is considered literature and what is considered philosophy, how they are read, and how they impact us and the world. Returning to the question of the relation between literature and philosophy, Gasché describes deconstruction as "invitation to rethink the relation between philosophy and literature as it has been understood by philosophers and, in their wake, by literary critics" (285). He reiterates the idea that both are particular institutions that control the identification of certain phenomena as literary or philosophical and the interpretation to which they are subjected. Gasché notes that "Before the Law" concerns "the constituting and differentiating function of the axiomatic beliefs about literature and philosophy and the law to which they yield in that respect" (289). Though it is not a critique nor literary criticism in the traditional sense, deconstruction intervenes, then, in the laws constituting institutions. It does so, first, by exposing the possibility and impossibility of meaningful units of experience, which is to say, it confronts us with the way they exceed and precede our experience and consciousness.

Gasché speaks frankly about "deconstructive" literary criticism's failure to measure up to the challenge of deconstruction, its misconstrual of Derrida's work as one theoretical perspective among others, rather than an analysis of the presuppositions of theory in general. Its terms have been transformed into concepts and methodically deployed in analyses and theorizations that propose new interpretations of the literary or cultural artifacts. At the beginning of "A Relation," Gasché considers the thesis that literature is philosophy's other and argues that it fails to appreciate the extent to which literature's singularity does not constitute *the* other, but a plural other, a heterogeneous manifold of others, some of which might be better considered nonliterary. In *The Tain of the Mirror*, Gasché takes stock of the difference of Derrida from his philosophical predecessors and insists that whatever new concepts of textuality and metaphor we might extract from Derrida should not merely go into a literary critic's toolbox. Rather, Derrida implies "a new kind of 'rationality' and a new practice of 'knowledge.'"[87] The novel practice in question would not merely incorporate new concepts but commit itself to the always singular construction of the conditions of possibility and impossibility of signification, of full meaning, and of questioning.

Derrida has left a brief and dense articulation of the relation between literature and philosophy in "Che cos'è la poesia?" The title quotes from the question posed to him by an Italian journal. Throughout the essay, Derrida explores the French and English idiom "learning by heart"—which does not exist in Italian (or Spanish)—suggesting that poetry is above all something we memorize, hold onto in its literalness, with a certain indifference to meaning. In one common practice associated with it, therefore, literature represents a privileged site to observe iterability at work. "Che cos'è" is framed by formulations that reiterate how poetry must stand in a particular relation to philosophy, a relating that might contaminate poetry as its condition of possibility for appearing at all. The first paragraph begins to answer the question "What is poetry?" by relating it to knowledge, with a paradoxical formulation: in order to "respond" to the question, Derrida says, "you are asked to know how to renounce knowledge."[88] The very person who speaks of poetry—marked already by Derrida as an individual by the use of the second person singular—must renounce the very knowledge that determined that she or he should speak in the first place. The person who responds to the question must have cultivated a knowledge of poetry in order to be able to renounce it in a definition of poetry. Thus Derrida calls it—in an allusion to Augustine's description of the approach to God—a "learned ignorance" (223). He further describes his response to the question as a repetition nearly devoid of understanding, the school exercise known as a "dictée": "*La réponse se voit dictée*" (222). Dictation is the writing down of something independent of understanding the whole; in order to write down a statement in French, one must know the conventions of writing and recognize the words, sometimes by recognizing a meaningful context, such as knowing whether "dictée" has a final "e" in the sentence quoted above. Rather than a demonstration of understanding, that is, of appropriation of knowledge, "taking dictation" connects the identity of poetry to iterability; it involves the inscription of the words before meaning, because there is no meaning without repeatable units.

"Che cos'è" describes a poetic utterance as a hedgehog, developing, without attributing it, the early German Romantic definition of the work of art as a fragment.[89] This analogy, after all, can be detached from its source and developed in its own right, which Derrida does, mentioning the danger a hedgehog runs of being curled up on a highway where it might be killed by traffic (223, 229). The significant trait of the hedgehog is the paradoxical action of turning in on itself, and the person with a concern for poetry, and what it might be, wishes to publicly celebrate and respect the uniqueness of the poetic work: "[you desire] to guard from oblivion this thing which in the same stroke exposes itself to death and protects itself" (229). Derrida thus proposes two mechanisms to carry out this strange, impossible effort. First, he develops a description of poetry as "the poetic" and "the poem" as the welcoming of the wholly other. Toward the end, though, he rejects the locution "the poem," preferring to use a French partitive article and speak of "du poème": "There is never anything but some poem [du poème], before any *poiesis*" (232–33). All discourse requires, before anything—before the different idioms, before genres or authorial intentions of creation or expression—that there be "some poem," the welcoming of the other that is uniquely poetic but also generalized in discourse and experience, in a poem, for example. Derrida immediately indicates that this alternative name to speak of "poetry" can incorporate its inextricable relationship to repetition without understanding: "When, instead of 'poetry,' we said 'poetic,' we ought to have specified: 'poematic' " (233). He thus integrates the mechanical and inhuman, the otherness of the nonhuman, into what is traditionally considered the most human of activity, our questioning and our involvement with *poiesis* in any type of creative activity. "Poematic" refers to the blind repetition of a machine with the irruption of singularity for which "poetry" can also stand, in its paradoxical way. Poetry is never simply invention of a unique work or voice, since these things must assure their legibility with a measure of the mechanical, the repetition of conventions. While this exposes it to abuse—the ideology of aestheticism or the political use of poetry, for example—this exposure is its only chance to appear at all.

The Ongoing Relation

As we can see from even a cursory glance at recent manuals on literature and philosophy or titles about the "ancient quarrel," much more could be said about philosophy's engagement with literature. Rarely has the question been posed in itself, as a merely theoretical question involving two elements and their relationship; rather, the question emerges as a matter that bears on the particular modes of activity that constitute thought, even while maintaining a reflection on the possibilities of activity per se. Each of the four moments examined in this chapter, like the four Spanish thinkers I have begun to discuss, notice that philosophers and poets act in relation to life and must live in relation to a larger element that they sometimes call *life*. What is unique to Derrida, perhaps, is the affirmation of the role of death, or the dead-ness of iterative marks in the constitution of life. *Perhaps*, because to demonstrate this would take us too far afield. The philosophers in this chapter do not merely seek to define the relation between philosophy and literature but explore that question in the context of broader questions, and thus the inquiry yields insights that bear on other matters. Plato thinks about fantasy and immorality, whimsy and trickery, with respect to the seriousness of truth, piety, justice, and virtue. Aristotle finds a role for fickle emotions within a well-ordered life, characterized by reliable and justified activities. The Romantics, after considering the relationship of affect to understanding, experiment with possibilities of putting into practice mutually exclusive sorts of activity, rational knowledge and original creation. All of these initiatives, seen in this way, suggest that the question of literature and philosophy's relationship drives us to issues of otherness, not just the alterity of these two activities, disciplines, or discourses, but other instances of otherness.

My concern that the characterization of the relation of literature and philosophy in Spanish letters as *synthesis* or *fusion* grows out of an understanding of a philosophical tradition in which *polemos*, *agon*, antagonism, incompatibility, difference, and exclusion play a necessary role, and in which that role itself is contested. Unamuno and Zambrano are especially vocal about the tyranny of absolute exclusions, such as those between life and death, understanding and feeling, truth and opinion. And while I agree with them that philosophers sometimes proclaim the necessity of simple dichotomies, the same philosophers bear witness to the relative or relational nature of such differences. That is, philosophy also explores—not always as extensively as we might wish—how differentiations are constituted by particular structures of contact and separation, the opening of a space between and the crossing of an interval. Heidegger's reflections on *Dichten* and *Denken* stand out in this regard, "proposing" that the constitution of a meaningful world (in which propositions of all sorts can be thought and vetted) is characterized by language and by something before languages, given or sent before poets and thinkers make something of it. Derrida will always challenge Heidegger's inclination to view this strange giving in excessively narrow terms, restricting its range and imposing unexpected limits on heterogeneity.

We are in a better position than before to acknowledge the extent to which Spanish thinkers fit in and connect with the philosophical inquiry into the relation of philosophy and literature. This is the case, even when they directly express disagreement with some of the philosophical figures or represent them in limited ways. Romanticism amplified and conferred unprecedented prestige on the idea that classical thinking needed to be supplemented by what it appeared to exclude. Unamuno, Ortega, Machado and Zambrano will all speak of what reason omits, and they will propose, in different ways, interpretations of the history of that exclusion. Their elaborations of salutary mechanisms whereby thinking can be rendered mobile, hence vital, owe something to the Romantic experiments with the fragment, occasional writing, fictional characters and narratives, and collaboration. It is probably the case that little more than the outlines of Heidegger's thought found their way into Machado, Ortega, and Zambrano: an attempt to look behind the subject at its constitutive structure; considering poetry and art as primordial events that beckon to us rather than constitute objects of perception; the evocation of time, essence, paths and clearings, sky and earth, mortality and the gods. I don't deny that these loose connections offer fertile ground for scholarly work, but I don't examine any of them at length here.[90]

Above all, my four Spanish writers share with this European tradition a concern with otherness and heterogeneity, with a difference. If the tradition I have outlined concerns itself with the otherness of literature and philosophy within language, the Spanish thinkers worry about the relationship of individuals to different sorts of others: other persons, lovers, strangers, family, friends, teachers and students, people from the same region or nation, the same language-community or the same cultural heritage, the "masses," generations, and levels of learning. They consider their relationships to other kinds of beings—objects, landscapes, animals, and instruments—and other realities—fantasies, dreams, hallucinations, fictions, memories, religion. In my discussions of them, I can only begin to do justice to the richness of this exploration of otherness. It confirms, however, in a way, the institutional concept of literature as an effort to say it all, without limits, with an ever-renewed overflowing of limits.

Chapter 3

Unamuno's Twins

Feeling Philosophy and Philosophical Aesthesis

Prologue: The Promise of Life

In a 1908 letter to Ortega y Gasset, Unamuno writes, "I am interested in you personally, not in your ideas. And the other, and another other, and the other who is even farther away [el de más allá], and everyone, but taken one by one. They step on my heart, those who raise a banner for the ideas that I subscribe to, and my heart bleeds."[1] When Nelson Orringer describes the correspondence between these two giants of Spanish thought, he points out how they hope to benefit from interaction, Unamuno from the publicity of the younger philosopher's journalistic enterprises, Ortega from the prestige of a well-established writer.[2] Because Ortega was receiving his letter in Germany, where he was studying philosophy, Unamuno feels moved here to an odd gesture of intimacy, distinguishing between ideas and the person who expresses them. Unamuno emphatically avows an interest in others, "one by one," before demanding that his own innermost core not be overlooked. The classic metaphor of the heart is also a figure for the limit of rhetoric, the passage from a representation to a real, living, mortal being susceptible to being obscured or forgotten. He goes on to appeal to "the concrete man, the individual with the beating heart" (el hombre concreto, palpitante, individual), and to warn Ortega that philosophy might point us all elsewhere.[3] Philosophy considers *logos*, discourse or thought, but Unamuno wants to hold fast to the *pro-logos*, the "personal" presence from which the ideas go forth, a *this* that *logos* conveys to a *beyond*. Unamuno aims to create a prologue that is not a speech before speech but a warm body this side of language. Look for ideas and this man might slip through our fingers, and, with Unamuno, just as surely, the possibility of understanding, in a nonideational way, what it means to be a human, *un humano*.[4] One raises a flag to declare victory or a sign to demonstrate on its behalf, but Unamuno worries, as Dorothea Veit-Schlegel did, about the moment when "one is more interested in ideas than in human beings,"[5] the way the intellect's products come to stand in for the person of blood and flesh. At the same time, he provides yet another occasion to replace him with ideas, in the wake of an already abundant corpus of essays, a pair of novels, miscellaneous plays, stories, and poems. After all, what is his "interest" in the "person," his defense of the unique life of each and every other, if not another "idea" exalted in his name?

Surely he, too, felt the contradiction in what he wrote to Ortega. As we will see, Unamuno intended to stand for nothing less than feeling and contradiction. It is his devotion to feeling himself and his commitment to bringing others to an experience back behind the representations that stand in for them (as ideas commonly do for a professional philosopher like Ortega) that determines Unamuno's investment in literature. Unlike a philosopher, defined by ideas, a novelists' personae are associated with characters and situations, and with the words in which they create them. However, readers of fiction often anticipate the transition to ideas from the title onward; although this passage may be the specialty of the philosophical novel, the dynamic of reading can always be conceived as a drifting between the particularities of the work and the abstractions they invoke. Compared to philosophy, literature allows for greater variety in approach and rhythm of exposition, more exploratory, open-ended, or free approaches to everything, even philosophical problems. In spite of every last one of his ideas, Unamuno stakes his name on that living person, whom one encounters, for Unamuno, only under certain rare and ephemeral conditions, which he attempts to provide in a variety of works that position themselves in a multitude of spots between literature and philosophy.

Unamuno's approach to literature and philosophy in his phase of most concentrated reflection on it does not only produce a literary theory, expressing his understanding of his writing, or a poetics according to which he creates literary works. More importantly, he generates a tension between those two orientations toward exposition of the human problem that he senses in himself and others. His work ex-poses him—puts him out there, as the Latin roots suggest—in varied com-positions that link up with literature and philosophy in different ways as he modulates forms, treats themes, expresses different tasks and ambitions, and debates with predecessors. Unamuno's corpus can emerge as a site of literature and philosophy's ongoing struggle to touch on something beyond or this side of philosophical themes and literary experience, a task Unamuno pursued by way of a philosophical discourse that claims to involve feeling by way of literary stratagems and a literary discourse framed in philosophical terms, a philosophical aesthesis. By following Unamuno's ambiguous and shifting points of view in personal and philosophical essays and in fiction, we can come to an appreciation of his attempts to reach back from the representations that stand in for him and other people to something behind the persona, this side of all conceptual and thematic inquiries. Literature has a constant, though varying, role in all of these gestures, both as his predominant muse and as the genre in which he stakes his claim for immortality. *The Tragic Sense* and *Mist* might seem to provide paradigms for harmonious interaction between philosophy and literature, but I will insist that Unamuno's uniqueness as a philosophical writer and a creative writer consists in the violent juxtaposition of the conventions that belong to the two traditions, as he understands them. *The Tragic Sense of Life* serves as the clearest document of Unamuno's conception of philosophy as dehumanizing rationality and advances his vision of a new philosophy that might let life—even the lives of the philosophers—live in such a way that we can sense or feel it better than we can understand it. We know that Unamuno sought to affirm our lives, as individuals, and to do so not only for his sake but for our own. Curiously, he will do this by arguing on behalf of the vitality of fictional characters and works produced by a certain kind of monological writing. That is, he tries to bring us round to see our own living core precisely by claiming that our vitality coincides with that which he ascribes to don Quixote and Augusto Pérez and to what he considers his mature literary production. Whether or not we accept his arguments or feel what he wants us to feel, Unamuno will have taught us something about life and its relation to writing.

Much can be learned from Luis Álvarez Castro's extrapolation of a literary theory belonging to Unamuno in *La palabra y el ser en la teoría literaria de Unamuno* (Word and being in Unamuno's literary theory) and of an ethics of reading in *Los espejos del yo* (The mirrors of the ego).[6] These two complementary projects illuminate what Unamuno thought he was doing, ironing out the contradictions that recur throughout the oeuvre by distinguishing between "fundamental ideas" and "mere passing intuitions"[7] and arguing for a distinction between a genuine poetics and the false one (belonging to mere "literatos") targeted for ridicule.[8] In a similar fashion, Pedro Ribas, in *Para leer a Unamuno* (Reading Unamuno), shows how Unamuno claims to differ from canonical philosophers.[9] For both, what set Unamuno's genuine literature and philosophy apart concerns his combination of the two: Ribas speaks of "integration,"[10] while Álvarez Castro favors the figure of "fusion."[11] Such figures do not prevent Álvarez Castro and Ribas from producing coherent and enlightening interpretations, but they inevitably reduce Unamuno's stake in the notion or experience of struggle. The Romantic inquiry into literature and philosophy presents a fertile and tireless movement linking interiority and communication, feelings and ideas. However, static figures like fusion betray the dynamic vitality of this connection. Unamuno and his readers face the challenge of doing justice to each one's individuality while speaking literary and philosophical languages that insistently restrict it.

Ribas and Álvarez Castro follow Carlos Blanco Aguinaga's claim to find an author-figure that is previous to and more comprehensive than the famed "agonic Unamuno."[12] For Blanco Aguinaga, in *El Unamuno contemplativo*, the "contemplative" man sought peace and reconciliation and was forgotten by scholars and readers focused on "war and will to war . . . or anguish and fear of death" (17), the themes that take over Unamuno's writing in the years spent writing *The Tragic Sense in Men and Nations* and *Mist* (85). By contrast, he interprets the figure of the "nimbus" (nimbo) as the ground out of which conflict emerges, a "fusion of the spirit of the contemplative man with the spirit of things and of other men" (252).[13] Blanco Aguinaga believes one can recuperate this more original Unamuno, an image he considers a "positive" one in contrast to the "selfish" and "violent" legend (9), by focusing on childhood as a guide to interpreting the symbols of equanimity that represent the contemplative man in the later work. Ribas, too, in *Unamuno: el vasco universal*, aims at a "first Unamuno" before what he regards as a "stereotype" of the "agonic man."[14] I hope to show that Unamuno's efforts at reconciliation serve as preludes to conflict, as conflict provides an opportunity to seek peace. Blanco Aguinaga says as much by the end of *El Unamuno contemplativo* when he breaks from his own characterization of genuine versus cliché figures of the writer to admit the existence of "two alternating and contrary facets of Unamuno's personality" (284). The critic will go on to ascribe them a unity within an "unconscious continuity of personal life and History" to which Unamuno "hands himself over" (se entrega). Such submission to a necessary turmoil does not seem in itself to resolve conflict but, rather, allows it to play out as the substance and process of life.

Unamuno's preoccupation with life and its precarious relation to words and ideas was well underway by the time he exchanged letters with Ortega. The 1902 essay "Escritor ovíparo" (Oviparous writer) describes writing as a process of engendering life in the forms of live-birth or an egg, representing his own 1904 novel *Amor y pedagogía* (*Love and Pedagogy*) as a live birth in contrast to his 1897 *Paz en la guerra* (*Peace in War*), which would, according to this metaphorical paradigm, complete its gestation, if at all, outside of the body of its creator.[15] Although it is not the beginning of Unamuno's meditation on writing and life, the 1904 essay "A lo que salga" (However it comes out of me) captures several of the motifs I would like to emphasize before moving on to the works where Unamuno most explicitly connects life to literature.[16] "A lo que salga" shows that writing always restricts the writer's life to the condition of writing, which, at best, reflects the writer's intentions, but also provides room for misinterpretation. In addition, it introduces the power of writing to signify something in a way that is independent from the truth, a power that troubled Plato and brought it to the fore in Derrida's inquiry into the enabling limits of philosophy. These factors, we might already suspect, have to do with writing's inseparability from time and death.

While scholars often cite "A lo que salga" in order to describe Unamuno's creative process and how he understood it, a comprehensive reading of the essay should focus on his effort to relate writing and life, and not only his own.[17] Unamuno explains his motivation to write an essay on "writing technique" by the concern expressed in the previously cited letter to Ortega: people misconstrue his writing, mixing up the person and the texts (1194). Although he has published seven "volumes" and countless essays, people don't read, and when they say they know "Unamuno," it is only the name that they know, not the man or his work: "With respect to me and my work, they had—the majority of those who said that they knew me [que decían conocerme]—the wildest preconceptions [los más disparatados prejuicios]" (1194). Unamuno proposes a description of the act of composition as a way of presenting himself and his work to his readers, "introducing himself," as we would more usually say in English, in order to distinguish his real self from "preconceptions" or "prejudices," which mistakenly apply commonplace conceptions to him. He therefore implores whomever might be reading this particular piece to put up with his writing about writing ("I beg the nonprofessional reader to tolerate it for my sake") and to trust him as he writes without certainty about his own ideas: "This is what I want to write about here, about putting pen to paper [ponerse a escribir] without knowing where it is heading [sin saber adónde ha de ir a parar]" (1195). At the same time, one might translate this more literally as a question of not knowing "where it will have to stop" (adónde ha de ir a parar), and observe, by way of anticipation, that, while what is written might remain, the writing will stop with the writer's death, if not sooner.

As the distinction between oviparous and viviparous writers suggests, Unamuno claims his work is unprecedented because of the closeness between his work and his soul. He mocks us writers who "lay eggs," that is, who research, take notes, make outlines and toil over the work (1196). The result would be a product that is, to follow his metaphor, inert on the outside, containing life within it and dependent on atmospheric conditions in order to thrive and emerge into the world. Such a concept reaffirms Unamuno's well-known disdain for learning and erudition. The verb "empollar," to sit on an egg, is still a popular Spanish idiom to describe, in a slightly scornful tone, intense studying, "cramming" in the United States. In "A lo que salga," Unamuno declares that he has been different from the egg-bearing, "oviparous" writers, from the moment he became a "viviparous" one and began to have live-births. What we read *about*, his approach to writing, is also exemplified performatively in the writing that tells us about it: "I put pen to paper, as I have done just now, and let her rip, to see what comes out" (me pongo a escribir, como ahora he hecho, a lo que salga) (1197). Literally, the phrase means "according to whatever comes out"; it can refer to living day by day, according to the opportunities and resources that may arise. It connotes immediacy, improvisation, and resourcefulness, something like the English idioms "let her rip" or "on the fly": "I sit to write . . . and let her rip" or "I sit down and write . . . on the fly," to translate idiomatically the last passage. Unamuno clearly means to capture the living spontaneity that Socrates sees as an essential trait to the philosopher in *Phaedrus*, and to transfer that spontaneity into the texts that he signs with his name.

According to this discussion of "technique," Unamuno claims that his texts genuinely serve as proxies for his own living interiority. In "A lo que salga," he relates this to people he meets who seem to have nothing inside because of their cold and empty utterances, and what he sees as the understandable English taste for biographies, for lives captured in writing (1198). He attributes the public's relative indifference to his own writings, up to this moment, to their being received as eggs. The Spanish public was unprepared, due in part to its intolerance for "metaphysicses" (*metafísicas*) and their preference for talk over thought. Unamuno worries about the phenomenon of prattle or chatter, empty speech that merely gives the appearance of thought, while in reality it merely rambles on: "Among us at least," he says, meaning Spaniards, "language serves to spare oneself thought; one speaks when one does not want to think" (1201). As Peter Fenves points out in *"Chatter": Language and History in Kierkegaard*, no language has the power to banish altogether the possibility of "idle speech." All language can be accused of thoughtlessness and all discourse, even the most conscientious, can descend into prattle.[18] Whether it is because of his own exposure to this concept in Kierkegaard or his own experience, Unamuno grapples here with the inability to control the reception of writing. Perhaps it is the realization that his thought relies on written language—"I put pen to paper," he says—that leads to a curiously remarked pause. Immediately after impugning language for its thoughtlessness, we encounter a paragraph break and the announcement, "Yesterday I walked away from this essay and now I want to finish it, but without looking back, without revising what I have already written. . . ." (1201). What is a brief interval for the reader—if she or he has not also, by chance, walked away between paragraphs—is a major interruption for the person of the writer, who has left the inert material inscription behind, but continued to live. What better illustration could Unamuno offer for the irreducible difference between written language and life? And yet the life appears in the interstices of Unamuno's writing, in the blank space to which he alerts us and whose meaning is given a surprising specificity by the resumption of discourse. It is thus not surprising that Unamuno continues with his description of a certain kind of writing that he considers an adequate proxy of life. This time he discusses diaries, contrasting those that gossip with those that, he says, take in the quotidian intimacy that he discussed earlier, "yesterday" (1201). The genuine "daily writing" (*diario* means both *diary* and *daily*) goes beyond an account of deeds to become a spiritual task: "Our diary should be our words, our writings, our letters, all thrown to the four winds with bursts of our own soul [lanzadas a todos los vientos con ráfagas de nuestra alma]" (1201). It need not present, then, the ephemeral activities of a life, as long as it captures something essential about a person and conveys that into a larger medium. As we have often been told, for Unamuno, this belonging of the individual speech to a larger cultural and historical unit permits a claim, even a hope, for immortality, a life that would not cease.[19]

"A lo que salga" offers a figure for this conception, so key to understanding Unamuno's work, in the fog (*la niebla*) out of which human beings emerge and into which "foggy orators or writers" (escritores u oradores nebulosos) bestow their work (1199). As long as the fog does not dissipate, the speech of individuals like Unamuno will live, lending them immortality. This does not prevent this essay from rising to a somewhat shrill ending that remarks, again, on the process of writing: "That is enough. That is enough for now. One has always to leave the thread of life hanging [hay que dejar siempre suelto el cabo de la vida]. Only in fiction, in novels, do things have a complete beginning and come to a complete end. May this essay never stop, may none of my works ever end, may my life never end, my God!" (1204). With that plea for immortality, Unamuno ends "A lo que salga." Immortality includes, in a series that infers continuity, his life, his work, and the very essay that he puts an end to with these words. Unamuno asserts that certain locutions leave a thread dangling, that his "that is enough for now" not only functions to provide a sudden ending before the piece is sent off for publication, but that it anticipates the resumption of his speech. This end, he suggests, is not a true end because it promises more. Only fiction, he says, can offer death in a complete form by declaring "the end," although his next novel—a foggy one if there ever was one—will not only refuse to end but revive a character from his previous novel, *Love and Pedagogy*. While all of Unamuno's speech claims to proffer living spirit to a public used only to seeing a dead outer shell, he implies here that he produces two kinds of discourse, the ongoing, open-ended essay and the fully formed novels, an infinite, living flow of words and a finite work. His writing, then, is not a homogeneous activity, but one that ties together the finite and the infinite, and that extends the link from one side or the other.

Unamuno will put this vision into play in the production of his two most acclaimed works, a treatise and a novel. In the final chapter of *The Tragic Sense of Life*, written in late 1912, Unamuno attests to the spontaneity of the composition; the outward form clearly seems tied to a desire to evoke the twelve months of the year and an indefinite cycle of life.[20] In 1907, during the preparations for that project—described as a period of intense reading and notetaking—Unamuno began *Mist* and abandoned it in a decision he characterized as an "abortion."[21] He later managed to finish the novel, aborting the abortion and delivering it to the publisher in 1913.[22] Valdés suggests that Unamuno nearly completed the novel in 1907, merely retouching the late, metafictional chapter 31 before its publication in 1914.[23] After noting different ink and paper in the manuscript, Roberta Johnson argues that Augusto's personality in the first seven chapters differs appreciably from the later ones, moving from a critique of Cartesian rationalism to a "trophic knowledge or physiological thinking" that denounces

Kantian skepticism regarding knowledge of things in themselves.[24] Such a shift reflects, for Johnson, the evolution in Unamuno's thinking over the time of composition of *The Tragic Sense of Life*. For his part, Unamuno appears to have finished the novel in 1913 on the condition he didn't have to reread what he had written seven years before, showing a certain devotion to the idea of the work as living offspring that the author released into the world, as explained by "A lo que salga." Although the process of the creation of the novel had been interrupted to work on *The Tragic Sense of Life*, Unamuno picked it up where he left off, so that the finished fiction addresses similar concerns in similar ways, with sometimes striking disconnection between early and late compositions. Unamuno reiterates his characterization of the relation between poetry and philosophy as "twin sisters" at the beginning of his 1913 treatise: "For poet and philosopher are twins [hermanos gemelos], or perhaps even one and the same thing."[25]

However, Unamuno refers to neither philosophy nor literature in an exactly conventional sense, since both declare their service to a more primordial principle than the apparent aims of these genres. In the final chapter of *The Tragic Sense of Life*, Unamuno explains: "But the truth is that my work [mi obra]—my mission, I was about to say—is to shatter the faith of men, left, right and center, their faith in affirmation, their faith in negation, their faith in abstention, and I do so from faith in faith itself. My purpose is to make war on all those who submit, whether to Catholicism, or to rationalism, or to agnosticism. My aim is to make all men live a life of restless longing [que vivan todos inquietos y anhelantes]" (E 349 [revised]; S 236). This manifesto includes a number of ambiguities or provocations. First, Unamuno hesitates to call his oeuvre a "mission." His oeuvre is, after all, something that has the definite contours of individual works, published texts, which ought to be distinguished from his intentions on composing them. But Unamuno strains Spanish usage by saying his *obra* "is to shatter the faith of men"; in this sense, *obra* coincides with the word *trabajo*. His *works work* to have a particular effect on his fellows. He conceives of his writing in terms of his own intentions, of particular ends that he has determined ahead of time. In this regard, he suggests that his work aims at a kind of revelation. Paradoxically, the end has the particularity that it has no end. Rather, he wishes all men (*todos*) to lead a certain kind of life, that is, to be "restless and yearning" (inquietos y anhelantes) as long as they live. In the prologue to *Mist*, Victor notes that this sounds like "unbridled romanticism," and, indeed, the vision of his work as an unending task with a religious resonance resembles that of the early German Romantics, as well as other authors often categorized as "romantic." But Unamuno warns that "putting a name to things does not resolve anything" (S 101; E 7). In fact, as happens with ideas themselves, labels tend to put an end to thought.[26]

Unamuno's mission, then, would never be done, and this makes the literary nature of his work key. If he is interested in everyone (*todos*) and in lives that survive into the future, Unamuno's work must be written and remain after his own demise, even if that turns out to be a passage to another world. In addition, he clearly aspires to speak beyond his immediate surroundings, to those with whom he cannot speak directly. Unamuno needs the written text's potential for futurity and dispersal. And he also needs, presumably, the ability of texts to take on different meanings with different people at different times, a characteristic not only of literary texts but of language in general. Unamuno's mission speaks of an end, assuming that his readers, real and virtual, start out from a state of blind self-satisfaction. Elsewhere in *The Tragic Sense*, though, Unamuno insists that his end is but the beginning. Genuine moral life begins with the contradiction between feeling and reason, with the heart and the head immersed in fog, not knowing which one should lead the other. Chapter 6, "At the Bottom of the Abyss," depicts a "tragic embrace" between reason and anguish—said to be siblings themselves—in which neither one conquers nor succumbs to the other (E 118; S 85). The word "sense" in the English title connotes a conclusion, a meaning, even if in the form of a sensation (*sensación*), and if the "tragic feeling" (sentimiento trágico) is this embrace, we would do better to call it a *feeling* and recognize that it comes *from* this original crisis. I will henceforth refer to the work published as *The Tragic Sense of Life in Men and Nations* with the abbreviated title *The Tragic Feeling*.

While Unamuno wants to drive all readers to a point of disturbance, one to which one must be pushed again and again, his stated purpose for such an experience is to leave it behind, discursively and practically, in the pursuit of an active life. In chapter 11, "The Practical Problem," Unamuno expresses an intention to demonstrate that this crisis can "form the basis for morality" (puede ser base de moral) (E 284 [revised]; S 194). But before "leaving behind" the crisis for this new topic, he revisits it, defining it clearly: "Leaving all of this behind, I want to show how . . ." (E 284 [revised]; S 194). One must enter the abyss, unless one is already in it, in which case, one must get out. This is one of the jarring aspects of reading Unamuno: we are constantly told we should be doing something else. One finds references to this experience in Alison Sinclair's mention of an "anguished love-hate relationship with the man and his text"[27] and Álvarez Castro's confession that Unamuno would not have appreciated his scholarly work, *La palabra y el ser*.[28] To state the case with an English idiom, as soon as we begin to digest what he is serving up, Unamuno disagrees with us. In his prologue to *Mist*, Victor will even say that Unamuno intends to make his readers "puke" (devolver), since "the meaning of life and the universe is seen more clearly with a stomach empty of sweets and excessive food."[29]

Unamuno further claims this life's work for himself in the novel. The fictional character Victor sets out to fulfill the conventional prefatorial function of informing readers of a variety of Unamuno's intellectual positions. Among them, he quotes Unamuno's statement, "My role is to un-define, to confound" (lo mío es indefinir, confundir) (E 7; S 101). Victor considers this an "attitude" that grows out of a particular "feeling of life" (sentimiento de la vida), thus suggesting a connection between the novel and Unamuno's treatise (S 101; E 7 [revised]). Victor goes on to specify that Unamuno refers to his attitude as "illhumorism" (malhumorismo) (E 8; S 102). His explanation begins by referring to it as "his rough and ready, his confounding humor" (este áspero y adusto humorismo confusionista) and goes on to describe it as a way of getting people to see "the meaning of life and of the universe" more clearly (E 8; S 102). Anthony Kerrigan's translation works hard to render some extremely idiomatic lines of thought. *Humorismo* is the common practice of inducing laughter, *comedy*. *Mal humor*, a bad mood, is indeed sometimes written as a single word; but Unamuno coined *malhumorismo* to refer to a practice of inducing a bad mood. The commonplace perception of Unamuno as a depressing writer is not, therefore, without a basis in his stated intentions. After its publication, Unamuno will refer to *Mist* as "an illhumorist novel" (una novela malhumorística).[30] By putting us readers in a bad mood, *Mist* should reveal the fundamentals of our lives.

A bad mood comes when we find ourselves at the mercy of "confounding" or "confusionist" (confusionista) humor (E 8; S 102), which, as we will see, has to do with forcing together two incompatible elements. Victor's prologue mentions the fact that Unamuno, the writer, determines what the character will say, and Victor further acknowledges that his own statements in the novel correspond to Unamuno's thoughts. Thus it is remarkable that Victor will later declare to Augusto, during a conversation on humor, "And it's also necessary to confuse. Above all to confuse, to confuse everything [Y hay que confundir. Confundir sobre todo, confundirlo todo]. To confuse sleep with being awake, fiction with reality, the true with the false . . . To confuse everything in one all-encompassing mist [en una sola niebla]" (E 210; S 272). Unamuno's project, let us be as clear as possible about this, is to submerge his readers in this state of nauseating unclarity. Because the English word "fog" captures more effectively this state of indeterminacy and confusion, I will refer to the novel henceforth as *Fog*.[31]

A philosophical work to provoke thought and a literary work to provoke feeling, such is a common representation of the relationship of Unamuno's treatise, *The Tragic Feeling*, and novel, *Fog*. Yet both works are meant to provoke both feeling and thought; moreover, we are meant to keep them separate, to think, feeling, how feeling yields thought, to remain attentive to sentiments while contemplating how our thoughts arise out of our feelings. Unamuno's use of narrative and argumentation constitutes an effort to provoke feeling by thought, or at least to provoke the feeling of those who are capable of it. Unamuno seems unable to decide whether the tragic feeling is universal. There are peoples whom it characterizes and, he implies, peoples who are incapable of it. But when he pushes himself to consider this most interior of intimacies—the "principle of principles, the reason of reason," he calls it—he gives up: "But we can't talk about these things" (S 43; E 54 [revised]). *The Tragic Feeling*, as we will see shortly, posits a beginning before the "point of departure" in "the man of flesh and bone," and Unamuno suggests here that one cannot be convinced of or brought round to this "principle of principles." It must, on the contrary, be felt. He may also be thinking of the scholastic axiom "Cum negante principia nequit disputari": there is no use debating with someone who denies principles. For Unamuno, one doesn't argue matters of principle, one provokes feelings.

Jean-Claude and Colette Rabaté's 2009 biography announces a Unamuno revival by drawing on journalism and correspondence to show his relevance for contemporary sociopolitical issues.[32] By contrast, Jean Cassou, in a "Portrait of Unamuno" included in *How to Make a Novel*, declares that "Unamuno does not have ideas: he is, himself, the ideas which the ideas of others have become—are made—in him."[33] In his reply, printed in Cassou's edition of Unamuno's book, Unamuno more or less agrees. However, the supposedly non-idea of the tragic feeling seems to present a clear, solid principle. Tragic feeling must be, after all, both an idea and not an idea. It is an idea if an idea can legitimately coincide with a human being, if "idea" is redefined so that one's identity and life could assume the modality of ideation. Ideas, however, achieve a certain kind of transmissibility and temporal extension that conflicts with human mortality, and it would be hard to see how that would be anything but a restrictive notion of selfhood. In *The Tragic Feeling*, chapter titles such as "The Point of Departure," "The Bottom of the Abyss," and even "Conclusion," preside over a rhetoric of certitude, a solid foundation of argumentation that arrives at a definitive end. Only on closer look do we realize that this rhetoric is undermined by the strange nature of these beginnings and ends, whose clarity is blinding, whose end is to send us to the beginnings, whose grounds facilitate collapse. It is no accident that the essential question is one of eternal life and death, and, as we will see, Unamuno's caricature of philosophy and philosophers underestimates the tradition's appreciation of death's peculiarity. It is the ever-present threat of annihilation that turns Unamuno's practice of both literature and philosophy into distinct efforts to bring about events in the lives of readers, beginning with those of the twin works.

Raising a Hand against Philosophy

In another letter to Ortega, Unamuno tells of reading the neo-Kantians who were Ortega's teachers, and confesses his repugnance: "I don't get Cohen [no me entra]: he is a Sadducee who leaves me cold. I understand his position, but, to me—a spiritualist of the rawest type, of the most Catholic type in matters relating to desire—[Cohen's] rationalism or idealism, and all of that stuff, disgusts me."[34] He is not impressed by its being *true*, Unamuno says; rather, what he reads affects him physically: "I cannot, no, I cannot bear anything pure [no puedo, no, no puedo con lo puro]: pure concept, pure knowledge, pure will, pure reason . . . all this purity takes my breath away" (111). The reference to Kant is unmistakable, both in the list of suffocating purities and in the title of the book by Cohen that Unamuno was reading, *Logik der reinen Erkenntnis* (Logic of pure knowledge). Unamuno does not deny the truth of pure concepts, saying, "It's not enough to me that it is the truth, if that is the case" (111). Instead, he appeals to the authority of his own body, his own apparent inability to *think* pure consciousness without facing the threat of losing consciousness. To really dive into Cohen's work, or Kant's—that is, to go beyond what Unamuno simply calls "understanding [comprender] his position"—would require a degree of asceticism that Unamuno cannot assume: "There's no point in using reason [no sirve razonar]—no, no, no!—I will not resign myself to reason" (111). Feelings form the basis of this renunciation of the purity of pure reason, the sensation of needing air, the impulse to preserve oneself in the face of a threat to personal autonomy. In another letter, Unamuno warns Ortega, during the latter's residence in Germany, to be careful with the Sadducees whose "acid" will "corrode" and "dry up your soul" (102).

For his own part, Unamuno says of the "Sadducee science," "It exhales such cold breath that I flee from it before it can speak" (102). Unamuno defines the adjective "Sadducee," at the end of the same letter, saying it means "normative, objective, corrosive" (102). The abundance of Sadducees in Germany, for Unamuno, indicates the restriction of spiritual activity to a pursuit of impersonal, lifeless ideas, from which all particular flavor, color and warmth have been removed, leaving a product that sucks the life out of any reader who might happen to have any left.[35] Who would not prefer to breathe the air of Spain, impure as it might be?

Philosophy has traditionally associated itself with particular emotions; the initial love and wonder are transformed in Aristotle into a discipline that distances itself from the senses at the beginning of the history leading to modern science. Unamuno seems to reject a particular kind of philosophy, a particular trend within philosophy, and by doing so, to define himself as an *impurist*, an advocate of a doctrine that would be insistently, emphatically personal and ethnic. But for a reader of Kant, Unamuno's response could be puzzling. In spite of the anecdotal legend of the near automaton from Königsberg, Kant did not promote the restriction of life to thoughts and actions that he qualifies as "pure." In fact, here and there he expressed a fondness for rich experience of life and a concern for vitality. In addition, he insisted on the validity, and, at times, superiority of popular reasoning, since one of his overarching concerns was reason's propensity to overstep its own legitimate bounds, the limits it imposes upon itself. In this sense, Kant reiterates Aristotle's and Descartes's suspicion that this abuse of reason is more likely in an educated elite than in the common people. The worry that motivated the *Critique of Pure Reason* was, by Kant's account, the tendency of reason, when immersed in the world of experiences, to make extravagant claims. In the first preface to the first *Critique*, Kant likens his work to a tribunal in which reason becomes conscious of "its own eternal and unalterable laws."[36] The idea of "purity" refers to "[independence from] all experience," and refers only to the discussion within this court of reason (9). "Pure reason" strives to isolate itself from the empirical; nevertheless, we would be hard-pressed to find another word but "experience" for the discursive and juridical activity that Kant performs in his critiques. He describes it as "the test of free and open examination," to which reason subjects itself, and he contrasts it not only with "groundless pretensions" but "despotic decrees" (9). His readers, he says, "cooperate" in the testing of reason as the judge in an act that requires "patience and impartiality," especially given the lack of "examples and other concrete illustrations" whose inclusion would have tried his readers' patience even more than his famously obtuse treatise already does (14). Rather than the model of moral or theoretical superiority that Unamuno portrays, Kantian purity aspires to provide a general foundation for the use of reason, a foundation that is always already functioning but that is logically *prior to* the use of reason in knowledge and practical action in a particular place and time. If we conceive of foundations as bedrock, deep in the earth, or as a distant ethereal realm, we might understand Unamuno's revulsion. But Kantian purity, instead, locates this region within every rational being, where it coexists with legitimate emotions, such as patience or passion. In this sense, his aversion to pure reason deprives Unamuno of a realm of experience no less than Kant's bachelorhood and childlessness limited his life experience.

When Kant writes his second preface to the *Critique of Pure Reason*, six years later, he reinforces the connection to both abstraction and to common, everyday life. He identifies pure reason with logic, which he defines as the formal rules of all thought (18). Compared to math and physics, which provide formal rules of experience, logic is at one farther remove from the empirical world. The insights of math and physics, he says, prove their validity through empirical testing, but the "completely isolated speculative science of reason soars far above the teachings of experience" (22). It can only be tested by itself, in isolation from experience, and such a procedure ought to assure us that "our objects [conform] to our knowledge" and not the other way around (22). That is, Kant intends to prevent our assigning arbitrary meanings to objects, assuming that we would prefer to avoid contradiction between the principles of our knowledge and the meanings we determine. This rational tribunal combats dogmatism and offers what Kant calls "genuine populism" in that it renders explicit what is implicit in all experience, not just that of a trained elite (27). Perhaps surprisingly, in the *Critique of Practical Reason* (which he says really should be called the *Critique of Pure Practical Reason*) (3), Kant goes on to acknowledge that the long detour through his revolutionary metaphysical treatise leaves us exactly where many modest citizens and dogmatic thinkers start out, with an affirmation of the Christian doctrines of the existence of God and immortality (4).

Kant's troubled and somewhat defensive prefaces give us a sense of the kind of opposition he faced well before Unamuno expresses his revulsion toward a particular type of thought. Although Kant concludes that reason and Christian religion are compatible, it is the reasonable part of human consciousness, not the part characterized by faith, that comes to this realization by methodically identifying its own boundaries.[37] Contemporaries like Johann Gottfried Herder rebuke the idea that the forms of thought might exist independently of culture and language.[38] The more vulgar problem recognized by Kant initially appears to be the one that applies to Unamuno: some people lack "patience and impartiality," preferring instead "groundless pretensions" and "despotic decrees." Such are the characterizations of Unamuno by readers who have also met him in person. María Zambrano describes his propensity to talk on and on without listening to his interlocutors.[39] Salvador de Madarriaga, for his part, takes no issue with Unamuno's contrarian "attitude," saying that it was "the shape of his being; not his thought, not his philosophy; but the root-cause of his philosophy and of his thought."[40]

Decades before Madarriaga's "Unamuno Re-read," François Meyer also proposed that we understand the "contradictory attitudes" and "excessive polemics" as the result of a principle of life and thought.[41] The "secret" of Unamuno's thought and work, for Meyer, is an intuition behind and before the texts, "detached from the texts themselves."[42] Accordingly, Unamuno experienced that the nature of being is antithetical, and he manifested this "ontology" by way of "alternative affirmation of opposites" in an effort to avoid settling on a static point of view.[43] Curiously, then, the form of Unamuno's oeuvre does not contradict but, rather, conforms to this primordial ontological antithesis. For Meyer, and not only for him, any contradiction to be found in Unamuno, no matter how ill-informed or despotic, thereby serves as a confirmation—not a contradiction—of his fundamentally consistent deployment of antithesis.

In *Para leer a Unamuno*, Ribas imposes some welcome distinctions and goes a way toward questioning the commonplace celebration of Unamuno's personal and ontological contrarianism. First, he insists on distinguishing between two kinds of contradictions: the "intimate" ones that have rightfully obsessed critics; and more ordinary contradictions that appear because Unamuno simply changes his mind.[44] In order to read Unamuno, Ribas says, we should understand how Unamuno reads. Ribas calls the products of Unamuno's idiosyncratic style of reading "peculiar readings," noting that they tell us more about him than they do about any of the writers he considers (133). Observing, among other things, that Unamuno does not seem to know what Kant means by "a priori," Ribas calls the interpretations "arbitrary" and adds that this applies to literary as well as philosophical texts (141). Ribas shows how Unamuno uses other writers to reinforce his own positions, going so far, in one well-known occasion, as mistranslating Spinoza's Latin in order to make it coincide with his point of view (143). Unamuno's readings are indeed arbitrary in the sense that his interpretations could just as well lead to appropriation of a specious point of view as to an overhasty rejection of a dubiously simplified proposition. Some of the most frustrating moments in Unamuno criticism are those commentaries that accept without critical distance his questionable interpretations of individual thinkers. For example, Meyer's best support for Unamuno's agonistic ontology comes from his reiteration of Unamuno's claim that Kant exposed the antinomy between theoretical and practical reason,[45] but such a representation of Kant neglects to take into account the effort in the *Critique of Judgement* to provide what Kant calls a "mediating link between understanding and reason" (4).[46] As Ribas reminds us, Unamuno tended to regard study and exegesis of philosophical texts as "philosophastry [filosofería] and philosophical erudition" (quoted 104), rather than genuine thought. Dispassionate, well-grounded reading might yield more ideas, but it stands in the way of presentation of a genuine human individual.

If we may put this impersonally, being oneself is, indeed, one of Unamuno's themes. He follows or attempts to follow the imperative, "be yourself"; his textual encounters with others and his strange reaction to purity are geared toward preserving his own sense of himself. Purity, as we have seen, disgusts him, suffocates him and does so because it enters into a conflict with Unamuno, body and soul. Such a conflict brings to mind Hegel's analysis in the *Phenomenology of Spirit*, of the unhappy consciousness. A result of the struggle between an independent "pure 'I' " and a dependent consciousness that works on things of the world, the unhappy consciousness represents the first appearance of a free self-consciousness. After establishing a relationship to otherness through perception and understanding, the spirit develops a form of consciousness that can, for a moment at least, claim itself for itself. As its freedom gains in determinateness and concreteness, the self-consciousness takes on strange, potentially irritating characteristics. It finds itself capable of remaining neither pure, in and for itself, nor directly engaged in the world: it is "therefore the unconscious, thoughtless rambling [bewusstlose Faselei] which passes back and forth from the one extreme of self-identical self-consciousness to the other extreme of the contingent consciousness that is both bewildered and bewildering."[47] Furthermore, "its talk is in fact like the squabbling of self-willed children, one of whom says A if the other says B, and in turn says B when the other says A, and who by contradicting *themselves* buy for themselves the pleasure of continually contradicting *each other*" (G 162–63; E 126). Unamuno seems intent on remaining at this raw point of the emergence of self-possessed self-consciousness, preserving the energy of genesis by turning incoherence into a principle. In this he resembles Georges Bataille, who, in his *Inner Experience*, complains of the same affronts to the individual identified by Meyer in his book on Unamuno: he will die and he is not everything.[48] While Hegel's consciousness propels itself toward the fulfillment or concreteness in the forms of natural science, politics, art, religion, and, ultimately, philosophy, Unamuno dwells in this moment of self-affirmation, in a movement that is restless and unhappy, claiming to be its own absolute in order to avoid being lost in the immensity of the absolute itself.

But an absolute that belongs to a singular individual would be no absolute at all. In any case, neither Hegelian phenomenology nor Kantian transcendental philosophy is primarily concerned with consciousness and the knowledge possessed by the conscious subject but, rather, with the enabling structures that provide a foundation for a variety of universally valid judgments. Kant's transcendental philosophy attempts to articulate for a possible consciousness what otherwise remains implicit, silent, or veiled. These characterizations of the matter of philosophy remain a part of what philosophy questions, and, as we'll see when we discuss the "theme" of death, a certain kind of transcendental philosophy also takes account of necessary structures of experience that must remain other, incommensurable to consciousness. It might always be possible to stubbornly refuse to entertain the possibility of thinking a priori conditions of experience. In an article about Unamuno's claims to be a follower of Hegel, Ribas quotes Unamuno's answers to his *oposiciones* (state examinations for a competitive teaching position) that profess a rejection of all "metaphysical" inquiries: "It is misguided to take up the analysis of the concepts of matter, force, life, consciousness, etc., deprived of [ayuno de] the results that physical-chemical, physiological and psychological sciences offer us."[49] Such a rejection, Ribas reminds us, is indebted to the predominance of positivism in the Spanish educational institutions. Although Unamuno eventually disavows this privileging of scientific inquiry (doing so in the name of Hegelianism), it is not in order to embrace the metaphysical. Rather, Unamuno appeals to the previousness or *priority* of the living, breathing, autonomous self, in particular, his own self.

When Unamuno renounces philosophy, then, he rejects the standards of argumentation, the traditional claim to identify first principles, and the possibility of articulating and grounding them in a nonempirical (pure) fashion. While this renunciation of philosophy is not uncommon, occurring both as a kind of popular phenomenon and a problematic intellectual position, what is strange is that it should be inseparable from Unamuno's philosophical prestige. In a magnificent irony, it is the effort to speak for the "man of flesh and blood," starting with himself, that, for some critics, justifies giving Unamuno an honored place in a pantheon of Spanish thinking. Madarriaga ascribes Unamuno's combative attitude—that basis for his "being," not his "thought"—to his Spanishness, claiming that the latter has fought against the fallacious "belief that thought presides over the council of ministers of the soul and decides what a man writes."[50] Some scholars take for granted that Unamuno was a philosopher with his own position. For Julián Marías, Unamuno deserves a place beside Ortega as one of the two philosophers—"born in Spain by an unexpected accident"—whose doctrines finally allow an approach to humanity's most pressing question, its finitude.[51] Mario Valdés titles the first chapter of *Death in the Literature of Unamuno* "Unamuno's Philosophy of Death."[52] Dezsö Csejtei calls him the most important of the "Spanish philosophers of life and existence."[53] More common, though, is the remarking of a distance from philosophy, which would imply a certain philosophical irrelevance for Unamuno's treatment of philosophical themes, such a death. José Ferrater Mora, in *Three Spanish Philosophers: Unamuno, Ortega and Ferrater Mora*, insists that his first philosopher is not one "in the traditional sense" but a "poetic realist."[54] That is to say, Unamuno's philosophy appears implicitly in his poetics. Paolino Garagorri refers to Unamuno as "the philosopher in spite of himself."[55] Miguel Cruz Hernández observes that literary scholars and writers consider Unamuno a philosopher, while philosophers consider him a practitioner of literature.[56] In whatever category he might belong, Cruz Hernández concludes, we should see Unamuno as someone who "[dissolved] his overflowing personality" in a variety of genres, the personality remaining the primary thing, the element suspended in his texts, awaiting us readers.[57]

How to make sense of this double gesture, the renunciation of philosophy and the assumption of standards that provide entrée into philosophy? Unamuno's essays are a testament to his refusal of philosophy, repeating the ambivalent relationship to philosophy by making propositions and arguments that fit into the very discursive tradition that he also rejects. Meanwhile, Unamuno's fiction is an attempt to establish a different form of address, one that maintains the propositional thrust characteristic of philosophy, while attempting to avoid the reduction of individual human beings to generalizations. As we will see in an analysis of *Fog*, this inauguration of a discourse this side of philosophy rejects certain received ideas about literature at the same time that it presents itself as a modification of a traditional literary genre. Unamuno's intellectual and cultural reputation rests largely on an equivocal praise of his accomplishments, literary or philosophical, without allowing the internal contradictions to disqualify him from either realm. Unamuno is undeniably philosophical and literary, separately and simultaneously. Let us take a deep breath and see how this works.

Literature on the Fringes of Philosophy: The Conclusions and Contradictions of *The Tragic Feeling*

The abrupt beginning of Unamuno's *The Tragic Feeling* stands out in an oeuvre so abundant in prologues and prefaces.[58] Nonetheless, the author does provide a sort of exergue, the "Conclusión" listed without a number in the table of contents, which, contrary to standard Spanish editorial practice, is printed before the first chapter, as if to provide guidance in the absence of a prefatory statement. Though it does not receive the name of *epilogue*, the chapter called "Conclusion" fulfills this function, summing up, providing guidance for the correct interpretation of the foregoing work, and sending the reader off (or back to the beginning of the book) with a polite farewell.[59] In spite of its title's suggestion that the book yields up propositions, the "Conclusion" actually claims to expound the convictions and preconceptions that *produced* the improvisational discourses that make up the book and, indeed, because of their anti-methodical character, render it worth publishing. The end of the book tells everything one ought to have known from the outset, even before the beginning, but it does so in the process of wrapping things up, saying what one must not have failed to gather in the reading. While the critical bibliography of Unamuno abounds in interpretations of *The Tragic Feeling* that quote selectively, extrapolate from Unamuno's statements and commentary on literary and philosophical predecessors, and impose a more systematic order of exposition,[60] I propose that we follow the reading protocols offered in the "Conclusion" and in the transitions between chapters to get a sense of the particular *ends* that Unamuno aimed to achieve with this work. It would not be inaccurate to say that he aims at avoiding an end, avoiding the lifeless stasis that he associates not only with physical death but with fixed ideas in general.

Unamuno begins his "Conclusion" by setting out the contradictory nature of *The Tragic Feeling*, investing the book with the values of casual spontaneity and the seriousness of a polemic with no less an adversary than European culture. He stresses that he worked with little concern for the production of a book, the act of writing being simply a manifestation of his life (as we saw in "A lo que salga"). The essays that make up the book "have gone from my hands directly to the printer in a kind of improvised commentary upon notes gathered over a period of years, so that I have not had before me, as I wrote each essay, those that preceded it" (E 322; S 219). Unamuno stresses the temporal character of composition, improvisational and discontinuous, but focused on drawing from the past in a present moment of composition. He continues, speaking of the essays: "And thus they go forth full of quintessential contradictions—apparent contradictions, at any rate—like life and like myself" (E 322; S 219). The notes he refers to appear to have been the sort one makes while reading, for he immediately apologizes for the abundance of "quotes from others" (citas ajenas) (S 219; E 322 [revised]). We already perceive a contradiction: the writing reaches the public all at once through print, but it could scarcely be more personal, more tied to separate moments of composition whose autonomous character Unamuno underlines: let no one suspect him of striving for consistency; he simply accumulated notes and, guided by these offhand jottings, turned out a series of essays. The text gets compared to other ostensibly spontaneous discourses: "In these essays . . . I proffer what springs from the deepest part of me as poetry, dream, chimera, or mystical whimsy [capricho]" (E 327; S 222). Notably, however, Unamuno has just quoted all of these elements from Galileo's self-defense against the Inquisition. Unamuno presents what flows from him in a mysterious, undisciplined way, so that it represents his deepest essence. Yet he appeals to others, in quoted passages, in order to bring his own inner experience to expression. His intimacy is as *extimate* as can be. If these are his *entrañas* (in his reading of *The Tragic Feeling*, Candelaria calls Unamuno the "Philosopher of Spiritual Innards")[61] they can only appear on the condition of becoming *extrañas*, put in words belonging to strangers, rendered strange by their incorporation into another's discourse.

Therefore, we not only hear about contradiction but encounter one. By noting a few others, we can get a preliminary image of the book as a whole. Unamuno's insistence on the book's extemporaneous character is perhaps an effort to distinguish himself from Phaedrus, whose discourse represented not genuine thought but a mere representation of thought. Yet *The Tragic Feeling* bears many marks of careful composition. If one does as Unamuno proposes and includes the "Conclusion" as one of the essays in what he calls a "treatise" (at the end of chapters 6 and 9), the whole appears less intuitive than Unamuno might suggest. In his prefaces to the English and Spanish editions of *Treatise on Love of God*, Orringer explains that the published book consists largely of rewritten passages from the earlier work and new statements and provocations inspired by his correspondence with Ortega.[62] While I have quoted from the more cordial moments of Unamuno's exchanges with Ortega, Orringer provides evidence that Unamuno took away from this episode a sharpened rejection of what he considered the faults of philosophy. Surprisingly, then, Unamuno neglects to mention a personal offense as a factor in the composition of a book about the pre-eminence of the life of the individual person over ideas and thoughts that are worked out by study and reflection. *The Tragic Feeling*'s twelve essays do wander, as Unamuno glosses and critiques statements by philosophers and literary writers, but they are all linked by an unmistakable procedure, according to which Unamuno concludes each chapter with a summary statement and formulates a clear proposition for the next chapter before stating—in almost the same words every time—"let's see" (vamos a verlo). In addition to the announcement of a conclusion, Unamuno ends chapter 6 by characterizing it as "a practical summary of the critique developed in the first six chapters of this treatise" (S 103; E 145 [revised]), suggesting that this draws together the preceding exposition before characterizing the following chapters as "fantasies" (S 103; E 145 [revised]). The second half of *The Tragic Feeling* continues from this "practical summary" of a "critique," that is, from an explicitly established theoretical position (whether Unamuno wants to call it that or not) to what he calls "the practical or pragmatic part" (S 162; E 235). That is, he moves on to show how the principles laid down "serve as the basis of a moral code" (S 194 E 284 [revised]). Unamuno highlights both spontaneity and its opposite, a method or system of the most conventional type.

 Let's take note, then, that the contradictions in manner of exposition go together with those of Unamuno's central convictions. The "fantasies" just mentioned are, says Unamuno, "not devoid of reason, for nothing subsists without reason" (S 103; E 145). The entire exposition must incorporate both reason and feeling even as it aims at establishing their contrariness. Indeed, he describes his project—in chapter 6, in the conclusion of this conclusion to the first, theoretical half of the book—as "a manner of setting down [dejar asentada] the practical position to which this critique may lead someone who does not care to renounce life and does not care to renounce reason either, and who must, consequently, live and work between these two molars [muelas] that grind our souls" (S 103; E 145 [revised]). In chapter 11, which also offers itself as a conclusion—this time one previous to the "Conclusion"—Unamuno mentions his "horror of definitions" before defining life as "strife": "It is precisely this intimate contradiction that unifies my life and gives it a practical reason to be [le da razón práctica de ser]" (S 193; E 282 [revised]). Aversion to definitions applies to what imposes limits, *fines*, and Unamuno's definition of life as a bone of contention ground down between two adversaries implies that a cessation of hostility would mean the end of life. Here lies the key to Unamuno's effort to survive into eternity: as long as his texts embody contradiction (and he claims they do this, in themselves), they might be said to keep him alive. To the extent that a methodical or systematic treatise avoids contradiction, its author misses the essential, that *life* survives through the contradiction between acquiescence to reason and a conscious desire for immortality.

Unamuno's aversion to definition afflicts the eponymous concept of his treatise, which he treats from the beginning as something that one feels by virtue of being alive but which is covered up by the work of description and analysis. The whole book can be seen as a denunciation of the philosophical prejudice of putting thought before feeling, but, as we have seen, a share of reason is necessary to make visible even what is contrary to reason. Indeed, the chain of arguments Unamuno presents is nothing if not logical: a flesh and blood human, endowed with speech, necessarily yearns for immortality, from which she or he can only be dissuaded by reason; God is a guarantor, though only a weak one, of immortality; we are left with the bare possibility of God by reason's incapacity to disprove his existence; that possibility takes the form of hope and serves to guide human actions towards virtue. From concrete human individuals, Unamuno proceeds to immortal souls, to God, and to hopeful, moral behavior on the part of the individuals. Although Unamuno describes right reasoning as part of moral behavior, he also explains that it has been invented for the purpose of serving life (S 29; E 33). That is, concrete, living humans invented both God and rational discourse out of yearning for immortality; in more recent times, they go about nullifying the possibility of immortality in the form of "rationalism" before they, finally, participate in the forging of a point of view that narrates this history and denies its own denial of immortality.

It seems one-sided to characterize Unamuno's discussion as "irrationalist" when every bit of it is colored by reason as the condition of possibility of all reflection. Instead, what Unamuno claims is that certain questions do not call for a rational approach. To dismiss, or simply call Unamuno a literary writer neglects the extraordinary ambition that characterizes his writing. Without focusing on the theme of contradiction, then, we can return to the "Conclusion" to see how a certain idea of Spanishness and literature brings

The Tragic Feeling to a close in a way that *Fog* reiterates when the novel concludes with a movement toward philosophy. Besides laying claim to a spontaneous speech on his own behalf, Unamuno's "Conclusion" intends to speak on behalf of Spain against what he calls "Europe." He explains that one of his chapters aims to "de-essentialize Europe," which means replacing "the ideal of progress, reason, and science" with the older ideal of "eternal ultra-terrestrial life" (E 323; S 220). Unamuno defines Europe by a commitment to terrestrial life, to theoretical knowledge and its application to practical problems facing humanity. He does not simply argue against reason, sensing perhaps that such a performative contradiction would give the victory to his adversary from the start. Rather, here and throughout his work, he preemptively dismisses all representatives of Europe, philosophers first. He is not above a sort of self-ridicule for his own "pseudophilosophical constructs," which contain "dilettante attempts at mysticism," "everything but patient study, objectivity, and method" (E 328; S 223). But this ironic self-deprecation paves the way for his claim that arbitrary reading, subjectivity, and capricious meandering guarantee the genuine character of his thought. As we will see shortly, this side of philosophy is another philosophy, truer for exploiting its kinship or twin-ship with literature. In a similar way, the Europe that Unamuno dismisses belongs to a more comprehensive Europe—more "essential," as a result of its "de-essentialization"—which Spain brings into focus, grounds, and aspires to lead. Unamuno's literary philosophy is more philosophical than philosophical philosophy; the Spain that surpasses Europe belongs to a more essential Europe, a de-essentialized essence of Europe.

The subtitle to the "Conclusion," "Don Quixote in the Contemporary European Tragicomedy," leaves some ambiguity about whether don Quixote arrives from outside or already constitutes a part of Europe's ambivalent, "tragi-comic" state. In *The Tragic Feeling*, the interpenetration of lightness and gravitas, and of worldliness and transcendence, suggest that Unamuno, too, takes part in Europe's ambivalent character. For Unamuno, scientific Europe stands opposed to literary Spain. He says he is convinced that "our philosophy, Spanish philosophy, is to be found diffused and liquescent in our literature, in our collective life, in our action, above all in our mysticism, and not in any philosophical system whatsoever" (E 336; S 227). Unamuno means to present, then, a quintessence of Spanish philosophy, and he runs down a list of the candidates that we may already assume he will reject: Seneca, "the pagan Stoic of Córdoba"; the scholastic Suárez; the Spanish humanists discussed by Menéndez Pelayo, including Luis Vives; his near contemporaries, Jaime Balmes and Ángel Ganivet (S 229–30; E

340). The real "hero of our thought," Unamuno avows, is not a flesh and blood man or woman but an "entity [ente] of fiction and action," Don Quixote, who is "more real than all the philosophers" (S 227–30; E 340 [revised]). In contrast to an individual who has devoted his or her life solely to rational discourse, a literary character is able, according to Unamuno, to embody the struggle in which individuals are engaged and the feeling that characterizes the individual soul. Here Unamuno gives the closest thing to a definition of the tragic feeling: "Is there not a place for another philosophical practice [oficio], and that would be the reflection [reflexión] on the tragic feeling of life itself [el sentido mismo trágico de la vida] such as we have studied it, the cultivation [formación] of the struggle between reason and faith, between science and religion, and the reflexive maintenance [mantenimiento reflexivo] of this struggle?" (S 232; E 344 [revised]). The tragic feeling only happens when one rests neither in the confidence of faith nor in the resignation of reason, but struggles with the two and sustains it *as* a struggle. One does not only "formulate" the struggle but teaches or trains individuals—according to the idiomatic meaning of *formación*—to perform this reflection of something that precedes philosophy's traditional talk of giving an account. Such a newly oriented philosophy would, indeed, incorporate literary strategies in order to restore affect, the love of wisdom, but also, clearly it would still convey lessons regarding *The Tragic Feeling*'s assessment of philosophical history, reason, and first principles. In other words, Unamuno would promote a rational and sentimental education in order to set his pupils up for an "intimate" strife of their own.

Life, Death, and the Need to Feel

Before shifting from Unamuno's philosophical approach to literature to his most celebrated effort to bring the novel to philosophy, it is worth assessing more carefully the place in philosophy that he stakes out with *The Tragic Feeling*. Even though he expressed an intention to generate confusion and contradiction, the state of suspension between opposites was to be an indicator of life rather than a thematization of it. He repeatedly insisted that he had a single concern. He says in a 1908 letter to Ortega, "You know *my only problem*, that of the immortality of the soul in the most Medieval sense of the word" (101 [emphasis added]). "All Sadducee philosophy," he continues, "tends to erase *the only problem*! *Memento mori*!" (102 [emphasis added]). In the schematic history of metaphysics that opens the *Fundamental*

Concepts of Metaphysics, Heidegger explains that Medieval philosophy maintains emphasis on just one aspect of human being: "not only, nor indeed solely and predominantly as a creature of this earth, but with respect to his eternal fate, his immortality."[63] Like Unamuno, Heidegger will express concern for post-Medieval thought's privileging of the earthly human, the one who knows and acts in the world, neglecting the genuinely temporal character of human existence. Unamuno's letter to Ortega condenses immortality and mortality into a single problem, a reminder of death and a defense of a Christian idea of the eternal soul that would survive death. Unamuno's most sustained discussion of this appears in *The Tragic Feeling*, where it shares the ambivalent kind of exposition that characterizes the discussion of philosophy and literature and the priority of his own living identity.

Oddly, *The Tragic Feeling of Life* does not begin with "The Point of Departure," which is the title of the *second* chapter. Rather, the first essay of the volume posits a *this side* of the explicitly designated beginning, something that must be present for even the beginning to begin. Entitled "The Man of Flesh and Blood" ("El hombre de carne y hueso," literally "flesh and bone"), chapter 1 sets forth Unamuno's conviction of the importance of death and immortality. "Flesh and bone" name the mortal, bodily human being, the one who will perish. Unamuno explains that "the only real and vital problem" is the "problem of our individual and personal destiny, of the immortality of our soul" (E 6; S 11). Mortal humans must find a way to assert their immortality when confronted with their apparent mortality. All human activity, Unamuno insists, responds, whether self-consciously or not, to this originary problem. His immediate reference is Kant, whose *Critique of Practical Reason* discusses immortality and the existence of God as "postulates of pure practical reason."[64] For Unamuno, "Kant the man" understood the essential connection between immortality and reason, but Kant "the professor of philosophy inverted the terms" (E 7; S 11). Instead of reasoning their way to a conviction about immortality, humans should feel their mortality and immortality, letting this primary feeling be the basis for reflection. "It is not enough to think, we must also feel, our destiny," he says later in the chapter (E 20; S 20). Unamuno regards feeling as a function of the mortal body. In a reading of *Fog*, we will see how he figures the feeling of mortality as a job not for the entire body but, in particular, for a hand, *una mano*, which writes and hands off work to a printer, and, especially, touches, feels, and pinches the body to which it belongs.

Hegel also attempted to end philosophy by completing it, by showing that philosophical history in its entirety culminates in his way of thinking, which takes up that history in its logical development and justifies the initial suppositions by grounding them in a concrete philosophical doctrine. As Ribas has shown, Unamuno's reading of Hegel was fairly limited, such that he seems unaware of his own similarity to Hegel's description of the unhappy consciousness and his failure to recognize the key role of death in Hegel's thinking. In *The Tragic Feeling*, Unamuno characterizes Hegel's thought of immortality as merely "abstract" (E 122–23; S 88), as if the passage between abstraction and concretion were not the very movement of history for Hegel. In his reading of Hegel in "Literature and the Right to Death," Maurice Blanchot characterizes Hegel's spirit as "not the life that shrinks from death and keeps itself untouched by devastation but rather the life that endures it and maintains itself in it" (336).[65] A brief digression into Hegel can help us appreciate how, in his concerns and approach to the philosophical problem of death, Unamuno would fit quite comfortably within the tradition that he routinely vilifies.

As in Unamuno, the question of death belongs to Hegel's concern for the potential lifelessness of abstract thought. In the preface of the *Phenomenology of Spirit*, Hegel too warns against the exaltation of "lifeless universals," abstractions that are not enlivened by concrete manifestations of their subject matter (G 13; E 2). His goal in the *Phenomenology* is to show how the highly abstract concepts that characterize the modern spirit and the realization of science in the system of absolute spirit are grounded in lived experiences; though religion and the state seem far removed from the experiences of perception and understanding of the natural world, the *Phenomenology*'s preface insists that the work shows how political and religious life possess all the richness and concreteness of immediate sense experience. But if the whole range of experiences of spirit are characterized by life or vitality, it is only because death inhabits the development of spirit from the start. This becomes especially apparent to readers of the chapters of the *Phenomenology* on self-consciousness. Although it is an account of how self-consciousness emerges from understanding of the sensible and supersensible worlds, it is also the moment when philosophy itself emerges as self-reflection, the consciousness of what is happening when the thinking subject thinks. Self-consciousness takes its point of departure from the achievement of understanding objects of consciousness. In the introductory section to the *Phenomenology*'s chapter "Self-consciousness," Hegel reiterates the results of his previous reflections. At the beginning of the *Phenomenology*, the very first experiences of objects gave the impression that the subject of perception kills the object, taking it up into itself as something that exists for it, in contrast to the "richest kind of knowledge," the immediacy of "what simply *is*" (G 82; E 58). But through the development of perception and understanding, a consciousness develops for which "the being-in-itself of the object [Ansichsein] and the being-for-an-other [Für-ein-Anderes-Sein] are one and the same" (G 137; E 104). At such a moment of spiritual development it could not be said that a living thing is supplanted by a lifeless one, a beating heart, say, for an idea. In "Self-consciousness," this passage occurs when the object becomes a part of a subject whose powers of appropriation reach an adequate level of complexity. Consciousness turns on itself, becoming an object of its own (subjective) act of knowing, and in doing so it revisits the possibility that the other's being must be arbitrarily restricted in order to exist for a subject. This dynamic takes the form of the master-slave dialectic; in it, the master represents the part of consciousness that wants to retain autonomous power and the slave maintains the consciousness's relationship to the sensual world. The latter threatens autonomy, since it implies that the subject can only exist as a relationship to objects. Hegel describes the struggle between two aspects of the subject, one that desires freedom ("immediate self-consciousness") and the part that maintains the relationship to objects, as a mortal combat within the subject: "In so far as it is the action of the *other*, each seeks the death of the other. But in doing so, the second kind of action, action on its own part, is also involved; for the former involves the staking of its own life. Thus . . . they prove themselves and each other through a life-and-death struggle" (G 148–49; E 113–14). In order to maintain within itself both independence and the dependence implied by its immersion in what Hegel calls "life," the subject must contain within itself two mutually incompatible parts.

Although the struggle for self-consciousness involves "the staking of [the master's] own life" in addition to the threat to the bondsman's, the two are aspects of the same subject, and the killing of the other would be a killing of self (G 148; E 113). This negation cannot actually happen, though; "death is the *natural* negation of consciousness" and the subject must "survive" and endure the "splitting into extremes with opposite characteristics" (G 149; E 114). It is in this sense that, as Blanchot says, the self "endures [death] and maintains itself in it." Nonetheless, for Hegel, the staking of a life reveals freedom, an impoverished freedom for a self-consciousness whose "essential being" possesses no solidity or permanence: "There is nothing present in it which could not be regarded as a vanishing moment" (G 149; E 114). Like perception and understanding, this characteristic of self-certainty as certainty of impermanence can be recognized in the description of sense-certainty at the beginning of the *Phenomenology* and follows spirit through its subsequent development. For this reason, one could regard the pathos of struggle as the fundamental motor of the development of spirit. Hegel says at the end of the chapter on self-consciousness, "Consciousness itself is the absolute dialectical unrest [Unruhe]" (G 161; E 124).[66] Whether philosophical, artistic, scientific, or religious, spirit develops only because of the constant threat of death. This threat must be maintained by both the slave and the master, both with respect to sensuous existence and free self-certainty. The subject must not die; the two sides of subjectivity must keep pressure on each other, without victory and without resolution. That is the condition of a free subjectivity that interacts with autonomous, living others. To the extent that Unamuno seeks to join human temporal finitude to a living theoretical and practical activity, this philosopher would seem to agree with him.[67]

Death in the master-slave dialectic might be abstract in the sense that the death of the master or slave does not correspond to the concrete death of a particular individual but of the possible death of an imagined human subject. By making it characteristic of every moment of our lives, it loses the particularity of the moment that sense perception and all forms of consciousness are extinguished. Critics mention, then, the death of Unamuno's young son in 1896 or of his mother in 1908, events that made him impatient with the notion that death is a part of life. He says that he does not care for an afterworld in which he and his loved ones have lost their particularity in eternity. He dreams, rather, as he says in the letter to Ortega in which he renounces purity, of "a *material* immortality of the soul, one in which I might, after centuries, encounter my mother, my children, my wife, and might have the certainty that the human soul, this poor human soul of mine, the soul belonging to my people, is the purpose of the universe [el fin del universo]" (*Epistolario* 111). Unamuno demands that his death retain a specificity that runs counter to reason, which he considers inseparable from philosophy. But it was not long before death's singularity also found a more elaborate role in another philosophical project.

In "La misión socrática" (The Socratic mission), Cruz Hernández tells of a conversation with Heidegger in which the latter expresses an interest in Unamuno: "And in Freiburg, Heidegger showed me the volumes of Unamuno lined up on the shelves of his library and told me that he was the Spanish thinker who had preoccupied him the most [que más le había preocupado]."[68] Cruz Hernández's further account of the conversation fails to distinguish between Heidegger's comments and his own dubious grasp of the matter at hand, speaking of Unamuno's "[rebellion] against the aseptic cognitive subject invented by Descartes and perfected by Locke and Hume, refined by Kant and deformed by the positivists,"[69] formulations that Heidegger is unlikely to have endorsed without much qualification. In any event, it is worth examining the echoes of Unamuno's "ideas" in Heidegger. *Being and Time*'s analysis of Dasein—with its attention to the "closest" phenomenon, average everydayness—claims to be this side of the human subject or "I."[70] Heidegger insists that his investigation into the structure of being that Dasein possesses does not come out of professional obligation or idle curiosity. Rather, Heidegger identifies inquiry as part of the very structure of Dasein: "This entity which each of us is himself and which includes inquiry as one of the possibilities of its Being, we shall denote by the term 'Dasein.' "[71] He also addresses from the start the sense in which something remains hidden, obscure or enigmatic in ourselves, even when it is described through ontology and phenomenology. Heidegger explicitly takes issue with "vague average understanding," which might be dismissed as lazy or indifferent (25), and wonders whether science and the entirety of the philosophical tradition provide adequate means of access to the being, Dasein, who could possibly provide access to the question of Being (29).[72] Indeed, Dasein is emphatically distinguished from traditional philosophical concepts of human consciousness, particularly subjectivity, precisely by its definition in principle as the Being that inquires not only into beings but into the possibility of an inquiry into Being. Since, like Unamuno, Heidegger thinks the philosophical tradition has failed to even notice this omission, he joins Unamuno in examining ways in which concrete existence might push us into particular strategies for avoiding disturbing conclusions about ourselves and to advocate for renewed attention to human mortality and temporal finitude.

More precisely, though, Heidegger agrees with Unamuno on the fundamental principle that something like feeling has been misinterpreted throughout history of philosophy, conferring on it a subordinate status to knowledge. Until the end of *The Tragic Feeling*, Unamuno exclusively characterizes philosophy as a pure consciousness that discerns the objects of the natural world and can turn its perspicacious viewing on itself, but a major part of the institution of philosophy shares skepticism toward this rarified gaze. In *Being and Time*, Heidegger's characterization of sciences might be condescending, but it is much less disdainful than Unamuno's. A reading of Heidegger's phenomenological description of Dasein—the type of being that the human individual is—might strengthen the philosophical credentials of Unamuno's premises in *The Tragic Feeling*. In general, for Heidegger, the theoretical scientist applies a particular way in which the world is disclosed; the great success of sciences and the virtue of certain great philosophical thinkers depends on the rigorous attention to this one particular conception of being that cannot be dispensed with. Heidegger wants to call attention to the limitations of the scientific orientation toward the world; in particular, philosophers appear to have conceived of human beings in the same manner as they conceived of other objects, according to the same kind of temporality. In *Being and Time*'s analysis of state-of-mind (*Stimmung*), Heidegger regrets that philosophy has made no progress beyond the Aristotelian reduction of affect to "the level of accompanying phenomena," secondary to ideation and volition, that is, to theoretical knowledge and practical action (178). In short, Heidegger's analysis of Dasein intends to restore affect, feeling, to the status of a primary phenomenon. Furthermore, he appears to place it, like Unamuno, *before* a division of human activity into theory and praxis. Cognition and decision-making operate for an individual whose world has already been disclosed to it, after all, and Heidegger's analysis of "Being-in as such" insists that the interconnected beings of a world in which we know and act are constituted for Dasein only in the disclosure of a mood or state-of-mind. It might appear that there are times when we have no particular mood; Heidegger calls this "undisturbed equanimity" (ungestörte Gleichmut), but notes we can pass from it to "inhibited ill-humor," or "slip off into bad moods" (173). He says these phenomena are "left unheeded as supposedly the most indifferent and fleeting in Dasein," but they are "by no means nothing ontologically" (173). Rather, "in every case Dasein always has some mood [gestimmt ist]" (173). In other words, there is no such thing as not having a mood, for mood is the way Dasein "is brought before its Being as 'there'": "In diesem 'wie einem ist' bringt das Gestimmtsein das Sein in sein 'Da'" (173). The idiomatic German helps Heidegger articulate this proposition that bears within it the very nature of the propositions we make about the world. "Wie einem ist" expresses something like "how it's going," which German articulates by a unique use of the dative case: how it is for one. To translate the above German phrase: "In 'how it's going,' being in a mood discloses the Being in Dasein's 'Da.'" Scientists or philosophers of purity do not lack mood; they merely cultivate "equanimity" as the most appropriate mood. The analyst of Dasein, in an inquiry into the particularity of the human kind of being, must take into account a wider range of states-of-mind, including "bad moods," fear, boredom, and, as is well known, anxiety, because these moods reveal something that "equanimity" or indifference—specious claims to moodlessness—obscure.

As we have seen, Unamuno makes much of his "malhumorismo," his effort to put us in a bad mood, to upset us, even disgust us, in the way that *humorismo* might make us laugh. Since he claims his "ill-humor" assures him an authoritative voice from the margins of philosophy, it is worth looking more closely at Heidegger's analysis of mood in *Being and Time*. Thanks to states of mind, we are aware that something happens within Dasein that is not self-consciousness but does correspond to our ontological structure. "States of mind" are not phenomena of self-consciousness or action on the self; rather, they show that we are at the mercy of something; they "assail Dasein in its unreflecting devotion to the 'world' with which it is concerned" (175). We do not choose our moods, although Heidegger does speak of mastering moods by replacing some with others. Presumably, we are also vulnerable to being put in moods by others. The phenomenon of mood reveals the need for an analysis of Dasein, beyond the philosophical analyses of self-consciousness of the "I" or the subject. Neither outside nor inside, they show that there is something like a structure of being, of being-in, that determines the range of Dasein's life from the start (176). In bad moods, says Heidegger, "Dasein becomes blind to itself, the environment with which it is concerned veils itself, the circumspection of concern gets led astray" (175); there is no self-regard, no awareness of the act of viewing, let alone self-consciousness. Such a state of mind would make possible the suspension of reason that might be required by Unamuno's belief in immortality. The bad mood creates the fog, which is not an understanding of Unamuno's point of view, nor a conviction, strictly speaking, about life or death. In fact, as we will see in a reading of *Fog*, it is a suspension of decision between despair and faith, consolation and hope, thought and feeling. Heidegger's philosophical innovation prepares for a "destruction" of the history of ontology and the overcoming of philosophy's forgetfulness of the question of Being, and his analysis will proceed to reveal the structure of Dasein based on other, more revelatory moods. Heidegger would designate as "resoluteness" this possible decision to hearken to an unpleasant facet of Dasein's Being, its "ownmost being-guilty."[73] Unamuno seems convinced that the threat of death calls not for further thinking but for stubbornly circling back to bad moods, to experience the suspension of ill-humor as the most essentially human experience there is.

Although feeling as mood or state-of-mind provides one key for Heidegger's inflection of philosophical history, it is neither an end nor a simple moment of revelation. In Unamuno, a certain mood makes possible the individual's affirmation of faith, the "My God!" that ends "A lo que salga," for example, or his farewell to the reader at the end of *The Tragic Feeling*, "May God give you glory but no peace!" (S 241; E 358 [revised]). Nonetheless, like in Unamuno, feeling's status is related to the problem of death. *Being and Time* addresses death because the being that inquires into Being is finite; that is, it ends; the eventuality of its end makes up part of its possibility for inquiry. His analyses of fear and anxiety might, indeed, recall Unamuno more than his mention of bad moods; Unamuno, after all, does not only want his reader to experience *fog* but also the "depth of the abyss" that gives the fog its meaning. But, like Hegel after the dialectic of the self-conscious spirit, Heidegger's analysis forges ahead from the mention of death, claiming that the finitude of Dasein provides the possibility of describing the temporal character of Being, and by doing so, contributes to the possible awakening of the question of Being. Along the way, Heidegger makes a comment on death that further resembles Unamuno. Specifically, death must not be understood in the abstract manner of the sciences, since what is important to every Dasein is its own death, or, as Heidegger writes, "that *possibility which is one's ownmost*" (294). Heidegger continues his analysis by observing that the necessarily inauthentic experience of death—by only having experience of the death of others—must correspond to a structure of everydayness, one he calls Being-toward-death (ch. 51). By contrast, Unamuno declares philosophical thinking on death invalid and resorts to fantasy, wishing for a "material immortality" in which he could both die and live. This comparison suggests that, in spite of similarities in the characterization of death, Unamuno's consideration of death as a human trait itself stops at the most solitary and threatening moment. What pushed Heidegger beyond the analysis of death was the focus on the temporal character of being, for which the anxiety of mortal Dasein could act as a clue or trail marker pointing onward in the phenomenological description and back to primordial structures of Being. For Unamuno, the thought of death calls us to suspend thought, and that suspension leads to *Fog*, with its representation of thoughtlessness propelled, in turn, into obsessive rumination on life.

The Form of Your Death: The Possibilities of the Novel

To borrow the metaphor from Unamuno's description in "A lo que salga," *The Tragic Feeling* and *Fog* gestated together during the same years, and by extension, they were born in quick succession, the treatise before the novel.

It might be tempting to apply the principle, dominant since Aristotle, that the ideas expressed in *The Tragic Feeling* found a means of sensuous presentation in *Fog*. It is thus common to describe Unamuno's 1914 novel *Fog* as a dramatization of Unamuno's convictions as expressed in *The Tragic Feeling*, published in the previous year. According to this conventional reading, the treatise expresses ideas directly, or as directly as possible, in the form of propositions. Through the story of Augusto Pérez and the episodes that represent the author in dialogue with his creations, we learn of Unamuno's belief in the importance of an anxious belief in immortality, of his exaltation of the individual soul, and of the way being Spanish provides a predisposition toward these views. Meanwhile, as a work of fiction, *Fog* acts upon the reader's consciousness, allowing for a free emotional response to Unamuno's ideas. We readers come to feel anxiety for our own mortality, our own contingency as individual, created beings at the mercy of a creator. As Augusto says, speaking directly to readers as he speaks to his interlocutor in the scene, "You will die, yes, you will die, even though you don't want to. You will die, and so will all those who read my story, every one, every single one, without a single exception!" (E 226; S 284). According to this paradigm, which hews to different reading protocols for literature and philosophy, *The Tragic Feeling* may help you know the idea of your mortality, but *Fog* attempts to render the form of your death, to make it possible for you to feel your death.

Critics say that *Fog* puts Unamuno's world view on stage, and that precisely this expository strategy constitutes Unamuno's legacy, a philosophical thinker who was devoted to a literary form. For Thomas Franz, *Fog* is a "dramatization of the will to exist and to go on existing," and it sets forth an ontology that might achieve survival.[74] Jan E. Evans claims that Unamuno's novels force readers to "appropriate for themselves" the philosophical point of view that is more directly proposed in texts like *The Tragic Feeling*.[75] She suggests that, by engaging only the understanding, philosophical discourse does not permit a free and profound reception. In *Death in the Literature of Unamuno*, Valdés divides Unamuno's texts into those that offer intellectual experience and those that offer "esthetic intuitional experiences."[76] The difference between knowing and feeling proposed by Unamuno seems to prescribe this division and give the privileged place to the texts that might make us feel. Brian Cope contends that *Fog* is an "artistic expression" of a skeptical position more directly stated in "Mi religión" ("My Religion") and *The Tragic Feeling*.[77] He describes the point of view as a "vitalist ontology" in which being alive requires a kind of vital agitation created by the individual's internal (conceptual) conflict, thus depicting, as a kind of ultimate position for Unamuno, "acceptance of the incessant internal conflict between the passions of the heart and the rationality of the mind."[78] The heart wants to live forever; the mind sees evidence against immortality and, moreover, might understand that an eternal life is not logically compatible with individual subjectivity. Cope describes this as a "state of perpetual uncertainty" and yet, it appears exactly the opposite, a definitive acquiescence to a difficult truth. As we have seen, Unamuno's nonfiction writing is not without performative aspects that can baffle and disturb an attentive reader. In fact, he seems intent on generating skepticism about all philosophy, that is, any discourse that might give us mere ideas instead of the feeling of flesh and blood human existence this side of what we read. To the extent that *The Tragic Feeling* attempts to accomplish this via "intimate contradictions," we would do well to ask exactly what *Fog* dramatizes that was not already exposed by its companion piece.

Fog aspires to be not merely a representation, not a secondary phenomenon, subsequent to determinations regarding human lives, but, rather, to be the "thing" itself, an event in its readers' lives. If, as Valdés says, Unamuno's novels offer an experience of death, we must be reminded (as in Heidegger) that our death cannot appear to us unalloyed. These characteristics of *Fog* point to the strange impression that the novel is a form filled in by the reader's consciousness, which actualizes the textual operations and, if successful, receives an experience of death. Not by being put to death, of course, but by being confronted by it: "You don't want to let me be myself, to get out of the fog," says Augusto to Unamuno. "We, you, too, will die . . . and everyone who reads my story will die, too, all of you. . . ." (E 226 [revised]; S 284). When Augusto expires within the pages of the novel, and when he reappears as a ghost, Unamuno seems to be saying, thus will we die, in spite of ourselves, even though we might continue to haunt the dreams of others. Whether we are in *Fog* or *Fog* is in us as we read, Unamuno's novel aspires to the condition of an event or incident more than an act of cognition about which we might be clear or certain.

Augusto's direct address to us readers is one of the bluntest means of impacting the reader, but others are more subtle and require a more careful analysis. The challenge of *Fog*, the challenge of a presentation of death, is that negation requires the formation of something upon which it can operate. Thus negation is always determinate, always negation-of, and thus it avoids arbitrariness. Unamuno's negation is negative, then, as dissolution, which presupposes an affirmation in the constitution of what is dissolved. On the most conventional level, Unamuno tells the story of Augusto Pérez and lets it dissolve as the difference between reality and fiction seems to disappear. With series of double gestures, *Fog* reiterates or repeats literary conventions as a prelude to dissolving them. Dissolution allows for the idea of what is dissolved to reappear in a precipitate. The creative solution is *dissolution*; solution lingers in its disintegration.

This dynamic can be seen in the most general outline of the novel. In his prologue to the third edition, Unamuno refers to it as a "biography of Augusto Pérez" (E 17; S 87), and, as such, it focuses on the unique events in this fictitious individual's life. The setting resembles Salamanca, with Augusto walking through the main park called La Alameda (see S 130, E 51; and S 173, E 99 [revised]); the real Salamanca has an important park called la Alamedilla. We might be surprised to find, later, that Augusto must take a long train ride to visit Unamuno, when the narrator has him travel "here [acá], to Salamanca" (S 277; E 217). His home city is and later is not Salamanca. He has inherited a home and assets that will allow him to live a modest bourgeois existence. He decides to marry, to seek meaning through love of a woman, with the emotional support of his friend Victor. We follow him through the process of choosing a mate, Eugenia, and courting her. His inexperience and indecision lead him to discuss the nature of social and individual life with several people. Ultimately, he falls victim to a fraud by Eugenia and her boyfriend, and he is tempted by thoughts of suicide. It is then that he seeks the advice of a writer whose perspective he respects, a certain Miguel de Unamuno who resides in Salamanca. Making the trip to see his intellectual hero, the unsuspecting fictional character walks into the office of a character who ostensibly coincides with the author of his story. At this point, the novel's conventional character dissolves; all the details of the biography become irrelevant in the crisis that ensues in the encounter between creator and creature. Augusto's temptation of suicide is now accounted for by the rational conviction that he must not exist. He despairs of his life not because of injustice or heartbreak but because his mind concludes that he possesses neither existence nor free will. The Unamuno in the novel reminds the character that he may not do anything without his consent; Augusto spends a few pages struggling to prove his autonomy before dying, in what appears a fulfilment of Unamuno's wishes.

From the title page on, Unamuno presents *Fog* as a novel that is at the same time not a novel. The first edition in 1914 includes the title, followed by a mysterious parenthesis: *Niebla (Nivola)*. Spanish readers might have noticed the similarity of the second word to *novela*, but otherwise they would have to wait until the prologue or the middle of the novel to make this connection (as readers of Unamuno might have waited until the first page of this chapter to realize that Unamuno is a slight alteration of "un humano"). Unamuno's translators have chosen to leave *nivola* as it is in the original, as if it were a proper name, rather than an idiomatic alteration of *novela*. In English, something like *nivole* or *novile* might have captured the operation that Victor carries out in a conversation with Augusto in chapter 17. He tells that the poet Manuel Machado altered the sonnet form and joked that, in order to assuage traditional formalist critics, the result could be called a *sonite* instead of *soneto*. Victor suggests, then, that his transformation of the novel could be called *nivola*, an option he chooses over other options, *navilo*, *nebulo* (E 130; S 200). The name he finally chooses is not entirely arbitrary, however; readers of Spanish can hear *niebla* in *nivola*, since the diphthong *ie* is commonly accepted as a rhyme with the vowel *i*, and the letters *b* and *v* have the same phonetic value. The *nivola* is not, thus, just any new genre but the one suited to the novel of fog, the novel which not only confounds reality and fiction but demands that we refuse to settle into habitual acceptance of conventions, such as an undifferentiated universe embracing two distinct modes of existence. In a similar way, I might add, Unamuno is not just one human (*un humano*) but the one most suited to considering life, insofar as he names the body part that writes, *una mano* (a hand).

Indeed, when Victor touches on this subject in the prologue, he does so in such a way as to set in motion the oscillation between different points of view that will characterize this genre of the *nivola*. First, Victor announces that he is a "good friend" of the story's protagonist (E 3; S 97). Victor says that Miguel de Unamuno insisted on his writing a prologue and "the wishes of Señor Unamuno are for me commands, in the full sense of the word" (E 3; S 97). In the prologue, Victor only indicates that the *novela* and the *nivola* resemble each other, referring to the book in passing as a "novel or *nivola*" and insisting that it was he who invented the notion, not Unamuno (E 4; S 98). Already we are confronted with incompatible visions: if Victor invented the *nivola*, it would only be at the behest of the writer who created him, Unamuno. In chapter 17, speaking of his own *nivola*, Victor admits, "Everything my characters say, I'm really saying myself" (E 130; S 200). As Victor both is and is not Unamuno, the *nivola* both is and is not a novel.

Victor speaks for Unamuno when he describes the *nivola* as a spontaneous exercise intended to capture life, in contrast to novels that construct mere representations. "There is no plot, or rather, the plot will unfold," he says, as if creation were a matter of passively recording the progression of time itself. Indeed, he continues, "I determined to write [a novel] as life itself, without knowing what will happen next," and he describes the creation of characters who simply converse (E 128–29; S 199). Unamuno reinforces this view of the novel in his letters of the time, going so far as to call it an "abortion" when he gave up on it, describing the manuscript, "stored in a blue envelope like one might store the fetus of one's progeny [un feto promogénito] in alcohol."[79] All of this echoes *The Tragic Feeling*'s claim to spontaneity and Unamuno's vision of himself on the edge of philosophy, both in and out, speaking in his own voice and in a fictional one.

Conventional interpretations have it that he eventually succeeds, that the lifelike *nivola* provides greater realism than the genre of realism. In a subsequent discussion in chapter 25, Victor says he achieves a "more penetrating examination of the reality of things" (E 186 [revised]; S 249–50). The focus on dialogues is the key to this perspicacity: characters are allowed to reveal their intimate inner existence, even when the result is vacuous: "My fictional characters will create themselves by the way they act and talk, especially in the way they talk. Their personalities will develop gradually. And sometimes their personalities will be not to have any personality at all" (E 129; S 199). In its attention to exterior reality, Victor/Unamuno contends, the realist novel neglects what the *nivola* offers: the fragile construction of human lives, speaking the language they have been given, grasping tentatively for meaning, and remaining always exposed to the possibility of failure. And in its attention to conventions of plot and character, the realist novel, according to Unamuno/Victor, denies that our most intimate concern is for the fate of individuals, who, ultimately share our own fate. Ironically, in *Fog*, the person who most forcefully expresses this position is Victor's wife, Elena, who condemns description and anecdote as superfluous and wants only dialogue (E 129; S 199).[80]

In a 1935 prologue signed in his own name, Unamuno takes aim, preemptively, at those who might defend novelistic conventions or complain about the tedium of endless dialogue. The best readers, he says, are the ones who simply say they have thought the same things before. They resemble the Unamuno who, when asked for this prologue twenty years after the novel appeared, reviewed the book, that is, reread it, and by doing so resurrected characters, including himself: "I have reread it and, in rereading it, have redone it within myself, I have remade it: I mean, I have relived it. For the past does live: remembrance revives, it relives and remakes itself. It is a new work for me. . . ." (E 15–16; S 86). For Unamuno, the *nivola* is the novel that permits a life to be engendered; this life can be repeated at will, but the repetition constitutes a new life. Lest we consider *Fog* absolutely different from the conventional novel, which presumably does not offer this living encounter, Unamuno also warns in the 1935 prologue against the "mental laziness" (pereza mental) that would separate it from the novel (S 88; the English translation omits this phrase, 18). Again, the *nivola* is different, but also not.[81]

In addition to the doubling of the figure of the novel, the fictional tale bears an ambivalent relation to paratexts, which Unamuno multiplies and subjects to transformations. Gérard Genette includes within the category all phenomena that act as thresholds (the French title of *Paratexts* is *Seuils*) to a particular text: "Paratexts enable a text to become a book and to be offered as such to its readers."[82] These include facets like the author's name, the title of the work, dedications, epigraphs and the various forms of preludial or postludial texts we know as prologues and epilogues, *inter alia*. A note alerts us that the "para" in "paratexts" removes them from the dull realm of convention, quoting J. Hillis Miller's description of it as a "double antithetical prefix, signifying at once proximity and distance, similarity and difference, interiority and exteriority" (quoted 1n2). It is appropriate, then, that Unamuno's 1935 prologue attaches itself to a novel that already has Victor Goti's prologue, a "post-prologue," and the postface "Funeral Oration by Way of Epilogue," which consists largely of an interior monologue ascribed to Augusto's dog.

For Genette, all prefaces and epilogues share the same function, "getting the text read and getting it read properly" (197). That is, the prologue serves as advertisement and authoritative interpretation. Victor's prologue shows a thorough awareness of prefatorial conventions. He expresses agreement with "don Miguel" that a famous author would do better to allow an unknown one to write a prologue, acknowledging that the practice has as much to do with the marketplace as aesthetic or intellectual criteria. As we have seen, he also provides guidance to the meaning of the work, referring to conversations with the author in which Unamuno expresses his intentions. Genette informs us that the fictional preface is not entirely original to Unamuno, Walter Scott having published many playful prefaces, including one to *Ivanhoe* signed by the fictional Laurence Templeton, who claims to be the author (279). Victor manages to provoke a response by Unamuno in what he calls a "Post-prologue," which is to say, in a discourse *after* the discourse *before* the text proper. This response is a precursor of Unamuno's appearance in the novel, which is to say, it generates a textual persona who seems to coincide with the flesh and blood Unamuno.[83] He refers to Victor as "my prologuist," after all, making himself out to be the man who composed and delivered the book to the printer (E 13; S 107). Wayne C. Booth's typology of author figures can help us distinguish here between the "flesh and blood author" and the "implied author" who is made up of the decisions that constitute the text.[84] Among those decisions is the one to include an author figure as a character in the novel, beginning with the "Post-prologue" (which, as we all know, and as Victor's prologue makes manifest, is composed after the text proper is completed). Nonetheless, in his 1935 prologue, Unamuno continues to speak as if his characters related to him outside of the texts in which their encounters are staged.

For Genette, fictional prefaces and epilogues expand the texts to which they are attached; they are at once outside and part of the fictions. Rather than invalidate the statements they make when they attempt to "get the book read properly" (197), Genette suggests that their conventional function is to appropriate the fiction into reality. The fictional preface, he says, brings all prefacing strategies "to their ultimate fulfillment by passing, in its own way, over to the other side of the mirror" (252). Implicitly referring to the Shakespearian dictum that art "holds a mirror up to nature," he claims that the fictional preface stops being the (fictional) reflection and comes to take a place *this side* of the mirror, in the natural world. Furthermore, he concludes his long discussion of this paratext by saying that it is the "most typically literary, sometimes in the best sense, sometimes in the worst, and usually in both senses at once" (293). "Literary," indeed, can mean a breakdown of truth in a state of indifference, or it can mean a celebration of creation. Genette does not elaborate, though we can imagine that Unamuno appreciated this dynamic, serious and comedic at the same time. After all, he will refer to *Fog* in the 1935 prologue as "tragicomic" (E 22; S 90).

Victor's prologue does not neglect to refer us to Unamuno's philosophical tract, although his indirection and commentary question its authority. As we noted, Victor tells of Unamuno's insistence that providing labels does not solve problems (E 7; S 101), but Unamuno himself dismisses "Hellenism" and its habit "of distinguishing, defining, and separating" before claiming his own goal, "to undefine, to confound" (E 7; S 101). Nothing is resolved, perhaps, but certain unmistakable (*inconfundible* is the Spanish word) positions are marked out. Paradoxically, this Unamuno practices Hellenism as he claims to be diametrically opposed to it. Victor attempts to provide a label, coming as close as possible to naming the title of Unamuno's previous book: "The background for this attitude is the conception, or better even than conception, *feeling of life* [sentimiento de la vida] that I dare not label pessimistic, knowing as I do how don Miguel loathes that adjective" (E 7 [revised]; S 101 [emphasis added]). "The tragic feeling," the locution that he implies, will have to wait until critics mention it in connection to the novel, unless we count Unamuno's own "Entrevista con Augusto Pérez" (Interview with Augusto Perez)—a newspaper article Unamuno published shortly after the novel—in which Unamuno explains that the key scene awoke Augusto's "tragic feeling."[85] Both fictitious character and the author-character composed in 1907 seem unaware that, by the time of publication in 1914, Unamuno has already raised the banner of "tragic feeling" over his thought.

This distance between the implied author and the author's proxies widens throughout the novel. Of course, Unamuno's first appearance proper—in chapter 25—seems to encourage our association of the author with Victor, and even with Augusto. The discussion of the *nivola* Victor is writing, the mix of narrative and dialogue, is followed by an italicized text, a sort of epilogue to the chapter. "I, the author of this *nivola* that you have in hand and are reading, dear reader," says this new narrative voice, "was smiling enigmatically as I watched my 'nivolistic' characters plead my case and justify my method" (E 190; S 252). He immediately mocks them, however, noting that they don't suspect he is manipulating them like a puppeteer. The personality of the Unamuno character consistently shows a lack of sympathy toward his characters, from the mortal threats to Victor in the "Post-prologue" to his verbal attack on Augusto in the last chapters. Because of this distance between the implied author and his homonymic character, we are encouraged to question the wisdom of *any* figure going by the name of Unamuno, even the one Booth calls the "flesh and blood author."

When well documented Unamunian ideas are represented in *Fog*, these ideas also suffer this parodic assault. As Roberta Johnson and Brian Cope have shown, the evolution of Augusto from an idealist—who believes his identity resides in his thinking—to a believer in an incarnate or material reality seems to follow the novelist's own trajectory. If we accept that Unamuno's text makes use not only of words but of their omission, perhaps it is not too much to note that when we meet Augusto in the first lines of chapter 1, he extends his hand, "extiende la mano," to check the weather; this *extensión de una mano* is in a sense an extension of Unamuno (E 27; S 109). By the end of the novel, Augusto and Victor both accept that the most profound self is the one that lives and dies, aches and cries, procreates and eats. They agree that "the second birth, the true one, is being born through pain into the painful consciousness of incessant death" (E 212 [revised]; S 273). Like an infant born into the world, the person who will genuinely live must know he is dying; as we've seen in *The Tragic Feeling*, Unamuno asserts that this awareness of mortality might become a condition of immortality. For Augusto, the "ferociousness" of Eugenia's betrayal confronts him with his own death: "Now I feel myself, I touch myself [me siento, me palpo]. Now I no longer doubt my own existence" (E 214 [revised]; S 203). Augusto will retain this insistence that he can best reassure himself of his existence by demonstrating his own physical being. In the final scene before his death, he speaks with his servants, eats, feels his limbs and falls asleep, all to assure himself of his physical existence. His mockery of Descartes might seem sincere, but only a fool would propose "I eat therefore I am" as an adequate revision of "I think therefore I am" (E 230; S 288). More profound, perhaps, by retaining the self-reflective kernel of Descartes's formula, is Victor's half-serious idea that he should "devour himself."

Merely eating (ham, foie gras, etc.) assures Augusto that he exists, in a way that taking account of himself, thinking himself thinking, does not. In Descartes this test of self-certainty occurs when he asks whether he might not exist, and he realizes that he is thinking even while he entertains the idea of not existing. To quote again the words of the *Discourse*: "I resolved to pretend that all the things that had ever entered my mind were no more true than the illusions of my dreams. But immediately I noticed that while I was trying thus to think everything false, it was necessary that I, who was thinking this, was something."[86] The same cannot be said of eating ham; the self-devouring subject that Victor imagines would at least qualify as a being that assures itself of existence by finding itself subsumed into another thing. Like the *cogito cogitans*, the man who devours himself is both the devourer and the devoured, but unlike the thinking *ego*, the eating *ego* could stop eating itself without continuing to eat itself.

It is perhaps excessive to take Unamuno and his characters seriously on this point. There are certainly moments in which Unamuno's appearance of seriousness falls prey to irony. If it weren't for so many connections between *Fog* and *The Tragic Feeling*, we could go along with the critical tradition that declares Unamuno's novels a site of irony and his treatises his real voice. What would protect *The Tragic Feeling* from the corrosive effect of irony? Our best candidate for this role would be the very institution of philosophical discourse that Unamuno disparages throughout his work, at least when he is not attempting to recuperate philosophy for the sake of life, by deflecting it toward literature.

The Ends of Unamuno

In his reflections on Unamuno's death, Ortega lauds his countryman for curing Europeans of their neglect of death and for achieving what he desired as an intellectual. Unamuno had a good death, says Ortega, because he "has inscribed his death in the innumerable death that is Spanish life today."[87] Aside from the oblique reference to the ongoing Spanish Civil War, Ortega shows that Unamuno's success went beyond the achievement of renown for literary and philosophical works. He also succeeded in creating a tradition that would pass on and protect his work according to its own premises. In spite of the disagreements that we looked at earlier, Ortega would not disapprove of the idea of a man inscribing himself, including his own death, within Spanish letters, to be preserved in the voices and consciousness of the people he considered his own. As we will see in the next chapter, Ortega develops this general idea by adding concepts and a vision of the historical nature of life. The contrast he implies between himself and Unamuno does not amount to a major disagreement: while Unamuno does not, like Ortega, produce a "doctrine," he exemplifies the role of intellectuals who live up to the modern era's determination of them by "finding ideas with which other men can live [con las cuales puedan los demás hombres vivir]."[88] Without entering into more detail, we can see that Ortega agrees with the reconfiguration of the relationship between philosophy and literature that Unamuno represented, such that his status as a thinker is not doctrinal but vital; his thinking contributes less to knowledge than to the lives of people. Ortega writes a farewell of sorts, praising his deceased colleague for the things he agrees with. One could also, after all, do otherwise.

Jorge Luis Borges, for example, wrote two necrological essays in which he sends the older Spanish writer off into posterity, declaring him, in both, "the top writer in our language" (el primer escritor de nuestro idioma).[89] In "Inmortalidad de Unamuno," Borges acknowledges that Unamuno presented himself as a writer with one single theme, immortality, but he clearly disagrees on several counts. Unlike Unamuno and Dorothea Veit-Schlegel, Borges worries about how the writer can get in the way of reading a work. This problem, he says, is especially acute in Unamuno, and he complains about scholars like Jean Cassou who refuse to interpret the words, merely adopting the personal style of the man (143). For Borges, Unamuno's desires should not be confused with his achievements, and he was "above all, an inventor of splendid controversies [un inventor de espléndidas discusiones]" (145).

Immortality itself counts as a central theme, but it is only, for Borges, "of a dramatic nature," that is, it is deployed for the sake of producing these "discusiones" (144). Let us note the prominence of this tricky Spanish word—which appears in the first and last sentence of "Inmortalidad"—and its challenge for translation. In Spanish vernacular, the verb "discutir" suggests controversy and heated argument, something absent from the more benevolent English usage of "to discuss." The latter meaning has gained some ground in Latin American Spanish, probably thanks to its proximity to "discurso," *discourse* or *speech*, and the corresponding verb "discurrir," which can mean *to give a discourse*, or even *to think*. "Discutir" and "to discuss" come from "discutere" and "di-quatere," *to shake things apart*.[90] For Borges, Unamuno deserves to be celebrated for the shaking apart of *discusión*. In "Presencia de Miguel de Unamuno," Borges associates Unamuno's survival with the effect of this characteristic: "His bodily death is not his death; his presence—argumentative [discutidora], garrulous, tormented, sometimes intolerable—is with us" (82). Unamuno remains, as it were, a *discussive* presence, a sort of specter, dead but not dead, and alive to the extent that he can still make us argue with him.

Borges has at least two disagreements with Unamuno, then, and the declaration of these disagreements provides another kind of afterlife for him than the one Ortega assured us of. First, Borges thinks that immortality was not Unamuno's "only problem" (as the latter said in a letter to Ortega); instead, he was committed to arguing, and immortality was one pretext among others. Borges even puts it in the middle of a rather long list: "He argued about [discutió] the ego, immortality, language, the cult of Cervantes, faith, the regeneration of vocabulary and syntax, the excess of individuality and lack of personality of Spaniards, humor, ill-humor [el humorismo, el malhumorismo], ethics . . ." ("Inmortalidad," 144 [Borges's ellipses]). Second, immortality itself does not live up to its promise. In "Inmortalidad" Borges observes that Unamuno's readers notice its prominence as a theme but "do not try to argue about it or imagine it [discutirla o figurársela]" (79). Borges joins those readers, but he also adds a parenthetical comment, "from this we can deduce that they do not believe in it" (79). In short, one could say of Unamuno what he said of the Nationalist forces who took Salamanca, "vencerá pero no convencerá," "he will conquer but he will not convince"; he is the "top writer" in Spanish, but few readers, even admiring ones, find themselves preoccupied precisely with the immortality of their souls. "Immortalidad de Unamuno" closes ironically, insisting that disagreement does Unamuno a great honor, one that still addresses him as a human being:

"I know no better homage than to continue the rich disputes that he started [discusiones iniciadas por él] and to unravel [desentrañar] the secret laws of his soul" (144). That law, as we have seen at length in this chapter, has to do with unrelentingly shaking apart what he also puts together.

By cultivating a disagreement that cannot be resolved, Unamuno continues the tradition of Romanticism. Hegel's *Phenomenology* describes the restlessly self-certain self-consciousness and the endurance of death in the wake of the early German Romantics' experiments with strategies and figures that attempt to preserve spontaneity and movement in writing. Unamuno maintains, after all, the original philosophical drive to give an account of principles and demand agreement. At the same time, while one senses Schlegel, at least, running up against the limits of rational discursivity, Unamuno proclaims an allegiance to something philosophy might not tolerate. He fails to make precise conceptual distinctions and permits himself patently simplistic readings of philosophical predecessors. He appears to refuse the difference between bodily death and textual death, mortal life and virtual life, the intimate life of the individual with heart, breath, and hand and the public life of a literary creation. By pushing this question as hard as he did, by insisting that there is no difference between a fictional character and a flesh and blood author, he seems to have achieved an especially sharp demarcation of that irreducible part of the other that we cannot know, its "intimacy" or conscience. This achievement was either accomplished by the twinning and intertwining of literary and philosophical texts and gestures, or it happened by accident while he was trying to negate a difference he, personally, could hardly abide.

After the experience of *The Tragic Feeling* and *Fog*, Unamuno continued to explore different ways of relating philosophical and literary writing. Notably, *Tres novelas ejemplares y un prólogo* (*Three Exemplary Novels and a Prologue*) joins three apparently didactic fictions with an essay that explicitly claims the status of a novel.[91] *Cómo se hace una novela* (*How to Make a Novel*) narrates the production of a novel, including both reflections on composition and original characters and narration.[92] *San Manuel Bueno, mártir* (*Saint Manuel Bueno, Martyr*) and *La agonía del Cristianismo* (*The Agony of Christianity*) comprise a set of twinned works that engage the experience of religion.[93] Perhaps it is appropriate to leave open the question of whether the movement inaugurated by *The Tragic Feeling* and *Fog* gave way to his following a set procedure of philosophizing literary experience and feeling thought, or whether Unamuno restlessly, compulsively repeated the unresolvable movement that he associated with life.

Chapter 4

Josué Ortiga y Gazette and Reason's Living Narrative

Prologue: The Genesis of Life

José Ortega y Gasset wraps up the first major exposition of his ideas on life, thought, and art with a joke. Only a *German* pharmacist, he says, would have to provide an entire theory of "universal harmony" in order to concoct a simple remedy, and only a *German* philosophy professor would have to develop a "systematic view of the universe" in order to explain the nature of the art of painting.[1] The German he mocks, however, for going so far afield for the sake of a practical task, is his own creation, Dr. Vulpius, whose voice occupies all but the first few pages of "Adán en el Paraíso" (Adam in Paradise). The fictional Northern aesthetician, in Ortega's telling, espouses a belief in national characters and their predilections, much like Comte's national typology. Accordingly, he believes that the definitive aesthetic theory will have to come from Spain; upon reading Ortega's brief exposition of the value of painting, itself presented with the title "Adam in Paradise," Vulpius undertakes a lengthy justification of the Spaniard's ideas, an exposition for which Ortega's Spanish nature does not suit him, even though it might lend authority to his understanding of art. The result, Ortega's theory, affirms Spain's unique power of thought but also its continued reliance on the Germanic for its capacity to articulate complex theories. The German target of his taunt is his own creation, allowing distance from his ideas and welcoming laughter at the same time that Vulpius expounds ideas from which Ortega will not diverge over the next forty-five years. Nor will he cease to construct scenes of friction between the North and the South, the studious and the artistic, generating his own philosophy as a writing that steps back into an antechamber of philosophy, an utterance before the philosophical logos, one that sometimes gestures without words and employs an ostensibly literary style to address the body before the spirit.

Earlier we reviewed how Ortega's work is commonly understood as a synthesis or fusion of literature and philosophy. Two texts unequivocally figure this unity as the organic relation of a body's surface and insides. In the 1924 article "Ni vitalismo ni racionalismo" (Neither vitalismo nor rationalism), he declared a shift in his work from speaking of philosophy in a literary way to "speaking philosophically of philosophy."[2] It used to be necessary to disguise the difficulty of his discourse with "lyrical means," a process he describes as covering up the "philosophical musculature" (musculatura filosófica) with "a flesh-colored film."[3] A decade later, in *La idea del principio en Leibniz* (*The Idea of the Principle in Leibniz*), he will complain of the incomprehension of his critics, who, for the past thirty years, "proclaim triumphantly that my writings are not philosophy." He continues: "It is clear that fortunately they are not, if philosophy is something that [the critics] are capable of distinguishing [segregar]. Certainly, I carried to an extreme the hiding of the definitive dialectical musculature of my thought, as nature takes care to cover fiber, nerve, and tendon with the ectodermic literature of the skin. . . ."[4] Notably, he drops the separation between a literary philosophy and a philosophical philosophy, embracing the idea that his distinctive style constitutes his philosophy and ought, therefore, to retain all the homogeneity he attributes to his thinking. Following up on this representation of his text as a living prosthesis—if there is such a thing—of his own body, Ortega tells the virtual readers of his "Prólogo para alemanes" ("Preface for Germans") that Spanish readers of his writings will enter into them and find Ortega there. No doubt recalling his correspondence with Unamuno of decades earlier, he claims to "make [the reader] feel that he is there for me, that I am concerned for his concrete, anguished and rudderless self."[5] Furthermore, Ortega assures the Germans that Spanish readers are bound to feel him as an "ectoplasmic, but authentic hand that touches their person, that wants to caress or, well, slap them in a very courteous way."[6] This representation of a living presence unifies Ortega y Gasset's oeuvre or, shall we say, corpus, and the abundance of Spanish philosophical work that summarizes and in its way resumes Ortega's path testifies to how compelling his loose and intuitive intermingling of literature and philosophy can be, not only to those toward whom Ortega would reach out his hand.

We should not let these figures of clarity and fully present meaning drown out the more dynamic figures of tension and ambivalence in Ortega's texts. Even though they appear at times of disappointment, these other moments occur frequently enough to demand our attention. As we know from several reference points, mystery and incompletion, even contradiction, need not discredit a body of thought but might constitute a part of its force. Rather than constituting a systematic image of his philosophy, my readings from different eras of Ortega's thought show the philosopher at work developing his signature propositions and axioms at the same time that he acknowledges a tension between philosophical mastery and artistic or literary creation. Although Ortega struggles to control the latter—to subject it to philosophy as Plato, Aristotle, and Kant might—his texts sometimes assert and sometimes demonstrate that the revolutionary force of literature can be both invigorating and debilitating.

In addition to a certain literariness manifested in the fictional character of Dr. Vulpius, "Adán" provides one of the most direct articulations of the theme of "life" in Ortega, of how it ties the most universal category together with the individual human as the preeminent living thing. This is the "systematic view of the universe" that provokes Ortega's mirth, although it also establishes the axiomatic status of a notion of life, the centrality of the concept of the organ, and the outlines of Ortega's totalizing interpretation of the history of philosophy. In sections 4 and 5 of "Adán," Vulpius describes the birth of life with the emergence of a creature equipped with organs for discerning the totality of life's modalities, among them, the organs that create "pictorial art," the topic that the series of articles Ortega collected and called "Adán en el Paraíso" expressly sets out to address (69). Although vision and manual dexterity belong to painting, he will also home in on what is unique to the painter's achievement in contrast to many other things that vision and use of hands might perform. "Every art is born out of the differentiation of the radical necessity of expression in man, which is man" (72). He understands the human as a "radical necessity of expression"; for Vulpius, we need to express ourselves as ourselves, and we do so in myriad modes and forms. Each one has an "organ" corresponding to it, so that the human can both express and receive these modes; vision, digestion, pain, and hunger correspond, says Vulpius, to a constellation of needs that he calls "the human problem" (73). At this point, a footnote claims this exposition for Ortega, in his own voice, so that we may begin to refer to this, with a minor adjustment, as his own: he rejects as "naive" the idea that the need precedes the means of satisfying it, explaining that "the function no more creates the organ than the organ creates the function: they are coeval" (72n1). This somewhat mysterious moment of genesis leads to the biblical figure of Adam in Eden and the beginning of life.

In what follows, Ortega attempts to describe the primitive state of life, previous to cognition and action: "To perceive something is not the same as to know it but merely to take into account [darse cuenta] that something presents itself before us" (73). He goes on, "a dark spot, far off, on the horizon, what could it be? Could it be a man, a tree, a church tower? We don't know: the dark spot waits, aspires to be defined by us . . ." (73). In this description we can already anticipate the axiom to follow, that everything in the world counts as life and as a living thing: "Rocks, animals live: they are life" (73). Without the human, there is no presentation, hence no questioning and no yearning to be recognized. Thus, "when Adam appeared in Paradise like a new tree, what we call life began to exist. . . . For Adam life exists as a problem" (74). As a problem, then, life breaks down into different modes, with all the richness of cognition, action, and feeling. While Comte dreamt of finding a simple principle from which he could deduce the laws governing human history, Ortega declares that he has found in the "problem of life" the "virtual focal point" from which all human activity derives (73). "In a word," Ortega says, "when man was born, when he began to live, universal life began in that instant [asimismo]" (74). However, the choice of *life* for the most universal category receives no explicit justification. Pedro Cerezo Galán and Nelson Orringer will point to an origin in Goethe and in Georg Simmel's book on him.[7] But this does not explain Ortega's preference over, for example, *ser*, being, which he will even have Vulpius use as a synonym: "A thing's life is its being" (la vida de una cosa es su ser) (76).[8] Ortega will not be discouraged by the inconvenience of dividing life into living things like animals and inanimate things like rocks. From this point on, life remains the basic "ontological" category, which serves as the postulate—expressed with syntactical variations on the Greek and Latin roots—on which all of Ortega's subsequent thought rests.

One might understand the privilege of life for the ease with which it translates into an organic conception of the human. In "Adán" not only do bodily functions correspond to particular organs, but art, too, functions as an organ, or, rather, is differentiated into organs belonging to different expressive genres. In later work, too, Ortega will describe the operation of vital reason as the activation and creation of new organs through metaphor.[9] In the "Preface for Germans" Ortega presents himself, surreptitiously, as an *ortiga*, a nettle, growing out of Spanish soil: "This little thing that I am, a tiny excrescence sprouted out of the granite folds of one of the oldest mountain ranges in the world—the Sierra de Guadarrama."[10] He may also have enjoyed the fact that his name shares two syllables with the Spanish word *órgano*. In any case, the idea that he and his national or ethnic community grow out of their surroundings had a special appeal to him, and the everyday meanings of *life* seem to offer compelling ways to elaborate this Weltanschauung. It does not seem inaccurate to say that Ortega lets intuitions govern his philosophical principles, in a manner more akin to literary and artistic practice. In this sense, what Juan José Lanz says bears repeating: literature is not just a pedagogical resource but "the very entrails of his philosophical thought."[11] To his mind, Ortega's thought lives, ingests, eliminates, and shares a body with other vital functions.

Although Ortega does not provide any references in "Adán" to the history of philosophy's treatment of life, several assert themselves. First, the genesis of life as the presentation of self and other, and Ortega's persistent reference to immediacy and richness of the most bare-bones event of encounter repeats the beginning of Hegel's *Phenomenology of Spirit*. There, too, we find a purity of consciousness as what Hegel calls "one 'This' as I and the other 'This' as object," beginning the long process of determination and differentiation that eventually confers on the human, the church, art, and philosophy their necessity and character.[12] Hegel speaks here of "the sheer *being* of the thing," the greatest certainty, the "truest knowledge," but also "the most abstract and poorest truth."[13] Only when the "I" obtains self-certainty does Hegel's conscious Spirit determine life as a simple yet self-differentiated whole that includes, as Ortega does from the start, "inorganic life" as one of its constituent parts.[14] Rather than taking stock here of his rather complex relation to Hegel, Ortega proposes a history of philosophy he will maintain throughout his career, viewing all philosophies before Descartes as "realism" and all after him as "idealism," guided by devotion to nature and Spirit, respectively (80–82).[15] What Ortega will eventually call "vital reason" or "ratiovitalism" will hold that, as Jorge García-Gómez puts it, "living itself . . . is already a 'rational' affair."[16] That which was vital had a rationality all along, one which could only be seen and more intensely incorporated into lived reality through an overcoming of the kind of restricted rationality offered, in only apparently distinct forms, by realism and idealism. Ortega does not discard these basic forms of philosophy but raises them to a higher power, a combination that hearkens back to their original unity. That being said, it is striking that Ortega's differentiations of life around a single "virtual focal point" organized itself before all else into the classical philosophical divisions of theory, practical reason, and aesthetics ("science . . . morality, and . . . art") (73). In outline, at least, Ortega adopts for himself Hegel's claim of the completion of philosophy's evolution.

We might also observe that Ortega's insistence on "life" rather than "being" violates Aristotle's admonishment of his predecessors, who sought first principles among the categories of substance and movement examined in his *Physics* (fire, water, magnitude, etc.).[17] For Aristotle, one should not take one kind of being as the first and most irreducible constituent of both itself and others. We could assume here, by the same token, one should not make one category of being, the living—which Aristotle discusses in *Peri Psyche* (*On the Soul*)—into the model for the rest. In the *Metaphysics*, Aristotle avoids these pitfalls by resorting to the resources of his own language, using *being* (*eimi, ousia, ōn*), a category that belongs not to any particular thing but to things as such. Heidegger will notice this, noting Aristotle's failure to inquire into the Being of beings, and the difference between *Sein* and *das Seiende*. Being (*Sein*), for Heidegger, cannot be said "to be" in the same way that a being (*ein Seiendes*) is. By the same token, Ortega might have asked whether "life" lives in the same way as a stone or a caterpillar (such as the *gusano de ortiga*). As we will see, the maintenance of *life* as a word for being might well be credited with a clearer inscription of temporality in the nature of things, and to assess Ortega's philosophical achievement, one would want to weigh that against the terminological difficulty that the word *life* presents and that Ortega does little to mitigate.

In a sense, Ortega simply denies allegiance to terminological decisions of past philosophers. They are, for him, products of another time and place. He presents his reflections as the thoughts of a German professor whose name, after all, suggests he might be a wolf in sheep's clothing. In *Meditations on Quixote* and other texts, we will see other modes in which Ortega introduces discursive distance, as if showing a readiness to retract his own statements. At other moments, though, he speaks as if he were the creator of Adam, the engenderer of life and its mouthpiece for a particular time and place. In "Adán," the eye forms because life is visual, and artistic genres appear because the human being is a "radical necessity of expression" (72). Ortega's unique essayistic form corresponds, in its turn, to life's need to manifest itself as such. The arts offer "methods of individuation and concretion" (78) for something, defined as "the concrete [and] the individual" (77). All artists, says Vulpius, must create, in their unique time and place, forms proper to where they are. It befalls Ortega, apparently, to create a work that declares the artwork's task of "[proposing] a fiction of totality," such as "Adán" (80). Let us not forget one final detail. While in a sense the first man simply appears—and with him the human problem and the rudimentary organs from which more sophisticated ones will develop—life and the first man are "coeval." However, there is God the creator, who is not a part of the world generated by Adam. God is pre-vital, not beyond but before, on His own side of life, and hence lifeless. Ortega's interest in life persists, but it stops, it seems, at the question of the possibility of life, that which, perhaps, without any necessity at all, let life be, and differentiated it from both the immortal and the dead.

Meditations, Meditations, and the Joshua Method

We know from "Adán" that for Ortega, "life" might mean something different from what we are accustomed to thinking: "Adam is anyone at all and no one in particular: life" (89). Indeed, we could keep the word within quotation marks for as long as we discuss Ortega. For him, it includes within it anything that we might encounter in our own lives and serves as a single principle, differentiated into an evolving multitude of modes. This transformation of a common word into several meanings in a hierarchical order occurs with all key terms in Ortega, to the point of constituting a methodological principle. The hateful Spaniards Ortega warns us about in *Meditations on Quixote* should not be confused with the more Mediterranean ones who exercise their sensuous powers as Ortega does and therefore "strive to make love again rule the universe" (S 15; E 34). The philosophies or philosophers Ortega discusses need to be distinguished from the implicit worldviews expressed in their styles, a task that he will attempt to realize in his own writing and thinking. Art, Ortega says, might be a picture on a museum wall, but we must also look for the element that represents its vital necessity, its character as an organ fulfilling a function on behalf of life. The work of art, however, is not one concept among others. Lanz, Molinuevo, Valeriano Bozal, Philip Silver, and others, have recognized how, for Ortega, the work of art provides an appropriate presentation of the whole, which means, it is the condition of possibility of a genuine philosophy.[18] "Adán" and its fiction of the German spokesperson can be seen as a first effort to give an account of the immediate relation of a unique "I" to a multifarious world of things and to provide an instance in which that event happens. "Adán" even presents philosophy as a discipline restricted by its limited, because conceptual, view of the whole and, at the same time, as a presentation of the whole this side of "scientific" philosophy's restrictions: "For he who has a consciousness of what an orientation in [painting or poems] means, aesthetics coincides with [vale tanto como] the work of art" (71). This statement is somewhat ambiguous in that we could translate "vale tanto como" as a statement of equal worth. *The Meditations on Quixote*'s reflections on presentation and comprehension of the work of art make it clear that thought about art ought to aspire to the condition of a work of art. In addition, it reiterates the privileged status of art in capturing life as life by reaching behind mere understanding for a prior level of what Ortega considers "consciousness." Ortega's "consciousness," like other key concepts, has a double that is not entirely conscious, and that will eventually be called historical or vital reason.[19]

Meditations on Quixote's two prefatory chapters both address conditions that would enable a reader to respond appropriately to the book, a response that, for Ortega, does not come down to a merely intellectual act of comprehension. In the "Preliminary Meditation," he develops the dynamic of Mediterranean and Germanic cultures and represents himself as Ortega y Gasset, a Spaniard on the borderline between the two. In "To the Reader" he addresses "younger" countrymen, excluding the "learned" (eruditos), and recommending love over traditional Spanish resentment (S 14; E 34).[20] Both prefatory chapters contain characterizations of Ortega's activity in the writing of the book that approximate it to the matter at hand—*Don Quixote* and "quixotism"—as a particular work and as the epitome of literary work. All art, Ortega says, combines "vital spontaneity" with the artist's distance and reflection: "[The artist] has soared above his own heart and above his surroundings, circling about like the eagle in majestic flight [se ha cernido en giros aguileños]" (S 69; E 100). Too purely Mediterranean, Spain's deficient artworks do not reach the proper heights: "We find ourselves facing them as we face life itself" (S 70; E 100). By contrast, though, *Don Quixote* provides a rich evocation of both life and its meaning, the latter being associated with a Germanic or "reflective" character. In fact, for Ortega, "There is no book more potent in symbolic allusions to the universal *meaning* of life" (S 71; E 102 [my emphasis]). The "meditation" contained in *Meditations*, he will explain, by illuminating *Don Quixote*, will bring out the Spanish character common to don Quixote and don José Ortega y Gasset, which corresponds to a joining of the sensual and the intelligible (S 73; E 105). Meditation occupies the tension between Mediterranean and Germanic in a movement in which "we abandon the surfaces . . . with a feeling of being thrust into a more tenuous element in which there are no material supports" (S 47; E 74).

While the artist wheels like an eagle over circumstances, in "To the Reader," Ortega characterizes this movement as cyclical, and the character of his thought appears to lose some of its fragile, tentative character. Here he describes a criticism that distinguishes itself from learned pedants and Germans, who only describe the surface of the work, yet he retains the word "criticism" to describe his own practice. It does not pose questions and master the work, but "intensifies" the existing traits, retracing the artist's own movement, creating a sense of shared mission and counting on the work to give itself up. Thus, he contrasts the old criticism with his own approach:

> The secret of an artistic masterpiece does not yield to intellectual attack in this way. It might be said that it is reluctant to be taken by force, and only yields to whom it chooses. . . . It does not surrender to weapons: it surrenders, if at all [si acaso], to meditative worship. A work as great as *Quixote* has to be taken as Jericho was taken. In wide circles, our thoughts and our emotions must keep pressing in on it slowly, sounding in the air, as it were, imaginary trumpets. . . . These meditations . . . do not, of course, aspire to invade the ultimate secrets of *Quixote*. They are wide circles of attention which our thought describes without haste and at some distance, fatally attracted by the immortal work. (S 31–32; E 52–53 [revised])

Mentioning Jericho, Ortega keeps to himself, like a well-known secret, that the conqueror of Jericho was almost his own namesake in Spanish, Josué (Joshua). In his description, he acknowledges, for the instant of "si acaso," that life's meaning, the essence of "quixotism" of the Spanish character, relies on the intervention of something outside the control of the meditator. In this biblical story, like the Garden of Eden, this other is God. This minimal, easily overlooked aspect of otherness creates the indeterminacy of a tension that does not resolve into fusion or synthesis, providing room for unexpected success and, ultimately, for possible failure. It also means that Ortega's text assumes the character of any text, calling for a retracing of its movements in a reading that ultimately, whatever its claims, produces nothing more than the next in a series of texts.

Ortega retreats from this insight about the temporality and textuality of thinking, speaking instead of moments of completion and full understanding.

In *¿Qué es filosofía?* (*What Is Philosophy?*), he applies the Joshua method again, identifying four separate trips around the essence of philosophy, providing a definition or two each time. Although he describes the "tension" that such a procedure entails, he also forgets the tenuous character, describing the movement as a spiral that approaches its target in ever-narrowing passes before "perforating [the crust of life]" and "entering into subterranean zones of our being."[21] It could also be seen simply as a way of introducing an element of intuition and feeling into the work of interpretation, and some of Ortega's readers take up that call.[22] Like Unamuno in what he calls the "Conclusion" of *The Tragic Feeling*, Ortega gives himself license to follow his instincts, renouncing a more certain kind of method that he considers anti-vital. Unlike Unamuno, who declares his inability to work otherwise, Ortega claims that the cognitive support for his thoughts has been covered up or held back, suggesting that his is simply a choice to remain closer to the spontaneity of life without completely renouncing the transcendence of reason.

Ortega's retreat from his recognition of the role of contingency in understanding may have seemed necessary; it certainly, in any case, would have seemed advisable for someone with ambitions to guide Spain out of marginal status, someone aspiring to lead European philosophy. These ambitions are well documented: Ouimette attributes Ortega's energetic activities in the twenties to Unamuno's absence, and Gracia describes Ortega's regret at having lost a competition to Heidegger.[23] It is worth noting the similarity between Ortega's description of the artwork and his philosophical touchstone, "I am I plus my circumstances," presented in *Meditations*. Art, as we have seen, is living things plus the artist's perspective upon them, joined in a single work, a new living thing. It is not just the artist, though, who attends to his surroundings. In general, Ortega says in "To the Reader," "Man reaches his maximum capacity when he acquires complete [plena] consciousness of his circumstances" (S 21; E 41). Although consciousness might be "complete," or, to translate literally, "full," such a state is only possible because our circumstances are limited. Ortega says, "We must try to find for our circumstance . . . *precisely in its very limitation and peculiarity*, its appropriate place in the immense perspective of the world" (S 24; E 45 [my emphasis]). This limit gives rise to the dynamic enclosed in the strange formula that he gives. It does not simply express a "synthesis" between the individual and his or her time and place. Self and other are "coeval"—as Ortega says in a note to "Adán" that we read earlier—but the consciousness of their connection belongs first of all on the side of the first

"I" of "I am I plus my circumstances." Because there are in essence two I's, the conscious one and the one engaged with circumstances, Ortega can speak of "the reabsorption of circumstance" as "the concrete destiny of man" (S 25; E 45). For Ortega, we individuals are charged with discovering the character of our time and place and applying ourselves to the realization of that character. This conviction leads in later work to predictions and presumptions concerning philosophy and art. In *Meditations on Quixote*, he ventures, "One of the most profound changes in the present compared with the nineteenth century is going to consist in the *mutation* of our sensibility to environment [mutación de nuestra sensibilidad para las circunstancias]" (S 22; E 42 [revised, my emphasis]). Using a biological term that had recently been coined, Ortega announces both an observable alteration and his mission to formulate that change as an overcoming of realism and idealism. The very necessity of approaching "full consciousness" when one is already, in a sense, constituted by circumstances suggests that, like with philosophy and other key terms, Ortega distinguishes between an old consciousness and a new consciousness within consciousness, a consciousness that Ortega sometimes calls "ethnic." In any case, as San Martín and others recognize, this consciousness is prereflexive, this side, even, of the individual in the everyday world.

Certainly it is surprising that Ortega's concern for the present takes him to *Don Quixote*. In "Goethe desde adentro" ("In Search of Goethe from Within"), he takes up the theme of life before addressing Goethe's life.[24] In *Meditations on Quixote* Ortega aims at a renewal of Spanish life by clarifying *life* and *Spanish*, and for him, the two come together in an especially intimate way in Cervantes's novel. Ortega was the first to observe, however, that he hardly discusses the book evoked in the title (S 29; E 49). It is ironic that Ortega's meditation on life defines it as unique ("life is the individual," he says in "Adán," 77) while his commentary remains so removed from *El ingenioso hidalgo Don Quijote de la Mancha* that its particularities go almost without mention. Instead of appearing through the lens of an expert observer, the book simply remains as a vague presence at the center of José's circular movements. While he does not mark them out, as in *What Is Philosophy?*, one could discern two volutions corresponding to the two prefatory chapters and two more that take place in the "First Meditation." They, indeed, approach the target incrementally: Ortega offers an orientation in living, then one in reading artworks, an especially vital instance of the element of life. Thirdly, he provides guidance for the novel in particular, and, in a discussion of Maese Pedro and the episode with the windmills, he indicates the essential, living tension of the novel *Don Quixote*. Presumably, the fall of the city of quixotism would come after the reader is sent off to read that particular novel.[25] Unlike *What Is Philosophy?*, where he narrates the fall of philosophy-as-Jericho, in *Meditations on Quixote* Ortega merely hypothesizes that the "mutation in our sensibility" that he envisions will eventually materialize, with meditative guidance (S 22; E 42). Through an encounter with his style and teachings, Ortega's readers would, in effect, grow an Ortegan organ that brings a wider reach and deeper penetration to their lives, as it interacts, grasping or probing, digesting or discerning the facet of life for which it is intended.

As in the first half of *Meditations on Quixote*, the "First Meditation" deploys a rhetoric of fullness and accomplishment alongside renderings of a dynamic movement that characterizes—or *should* characterize—the contemporary novel insofar as *Don Quixote* serves as its model. In the end, what is true of the novel ought to be true for the *Meditations*, too, since both aspire to display "the present as such" [la actualidad como tal actualidad] (S 89; E 127). Ortega begins by laying down a principle familiar from "Adán": "form is the organ and content the function that creates it on an ongoing basis [lo va creando]" (S 78; E 112 [revised]). That is, the purpose creates a form in the process by which it is constituted. Form allows a particular content to "[reach] fulfillment [plenitud]" (S 78; E 113). Using another biological term, he'll define the novel as the "absorption" or "intussusception" (intussuscepción) of the "things of the world," comparing it to an organism's integration of others into its own systemic whole (S 100; E 139). Notably, Ortega does not consider the wholeness of a life within the context of its possible death, but within the continuum of organic decomposition and regeneration. Unamuno might have reminded him that many life forms do not take kindly to being treated as the mere building blocks of subsequent lives.

However, the culmination of Ortega's prehistory and history of the novel tells a different story. We need not recall the characteristics of myth and epic in its particulars, although it is interesting to note Ortega's repetition—without attribution—of Aristotle's account in the *Metaphysics* of science supplanting myth as an effort to understand the world (S 92; E 130). The novel, for Ortega, coming after myth, takes in, intussusceives, not only the things of the world but myth itself. The process of encountering and comprehending the world becomes part of the product. For Ortega, this process essentially deals with what he calls "two sides [dos vertientes] of things," meaning and matter, idea and reality (S 101; E 141). In a first look at *Don Quixote*, Ortega refers to a scene in which don Quixote watches Maese Pedro's puppet show, a moment that separates two spiritual "continents," the real and its representation (S 96; E 134). Between the two, Ortega posits an organic movement tending toward equilibrium: osmosis (S 96; E 134). But, later, after recalling the scene of don Quixote and the windmills, he decides the relationship is one of "everlasting conflict" (S 102; E 143). Ideal and real are joined in things, but their mode of togetherness is not a stable synthesis. Rather, the thing persists as "itself" only by the juxtaposition of two differends and by their ongoing struggle to overcome each other. Things are constituted by agonistic irresolution. As in Unamuno, we clearly need both sides of the conflict and thrive when neither neutralizes the other, takes in the other, takes the other over, or melds with the other. Neither one has any attraction in itself or by itself. Ortega says the idea subjects us to hallucination, and materiality makes us disillusioned, calling this a struggle between an allegiance to "phantoms" or "ghosts" (fantasmas) and a perennial and irremediable immersion in a "mute, terrible materiality" (S 103; E 144).[26]

Ortega concludes the "First Meditation" and the *Meditations on Quixote* as a whole with a vivid return to this theme. Ortega describes the novel not as a simple modification of myth, but as a combination of tragedy and comedy in "tragicomedy." The concept is not, however, a simple combination or synthesis of comedy and tragedy but, Ortega says, a response to the crisis that threatens to eliminate their difference. Tragicomedy, then, is not synthesis but a dynamic relation in a structure in whose gaps the work unworks the opposition on which it is based. Ortega concludes that the contemporary novel fails where *Don Quixote* succeeds, not because it fails to join tragedy and comedy but because the distance between them is too small. Hence the striking image: "the strain is too weak: the ideal falls from too low a height" (S 117; E 163 [revised]). His final topics of discussion involve the examples of Charles Darwin and Gustave Flaubert's Bouvard and Pécuchet, who represent for Ortega the victory of the so-called ideal over the richness of the real. Like María Zambrano, he associates with poetry the richness of reality that ideality threatens to obliterate (S 119; E 165).

What are we to make of these figures of tension and destructive, unresolved motion? Ortega's later work also displays an effort to project a movement of completion and realization of an epochal change. He preferred to describe this in biological terms like "mutation," which give the impression of something profound and inescapable, for which he would be a witness or a prophet, while also describing himself as an agent and advocate. Twice in the "First Meditation" he invokes the characteristic of *Don Quixote* that Cerezo has used to describe Ortega's work: "the will for adventure" (see S 98, E 136 [revised]; and S 106, E 148). While it does not offer much promise for a practical philosophy, this term describes how Ortega hoped to engage with the world through continued lecturing and writing, since making his thought public was itself an action, not a withdrawal into mere commentary on actions. The times offered many opportunities for activism in workers' rights, economic inequality, gender, war, corruption, and other things we might call "radical politics," but none would have seemed as vital or radical to Ortega as his continuing to speak his mind in his own name and to promote his perspective as itself paradigmatic of a will to adventure that coincided with the character of life in general.

The Theme of Our Time, Vital Reason, and the General Biology to Come

In spite of occupying a place in a third stage of Ortega's work, *El tema de nuestro tiempo* (translated as *The Modern Theme*) shows continuity with "Adán" and *Meditations on Quixote*, introducing the well-known notion of vital reason and amplifying the role of biological rhetoric in proffering a coherent philosophy. While "Adán" complains that science reduces life to "biology" as the object of "one particular discipline" (75), *The Modern Theme* continues, as does *Meditations on Quixote*, to privilege biological metaphors to describe the differentiations arising within the processes of "life." It even goes so far as to propose what Orringer calls a "metaphysical anthropology" in the name of a "*general* biology" that would usher in a new age.[27] Since that new age is defined in contrast to the "rationalist" one Ortega associates with all philosophy (except his own) since Descartes, often called "modern," we will refer to the book henceforth as *The Theme of Our Time*, or simply abbreviate as *The Theme*. The prefatory note that Ortega calls a "Warning" (Advertencia) explains that the text contains his "doctrine," and yet it also stresses the book's occasional nature, a set of lectures of a largely improvisational nature.[28] The publication is based on transcripts provided by audience members and, Ortega is glad to note, captures the living spontaneity that is implicit in his idea of the writer as a fully functional organ belonging to life as a whole.[29] *The Theme*'s topics of discussion include, thus, familiar motifs, and, in addition, it reiterates the principle of an unresolved tension before retreating toward complex and somewhat tenuous figures of synthesis.

Ortega again conceives of literature and philosophy explicitly as parts of a greater unity originating in life. Everything, Ortega says, including art, knowledge, and justice, is a "[pretext] invented by vitality for its own use, just as an archer seeks a target for his arrow" (S 188; E 72). Not just philosophy and literature, then, correspond to specific "vital functions," but also politics and art, the natural and human sciences, would form a part of this unit. As in contemporary interdisciplinary theories of the humanities, every sphere of activity is connected back at the origin. But we should note that from this point of view the connection of literature and philosophy seems to have no special status, as it does throughout the history of philosophy, or as it does for Unamuno, Machado, and Zambrano. The relation of literature to philosophy is simply one among other relationships within life. With such a view, expressed at times by Ortega, he takes away the suggestion that art's inventive character distinguishes it from other types of human activity and defines the particularity of his literature-philosophy. At best, his philosophy embraces a relationship that other writer-philosophers denied, minimized, or merely intuited.

It is surprising, then, that the traditional place of poetry is taken by *life* when Ortega speaks of an "ancient discord" between truth and life. Echoing the theme of the struggle between idea and matter in *Don Quixote*, Ortega uses this locution from Plato's *Republic* to characterize the new era he represents: "So far as we are concerned the old dispute has long ago been resolved, of course; we do not now understand how it is possible to speak of a human life from which the organ of truth has been amputated, or of a truth that requires vital fluidity to be dislodged in order for it to exist [que para existir necesita previamente desalojar la fluencia vital]" (S 163; E 37 [revised]). In its association with life, poetry has always had a particular power to question the limits of philosophy, and Ortega claims it as a part of what he will call, in *The Theme*, "a radical reform [reforma] in philosophy" (S 200; E 90). He resolves the "old dispute" by the combination of life and philosophy into a single term, a biology more basic than a scientific discipline: "The science of life, the *logos* of the *bios*, is converted into a fundamental science, from which the other sciences depend, even logic, and, clearly, physics and traditional biology" (S 164n1, not included in the English translation). The logic of Ortega's description of the new biology confirms his characterization of his own thought as a metaphysics, providing principles that ground different orders of thought, a first philosophy for natural philosophy, to which the conventional "life sciences" belong. While the very existence of a single word suggests that we have a synthesis of life and logic, the subsequent sections continue to describe their relation as an unresolved conflict. Once one overcomes the confusion caused by biology representing *both* the universal matrix of "life" or being ("general biology") and a discrete subdivision of the whole ("traditional biology"), one can understand what Ortega calls the "double imperative" to which the human is subjected. The human must answer to biology and spirit, the necessity for survival and the "ultra-vital principle of logical laws" (S 169; E 45 [revised]). He attributes Europe's unique place among cultures to the energy generated by this conflict between the vital and the ultra-vital, the dependent infralogic and the sovereign bio-logic: "This condition of extreme tension [esta superlativa tensión] inaugurated the unique dynamic quality and the permanent restlessness [vibración] of our continental culture" (S 175; E 53).

We might expect such an account of the charm, adventure, and fecundity of Europe to lead to the need for preserving differences, even heightening them. Ortega indeed pauses to draw conclusions here, pronouncing for the first time the title of his book, after noting that the present moment seems a historical high point in the conflict between life and reason (S 175; E 53). This is the theme of *The Theme*, he says, adding, surprisingly, that what seems like a final, permanent break, in fact, calls for one term in the conflict to be subsumed by the other: "the subjection of reason to vitality" (S 178; E 58). Life, in this case, is the *bios* that has already been absorbed into the new "science of life," a new metaphysics, in effect, a new philosophy. To continue the last quote, "vitality" has already been "localized within the biological." Not life per se but the *forms* of life would be brought, for Ortega, into a new understanding of life, he says while invoking our place in the title: "The mission of the new age is, precisely, . . . the demonstration that it is culture, reason, art, and ethics that must enter the service of life" (S 178; E 58). According to Ortega, they already come from life; "biology" will now provide directives and guidelines so that they can serve life better, serve *today*'s life. Once the laws are made clear, the obligation can be put in place so that "pure reason [might] surrender its authority to vital reason" (S 178; E 59). Ortega considers all modern philosophy "rationalist," which Kant's pure reason appears to epitomize and which occupies only one side of the tense unity of the human being. He claims to champion a form of life that will integrate reason into a larger whole.[30]

We will return to Ortega's exposition of this ostensibly broader reason, which he will designate "general biology," a term that we now have to understand not as a synthesis but as a pleonastic expression referring to an uneasy concept. Biology has been at issue in *The Theme* since the first section, where Ortega indirectly invokes his other surname. "The Idea of Generations" explains one of the concepts frequently applied in histories of Spanish thought. Ortega does not claim to have invented the concept, but he raises it to a metaphysical principle. Raw life, "existence in its undifferentiated totality," gets broken down, he says, into "consequences or specifications of the root feeling that arises in the presence of life [la sensación radical ante la vida]" (S 146; E 13). The human individual is always born into a generation; like *genre*, with which it shares a root, Ortega defines *generation* as a form that life fills, into which life "[lets] its proper spontaneity flow [dejar fluir su propia espontaneidad]" (S 149; E 16 [revised]). In *History as System* and *En torno a Galileo* (*Man and Crisis*) Ortega will provide more concrete traits of this process, but it is striking that he places himself within a particular generation as a way of accounting for his ideas, which he also attributes to a necessity of life itself.[31] But in *The Theme*, his time, if not our time, is not one moment among others; it is a "turn" or a "veering" (viraje), leaving the last generation behind (S 153; E 20). How does he know where his generation is going? Ortega y Gasset will regret that this is so difficult for his audience to grasp, but he describes it as a "[descent] to into our own hearts, eliminating all individual projects, private predilections, prejudices, or desires" (S 155; E 25). Ortega implicitly claims that such an experience belongs to him, such that time expresses itself through him, as a *gazette* contains the events of the present day. If we recall his self-characterization as an *ortiga* or nettle rooted in the ancient rock of Castile, Ortega y Gasset will appear the individual destined to deliver to humanity the double imperative of age-old truth and spontaneity of the living present.

Ortega y Gasset identifies his time, then, as the one in which life begins to assume its proper place, and he is not only the theoretician or philosopher of that time but also a part of it. In the conclusion to *The Theme*, he will again get out his favorite figure, although it is not only a metaphor, the organ: "Each individual, whether person, nation or epoch, is an organ, for which there can be no substitute, constructed for the apprehension of truth" (S 200; E 91). Ortega belongs to an epoch—the dawn of one, as commentators have noted[32]—in which science comes to expose itself as science, to show not only its organs but its organic nature, its organicity. Philosophy as a science has been an organ for creating organs and the new general biology will coordinate the combined labor of all creative practices on behalf of life. The organ is not just a metaphor, then, to the extent that even metaphors are governed by its law. Rather than an organ coming to articulate an original meaning, the law of organicity originates all meaning, including all of those in which rhetorical figuration can function.

In his 1924 article "Ni vitalismo ni racionalismo," Ortega returns to *The Theme* to clarify the relationship between reason and life, explaining that he does not merely mean to exalt life but to reverse the hierarchy and preserve reason as a subordinate term. Published two years after the book, this essay sets out to explain Ortega's "philosophical ideology" and to correct the impression that it is characterized by "vitalism" alone (271). Ortega says he prefers the term "biologism" to various doctrines he associates with vitalism, and his reasoning suggests that what interests him is the relation that the name for this life science sets up between *logos* and *bios* (271). Commenting on Plato's definition of philosophy as *logon didonai*, he explains that reason gives principles. He attributes to Plato the "antinomy" that "to know an object would be to reduce it to unknowable elements" (conocer un objeto sería reducirlo a elementos incognoscibles) (274). Philosophy is a rational movement towards the irrational; "unknowables" would be the Platonic ideas, which he does not consider objects of knowledge because they require indirect or mediate experience. Ortega describes Plato's and, later, Leibniz's surprise at philosophy's essence, and says that they react by inventing a perfect being who possesses the rationality that comprehends the unknowable (275–76). Ortega's title refers to his insistence that we acknowledge the irrationality of life as vitalism would have it, without discarding the methodical procedure of rationality. A positive version of the title, "Both Vitalism and Rationalism," would misleadingly suggest that the interest of the two could coincide. This is certainly the impression made by "vital reason" and "ratio-vitalism," that life and rationality can combine. The formula "Neither vitalism nor rationalism" places Ortega in an in-between, where he attempts to recognize the rights of both, as separate and related elements engaged in a movement of "counterposition" (273). Also, it authorizes him to advocate for one or the other according to criteria that are not explicit and seem, in fact, to belong to the secret movement of life. When, at the end of *The Theme*, Ortega speaks of a day when "culturalism and vitalism, on fusing together, will disappear," he mentions this disappearance as the goal for which his work is "only the preparation" (S 197; omitted from the translation, E 86). Life and reason do not "fuse" in ratio-vitalism but will do so in the general biology to come.

That being said, *The Theme* also represents Ortega's philosophy and its goals in terms that are consistent with the in-between indeterminacy of "Ni vitalism ni racionalismo." Generally, Ortega is rather dismissive of Freud, but he seems to agree with a principle of psychoanalytic desire as "the vital function which best symbolizes the essence of all the rest" (S 187; E 71).[33] He defines it as "a constant mobilization of our being in directions that lead beyond it" (una constant movilización de nuestro ser más allá de él) (S 187; E 71). That is, a living being must always be on the move toward what it is not, what is other. For this reason, Ortega invokes an ethical term, whose practical value he never elaborates: "Life is the cosmic realization of altruism, and it exists only as a perpetual emigration of the vital ego in the direction of what is other [del yo vital hacia lo otro]" (S 187; E 72). Life's "transitory" nature means that the ego remains itself as it approaches what is other. For Ortega, there is no indication that the root of altruism aims us at the other *person*; rather, we are compelled to what is different from us in general, to approach alterity and to make of life this passage toward others. It is remarkable that Ortega does not make a theme of what must remain other for the living self, its own death. Clearly, here, death would be not just an arrival at death as other but the definitive closure of the gap—held open by life—that separates us from any other at all.

Taken with the notion of life, in *The Theme*, Ortega proposes the term "general biology" for the vitally rational project that will grow out of the present time. Rather than a philosophical practice of riding the hyphen in "ratio-vitalism," the discovery of general biology lies in a future whose general feeling would give rise to new ways of knowing and thinking, motivating and evaluating actions. In other words, "general biology" is not a new philosophy but a philosophical poetics, describing not what discourses are but what they should be. In the Spanish text, Ortega italicizes this prediction and prescription for his readers:

> Good fortune [bienaventuranza] has a biological character, as does the day, perhaps less distant than the reader suspects, on which a general biology is elaborated, in which contemporary biology will only be a single chapter, celestial fauna and physiology will be defined and studied biologically, as comprising one of so many "possible" forms of life. (S 189; E 74 [revised])

"General biology" might come about not as an effect of hard work or insight but good fortune, a blessing that echoes the Messianic promise of the biblical Beattitudes ("las bienaventuranzas" being plain Spanish for the Sermon on the Mount, the list of blessings in the book of Matthew). Biology determines our luck and our destiny; the logic of life, one presumes, includes for

Ortega the day when the series of nonvital principles surrenders the place of privilege to the principle that has governed the chain all along. This is not, as it might appear, merely self-consciousness, but a coming into itself of life. Ortega will insist to the end of this book and the end of his life that this future self-realization of life remains the project that will resolve the political, social, and intellectual crises that affect modernity.

A new type of thinking prepares for the arrival of the "general biology"; although Ortega retains the nomenclature of "philosophy," the character of the new bio-logy resembles the *patho*-logy of literature. Reason "lets itself be dragged towards the ultra-vital," but the future philosophy stays this side of the "ultra" and "maintains its gaze upon living itself [el vivir mismo]" (S 188; E 73 [revised]). He calls for "a radical reform of philosophy and, more importantly, of our sensation of the cosmos [sensación cósmica]" (S 200; E 90 [revised]). Recalling Ortega's early description of the operation of life, we know that a new sensation ought to produce new "ideologies, tastes, and moralities" (S 146–47; E 13). In *The Theme*'s final chapter, Ortega speaks of creating a new human perspective through a new organ to discern truth, a means of knowing and thinking that would correspond to the sovereignty of life, in contrast with the "anonymous pupil" of the rationalist age (S 201–2; E 93–95). In "Goethe from the Inside," the task of the "biographer" was to "witness [asistir a]" life.[34] Written a decade after *The Theme*, the "Preface for Germans" gives a better idea of how a manual of general biology might look. After recalling the "theme of our time" and reiterating the necessity of remedying life's submission or subordination to culture, Ortega calls phenomenologists of his time the last proponents of an idealist delusion. To himself he attributes a point of view that sees the world as it is, as a "strange and radical reality," and that bears witness to life's "pure happening."[35] A doctrine that would let Being be life, he notes, would require a new language and hence a new dictionary: "Since all language is in its entirety constituted by an ecstatic inspiration, it is necessary to retranslate it in its totality to the fluid significations of pure happening [puro acontecer] and to convert the whole dictionary into a calculus of tensions [cálculo tensorial]."[36] Only "fluid significations" of "ecstatic inspiration" live up to life's spontaneous, infinitely mobile character. Our lists of words and their meanings must reflect a combination of interrelated tension and calculability, the relation between rationalism and vitalism held open in "ratio-vitalism."

Remarkably, the composition of this new dictionary does not translate the old rationalist language into a new ratio-vitalist or biological one. Ortega's projected "retranslation" returns language to a primordial condition, making it once again what it has always been. The very project suggests that words will not mean something different but will achieve meaning in a different way, according to new protocols of signification. That is, the new dictionary, following Ortega's ratio-vitalist poetics, will aim less at understanding as rational mastery than as participation in a network of reference and tension. Such a conception certainly sounds like the structuralist revolution ushered in by Saussure, replacing a linguistics governed by signs' relations to real referents with a system of differential references between signs. Signification as "tensorial calculus" in this sense already exists and is indistinguishable from our current dictionaries and grammars; indeed, we may all already speak dialects of this language. Ortega's style suggests that "calculus of tensions" does not refer to the relations between words but to the way he connects words—as rational, calculable, differential markers—with life's secrecy, to which words can relate only as mathematical symbols relate to the daunting complexity of tensors, the objects of a branch of differential calculus. It is perhaps no surprise that Ortega opted not to produce such a manual for general biology. Instead, he appears to have contented himself with speaking in the original, strangely cryptic style for which he is applauded, apparently believing that his combination of impulsiveness and deliberation was itself already living speech.

In addition to the tenuous, if not mistaken, impression that biology represents a synthesis of life and logic, "general biology" gives the impression that it might function like a discipline, providing stability and firm guidance for production of knowledge. In the final sections of *The Theme*, Ortega seems to have given in to these impressions and failed to address some of the more radical implications. His own "doctrine of the point of view" repeats the principles of his historical and philosophical intervention, but they are presented as the solution, the "perfect synthesis" that the crisis of his day demands (S 198; E 88). A sense of irresolution remains, however, in his representation of his doctrine as merely preparatory for the general biology to come: "What I have said up until now is only the preparation for this synthesis in which culturalism and vitalism, fusing together, will disappear" (S 197, omitted from the English translation). His generation, he implies in the last chapter of *The Theme*, can complete the task. One cannot quite tell whether he is effecting change with a "radical reformation" analogous to Luther's shake-up of Christianity, or merely manifesting, "transcribing," as it were, a change that happens on its own, according to the "logic" of life's historical flow. Moreover, Ortega recognizes that his hypotheses require a countersignature on the part of others, who will have to confirm and continue his thought. In spite of the irresolution such a situation highlights, Ortega's concluding words suggest that we have an obligation not only to ourselves and our communities, but to God, to fulfill Ortega y Gasset's outline for the future. We are "the visual organs of God" and we should "open our eyes wide to our environment with a profound faith in our own organism and vital nature, and accept the task [faena] that destiny assigns us: the theme of our time" (S 203; E 96 [revised]). Accordingly, we would become receptive, but, paradoxically, passive receptivity is the activity we must take on. Readers of the original would possibly hear in "faena" a reference to the phases of a bullfight in which the torero confronts the bull alone. In addition to an indication of Spain's place with regard to the possibility of humanity's fulfillment of its potential, it should remind us that the "task" combines elements of art, physical effort, and mortal danger. That God's eyes should perform or engender things is perhaps not as unusual as the suggestion that they might be capable of failure.

"Behind Itself": *What Is Philosophy?*

As a direct approach to a definition of philosophy, one would expect *What Is Philosophy?* to provide clear indications about its relationship to literature. The "Preliminary Note" by the editors of the *Obras completas* (Complete works) explains that Ortega prepared this text for publication in the 1930s based on notes for a 1929 lecture series. While it is not a final statement on philosophy, it establishes the beginnings of the phase Orringer calls an "ontology of human life" by reiterating the association of *life* with the most general concept, and, also, an anthropocentric understanding of that concept, being, *ser*.[37] Ortega allows the interconnections of literature and philosophy to appear almost entirely in an implicit way: he organizes the discourse around four circumvolutions of the theme, like the story of Joshua's conquest of Jericho; he deploys metaphorical descriptions of his topic; and he allows anecdotes and literary allusions to work on the minds of his audience. The content, meanwhile, consists of the presentation of Ortega's own philosophy as philosophy itself, including a reiteration of the formula, "I am I plus my circumstances" from *Meditations on Quixote* and the "doctrine" of "perspectivism" from *The Theme of Our Time*. Alongside echoes of earlier texts, we can observe a moment of significant tension between the desire for definite synthesis and a recognition of the value of openness and irresolution.

Ortega infuses drama into the public lectures that comprise *What Is Philosophy?* by associating philosophy with adventure and sport, activities that require dedication and offer happiness and fulfillment.[38] The first three lectures warn the public that they will be difficult, promising a "vigorous analysis" of "philosophy as a whole" and a "maximum of philosophy" to countervail the "minimum" that positivism imposed on the last hundred years of European thought (S 286–87; E 28–29). But he also speaks of a voyage of discovery—"exploring terra incognita" (S 374; E 157)—and repeats *Meditations on Quixote*'s evocation of early evangelicals "in partibus infidelium" (*What Is Philosophy?*, S 288, E 30; *Meditations*, S 11, E 31). He recommends philosophical reading and describes it as deep-sea diving, with a reader returning to the surface "master of [a text's] secret heart [dueño de su secreto interior]" (S 318; E 75). In these metaphors, it should be noted, he neglects to mention the possibility of failure, injury, or death that plague all such pursuits. If one suspects that Ortega means to invoke Spaniards who founded colonies—such as those on the Río de la Plata, where Ortega delivered these lectures—one might also wonder at the moral ambiguity of the results of adventure. As Bruno Bosteels suggests, Ortega seemed—like Hegel—perfectly comfortable with the destruction of native cultures, since it brings them into the present day of the most vigorous of the world's cultures.[39]

The explicit organizing principle of *What Is Philosophy?*, however, is the Joshua method described in *Meditations on Quixote*, with Ortega's discourse making mention of Jericho in the first two sections, modifying the story to suit his certitude that the right approach on his part can provide the same assurance as God's promise to the Hebrews. After the first round, Ortega sums up the difference of philosophy as a personal attunement to the whole of being, describing both a kind of receptivity and an ambition that, in accordance with its general character, makes philosophy "heroic" and "dangerous" (S 328; E 90). Philosophy is "an integral system of intellectual attitudes in which the desire for absolute knowledge is organized methodically" (S 310; E 63). It is not a discipline or a tradition but, as we have seen before, a set of implicit structures that can distinguish one individual from another. After a second round of meditation on the topic, Ortega offers a new and distinct definition, this time of "philosophizing" (the verb "filosofar"), an action belonging to a philosopher: "seeking to give the world its integrity, completing it as a Universe, and taking part in the construction of a whole in which it can lodge and be at rest" (S 333; E 98 [revised]). The definition bears elements of affectation and idiomatic language that suggest it is a carefully considered linguistic structure. What stands out in this new definition is the continual presence of desire, a desire for a whole and the necessity of human interaction, by means of a philosophical function, in order to achieve cosmic wholeness. Ortega adds that the result is a "system of truths" (S 333; E 98). Already, then, we are faced with an ambiguity within philosophy: it appears as both a temporal human activity and a doctrine, both something highly concrete and even personal and something general, categorical, and formal. Ortega highlights this tension when he describes the philosopher's "monstrous and even frenetic character" (un carácter desaforado, frenético) shortly before including domesticity and rest within the definition of philosophy (S 329, 333; E 92, 98). He seems to acknowledge this tension when he calls philosophy "paradoxical," a few lines later. However, his understanding of paradox as a passage from one *doxa* to another neglects to mention that the *doxas* at issue are themselves contradictory and constitute the poles of an unresolvable movement back and forth.

In the fourth trip round the theme of philosophy, Ortega's aims to formulate a definition but instead produces a series of propositions that intensify philosophy's internal tension and hearken back to the presentation of life in "Adán." Ortega emphasizes that the previous definitions were anchored in a person, "the fact of a person who philosophizes, who wants to think about the Universe and to that end seeks something which cannot be doubted" (S 404; E 202). Thus, as in Unamuno, one finds a human being this side of philosophy: "not a philosophic theory but a philosopher in the act of philosophizing, that is, in the act of living the process of philosophizing" (S 404; E 202). Before a determinate philosophy, Ortega highlights the philosophical activity, and prior even to that, he says, there is the form of life that belongs to the philosopher. "Philosophy goes behind itself [va detrás de sí misma]," he says; it goes back of itself as an action and it finds itself as primordial life (S 405; E 204). At this moment we can gather a solution to the mystery of why Ortega omits the definite article of philosophy in the titular question, "¿qué es filosofía?" Normally in Spanish, the article accompanies a concept or a discipline, a determinate thing. Without the article, *filosofía* becomes a mere word, one seemingly derived from another concept, like *peluquería* is from *peluquero* or *taquería* from *taco*. Somewhat like Unamuno's coinage "filosofería," "filosofía" is the site of the philosopher's activity. Should one shudder at the tautological form of his description, Ortega's final definition of philosophy offers a similar formulation, this time involving not philosophy but life and being: "[Philosophy] sees itself as a form of life, which *is what it truly and concretely is* [es lo que es, concretamente y en verdad]. . . . It is . . . *meditation* on our life" (S 405; E 204 [my emphasis]). The subjective and objective genitives combine here: meditation *comes from* life and renders life present *for the first time*, and life is the apparent self-identity of "it is what it is." As in "Adán" the forms of life that constitute its organs occupy the very same whole as that which the organs receive. In this regard, life fulfills itself; it is absolute, needing nothing else but itself in its own organic self-constitution. Besides reminding us of his first book, *What Is Philosophy?* insists that this philosophical discourse corresponds to the exposition of "vital reason" and "general biology," saying that this is a "discovery of our time" (S 406; E 204).

Life is life *itself*, and it is also *differentiated* into distinct units, intelligible as different within the systematic whole that they constitute. Such a description of life coincides with Aristotle's exposition of time in the *Physics*, an analysis that seems to be maintained for the most part by all subsequent thinking about time. As Jacques Derrida points out, Aristotle's inquiry into the question "What is time?" takes place in the context of a study of *physis*, of a natural world with a richness and variety of beings that exist without human intervention.[40] While Aristotle seems not to be concerned with the question of things' otherness to humans, Derrida notes that the inquiry winds up describing how time allows beings to be in the predominant mode of presence (38). Because beings must be in time, they have an essential relationship to other beings, including those ostensibly copresent at the same moment and, in addition, the former self and present self that lend a particular being continuity and identity. As Derrida explains, when Aristotle attempts to account for the motion or mutability of a singular being, he observes an aporia: the present moment must function as a discrete unit of time, *and* it must submit to immediate destruction by the future, which constantly and relentlessly comes along to destroy that "point" in time even before it can constitute itself. Aristotle solves the aporia by appealing to mathematical concepts, determining the present moment as a number and point on a finite line (39–40). Ortega, as far as I can tell, saw no need to explain how the present moment coheres with the things it constitutes. This leaves us without an attempt to think the connection between the philosopher philosophizing, the meditator meditating, or the being *being*, on the one hand, and, on the other hand, the doctrine, the meditation, or the thing. Nevertheless, Derrida suggests an explanation for Ortega's omission. The continuity between these elements seems as self-evident as the way points seem to constitute a line and the countless nows that we live make up our lives. Derrida surmises that this self-evidence leads to Hegel's mere repetition of Aristotle's geometric argument (40–41). Ortega's signature gesture is to call this aporetic structure of time "life," to say, as Aristotle might have, that time/life provides the room or space in which things can *be*. When he says in *What Is Philosophy?* that one must "invalidate the traditional meaning of the word 'being'" (S 394; E 185), it is because *being* ought to be understood in the context of temporality, understood on the basis of the *life* of self-presence, presence's continual passage into the future.

As a "this side," back of philosophy, Ortega's notion of life also differs from Aristotle in not constituting a system of principles. Ortega is in some ways never closer to Unamuno than in this moment. His dogmatic positing of *life* as a principle even echoes *The Tragic Feeling of Life*'s quotation of a Latin proverb, "primum vivere, deinde philosophare."[41] Except that for Unamuno life's limit is never far from sight. In spite of his evocations of philosophy's adventurous character, and the long tradition considering philosophy as the art of dying, Ortega's life only elaborates on its own internal borderlines, not on the one that would separate it from an other, from an alterity that is irreducible to its conscious attempts to grasp it. And the internal differentiations of life include such rich and intricate facets as one would expect from a text so devoted to literature. Ortega suggests here that his notion of life comes from Dante's evocation of a "vita nuova," perhaps another wink at the Argentine public and its well-known links to Italy (S 408; E 206). From what we can tell, Ortega would have relished the suggestion that the answer to the question "What is philosophy?" might come not from the philosophical tradition but from literature.

Ortega's Life and Limits

In his homage to José Ortega y Gasset, Octavio Paz praises the effort to put thought in the context of life, with a view to something behind ideas and concepts, their "why and wherefore."[42] Paz notes character traits often also associated with Unamuno: dialogue with him often consisted of listening to his monologue (145); he shamelessly displayed cultural prejudices (150); and he bragged of his own physical and intellectual vigor (150). Yet

Paz credits Ortega with stimulating his own thinking about literature and philosophy, and he offers some brief comments on their relation that echo those of his friend María Zambrano (150–51). Paz identifies "three omissions" that coincide with aspects I have noted. First, Ortega's conception of philosophy favors the theoretical over the practical, taking a greater interest in true understanding than in virtuous action. In addition, Paz regrets that Ortega's thought has little room for death, or for other worlds, that is, for the divine (146–48). When Paz concludes that "ratiovitalism is a solipsism" (148), we might even add, and a narcissism: it is Ortega's elaboration of a total vision of the universe corresponding to his own life, from his parentage to his given name. That is not to say that it lacks philosophical seriousness.

Let us observe that the omissions of God and death bear on the status of otherness in Ortega's thought. Cerezo says approvingly that Ortega regarded death as "a dimension of life," yet, as the end of life, it is certainly not just one dimension among others. In fact, Heidegger's and Unamuno's thoughts about death highlight the extent to which it should be regarded as an other of life, a fact whose place *within life* must be defined by its not yet appearing as such. In their analysis of the role of death in Ortega's work, Jesús M. Díaz Álvarez and Jorge Brioso observe a tendency to avoid the topic, which leads them to reflections on death as a radical other in Heidegger, Blanchot, and Spanish philosopher Antonio Rodríguez Huéscar.[43] In general, Díaz Álvarez and Brioso conclude that the "taboo" under which the question of death stands, for Ortega, results in a limited ability to think the future, to "expect the unexpected" by overestimating the human capacity to conceive of death.[44] In a similar fashion, Ortega regards God only with regard to human life, as a character in mythological attempts to understand the world. Such a manner of thinking about God does not take into account the radical distinctions—between finite and infinite, mortal and immortal, temporal and eternal, and so on—that the notion of the divine or sacred demand for so many contemporary philosophers. Zambrano will later claim that the entire philosophical tradition excludes the radical alterity of the divine, and this appears, at least, to be true of her teacher. The "omission" of a more sustained reflection on otherness probably belongs to that lack of introspection pointed to by Paz, and it can be logically connected to the casual prejudices he sometimes expresses against non-Spanish thinkers—including the young Mexican Paz—women, "the masses," and the aged.[45]

Whatever we make of Ortega's attitudes toward specific types of human others, it is worth considering that for Ortega, all otherness occurs within the whole of life. With that in mind, Ortega's followers see life's evolution behind contemporary changes in cultural practices and beliefs. In *El legado filosófico español*, Manuel Garrido notes that generations have different contours than in Ortega's day.[46] The inclusion in his manual of Spanish philosophy of a section devoted to women suggests that life has developed a thing for women, minimizing the extent to which women expressly fought to be even considered as thinkers.[47] After the patriotic gesture of his *Historia crítica del pensamiento español*, José Luis Abellán embraces as a ratio-historical phenomenon the passage from promoting Spain to promoting multiculturalism around the world.[48] The great danger in ethical discussions framed by the problem of otherness is the feeling of reassurance that one has taken the other adequately into account, comprehending and appropriating the other's interests and perspective. As a counterweight, the notion of utter alterity promotes greater openness and vigilance and a broader appreciation of the possibilities of future thought and life, even though it requires ever-renewed questioning of the way "alterity" is framed, addressed, evoked, even named.

The limitations in Ortega's thinking of alterity impact the relation between philosophy and literature. It is true that, like Heidegger, he relates both discourses or activities back to a common source. For Heidegger, that original element yields *Dichten* and *Denken* in the event of opening up worlds, structures of possibilities of beings, and various modalities of human activity. For Ortega, though, literature and philosophy belong together like skin and muscle, constituting a unit with other organ-like functions. Paz's first "omission" rightly suggests that Ortega is most interested in their relation as it bears on what is external to the human subject, as if life were more about perceiving, grasping, and ingesting than other more intimate functions. (What of Unamuno's favorites, spleen, digestion, rumination, or gestation?) Ortega's affection for sociologies, psychologies, and anthropologies of literature could obscure how literature engages with the principles of human life, but only if we neglect the extent to which Ortega attempts to radicalize these disciplinary discourses in the same way he reimagines biology.

Our discussion of Derrida in chapter 2 emphasizes the extent to which literature engages the question of otherness in ways that can help us assess Ortega. His vision of a fluid ratio-vital or ratio-historical unfolding of life postulates enduring laws, like Comtean positivism. It is on the basis of these that he can declare the death of the novel, for example, or the impotence of Krausism. For Ortega, the elite perceives and institutes what "life" determines, and invention is passive reception of life's newest determinations. By contrast, Derrida describes a more radical openness to the future as the unforeseen and unforeseeable. Literature provides a glimpse of what might come *as* unforeseen. Such a structure has implications for politics, individual and interpersonal life, and art. We could also associate such openness with ethics, and, again, Ortega's limitations suggest that one might do well to remember that our ideas of what others should be can blind us to what they are and have a right to be: different.

In that sense, Ortega's engagement with literature was not deep enough or "radical" enough to impact his life. At the same time, what other name could we attach to the writings that challenge us to think an extreme otherness and to do so more insistently than José Ortega y Gasset did? Did Ortega not also, to an extent he might not have appreciated, advocate for inventiveness in philosophy? And find the means for it in the encounters he staged with the natural sciences, social sciences, painting, popular culture, and so on? From Ortega, we learn not that literature and philosophy are each other's other, but that they should be thought in relation to innumerable others. Looked at from another angle—one that is not Ortega's, nor one that he would have foreseen—we might see that philosophy has many others with which it must cultivate relationships of separation and linkage. Or that philosophy is not one. From there, perhaps, we could begin to think of life's plurality, too. Paz's praise of Ortega's work, beyond his misgivings about the man, point in this direction when he asserts that one can learn from him how ideas and concepts teach us "not to know ourselves nor to contemplate essences but to open for ourselves a passage in our given circumstances" (145).

Chapter 5

Antonio Machado, Writing Ephemeral Passages

Philosophical Poetry

In whatever language we read it, Antonio Machado's 1914 book *Campos de Castilla* (*Fields of Castile*) shows him as a paradigmatic thinking poet, grappling with the interrelation between concepts and experience with dense, formally precise language. Among his best-known lines are these from the section "Proverbios y cantares" ("Proverbs and Songs"):

> Todo pasa y todo queda
> Pero lo nuestro es pasar
> Pasar haciendo caminos
> Caminos sobre la mar.
> **
> Everything passes and everything remains,
> But passage is our thing.
> We move along, making our way,
> Making pathways on the surface of the sea.[1]

With this poem Joan Manuel Serrat opens the medley he calls "Caminante" (Wayfarer), perhaps because it seems to propose fairly distinct ideas. We form part of a single, selfsame world, an "all" or "everything" (todo) that "remains" (queda). Machado's statement takes on a traditional philosophical problem, the characterization of beings as a whole and of the relationship of human beings to the oneness of what is, a whole to which we belong.

Immediately after the invocation of the being of the cosmos, Machado's verse evokes time: everything constantly changes; it "passes" (pasa); it is rendered other without losing its unity and integrity. The first line captures the challenge of metaphysics since ancient Greece to account for existence in a particular place and in the flow of time. The poetic voice turns quickly, then, to the specificity of the human in the whole of beings: time pertains to us in a special way. Certainly, we belong to the "everything," which includes the passing and the remaining, but *passing* is proper to us, "our thing" (lo nuestro). "Pasar" can also be translated *to happen*; human lives "take place" or occur as events, defined by their finite emergence and disappearance in an event we can call a "passage." Thus, the quatrain's appositional image of human existence: in the midst of everything else, we inscribe our own lives in a form as ephemeral as the wakes of vessels on the sea. Our way of remaining is also a sort of passing; it leaves something behind, a "pathway" (camino), not as a preexisting trail that we have followed but as a road that has been broken open by our passage. In the Spanish poem, "pasar" rhymes with "mar," which since Jorge Manrique is the traditional Hispanic symbol for death. Living, we human beings hold out for a time, tracing a singular trajectory through some particular site in the world, and we finally return, along with the evidence of our passing, to the undifferentiated state from which we emerged. The immense whole bears our signature for a while, markings on a sea dotted with ships and crisscrossed with their wakes, the signs of their passing. But, in time, oblivion will overtake every human life.

Machado stakes out a philosophy here in the sense that he pronounces time and being to be the fundamental axes on which everything occurs, and he distinguishes humans as the only being especially characterized by mortality.[2] One particular aspect, temporality, although characteristic of everything, belongs especially to the human. Machado's theoretical writing has taught us to pay attention to the temporal character of poetic rhythm and rhyme, how it causes a reader to remember a word at the end of a line and anticipate the partner that will fulfil the formal structure of the poem. "Everything passes," like many of the "Proverbios y cantares," conforms to the Spanish *romance* form, with eight-syllable lines and feminine rhyme in even numbered lines. As I mentioned in chapter 1, the "Cancionero apócrifo: Juan de Mairena" describes rhyme as a tool available only to poets to accomplish a "feeling of time" (sentimiento del tiempo).[3] According to Machado, writing poetically allows for a discourse to relate to a philosophical theme in a way that conventional philosophical discourse cannot.

All the same, a poem like "Everything passes" hardly takes up a dialogue with Aristotle or Kant. Its philosophical force depends on its literary power, the brevity and simplicity of the *romance* form (similar to the English ballad) harmonizing with the minimalism of the concepts of space and time. It is true that Kant calls space and time the two "pure forms" necessary to all possible experience, and Aristotle describes motion as the essential characteristic of the soul (*psyche*).[4] But the brief poem does not define a relationship to the philosophers and their discussions; instead, repeated words and a canonical poetic allusion contribute to the feat of a popular poem combining metaphysics with comprehensibility, a conceptual meditation with a particular feeling within an idiom. Machado is not unique as a poet who integrates philosophical meditations into his work. Certainly the classical ideal of *dulce et utile*, not to mention countless works before and after Horace's celebrated *ars poetica*, have provided sensuous, pleasing presentations of ideas. Although we may interpret this poem as an example of philosophical poetry, Machado's subsequent work does not stop at the reiteration of this classical model, but, rather, subjects it to intense scrutiny involving theoretical reflections on the relationship between poetry and philosophy. His commentaries on the whole range of philosophical history include Aristotle and Kant, as well as Hegel and Heidegger, in addition to Spanish-language philosophical poetry like that of Gustavo Adolfo Bécquer or Francisco de Quevedo. His inventive late work, presented under the rubric of "apocryphal teachers" (profesores apócrifos), constitutes an effort to restore the autonomous force of literature and philosophy both, after Unamuno and Ortega appear to subject philosophy to the demands of a *life* more attuned to literary expression. Philosophical poetry in the manner of "Everything passes" remains part of his repertoire, but Machado adds innovative theoretico-literary texts that constitute a unique intervention in the debate on the relation between literature and philosophy.

In chapter 1, we looked at one facet of poetry's engagement with philosophy in "poetic thinking," granting access to a primordial heterogeneity this side of theoretically defined reality. If we intend to give heterogeneity its due, we might begin by distinguishing between different phases and facets of Machado's philosophical-poetic discourse. By contrast, the mainstream of Machado criticism has tended to impose a homogeneity based on a presupposed unity of Machado's oeuvre. Studies that excerpt passages from a variety of his theoretical works implicitly assume a simple identity of Machado and the fictional poets he creates, as well as the relative consistency of their discourses. When individual works receive explicit attention, the 1926 "Cancioneros apócrifos" typically represent the appearance of a mature philosophy, which *Juan de Mairena* can then be said to reiterate, expand, or clarify.[5] In what follows, I distinguish three phases of Machado's inquiries into literature and philosophy: the 1917 prologues to his celebrated poetic anthologies, the two "Cancioneros apócrifos," and *Juan de Mairena*. While a reader who searches for the expected figure of fusion between literature and philosophy can find it, my reading seeks to demonstrate the heterogeneity of Machado's text and to discuss the limits of his approach to otherness and temporality. In addition, the two songbooks themselves do not combine to provide a straightforward exposition of a philosophy, nor does *Juan de Mairena* merely develop the themes at greater length. Instead, the book radicalizes two of contemporary philosophy's most important motifs by introducing a multiplicity of voices and perspectives and casting the relation of poetry and philosophy as a finite movement of human life.

Machado's earliest programmatic texts served as presentations of his celebrated collections *Soledades* (*Solitudes*)[6] and *Fields of Castile* and showed the influence of Unamuno and Ortega, whose work Machado knew and admired. In these prologues he formulates the intentions of the two volumes, while indicating his suspicions toward theoretical modes of speech, including his own. The prologue to *Soledades* contrasts two ideas of poetic creation. In the first, the writer of verse deliberately applies concepts concerning language and poetic technique: sound, form, imagery, narrative, contemplation.[7] One could certainly speak of Machado's work in this way, but he associates himself much more with another, almost mystical approach. The "poetic element," he says, is not a particular characteristic of poetic language but "a deep beating of the spirit" (una honda palpitación del espíritu) (68). Poetry's object is not communication in the medium or fabrication with the resources of an idiom but the manifestation of a primordial feeling: "I thought that man could catch by surprise some words of an intimate monologue [sorprender unas palabras de un íntimo monólogo], distinguish the living voice [la voz viva] from motionless echoes; that he could, by looking inside himself, glimpse cordial ideas, universals of feeling [ideas cordiales, universales del sentimiento]" (68). In a gesture of apparent modesty, Machado admits that he is reporting on his intentions, not laying claim to his achievements, but we can hear the ambition of maintaining contact with a pristine world of sentiment and life, one previous to the imposition of analytic concepts or technique that might subsequently obscure the properly poetic instance. It is worth noting Machado's recognition that *Soledades* did not aim at anything as precise as the "tragic feeling" that gave title to Unamuno's philosophical treatise but, rather, seems to aim at a multiplicity of feelings.

The prologue to *Fields* reiterates Machado's devotion to *life*, pitting it now against reason and defining his role, like Unamuno did, as a quasi-divine creator, not merely as an observer. "Reason analyzes and dissolves," he says, implying that his role is to forestall this fatal dissolution (69). *Fields* not only bears witness to life within the poet, but gives birth to new, autonomous life: "I thought that the mission of the poet was to invent new poems of eternal humanity [lo eterno humano], animated histories that, while belonging to the poet, might nonetheless live in their own right" (69). Like Unamuno's creation of Augusto Pérez, Machado's fictional figures would lay claim to their own living existence. This creation of living things would be, for Machado, a continuation of a literary tradition he links to the popular collection of ballads called the *romancero*. If he managed, as the *romancero* did, to engender new living poems out of the Castilian landscape, Machado, too, would attain an especially vital existence (69). As critical readers, we must take notice of this aspiration, but we should also continue to ask about the legitimacy of the claim that writings and written discourse might, literally, come to life. As in the cases of Unamuno and Ortega, such an ambition might be tied to a vague restriction of the notion of life and a failure to appreciate language's essential link to death. At the same time, Machado's figuration of life as an ephemeral passage effectuated in writing can be understood in different ways, including the vacillation between literature and philosophy that he will describe later.

In the twenties and thirties, the verses signed by fictitious, "apocryphal" poets were rivaled in their importance by prose texts, the commentaries in which some of the poems were initially imbedded, the "Cancioneros apócrifos" of Abel Martín and Juan de Mairena. Later poems were attributed to these two major figures and several other poets, in a practice that resembles Fernando Pessoa's creation of what he called *heteronyms*.[8] In the thirties, Machado devoted most of his work to the prose pieces collected as *Juan de Mairena: Sentencias, donaires, apuntes y recuerdos de un profesor apócrifo* (*Epigrams, Maxims, Memoranda, and Memoirs of an Apocryphal Professor*). *Juan de Mairena* includes many different voices. The poet-philosopher-teacher named in the title speaks directly in sections whose titles ("Fragments of Lessons," "From a Speech by Juan de Mairena," "Mairena Speaks to His Students," etc.) identify him, but he also converses with students, reports, and comments on the writings and teachings of Abel Martín. In addition to students and Martín, other voices occasionally appear, such as that of an anonymous reporter from an "apocryphal" newspaper, *La Voz de Chipiona*. The narrative voice of a critic often predominates, as in the "Cancioneros apócrifos," from the retrospective point of view of a contemporary of Antonio Machado. While the commitment to prose, fiction, literary and philosophical commentary, and meditation upset some of Machado's contemporaries, it appears that they did not appreciate the way the new work spawned a multiplicity of new literary voices. Whether a commitment to philosophy seemed of dubious Hispanicness or a regrettable drain of a great poet's time and energy, the complaint that Machado's interest in philosophy altered his poetry fails to take stock of the unique encounter of literature and philosophy in Machado's work. Nonetheless, the singularity of this case does have to do with a certain contrariness between literature and philosophy, a rivalry and incompatibility that has not escaped the notice of Machado scholars.

Critical responses can be divided into three ways of reckoning with the philosophical and poetic aspects of Machado's work. First, a venerable mode of interpretation insists that the man guarantees a synthesis of the literature and philosophy or, at least, understands the philosophical contributions within the framework of the poet's freedom from philosophical seriousness. Abellán and Patrick Durantou assert that the debate about Machado's philosophical character originates in an anachronistic and "arrogant" concept of philosophy, one that speciously denies his right to be "both a philosopher and a poet at the same time."[9] Sánchez Barbudo implicitly agrees when he applauds Machado for pioneering the same philosophical themes that later brought renown to Heidegger.[10] Cerezo Galán finds harmony between philosophy and poetry by attributing a poetics to Machado's prose, but he also ascribes a philosophical achievement to the man Machado in a "permanent leap of transcendence" (permanente brinco de trascendimiento) that he links to a living presence behind or beyond the texts.[11] Fellow poet and scholar Jorge Guillén attributes to a philosophical Machado and a poetic Machado the quality of "complementarity," suggesting, by using a word dear to Machado, that he was fulfilled by the combination of distinct but compatible spiritual pursuits.[12]

A second, closely related, position privileges the moments in which Machado's theoretical writings maintain a superiority for poetry over philosophy in matters that we will have to call, for lack of a better word, "philosophical." For the poet Aurora de Albornoz, Machado and Unamuno both practiced a writing that "put life above art and feeling above reason," and it is, in short, this attitude that makes poetry truer than philosophy.[13] Such a contention does not necessarily lead to the assumption of a polemical relationship between literature and philosophy, which we will consider in a moment. Biruté Ciplijauskaité speaks of a "symbiosis" of philosophy and poetry but proposes that the cooperative life between them is predicated on the "supremacy of poetic experience over logic and plain reasoning."[14] Steven Hutchinson writes of a "disjunction between philosophy and poetry," but his analyses of motion in two poems confirm the superiority of poetry in the thematization of temporality.[15] In a similar fashion, Rafael Gutiérrez Girardot declares a similarity to Heidegger and invokes a shared "neighborhood" of poetry and philosophy. For Gutiérrez Girardot, the close relationship between the two has always been characterized by the supremacy of philosophy, but Machado's writing effectuates an "inversion and fusion, at the same time"; that is, poetry gains the upper hand as its difference from philosophy disappears.[16] Nothing in language itself prevents us from speaking of simultaneous "fusion and inversion" or a "permanent leap," but these characterizations of Machado and his work betray a devotion to poetic freedom that shows more indifference to philosophy than respect for its claims of difference from poetry. Although the philosopher Julián Marías would not be one to embrace the superiority of poetry, he denies philosophical credentials to Machado at the same time that he attributes the poet's "extraordinary" quality to his practice of "literary thinking."[17]

Finally, scholars have explored ways of articulating the uneasy relation of literature and philosophy in Machado's consciousness and writing, emphasizing the strict difference in such a way that the name comes to represent neither the poet nor any preestablished human type. For the poet and critic Guillermo de Torre, Machado considers poetry and philosophy as distinct pursuits with their own traits and demands. De Torre begins by saying that Machado "came to dream of a sort of osmosis or exchange between the two," implying a progression toward neutral equilibrium, only to reveal that Machado also envisioned a reconstitution of difference, according to which "poets and philosophers would have to switch roles."[18] We will have to reread the texts to which de Torre refers, which show that the idea of fusing philosophy and poetry finds its first opponent in Machado's oeuvre itself, in the very place where the erasure of difference is said to occur in the person of Machado the poet-philosopher. Eustaquio Barjau and Antonio Fernández Ferrer both approach Antonio Machado as the hyphen in that figure of fusion, a graphic mark passing in between literature and philosophy. In his book about Machado's practice of creating "apocryphal poets," Barjau identifies for Machado "two ways of access to the same intimate experiences of his spirit: poetic expression and conceptual structuration."[19]

These experiences are "this side of [más acá de] philosophical reflection" but they do not fully qualify as poetic, since they occupy a time when, Barjau says, quoting Sánchez Barbudo, "the poet in [Machado] had begun to die."[20] Fernandez Ferrer, for his part, speaks of a "disposition on the border between [talante fronterizo entre] literature and philosophy," that is, a refusal to commit to one or the other, dwelling, instead, in a zone between two incompatible realms.[21] For Fernández Ferrer, the tension between the two constitutes the unique basis for Machado's late work, a "contradictory basis, always fleeting, eternally mobile, defined by lack of system."[22] How can a basis, which by definition provides stability, be constantly in motion? It appears that critical accounts of Machado's literary-philosophical work seek to come to rest on concepts that are themselves paradoxical, as if this would suffice to account for the apparent paradoxes of Machado's work, including the literary-philosophical character. Fernández Ferrer ultimately describes the borderline quality of Machado's work as "wisely indefinite" or "wisely undefined" (sabiamente indefinido).[23] Neither one nor the other, nor both at the same time, but some undefined or other discourse, Machado's perceived attitude authorizes critics, too, to use sometimes one, sometimes another definition of literature or philosophy and perhaps to consider this indeterminacy wisdom.[24]

The figure of the border as an in-between should not be interpreted as a wholly beneficent "position," if it is a position at all. The border imposes a dividing line and a defining limit, rather than constituting a third space. Barjau's and Fernández Ferrer's perceptive readings privilege the metaphor of border but don't go far enough in elaborating its consequences for literature and philosophy. I suspect that one hindrance is the predominance of traditions of interpretation that eliminate the difference, whether they attribute this move to the person of Antonio Machado or make it into a proposition of philosophical generality. Chapter 2's discussions of the ways of understanding the gap between literature and philosophy prepares us to look more carefully at Machado, considering the figure of the border in a new way. According to this figure, literature and philosophy give each other occasion to be themselves, which means to assume institutionally determined traits (even impossible ones) and accomplish the rupture that they both demand of a work that makes claims to originality. We will see how Machado comes to formulate this double demand shared by literature and philosophy and operative within their own separate conventional contexts. It is worth dwelling a bit longer, however, on Machado's two interventions, the supposed superiority of poetry and the conceit of "apocryphal poets," to assess their claims on literature and philosophy.

The Form of Life: The Possibilities of the Poem in the "Cancioneros apócrifos"

In the 1931 "Poética" (Poetics) written for an anthology assembled by Gerardo Diego, Machado defines poetry as "essential word in time" (la palabra esencial en el tiempo).[25] Five years before that, in two curious texts published in Ortega's *Revista de Occidente*, he had begun to articulate poetry's philosophical superiority to philosophy in a way that expands his ideas in the 1917 prefaces. Rather than its access to life, Machado speaks of poetry's ability to capture the fundamental character of being and becoming, essence and time, or, as the "Poética" says, "essentiality and temporality."[26] For the moment, we will disregard the fact that the "apocryphal songbooks" attribute these ideas to fictional characters and develop a narrative voice belonging to an interpreter and commentator. "De un cancionero apócrifo: Abel Martín" appears in Machado's *Poesías completas* in 1928 and describes Martín's conviction that everything that is must be understood as a medium of primordial heterogeneity, to which poetry provides privileged access. While "Cancionero apócrifo: Juan de Mairena" describes the "poet of time," these "apocryphal songbooks" agree with the 1931 "Poética" in describing the inseparability of beings and time in a protoconceptual exposure that finds its best expression in poetic language.

Both Martín and Mairena are described in these texts as poets and philosophers, and Machado invents poems and philosophical treatises for each, represented in a commentary that names titles and describes, paraphrases, and quotes from fictitious works. Ironically, this critical commentary implicitly ranks the poetry above the philosophy, as a more adequate manifestation of their thought. The critical voice of the Martín songbook proposes, "Let us say something about his philosophy, as it appears more or less explicitly in his poetic work" (305). The songbook indicates Martín's key concepts and propositions by providing the titles of his philosophical treatises: *Las cinco formas de la objetividad* (The five forms of objectivity), *De lo uno a lo otro* (From what is one to what is other), *Lo universal cualitativo* (The qualitative universal), and *De la esencial heterogeneidad del ser* (On the essential heterogeneity of being). However, the critical or narrative voice expounding on

Martín's work chooses an indirect approach to his philosophy via the poetry. He does not justify his choice, except to imply that the "new thing, poetic thinking," must inhere more in poems than in philosophical discourse. Once again, "let's say something about his philosophy, as it appears, more or less explicitly, in his poetic work, and leave the systematic analysis of his purely doctrinal treatises for someone else [otros] to do" (305). The narrator of the songbook thus sets out to reappropriate poetic thinking for a traditional philosophical mode of discourse, rather than to remain in one discursive realm. In fact, the propositional language of the Martín songbook comes as a surprise after the narrator's announcement that he will concentrate on Martín's poetry. The narrator begins, "With Leibniz he conceives the real, substance, as something constantly active. Abel Martín thinks substance as energy . . . ," and so on (305). After nearly two pages of philosophical exposition on the self-consciousness of monads, the narrator quotes the three short lines of verse out of which Martín "worked out, by reflection and analysis, his entire metaphysics" (307). The text alternates between dense philosophical exposition and quotations of poems, such that one can easily get the impression that the narrator considers Martín's true achievement to be the metaphysics, rather than the brief, concentrated verses he quotes and claims to be glossing.

The Mairena songbook appears to be a mirror image of the previous one. Its narrator seems to embrace a discussion of the philosophical treatises, rather than the poetry, devoting the piece's two sections to Mairena's expository *Ars poética* (327–37) before briefly summarizing the "metaphysical treatise" *Los siete reversos* (The seven setbacks or reversals) (337–39). Again, though, the narrator forsakes his stated purpose by digressing, first about baroque poetry and later about the composition of Mairena's book of poems, *La máquina de trovar* (The versification or troubadour machine). Still, he only discusses a handful of poems in order to address, as the Martín songbook does, the contribution made by poetry to philosophy. Both point to themes of heterogeneity and time when discussing poetry's power, and this is not surprising, since Mairena, here and in the book bearing his name, suggests that his own thinking follows and reiterates that of his teacher. One might even suspect that Mairena began as the narrative voice of the Martín songbook. Machado's intervention in the apocryphal songbooks can be detected, however, in the clear thematic division between the two: the Abel Martín songbook concentrates on heterogeneous being and Juan de Mairena's on time.

The Martín songbook ends with an acknowledgment that it has only managed to explicate the problem of heterogeneity but suggests that the other two points cannot begin to make sense without first exhausting this subject. Its narrator offers a three-part outline of the poet's sole collection of poems, called *Los complementarios*. After opening with a summary exposition of Mairena's philosophy through his poetry, it ends by admitting that it has only treated at length the first of the three "sections" in the poet's oeuvre. The first, he says, has to do with "homogenizing thought" and its derivation from a more inclusive "totality" that he associates with poetry and the divine (325). He merely mentions the other two sections, perhaps because they pose too much resistance to his translation into philosophical speech. A "song of the border, to death, silence and oblivion" separates the first division from the last, whose theme the narrator does not so much as name. Instead, he cites a poem entitled "Al gran pleno o conciencia integral" ("To the Great Plenitude or Integral Consciousness") with a statement that it serves "in the guise of a prologue" (325–26).[27] This structure suggests that the "border" lies not just between life and death, speech and silence, monumentality and nullity, but between the first and last sections of *Los complementarios*, explaining the concern for a history that has homogenized and, in so doing, excluded a new consciousness that will integrate time and the other. With a textual gesture, Machado's narrator suggests that no language that is not poetic—such as his own, the narrator's—can stand in for poetry and replicate its quasi-philosophical force. But what does "heterogeneous" mean and how does poetry approach it?

It is worth considering heterogeneity as a problem, rather than a mere trait or a concept, because it refers, for Machado's apocryphal poets, to the character of "the one-and-only substance," of what genuinely *is*, before being broken down into different things by conceptual categories (310). Such a logical priority for a single "one" multiplicity announced with a name, obviously strains language's referential function, especially to the extent that language traditionally has been grounded in a conscious subject. Martín's treatise *Las cinco formas de la objetividad* treats four "pretensions" to universally valid knowledge, subjective acts that merely appear to grasp the true being of reality (308). The "fifth form" offers access to what foils the first four types, "the essential heterogeneity of the one-and-only substance" (310). The first four "objectivities" turn out to be nothing more than "subjective acts" while the fifth appears "on the borders of the subject," where, Machado's critical voice explains, "a 'real other' [is] not an object of knowledge but of love" (309). Machado is grappling here with the problem of the otherness of the other, that when knowledge is defined as the appropriation of an object by a subject, any traits that do not conform to subjective structures not only disappear but are obliterated. In terms of traditional epistemology, the other gets translated into the same or the one. Hegel addresses this in the *Phenomenology of Spirit* as the problem of "Force and Understanding," where he discusses a problem that concerns modern Spanish writers: the impression that the primordial complexity of "life" must undergo a process of reduction in order for the understanding to function. The understanding, as philosophy conceives it, would thus always remain vulnerable to the charge that it deals with idealities rather than reality. Hegel contends that there is no reality before understanding, only "force" (Kraft), which drives things apart and unites them in a process he refers to as *Äußerung* and *Begriff*, expression and concept. The German words evoke a spreading out (from the root *aus*, out) and gathering in (from the root *greifen*, to grasp).[28] Hegel will also call force, this strange pairing of dispersal and unification, "the simple essence of life, the soul of the world, the universal blood" (das einfache Wesen des Lebens, die Seele der Welt, das allgemeine Blut).[29] For Hegel, a primordial movement associated with life's simple facticity pushes the network of ontological structures through its historical development. Hegel will eventually argue that conceptuality developed to its fullest captures all the richness of this originary energy, converting all heterogeneity to homogeneity, but only at the ultimate limit of the dialectic's movement.

Closer to Machado, the relation of same and other provides the guiding question for Henri Bergson's *Essai sur les données immédiates de la conscience*, known in English as *Time and Free Will: An Essay on the Immediate Data of Consciousness*. For Bergson, the theme of free will is a mere example of a more general issue, the incompatibility of conceptual language with respect to a primordial world he refers to as "concrete" and "living." Human beings "assimilate thought to things," using "clumsy symbols," and neglect the autonomy of the "organic whole" in and of which the "concrete and living self" is a part.[30] The self imposes the homogeneity characteristic of language upon the heterogeneity of the primordial world, a world characterized by *durée* or "heterogeneous time."[31] Machado's debt to Bergson is well known; Sánchez Barbudo and Cerezo, especially, have explained at length how Machado attempts to overcome understanding's "freezing" effect on all that it encounters in order to provide an "experience of heterogeneity."[32] As we will see, this includes the temporal displacement of the voice advocating for such an experience from Martín to Mairena, and to a critical narrative voice so naturally associated with Antonio Machado. The songbooks do suggest that such a problem is not simply theoretical but practical, trying to work out some of the ethical implications of reduction of other persons to *alter egos*.

The Martín songbook addresses the problem of heterogeneity through the motif of the "love object" (310). Machado's critical voice deploys this action by citing and explicating Martín's "erotic poems," which, again and again, insist that the "erotic object" is "that which is unmistakable with the lover" (312). "Unmistakable" (inconfundible) has a double value here. For one, the object possesses the singularity that prevents it being confused with another, another *other*, that is. But Machado adds, clarifying the strange preposition "with," that the object of love is "that which is impenetrable, not by definition . . . but really" (312). That is why the lover and loved do not "fuse" (fundirse) but remain side by side, *with* rather than *for* one another. The beloved retains the value of "what is essentially other" and is felt as absence or "thirst" rather than possession (313). One experiences the beloved as a presence that includes absence, as an unfulfilled yearning for a very particular, but unassimilable other. This experience stretches out into time, activating a particular identity found in the past and projected into a future of unfulfillable desire. While the beloved's concrete existence seems to play a role in this experience, Machado's critical commentary coins a curious paradox, the "autorevelation of essential heterogeneity" (310). Accordingly, the self experiences an irreducible other as a revelation to self; the self in itself, in the space of *auto*, enacts an encounter with the other. One wonders, then, how the other can be absolutely distinguished from self, if it is in the self and on the self's own terms that the encounter takes place.

Machado's commentary turns what might appear a failure to identify the other with the one into a philosophical success. Although these poetico-erotic acts constitute a "new logical form," they do not yield words or concepts, because concepts still homogenize heterogeneous entities by fixing them in time. Machado's critical voice says, paraphrasing Martín,

> But he believes that poetic language can suggest the evolution of the established premises, through conclusions that are oblique and incongruent enough that readers or listeners might calculate [para que el lector u oyente calcule] the changes that, of necessity, these premises have to experience, from the moment that they were fixed in place to the moment they are concluded, so that they might see clearly that the immediate premises of their apparently inadequate conclusions are not, in reality, the ones

expressed by the language, but, rather, others that have been produced in the constant mutation of thought. (314)

By making use of the movement from premises to arguments and conclusions, and by refusing to use clear and direct language, poetry indicates something that it does not say or signify. Here, this "something" is named "the immediate premises" "produced in the constant mutation of thought"; that is, the principles of constancy and change experienced in the movement of a logical discourse, but whose immediacy is betrayed by precise designation. Poetry performs in language in such a way that the homogenizing effect of language loses its validity in the face of a "calculation" that every individual subject must make for his or her self. In so doing, poetry bears witness to the otherness of a reality that is in constant flux. As we might suspect, the respect of the other's otherness requires an enactment of time, not just a thematic treatment of it. We could express another reservation here. Martín's prescription implies that only willful indirection and discontinuity deserve credit for turning us readers from the frozen time of words to the heterogeneous time of primordial experience. We could well wonder whether it could not be carried out either in a poetry that doesn't pose time as a theme or in theoretical texts that themselves struggle, deliberately or not, with the passage from premises to conclusions. The reference to authorial intentions—in as minimal a way as the belonging to a particular discourse or producing a familiar genre—already assumes that otherness remains constricted to what can be rendered conscious as a meaning, whether poetic or philosophical. In this regard, the limits of Machado's thinking are the limits of all metaphysics of consciousness and will.

Juan de Mairena's "Cancionero apócrifo" presents him as a student of Abel Martín, and it should not be surprising that his inversion of the relative importance of time and heterogeneity attributes a similar ethico-metaphysical privilege to poetry. Mairena calls himself "the poet of time" and claims that in his verses time gets "fully expressed" (plenamente expresado) (329). All art, Mairena admits, strives for eternity in a transcendence he calls "atemporal." Paradoxically, the poet also attempts to "atemporalize" time (329). He specifies this time as "the living time [tiempo vital] of the poet with his own vibration" (329). Throughout his songbook, Mairena contrasts the poetic with the logical, dismissing Spanish baroque poetry for imposing logic on poetic form, "discoursing" and "reasoning" when it should "sing" (331). Poetry is most itself, says Mairena, when it "has a marked temporal accent" (marcado acento temporal), that is, when the poet takes advantage of the many "temporal elements" at his disposal (329). He lists them, and they are familiar as formal, linguistic traits of poems: "quantity, measure, accentuation, pauses, rhyme, images themselves enunciated in series" (329). Poetry realizes its philosophical potential when it emphasizes that the meaning of any moment relates forwards and backwards in time, and that reading and writing, along with thinking, are irreducibly temporal experiences.

The songbook's narrator describes how Mairena "starts out from Martín's magical thinking, from the essential heterogeneity of being, from the immanent otherness of the being that is itself [del ser que se es], from the one-and-only substance, calm and in perpetual change, from the integral consciousness, or great eye . . . , etc., etc." (339) Once again it is worth pausing to note Machado's placement of otherness within the self. Mairena's contribution to thought consists of a demonstration of *Los siete reversos*, the origin of "logical thought, of the homogeneous forms of thinking," in the more comprehensive form of "poetic thought" (pensamiento poético) (339). This would be no small feat, including an exposition of the seven "pure forms": substance, space, time, movement, rest, "being that is not," and nothingness ("nada") (339). Their designation as "homogeneous" suggests some deficiency, as does their status as "setbacks or reversals" (reversos): they seem to be the precise contraries of a more primordial, and hence more exalted world associated with poetry. Machado's narrator chooses not to provide an account of the derivation of theoretical or philosophical knowledge from poetic sources. It may even be said that poetry and philosophy retain a nonhierarchical relation as a dialectical pair. Ironically, the voice of this songbook chooses instead to describe *Los siete reversos* in material terms, as having "nearly 500 pages," before settling into a commentary reminiscent of the history of ideas. No one read Mairena's treatise, he says, not even Menéndez Pelayo, whose work is described as an "expurgatory index of Spanish thought," that is, perhaps literally, the list meant to lead Spanish philosophy out of its purgatory into the bliss of canonical status (339). Instead of relaying how Mairena accomplished this most transcendental of philosophical tasks, the narrator prefers to turn to Mairena's poetry, since "analyzing it in detail would distance us from the poet" (339). While the narrator says, "let it wait for another occasion," it is worth our noting that Machado's narrative voice genuinely behaves like a fictional one here: we will not read the derivation of philosophy from poetry because this treatise only exists as a reference to a fictional realm. As we will see, María Zambrano attempts to tell this genealogy throughout her oeuvre. Like Unamuno and his characters, Machado and his treat philosophy as if it were only valuable up to a point. One must know when to abandon philosophy, with a "knowledge" perhaps indistinguishable from whimsy or fright.

Machado's commentaries on poems provide an even more precise account of the experience of heterogeneity as the unrepeatable living moment of "vibration" in the unique individual. Mairena praises Jorge Manrique for offering an intuition of time and singular being: "When the stanza is over, the whole thing remains vibrating in our memory like a unique melody, which cannot be repeated or imitated, because to do so would require that we lived through it" (331–32). Machado relates the genuine poem to the moment of resonation, compared to a melody that can be transcribed and reiterated in different moments and on different instruments. In a similar way, each reading sets up its own new vibration. We cannot communicate our lived experience, just claim it, bear witness to it, and recommend to others that they experience their own momentary possession of something irreducibly singular. For Mairena, this experience of intimacy, the unrepeatable vibration, is induced only by a particular kind of poetry. Manrique is superior to Calderón in that in the former "poetry has a future [porvenir]" while the latter's baroque verse "abolishes its past" (332). Manrique invites the impossible repetition, while the baroque seems to issue a kind of prohibition of it. This is visible on the thematic register of the poems quoted: Manrique's poetic voice asks "What ever happened to the ladies . . . ?" while Calderón pronounces, to paraphrase, that the ladies are dead and gone (332). The failed repetition of the Manrique verses accomplishes an "emotion of time," an emotion felt in failure. The promise of a successful communication comes in a misfired communication with a shared content, the nature of time. Calderón states too forcefully the nature of time, while Manrique asks a question and lets the reader form a response. That conclusion might indeed be the same for me as for you, and be apparently the same as for the reader of Calderón: the past cannot be recuperated. But in each case what is the same will remain marked by the occasion and by the individual consciousness, its decision to read, its inclination to feel time. Consequently, not all poetry captures time, but among poetry's ways of discussing time lie both thematic treatment and this possibility of letting a future reader share in time's temporalizing.

In short, the two 1926 *Cancioneros apócrifos* attribute to poetry the power of evoking the irreplaceable, unmistakable and unrepeatable, an instance of singularity defined by temporality and what we could call categorical uniqueness. According to the texts' descriptions, this power comes from poetry's formal character—it occupies a place in a tradition, creating a sensation in the present of a connection back to tradition and forward to fulfillment of expectations. In a similar fashion, the evocation of the other includes an intimation of the irreducibility of the other to the same, the elements of desire, surprise, eroticism, and exoticism alerting us to the impossibility of replacing the other. It is worth noting that the question of otherness is limited to interactions of discrete individuals, who seem already constituted before, outside of this dynamic. A conventional vision of Machado emphasizes his inclination to formulate a communal character of the Spanish race, a product of history and environment and, thus, even prehistory. Juan de Mairena, by contrast, expresses misgivings about any effort to "add individuals together" (sumar individuos) into a collective (*Juan de Mairena*, S 79). The very nature of expounding these ideas signals that poetry's meaning is capable of repetition and subject to misapprehension. When the critical voice of the songbooks—assuming it is single voice, from start to finish, let alone from the first to the second—refers to specific poetic passages, it is to specify, to define, that is, to place a limit on their meaning, in order to preclude a possible departure from the philosopher-poet's intentions. This gesture is so familiar that it hardly seems worth mentioning, except that Machado's philosophical voices insist, in a more declarative than descriptive mode, that poetry bears extreme singularity. Could it be that, in addition, poetry's most potent resource consists of speaking about the impossible? That is, even though Machado's voices proclaim the capacity for poetic language to evoke absolute singularity in the form of the unrepeatable or unmistakable or irreplaceable, is it not the case that such a capacity can only be spoken of as a fiction, referring to a text that cannot be produced, be put on display, or function as such?

After the apocryphal songbooks, Machado's thought was presented primarily as the speech and writing of others, signed otherwise than "Antonio Machado." Hence Oreste Macrí, the editor of Machado's complete works as *Poesía y prosa*, considers the apocryphal songbooks the "true and authentic [dimension] of Machado's poetic spirit."[33] Rather than a simple ironization of thought—comparable to all fictional characters with literary or philosophical aspirations—Macrí views the creation of Martín and Mairena as an act of self-fragmentation that constitutes a "border zone between the heterogeneous and the homogeneous" (74). However, Macrí believes that Machado must have lived and documented in writing a moment of mastery of this strange project, and he regrets the loss of the poet's notebooks that might bear witness to this experience (83).[34] For Macrí, the literal record that would map out this "border zone" must be possible and distinct from the documents we possess. He does not consider that the Mairena songbook posits an extreme, perhaps absolute difference between the discourses of homogeneity (philosophy and most poetry) and the hypothetical discourse of heterogeneity. Macrí tells us how much of what appears in the apocryphal songbooks and *Juan de Mairena* can be found in notebooks published posthumously as *Los complementarios*. Anticipating their publication, Machado wrote a prefatory note that warns that "no one has a right to publish [publicar] them" (74). He adds, if you will forgive a literal translation for a moment: "Before bringing the notebook into the light [darlo a luz], the author would have revised it and put it in a correct literary form" (74). Machado distinguishes between "publication" and "giving to the light" (dar a luz); the latter could refer to the light of the public realm, or, using a very common Spanish idiom, giving birth. Literary form, then, might seem simply to be the price of dialogue with others, a threshold of correctness expected by editors and recognized by Machado. It could also be the process of giving life to the texts, which, for Machado, meant attributing words and thoughts to a fictional character, as if they were not first of all his own, as if the very thought of poetry's originary force were itself fictitious.

Machado's concerns resemble those of his contemporary Edmund Husserl. From *Logical Investigations* to his work in the decade before his death in 1938 (such as the *Lectures on the Phenomenology of the Consciousness of Internal Time* and *Cartesian Meditations*), Husserl worked at providing unmistakable, unshakeable ground for knowledge through the description of pure idealities of experience.[35] For Husserl, only a transcendental ego possessing a structure of cognition susceptible to phenomenological confirmation could empower a researcher to go "to the things themselves." Jacques Derrida's *Speech and Phenomena* assesses Husserlian phenomenology as both a "critique of metaphysics" and "a moment within the history of metaphysics."[36] Derrida identifies two elements that "torment" phenomenology, and they are precisely the two metaphysical problems that Abel Martín and Juan de Mairena claim to solve with poetry: the "movement of temporalization" of the ego and "intersubjectivity," one framework for the relation to others (6–7). In other words, Husserl proposes a new, definitive grounding of knowledge through the phenomenological description of the relation of the self to time and alterity. Needless to say, he does not need poetry for this.[37] What requires analysis for Derrida and could be identified with his signature contribution to philosophy, is Husserl's determination of being as presence.[38] For Machado, however, poetry sometimes seems to achieve precisely this event of self-presence, an occasion for a subject to be present to itself within the flow of time and alongside irreducible others. In *Speech and Phenomenon* and elsewhere, Derrida acknowledges the technical accomplishments the metaphysics of presence has made possible while exposing and analyzing its limits, as they become legible in particular philosophical texts. In the case of Husserl, he notes aspects of specific phenomenological descriptions, especially in the *Logical Investigations*, that do not square with Husserl's programmatic conclusions. Such a disjunction also characterizes Machado's discourses on otherness and temporality, especially, as I have already suggested, the accomplishment of an adequate link between "philosophical" homogeneity and "poetic" heterogeneity. That "border zone," if it appears at all, constitutes a place that may be referred to but never presented. Derrida's conclusion that Husserl's descriptions of presence hint at the "nonpresence to itself of the living present" (37) could also be said of Machado: the text, or even the conscious instance in which the self unites with time and alterity, must always be elsewhere, at the absent place toward which his textual indications point.

Derrida follows what Husserl's descriptions suggest, without merely letting himself be guided by the conclusions Husserl will draw from them. While his analysis tracks the question of meaning and its relation to expression, Derrida's account dwells on Husserl's conviction that meaning is rooted in a pre-expressive ego, structured in a way that opens it to otherness and maintains its integrity though the passage of time.[39] Such a living ego, for Husserl, is endowed with "living speech," which would guarantee the possibility of unequivocal knowledge and mastery of techniques of communication in a voice that hears itself speak. If Machado agrees with Husserl on the basis of knowledge and normative communication in the auto-affective self-consciousness—an "I" that sees itself, feels itself, and knows itself—he belongs also to the tradition of Hegel, Kant, and Descartes, reaching back to Aristotle, each of whom have unique ways of reassuring themselves of the autonomy of the self. The self that immediately hears itself may not, according to Husserl's descriptions, appear phenomenologically, except in a situation that introduces *différance*, the internal self-othering that delays and disconnects the self-that-discerns from the self-that-appears.[40] This movement "itself" is irreducible; there is no discourse that escapes the movement of *différance*, that would therefore possess a ground in presence along with the reassurance it would produce. It is in this sense that Derrida refers to a self-assured self as characteristic of metaphysics, repeated throughout the history of philosophy, as a fiction. But it is a fiction with powerful effects, including, of course, the mastery of nature and an entire history of politics and intellectual activity whose closure, Derrida suggests, may be coming into view (102).

The name "Antonio Machado" refers, then, to a particular attempt to think through the possibility of self-identity in relation to otherness and temporality. The songbooks indicate, without directly stating it, the difficulty of speaking a language of the other or even expressing thoughts that address something wholly other than philosophy's supposed "homogeneity" without exploring alternatives to traditional genres, concepts, and modes of address. By attributing many of his thoughts and propositions to fictitious characters, he suggests, he might detach from the "homogeneous" tradition without forfeiting relevance for theoretical and ethical discussions. As we have begun to see, not all applications of heteronymity have the same functions or meanings.

Thinking by Another Name: Pseudonymity, Heteronomy, and the Apocryphal Writers

In 1928, Antonio Machado received a letter from Ernesto Giménez Caballero from the *Gaceta Literaria* requesting a submission for publication from the well-known poet. Machado responds in the negative but promises the editor, "The first thing that I write—verse or prose—will be for you."[41] He then offers the following explanation. Giménez Caballero was no doubt familiar with the recent publication of the "Cancioneros apócrifos" and the presentation of Abel Martín and Juan de Mairena as fictional predecessors of the poet Antonio Machado. "They did not exist," he clarifies, "but they should have existed and they would have existed, if Spanish lyric poetry had lived its time [si hubiera vivido su tiempo]" (314). Machado takes up Ortega's proposition that history follows set, formalizable laws, although he implies that reality does not always conform to what the laws say should have happened. Also, as we will see shortly, he begins to consider whether poetry's temporal character does not extend beyond the poem to literary history, and whether thinking, too, might have a potential for marking its temporal nature. In more concrete terms, Machado suggests to Giménez Caballero that his recent effort has been devoted to the development of the already familiar "apocryphal" figures, to which he adds a third, named Pedro de Zúñiga. Although he has the latter "between his hands," like a god shaping a human being out of clay, Machado himself has not yet produced the poems that would speak for Zúñiga; he nonetheless deserves to be called "present-day poet," in contrast to Martín and Mairena, who belong to the nineteenth century. Machado's current projects constitute a "new objectivity," in accordance with which he is not writing poetry but generating or even gestating poets whose eventual birth would coincide with new poetic productions, in their own names. While Machado had previously spoken of poems coming to life—in the 1917 prologue to *Fields*—here his stated goal is the creation of creators: "New poets—not new poems [poesías]—let them sing for themselves [que canten por sí mismos]" (314). In the words of Jordi Doménech, the editor of the *Escritos dispersos* (Scattered writings) in which this letter is published, Zúñiga "remained unborn" (quedó nonato).[42] By this, presumably, he means that Zúñiga never took on the kind of life that we might ascribe to Abel Martín or Juan de Mairena, since no poems appeared in his name.[43] Machado sends Giménez Caballero his regrets, then, somewhat like Dr. Frankenstein after yet another failed experiment. The irony, of course, is that *La Gaceta Literaria* received its piece, "in prose," from Antonio Machado, "the first thing that he wrote," and published it accordingly.

Machado's choice of terms for his "apocryphal poets" is potentially confusing. Gérard Genette's *Paratexts* devotes a chapter to "The Name of the Author," announcing that the name has a "contractual function," connecting the text proper to a particular legal name (40). He later adds that it is a sort of "owning up to" or assuming responsibility for a book as a reflection of the subject who inscribes her signature on the "threshold" of the work (51). He calls this function "onymity," working back from the common word "anonymity" and noting the "deceptive ordinariness" of a text being signed with the author's name (39). Genette explains that *pseudonymity* is what we call the mitigation of the onymic effect by providing another name than the legal name of the author. In *Paratexts*, an "apocryphal" name is "fallacious attribution of the text to a known author" (47). "Fallacious" implies an innocent error, such as one might make by attributing to a writer a work that she might plausibly have produced but that turns out to be skillful pastiche or accidental similitude. It might be entertaining to play along with the "Cancioneros apócrifos" and insist that Juan de Mairena and Abel Martín falsely attribute their work to the true author Antonio Machado. However, in the accepted terms of literary study, Machado practices pseudonymity. Not the pseudonymity of Cecilia Böhl de Faber, María Lejárraga, Aurore Dupin, or Karen Blixen, whose pseudonymity was motivated by the need to subvert the exclusivity of the literary marketplace by supplying a more acceptable, male name. Rather, Machado's pseudonymity, and his substitution of the term "apocryphal" seem motivated by the possibility of being "less himself" when writing of philosophy and reflecting *on* literature instead of producing it directly. Needless to say, Machado's insistence on "apocryphal" instead of "pseudonymous" participates in his textual performance, making the claim he expresses to Giménez Caballero: that Martín and Mairena "should have existed and could have existed" and that it is thus wrong to attribute them to Antonio Machado. Rather, as Augusto Pérez argued against Unamuno, one should perhaps attribute the existence of the real author to his fictitious creations. In such a way, a given instance of poetry, too, could retain both identity and alterity. Often it merely seems that poetry's heterogeneity only concerns its inexhaustibility by knowledge, but myriad processes of othering contribute to what Abel Martín, Juan de Mairena, and the anonymous critic-narrator refer to as *heterogeneity*.

For some, pseudonymity offered Machado a means of achieving a kind of absolute irony. This distance allows Mairena to affirm, "I am incorrectness itself" (yo soy la incorrección misma) (*Juan de Mairena*, S 105; E 16 [revised]), while Machado maintains the necessary rectitude and—in accord with specifically Spanish connotation of "correcto"—respectability to publish Mairena's words. In general, though, it is worth observing that Mairena's and Machado's words coincide in style and content, supporting the common attribution of Mairena's jokes and thoughts to Machado. To mention just one brief example, in the 1917 preface to *Campos de Castilla*, after a precise description of the character of his poetry, he declares, "You will find many compositions that don't fit with these propositions that I am declaring to you" (69). However his work is signed, Machado claims and carries out his right to contradict himself, to be sloppy, or simply to be wrong, as Unamuno does in "A lo que salga."

But why invoke another's signature, indeed, the signature of a fictitious character? The signature is no mere game. J. L. Austin, in *How to Do Things with Words*, the founding text of speech-act theory, grounds communication in the attribution of a locution or linguistic utterance to a particular human subject. That any statement has a particular, determinable meaning at all derives, for Austin, from "being the person who does the uttering," in the case of speech, or else from providing a signature in writing.[44] For Austin, such a moment of authorization provides a connection between words uttered and their subjective origin, and an utterance gradually loses its grip on meaning as speech distances itself from its source. By contrast, Mairena celebrates the disconnection of the "apocryphal" from any incontestable point of view: "We live in an essentially apocryphal world, a cosmos or poem of our own thinking, ordered and constructed completely on suppositions postulated by reason" (*Juan de Mairena*, S 166; E 50 [revised]). His usage here suggests that "apocryphal" signifies not fallaciousness, but contingency and provisionality. The utterances of Abel Martín and Juan de Mairena, then, do not need to be ascribed to "apocryphal teachers" in order to be apocryphal, for all efforts of speech, logical or poetic, remain suspended in discussions that on some level include the problem of their own status. Mairena says, "The apocryphal character of our world is proved by the existence of logic—our need to put our thinking in agreement with itself, to compel it, in a certain way, to see nothing but the suppositions or its postulates [lo supuesto o puesto por él] to the exclusion of all other things" (*Juan de Mairena*, S 167; E 50 [revised]). If the world were not "apocryphal," if there were solid grounds for logic, philosophy would not be necessary. In any case, while Machado's practice of pseudonymity puts the reflections in the songbooks and *Juan de Mairena* at a remove from his own point of view, he also uses Mairena to discourage us from reinstating the authoritative, unifying authorial figure of Antonio Machado.

Juan de Mairena includes several other reflections that are relevant to the practice of pseudonymity and heteronymity. Mairena imagines the poems that Shakespeare's characters might have written and notes that Hamlet, Macbeth, Romeo, and Mercutio all would have produced very different poems outside of the plays in which they figure. Shakespeare would have been "the author of them all, and the author of the authors of the poems" (S 190; E 47). He then asks his listeners, "Would you say that a man can carry no more than one poet within himself? The reverse would be much more unlikely: that he carried inside himself only one" (S 190; E 47). Abel Martín had called on young poets to write verse with a "marked temporal accent"; the use of heteronyms allows for a marked heterogeneity for a poet's production; it is a technique for marking irreducible alterity. In so doing, this practice strains the unity of the creator, working at overcoming the limitations imposed by the common idea of a homogeneous oeuvre by a single unified consciousness. By presenting thoughts and ideas under another name, Machado strives for the same effect on thinking. One part of *Juan de Mairena*'s chapter 18 reflects on the proprietary character of thinking: "Our own ideas seem hostile to us when expressed by others, because we think they are no longer ours. The truth is that ideas should not belong to anyone" (S 168). Mairena goes on to compare ideas to a beloved article of clothing that looks strange on another person, and to acknowledge the autonomy of thoughts that, like fighting cocks, go off to sharpen their talons and return to attack their owners. Such comparisons suggest that one ought, indeed, to attempt to detach ideas from the human thinker, that such an effort would remove obstacles to frank and rigorous thought. Ideas, too, can be the victims of homogenization, in this case, by the restrictions imposed by the framework of authorship. In Chapter 18, Machado allows that philosophical thinking enters into a relation with the other and thus might not always commit the homogenizing atemporalization elsewhere attributed to it: "Only philosophical thought has some nobility. Because it is engendered either in the loving dialogue that presupposes the thinking dignity of our neighbor [el diálogo amoroso que supone la dignidad pensante de nuestro prójimo], or in man's struggle with himself" (S 169). Machado's songbooks not only represent dialogues—between Mairena and students or between Mairena and his teacher Martín—but themselves enact a dialogue between Machado and his characters. Such an arrangement might appear to merely emulate a relationship of self to other, since Machado indeed authored Martín and Mairena. But Machado's writings, like his comments on Shakespeare, expressly indicate and highlight heterogeneity and temporality within the self, while also acknowledging the fragility and ambiguity of this philosophical gesture.

A return to a previously discussed quote can give us another, broader interpretation. Chapter 3 of *Juan de Mairena* speaks of our "essentially apocryphal world," adding the following definition by apposition: "a cosmos or poem of our own thinking, ordered and constructed completely on suppositions postulated by reason, which we have come to call principles of logical discourse" (S 195; E 50). Mairena then continues, "It is these principles, compacted and synthesized into a principle of identity [el principio de identidad, que los resume y reasume a todos], that constitute the master supposition of them all: that all things, by the mere fact of their having been thought, remain immutable, anchored forever, as it were, in the river of Heraclitus. (S 195; E 50). "Apocryphal" indeed means, as Genette points out, false, but it is a necessary falsehood, the imposition of logical principles organized around the principle of identity. Hence the power of that transcendental identifier, the proper name. Machado and his apocryphal teachers question the notion that "being thought" stops time, and they attempt to alert us—those who live in this apocryphal world—to the constant flow of time, according to Heraclitus's celebrated metaphor. They also attempt to alert us to what logical principles block from view: "The apocryphal character of our world is proved by the existence of logic—our need to put our thinking in accord with itself, to compel it in a sense to see nothing but what it itself *presupposes* or posits, to the exclusion of all other things" (S 195; E 50 [revised]). Mairena's meditations on identity alert us to the impression that all attribution tends to cover up the raw fact of time's flow and logic's exclusion of radical otherness. The creation and development of apocryphal poet-philosophers provides a formal means—analogous to rhyme, meter, and other poetic devices—of writing philosophy with a "marked temporal accent."

Difference, Relation, and the Poematic Metaphysics to Come

In the apocryphal songbooks and *Juan de Mairena*, Machado proposes ways to temporalize the philosophical, lending poetry a temporal meaning and providing a temporal character to philosophical discourses that already speak *about* time. He does not propose, then, a new interpretation of poetry and philosophy; they do not receive a new definition of essence. Like Unamuno and Ortega, Machado continues to speak of philosophy both as the rule of rationality and of poetry as the realm of emotion and careful linguistic invention, even as he envisions a new philosophy and a reinvigorated poetry, modeled on the best of the tradition. Machado proposes an expansion of traditional institutions in the form of an amplification of characteristics that were already there, a marking of the temporality and heterogeneity that were already there, in a language whose structure naturally favors uniformity and stasis. Yet Machado's poems and contemplative works are not radically different from predecessors' with similar concerns. *Juan de Mairena* resembles fragmentary or aphoristic texts like Pascal's *Pensées*, Nietzsche's volumes of aphorisms and fragmentary essays (*Human, All Too Human, Beyond Good and Evil*, etc.), and the early German Romantic fragment collections. Furthermore, his use of heteronymous thinkers can be compared to Kierkegaard, Unamuno, or any writer who put philosophical discussions in the voices of fictional characters (like Dostoyevsky's Ivan and Alexei Karamazov, Flaubert's Bouvard and Pécuchet, and Joyce's Stephen Dedalus). The premise of the "Cancioneros apócrifos" resembles that of some of Borges's more famous "fictions" from the 1940s in the construction of fictitious writers and glosses of their works (Herbert Quain, Pierre Menard, Carlos Argentino Daneri, and Ts'ui Pên, to name some prominent examples). But although *Juan de Mairena* also reworks materials that Machado explored first in his private notebooks, the volume is also more diverse and polyvocal than previous models and the earlier songbooks. Its fifty chapters are subdivided into sections that sometimes stand alone and sometimes form groupings of thematically related discourses. It includes a narrator speaking about Mairena, who is sometimes speaking about Martín or about other poets and philosophers (Góngora, Calderón, Fray Luis, Kant, Hegel, Descartes, Heidegger, Plato, da Vinci, etc.). It includes some miniature dialogues in which Mairena speaks with a student, sometimes taking the role of a listener to the student's ideas. Sometimes one cannot tell who is speaking; a narrative voice like the one in the "Cancioneros" sometimes interrupts to say, "Juan de Mairena said," but one also encounters the words "my teacher said," which suggests that the narrator is Mairena. These indications are absent at times, and in others a section title informs readers that they are reading extracts from lessons, presumably the titular character's. The relay and detachment created by the apocryphal nature of the text is intensified, in spite of the impression that a single volume christened with a single proper name might give us.

Curiously, other conventions of philosophical and poetic readings remain intact. For one, Machado and his many speakers place trust in summaries of philosophical texts, as if the primary sources of thinking were transcended in the reading. We also find various expressions of distrust in writing, reminiscent of the passages from the *Phaedrus* discussed in chapter 2. Mairena voices a suspicion toward language that has been separated from a speaker (S 347; E 115) and warns his students that this denunciation appears hypocritical: "Never trust a literature teacher who declares . . . that he is an enemy of the written word" (S 348). If writing does not allow for the spontaneity of living speech, Machado says, one should still strive to give the impression of spontaneity in writing. This is aligned with the value of what is called "metaphysical spontaneity" (S 317) the ability of his students, among others, to think for themselves.

In addition to the multiplicity of voices and formal eclecticism, *Juan de Mairena* differs from the songbooks in the *Poesías completas* in the proliferation of topics of discussion. Most deal with intellectual topics: theater, oratory, folklore, diaries, and poetry in general and particular cases; historical periods and moments in intellectual history; interpretations of a long list of philosophers, concepts, and controversies. But one also reads witty and insightful discussions of painting, everyday language, pedagogy, clothing, exercise, the natural sciences, society, and politics.[45] One could interpret this as a performative intensification of the theme of heterogeneity in the apocalyptic songbooks, even though the theme of heterogeneity remains consistent with earlier work. Even the temporal character of the work appears emphatically heterogeneous, as we read words attributed to Abel Martín and Juan de Mairena as well as a retrospective commentary and interpretation. Martín is supposed to have died in 1898, while Mairena lived to 1909.[46] The anonymous narrator of *Juan de Mairena*—assuming he is a single nameless voice, and a male—positions himself in the time of Machado when he proposes that Mairena "got ahead of himself by thinking vaguely of a poet like Paul Valéry and a philosopher like Martin Heidegger" (S 263; E 79 [revised]), intellectual figures whose renown began in the 1920s. We will return to consider Mairena's long exposition of Heidegger's "philosophy," published 1936–37, where the narrator proposes "imagining" how Mairena might have interpreted *Being and Time* from 1928 (2:89). The temporal heterogeneity in *Juan de Mairena* includes speculation and imaginative anachronism.

Nonetheless, *Juan de Mairena* contains and reiterates major themes of the songbooks, formulating the idea of a poetic thinking that would integrate temporality and heterogeneity into philosophy via a new vision of its relation to literature. In chapter 1, we looked at two characterizations of poetic thinking, a "creative" thinking in contrast to a "logical or mathematical" kind. The collection distinguishes itself by providing—mixed among a greater thematic variety—many propositions regarding the relationship of poetry and philosophy, and this multiplicity cannot be reconciled without violently imposing a unitary idea. Indeed, reconciliation does not seem to be the point. In order to provide a more detailed account of this problem in *Juan de Mairena* and to prepare for an appreciation of the surprising characterization of human life as a movement between philosophy and poetry, let us look at their common traits and the frequent contrast between poetic openness and philosophical restriction.

Antonio Machado and his poets already pose a resemblance of poetry and philosophy by associating them with two "logics," different kinds of an identically named procedure or perspective. Mairena will speak repeatedly of this common character in statements intermingled with other comments on their difference. Toward the beginning of the volume, one reads that poetry and philosophy both engage with the problem of the relationship between consciousness and "things themselves." For Mairena, philosophy's concern with the operation of representation "evades" the "eternal problem" that persists as a result of "absolute heterogeneity" of a thing that is other because it is "in itself," as opposed to "in" the representing subject (S 83; E 6). But poets "also," says Mairena, "have to grapple with presences and absences, not in any way with copies, translations, and representations" (S

83; E 6 [revised]). Later in the same chapter, the narrator identifies this problem with the title of one of Abel Martín's books, "De lo uno al otro," "From the one to the other" (S 85; E 6). Here "human reason attempts to eliminate the other," but poetry retains "faith" in what is referred to as "the incurable *otherness* that *the one* suffers" (la incurable *otredad* que padece lo *uno*) (S 85; E 6 [revised]). Poets also engage in the movement "from one to another," but suffer the impossibility of incorporating the other into the unity of their individual consciousnesses. Philosophy's claim to accomplish the passage once and for all is perhaps a claim that is made again and again throughout history. If it were to accomplish this particularly philosophical desire, Mairena says, it would no longer need to exist, because otherness would be the object of complete mastery, would cease to trouble anyone and obviate the drive to philosophy and literature both.

In later passages—the closely related chapters 22 and 23, where the motifs of translation and representation reappear—Machado ascribes faith to the philosophers. Both poets and philosophers construct a means of passage from consciousness to objects, yet only philosophers believe in the truth of their creations. Again, "what is inevitable is going from the one to the other" (S 195). Besides this movement, poets and philosophers share an inventive language that provides a link between subjects and object, and a skeptical attitude that puts their abilities to the test. Chapter 22 is especially insistent on statements that establish attribution to a particular subject: "Mairena said," "Mairena added," "my teacher said," and the first attribution of chapter 23—doubled to emphasize the potential distance from the author writing in 1936—"my teacher said—Mairena is speaking to his students" (S 199; E 50 [revised]). Although philosophers and poets share skepticism and rhetorical skill, each type enriches the other with its own particular strength. The poets learn from philosophers how to forge metaphors that compel belief (S 191; E 47–48). Meanwhile, philosophers learn to intensify skepticism, which in poets "tends to be the deepest and hardest to refute" (S 190). Mairena notes, then, that the movement from the self of "one" to the alterity of "other" not only characterizes poets' and philosophers' activity in general but in the specific instance of their relationship to each other. They appear to be doing the same when they benefit from the other's example. Let us note the irony in this observation: "There are men, my teacher said, who go from poetry to philosophy; others go from philosophy to poetry. What is inevitable is going from the one to the other, in this, as in everything [en todo]" (S 195). Speaking for the moment, then, as a philosopher, Machado finds the unifying instance in the movement from one to the other. But the same text and its surrounding aphorisms and essays point out, at least, differences within the same, associating differences with movements. In this way, the site of differentiation is associated with temporality as the displacement between relatively stable differends. Conceiving of the relation between literature and philosophy as a series of instances of movement, rather than a single pathway or structure, also suggests that there is no "relation" in general but, rather, singular trajectories sketched out in a space between, a relation that can be effectuated but cannot be theorized, in the traditional sense of the word.

This vision of alliance and enrichment clearly gives priority to difference, to what Machado and his apocryphals will continue to associate with poetry, and *Juan de Mairena*'s passages on the relation between poetry and philosophy continue to connote a negative character for philosophy. In a lesson on Democritus, Mairena describes the process of emptying the world of life by reducing it to the drab uniformity of atoms, while poets capture "the colors of the rainbow and the painted plumage of the peacock's feather" (S 131; E 26). In an exposition of lessons devoted to the poetics of Abel Martín, Mairena speaks of philosophical "explanación," a homogenizing leveling out, *explanación* relating to *plano*—flat and featureless—instead of *explicación*'s root in unfolding (S 240; E 69 [revised]). Again, we can hear an ironic overstatement that associates the voice of Mairena with philosophy even as he disparages it: "All human reason militates against the diversity and richness of things" (S 239; E 69). Meanwhile, Mairena explains time and again that poetry embraces time and life. A "poetry teacher," for example, "teaches his students to reinforce the temporality of their verses" (S 111). Poetry is "man's dialogue, his dialogue with his time"; a poet is a fisherman seeking "fish who go on living in the aftermath of the catch" (S 121; E 21). As "word in time," Bécquer's poetry remains foreign to the temporal logic of inference or deduction, bearing witness instead to the "irreversible time of the psyche" (S 319; E 102). Poetry indeed often seems to have accomplished philosophy's founding task of giving an account of being by attending to its own mode of exposition and embracing its necessarily provisional and partial nature.[47]

In spite of his design to inject temporality and heterology into philosophy and poetic discourse, the project actually consists of calling attention to elements that already inhabit them, in short, an embrace of that which philosophy considered a contaminant, and an amplification of what is most particular—and least philosophical—about poetry. As with Ortega's "general biology," one would gather from the tradition of interpretation that Machado accomplished this "poetic thinking" and left it as the legacy of Hispanic thought. The ensemble of Martín, Mairena, and Machado's critical narrator begins to lay claim to such a poetic logic in the "Cancioneros apócrifos," but, already half way through *Juan de Mairena*, it starts to appear a distant goal, a poematic metaphysics located in an uncertain future. The traits from the book's description of "our logic" are already familiar: freedom from the restrictions of syllogistic logic, an aversion to reductions of the other to the self, an embrace of self-contradiction, openness to everything that logic is not, and an appreciation of the primordial necessity of otherness (see S 206–7). In spite of the possibility, apparently realized, of stating new logical principles, Mairena goes on to warn of the "long and difficult apprenticeship" to learn and understand the principles of the new logic (S 207). After that, one would have to learn to apply them strictly. Only after this process, says Mairena, "*which we have not yet begun*, will we be able to know whether or not we are capable of truly original thought" (S 207 [my emphasis]). This image of thought, whose rough outlines suffice to evoke it and propose it as a project, might indeed be not only impractical but impossible. Jochen Mecke and Nicolás Fernández-Medina have connected Mairena's concern for otherness with the thought of Emmanuel Levinas; perhaps no one else has taught us so insistently what a challenge the thought of otherness poses, when all speech and knowledge necessarily carry out a violent domestication of otherness.[48] Machado's sense of this difficulty is inscribed in many ways in his work, in performative gestures as well as thematic passages. Accordingly, contributions to Machado studies may seek to render him other but still do so in order to bring new possibilities of understanding and experiencing the figure of Machado, still making him ours, but doing so in an unprecedented way. "Poetic thought"—described as "*heterogenizing, inventor* or discoverer of reality" (S 207)—appears to correspond to motifs of existing texts, quoted and discussed in the apocryphal songbooks and in *Juan de Mairena*. Yet, again, Mairena proposes an entire program that would merely prepare us for a new logic, anticipating some traits of Foucauldian archaeology. We ought, he says, to familiarize ourselves with "the old logic," the one to be overcome (S 208). We also should study, methodically, a long list of other discourse types, including "the verbal confusion of drunks and the mentally deficient" (S 208).[49] These "other logics," says Mairena, "still do not fall within the new [logic]" (S 208). His conclusion to this important chapter (the only passage included in the English edition) reiterates that the goal for thought remains distant: "Our aim is to strengthen and sensitize thinking, and thereby discover its real limitations and potentialities: the degree to which thinking is free, original, self-initiating, and the degree to which we are blocked by inflexible criteria, unaltering habits of mind, or the sheer impossibility of thinking differently" (S 210; E 56). Mairena seems to suggest, in other words, that we stay, in a sense, on the move, working with what we have available, not yet using the new logic, the poetic thinking to come, but exploring the limits of the old logic in a quest for "the liberty of thinking as such" (S 210; E 56). Typically, the narrator reports that this statement is taken from a transcript of an "auditor" (oyente) in Mairena's class, who would have slavishly copied these words down, recognizing that among the incapacities of a free thinking would be preventing quotation. While the effect here is to distinguish the "stenographer's apprentice" from the thinking speaker, Machado's text remarks, with an implicit chuckle, that the nature of language prevents us from establishing an absolute difference between free and servile utterances (S 210; E 56).

Machado presents another version of a poetological task oriented toward the future in *Juan de Mairena*'s chapter 34, looking forward to "one day" when the relationship of poets and philosophers will be different, as poetry and philosophy will undergo transformations. This appears to be a distant, indeterminate future for Mairena. At this time "the great metaphysical deed" of "[thinking] being outside of time" will be sung of by poets present as an event accomplished by philosophers past. Philosophers, for their part, will create "an existentialist metaphysics . . . rooted deeply in time; something, in fact, more poematic [poemático] than philosophical in character" (S 263; E 78 [revised]). Because philosophers will assume the poet's privileged relationship to time and poets will focus their attention on the restrictive separation of being and time, Mairena declares that in this moment they will have "traded places" ("se trocarán los papeles entre poetas y filósofos") (S 263; E 78). Rather than eliminating difference, they accentuate it, relating as others in a genuine encounter: "And poet and philosopher will meet face to face [estarán frente a frente], never being hostile [nunca hostiles], each carrying forward the great labor from the point where it is relinquished by the other" (S 263; E 79 [revised]). Poets will continue to sing of fictional accomplishments and philosophers to produce metaphysical representations of being; the first a philosophical poetry and the second a poematic, rather than philosophical, philosophy. "Poematic," in contrast to "poetic," emphasizes that the poetic will combine with *mathesis*, the Greek word for learning or acquisition of knowledge. Since Mairena would have to be speaking, realistically, before his death in 1908, it becomes questionable whether this future moment might be the time of Antonio Machado's writing.

In the Meantime:
Adopting Valéry and Truncating Heidegger

Machado's philosophical voices certainly do propose, at times, that poetic and philosophical activities might be blended in or fused by a single human subject. Such a premise could even seem to prevail in the "Cancioneros apócrifos" and *Juan de Mairena*, not to mention the biography of Antonio Machado. As we have seen, however, Mairena also serves as a means to impose or enforce a differential or even disruptive approach to what is sometimes imagined as a potentially harmonious relation. The restoration of a unitary and cordial relation between points of view and personae threatens to close down this advocacy for heterogeneity by, among other things, attributing the whole play of perspectives to a singular Antonio Machado. Mairena proposes, curiously, a poetic thinking or poematic metaphysics occupying a future moment, when poets and philosophers "will trade places" (S 263; E 78). Until the time is ripe for that, he says, poets and philosophers may make preparations. In the meantime, then, poetry and philosophy will continue to do what they have always done, more or less: philosophers elaborate plausible but fictional connections between consciousness and the world, seeking to convince themselves and to compel belief in others. Poets compose tentative, elliptical works that remind themselves and readers of the irremediable gap between the unity and homogeneity of consciousness and the variety of the world. Such a maintenance finds models in the past, making the most of the archive, in spite of its flaws and incompletion and the ambiguities found in poets and philosophers. Juan de Mairena sets out to distinguish which philosophers and which poets perform the traditional tasks best. Also, a kind of training takes place, both of thought and sensibility, preparing not only for continuation of the propaedeutic activity but its advance toward the poematic metaphysics to come. Whether this is a finite process might have to remain one of the uncertainties required by the irreducible otherness of the destiny Machado and his poets prophesy. One could even hypothesize a messianism of literature and philosophy, a moment in the future in which a solution to their antagonism would be given, when the lamb would lie down with the lion and time would come to an end. Until then, philosophy and poetry remain engaged in adventures of approximation, crossing the space between them in ways that are unique every time, that aspire, at least, to connect what must remain apart. What Mairena says of philosophy's effort to reconcile one and the other can be said of this particular pair: neither philosophy nor poetry will exist when their difference ceases.

It could be said, however, that Machado had a very particular moment in mind, when his nation's literary tradition met the challenge philosophy poses to poetry and resolved it with the fusion of literature and philosophy, a poetic thinking that answers the criteria set out by Abel Martín, Juan de Mairena, and Machado's critical narrative voice. Such a claim seems based on a selective reading of Machado's oeuvre and an identifiable set of protocols for readings, involving patriotism, devotion to the history of ideas, and a focus on reconstituting a homogeneous vision of the author's concerns and accomplishments. Before a last look at Mairena's vision of a final attainment, let us consider the suggestion that Machado's task had already been realized by others within his lifetime. Mairena pictures poetry and literature "face to face," happy to see the other occupied by what the partner has left behind, a preoccupation with time and existence, a concern for anguish. *Juan de Mairena*'s narrator concludes, then, with the ironic observation that Mairena "was getting ahead of himself" (adelantándose) (S 263; E 79 [revised]). He is not himself the philosophical poet he has in mind; however, the one the narrator mentions, as well as the poetic philosopher that he envisions, are contemporaries of Antonio Machado. According to the narrator, Mairena "[thought] vaguely of a poet à la Paul Valéry and a philosopher à la Martín Heidegger" (S 263; E 78 [revised]). An understanding of what these figures represent in Machado's text indeed promises to provide a definitive idea of what might be accomplished in the name of a union of literature and philosophy.

Whereas Machado published a long piece about Heidegger in his *Juan de Mairena* column in *Hora de España* (posthumously collected as a second volume named after the apocryphal poet-philosopher), the archive offers only brief and scattered references to Valéry. The Heidegger commentary includes a reference to the Valéry poem "Ébauche d'un serpent" ("Silouette of a Serpent") (2:93). In *Los complementarios*, Machado copied out two of the French poet's verses and a long passage from "Le Crise d'esprit" ("The Crisis of the Mind").[50] One also finds there the draft for his 1925 book review, "Reflexiones sobre la lírica" (Reflections on the lyric), in which Valéry forms one of the two "complementary" positions driving contemporary French poetry, the other being represented by Jules Romains.[51] None of these moments account for the privileged position given to Valéry in the two *Juan de Mairena* passages. Nor does it seem especially insightful to group Valéry with other examples of "philosophy and poetry intermingled," for his creation of monsieur Teste and his later devotion to both verse and prose.[52] One certainly might assert that Valéry belongs among the figures that reassured Machado of the viability of his own cultivation of both verse and essayistic prose. Moreover, like Machado, Valéry's fame for his poetry launched a career celebrated for the thought-research of his *Cahiers*. If our goal is to learn from Machado something about the relation between literature and philosophy, we need not be as embarrassed as Carlos Clavería that Valéry's most pointed statement on the matter, "Poésie et la pensée abstraite" ("Poetry and Abstract Thought"), appeared slightly after Machado's death.[53] The two shared an interest, along with an attitude. For example, Valéry's narrator for *Monsieur Teste* expresses misgivings about thoughts that have been expressed in words, saying that they cease to represent him insofar as they become "invariable" in a fixed text.[54] In "Poetry and Abstract Thought," Valéry explicitly sets out to question the "alleged antithesis" between the two elements named in his title and proposes they be considered as extraordinary states of mind that give rise to distinct sorts of products.[55] Furthermore, Valéry says, not only may the two coexist within a single individual; human existence even depends on interchange between them and other ways of being: "If each man were not able to live a number of other lives besides his own, he would not be able to live his own life."[56]

Machado's brief references do not explicitly reflect upon this kinship to Valéry, and, in fact, they hardly say anything about the French writer beyond placing him in relation to Heidegger. In "Reflexiones sobre la lírica," Machado places Valéry in relation to Romains, contending that the former's focus on individual, visionary intellect and the latter's on shared rational structures together "announce a rebirth of man, whose thought is defined as a faculty for direct relation to the real."[57] Together with Heidegger, Valéry represents the position of the poet who takes up what philosophy leaves behind. Mairena's description of this philosophical poet appears before the assertion that he was thinking "vaguely" of poets like Valéry. It might be excessive, then, to apply that description too carefully. Clearly, though, what defines poets is their commitment to singing, a word that Mairena applies to them twice in *Juan de Mairena*, chapter 34: "They will sing of their wonderment in the presence of the great metaphysical adventure, especially the supremest of marvels, the power of contemplating *being* untrammeled by time"; "to sing of the old miracles of human thought" (S 263; E 78 [revised]). Philosophers "think"; "they will arrive at an existentialist metaphysics"; and they "speak to us"; that is to say, in the most classical of definitions, philosophical discourse subordinates what it is saying to what has *already* been thought (S 263; E 78 [revised]). Later, in the section devoted entirely to Heidegger, Mairena evokes Valéry by quoting two lines from "Ébauche d'un serpent," reinforcing the impression that Valéry's primary significance remains tied to his verse, poetry wherein song elicits philosophical activity without exactly engaging in it. Poetry provides a relation to thought that philosophical speech itself obscures, as if thinking stopped when philosophy begins to speak and, by contrast, remained on the move in the lines and stanzas, narratives and personae of verse.

"La Jeune Parque" ("The Young Fate") could indeed be understood as a case of nonphilosophical thinking and as a sort of song to time.[58] In it, to give a broad characterization, we read a monologue by one of the divine figures in charge of human lives, the Parca or Fate who cuts to measure a length of thread representing an individual's finite lifespan. A snakebite motivates the Parca to reflect on the possible effects of mortality, highlighting the impossible experience of temporality by an immortal being. This impossibility is a philosophical theme, but Valéry embraces the additional impossibility that she, as an immortal, might speak of and yearn for all that time makes possible: emotion, sensuality, desire, regret, and so on. Most egregiously, Valéry's Parca is said in the title to be "young." But the origin of the essence of temporality may not itself be temporal, as the poem eventually suggests by having the Parca gradually return to silence and an atemporal state. That is, for philosophy, the essence of time may not be temporal, but poetry has the ability to defy—for the duration of a poem—a philosophical premise. The bite of the serpent creates a double who appears for almost the duration of the poem and then departs. Toward the end, the Parca says, "Farewell . . . mortal ME, sister, falsehood"; she gradually loses her fascination with mortality and its "divine sorrow."[59] "The Young Fate" is nonphilosophical in that it does not explain or expound upon time and life. Its speaker-protagonist's implicit understanding of time recalls Bergson in its expression as an exposure to otherness, but it does not methodically reflect upon time. After wondering whether "Time" will "dare" to impose a recollection upon her eternal mind, she calls upon her own memory to act as a "bonfire" in her "refusal / to be, in myself aflame, another than I was."[60] She remains herself, but only as the conflagration that destroys all other selves that she might have been, had she been mortal. In a like manner, Bergson describes the impossibility of a temporal reversal, claiming that traditional notions of time erroneously authorize us to conceive of the past in the manner of a spatial representation preserving the integrity and accessibility of events. Bergson contrasts with this a notion of "true time," "durée," characterized by a "heterogeneity" that renders all repetition impossible.[61] In Valéry as well as Machado, the impossibility of temporal identity, of the present self joining with past selves in a single unit, finds an especially economical form in the figure of a consciousness that sees itself seeing. Toward the beginning of the Parca's rumination on mortality, she characterizes the serpent's bite as an event that makes her "see herself seeing" (je me voyais voire) that breaks her into a seeing being and a seen being.[62] Such a fragile consciousness also appears in *Juan de Mairena*, which would attribute to the Parca's brief scission a poetic achievement in its "seeing that sees itself" (ver que se ve) (S 238). Such a moment, says Mairena, is simultaneously "seeing and blinding" (ver y cegar), since the consciousness divides into that which sees and that which merely, blindly, gets seen.[63]

By definition, a poetic act—even though it is an interpretation of time and identity—lacks systematic conceptuality and terminology. The narrator of *Juan de Mairena* draws the outer limit of poetry's philosophical character at being an "emphatic expression of thought," such as he finds in a quatrain by Abel Martín.[64] Without stating it directly, Machado's texts, with their own gaps and methodological shortcomings, resemble Valéry's position in the dichotomy sketched in *Juan de Mairena* chapter 34. The text posthumously designated chapter 61 in volume 2 stands out for being a lengthy exposition of a contemporary philosophy, one actually developed during the life of Machado, during the time he composed his narratives, though not the historical moment ascribed to the characters he creates. These ten pages in the standard edition of *Juan de Mairena* form the most sustained piece in a collection more characterized by aphoristic and fragmentary writing. Nonetheless, it has been taken as a nonphilosophical exposition of philosophy by no less a figure than Julián Marías, for whom it represents Machado's engagement with the history of philosophy rather than philosophy itself, a task for which he was not suited and cannot be blamed.[65] This assertion results from Marías's detailed and convincing demonstration that Mairena's explanation of Heidegger merely rehashes that of the scholar Georges Gurvitch. However, it is relevant to point out that an important part of Heidegger's work had already questioned the identity of philosophy as a discourse susceptible to being glossed in the traditional manner pursued by both Gurvitch and Marías. Heidegger's review of Karl Jaspers's *Psychology of Worldviews* was especially clear on this, though probably not widely available outside of Germany.[66] What would be hard to miss for a reader of *Being and Time* would be the introductory efforts to distinguish the pursuit of the question of Being from anthropology and the announcement of a project of "destruction" (Destruktion) of the traditional disciplines of ontology and metaphysics.[67] That Heidegger proposes calling this project "phenomenology" does not mean that he joins a school or simply follows predecessors such as Husserl and Max Scheler. For the Heidegger of *Being and Time*, the conclusions of the analysis of Dasein mean little without the transformative action of thinking phenomenologically, in the manner of letting things show how they are. Thus, Machado's treatment of Heidegger does an injustice for more reasons than the one Marías mentions. First, he too quickly assigns Heidegger to the school of "phenomenologists of Freiburg" (*Juan de Mairena* 1:237), enclosing his thought within a frame that is itself one of the stakes of *Being and Time* and later work. In addition, Machado treats Heidegger as though his thinking were adequately captured as a set of propositions and themes, a doctrine or an "ideology" of the nature of a worldview. Having limited the lens through which Heidegger's thought appears, Machado's philosophical-critical voice—Mairena—will lay the fault for those limitations at Heidegger's feet and propose going beyond Heidegger by holding back at the "threshold of [his] thought" (2:96). This strange prescription, offered by one poet to others, entails taking from philosophy only what the history of philosophy has already taught the poets to seek.

Chapter 61 of *Juan de Mairena* reiterates several motifs from earlier Mairena texts. Chapter 30 notes that Mairena could not measure up to what the critical-narrative voice credits the "Freiburg phenomenologists" with achieving, "the ultimate consequences of Bergsonian temporalization, the faith in the ontological value of human existence" (237). Later, in chapter 61, the narrator will praise phenomenology as an "intuitionist movement" that "reaches, with Heidegger, in our time, an extreme approximation to Bergsonism" (2:88). When the narrator introduces his effort to imagine "how Mairena would have explained [Heidegger]," he again refers to Bergson, saying that his Spanish philosopher-poet would be adept at such an exposition "on account of [Heidegger's] Bergonism" (2:89). Without following that lengthy presentation, we can note that it largely depicts *Being and Time*'s Dasein as a human figure with something like a divided contact with the world, one direct and one highly mediated. Like the common interpretation that Heidegger will eventually critique in "The Letter on Humanism," Mairena will view *Being and Time* as an anthropology that aims at establishing more authentic, because more direct contact with beings through an appreciation of time. In line with what Mairena says when he invokes Heidegger together with Valéry, chapter 61 describes how the philosopher takes up themes beloved by poets, primarily anguish and mortality. Throughout *Juan de Mairena* one can read the narrator's praise of an implicit metaphysics that manifests itself in folklore and popular poetry such as ballads, ideas that Machado also expressed in his 1917 prologues. Remarkably, the posthumous Mairena also offers a more precise outline of that implicit philosophy when he claims that "Heidegger's doctrine" is "somewhat sad" and asks whether Spaniards—especially Andalusians—might not be "somewhat Heideggerian without knowing it" (2:92). Along with this provocation goes the claim that Unamuno "was ahead of Heidegger's existentialist philosophy by a few years," and he goes on to praise Unamuno's "rebellion" against mortality in comparison to what he sees as the German's mere "resignation" (2:94).

As he winds down his exposition, Mairena returns to the theme that poets are failed metaphysicians and philosophers naive poets. In the original volume of *Juan de Mairena*, he offers a list of the "great metaphors" of philosophers, "immortal for their poetic value": "Heraclitus's river, Parmenides's sphere, Pythagoras's lyre, Plato's cave, Kant's dove, etc. etc." (191). Naturally, then, chapter 61 comments on the consummate phenomenological attempt to fit into this legacy. Mentioning again some of the same philosophical metaphors, he calls them the "eternal viewpoint" from which the universe may be taken in. Yet Mairena does not find an apt metaphor in Heidegger. He returns to settle on the abstract description: "a new humanism, humble and as sad as it is deeply submerged in time," a "primordial time, as in Bergson . . . finite and limited" (2:98). For the last words of this piece, though, he suggests that a Spanish proverb could provide Heidegger's great metaphor: he attributes to "das Man" the words "aún hay más días que longanizas" (still there are more days than sausages) (2:99). The proverb suggests that our temporal existence requires that we impose measure on our everyday lives, that as living beings we must reckon with finite time, lest we run out of sustenance before the end of our lives.

Mairena, the critical voice that presents him, and, by all appearances, Antonio Machado, thus seem to approve of Heidegger's thought, at least in some of the principles, such as mortality and anxiety before death, as well as the definition of the human as an emphatically temporal being in the world. But for Mairena, philosophy is bound to err to the extent that it remains philosophical in its exposition, since it proceeds through either pedantry or scholasticism. The latter, says Mairena, characterizes Heidegger and will inevitably lead him to superficiality in spite of his pretense to provide a deep description of the human (2:94). For Mairena, Heidegger the philosopher will inevitably build a "path of perfection" (camino de perfección) or a set of "conclusions" (2:96). By nature, a philosopher's conclusions draw consequences from the principles that so attract Mairena and other poets, and such deductions "tend to be false" (2:96). This passage seems to suggest that a philosopher who draws conclusions to form a "doctrine" speaks philosophical falsehoods; but a thinker who did not draw conclusions would not even deserve to be called a philosopher. In this sense, like Unamuno, Machado's philosophical voice recommends not going full philosophy, but returning to poetry or to life, where one savors sausages and may always defer conclusions until death arrives. Conclusions commit a theoretical and practical error by imposing an arbitrary limit where the only legitimate one is death.

It is worth noting that Heidegger's work is mostly devoid of the kind of determinations that preoccupy Machado's narrator and character and their representations of it. One does not find, in any case, much advice for living and thinking, although he does vaguely express a preference for determinate poets and kinds of poetry and voice suspicions about science and urban society. More commonly, Heidegger attempts to fashion a new mode of contemplation, warning against scientific habits of thought and the conceptualization of philosophy in terms of positions and worldviews. The shortcomings of such modes of thinking correspond to what concerns Mairena: the closing down of possibilities of human existence, treating principles of life as something settled once and for all, an itself atemporal structuration of the possibilities of a thoroughly temporal being. *Being and Time*'s novelty lies in a phenomenological-ontological method, setting out structures that would have to belong to any research into Being. The latter takes surprising forms throughout Heidegger's life, including crossing out the name of Being with a silent, written *X* and elaborating a myth of the fourfold clearing. It often affirms the achievements of science and technology, the greatest dangers to human life, but always aspires to keep open the possibility for thinking *who* the human can become, for decision according to a thought that responds to a primordial offering that humans, perhaps alone among beings, receive. For the Heidegger of *Being and Time*, a kind of Dasein he calls "authentic" resolutely remains open to the otherness from which it might receive unexpected insight or experience; among the others we would have to count not just other beings but "Being," and not just the time of life but time in general. In their conviction that openness to otherness is the primary challenge for humanity, Heidegger and Mairena concur, as they do in their interest in both philosophical and poetic activity. In fact, Mairena suggests that no philosophy, even Bergson's or Heidegger's, could provide a better account of time and the world than poetry does, and in this he anticipates María Zambrano.

Heidegger's shortcoming turns out to be the supposedly simple fact that he is a philosopher. Mairena wants his own listeners to remain focused on principles in order to avoid the dehumanization of philosophy: "I advise you, my dear friends, to pause and meditate on the threshold of this philosophy, before you penetrate within it. May your position be more human than scholastic [escolar] and pedantic" (2:96). In the name of humanity, then, his followers should remain cautious and skeptical, Mairena continues: "You do not need to take the conclusions of philosophers very seriously, since they tend to be false, and, of course, inconclusive, but, rather, their beginnings and their visions, the latter above all" (2:96). For Mairena, Heidegger has started out from anguish, a "radical psychic fact" (hecho psíquico de raíz) (2:93). Heidegger's strength, then, lies in the root and its first growth, and for Mairena all that extends from there may be and should be cut away, for the sake of poetry and humanity.

Passages: Poetry to Philosophy and Back

Machado's readers and critics struggle to define the relationship between literature and philosophy, proposing figures of fusion, clinging to visions of an absolute difference, or elaborating formulations that combine gravitation and repulsion, sameness and otherness, though figures of an in-between. The difficulty lies in the nature of Machado's texts on literature and philosophy, which represent all of these positions and require us to find a way to come to terms with heterogeneous but related utterances. Although the device of apocryphal poets conditions us to think of Antonio Machado as the site of different, distinct human perspectives, it is remarkable that even the ostensibly univocal work *Juan de Mairena*—which appears to center on one of the poet-philosophers—incorporates a number of conflicting perspectives. While some moments project an amicable partnership between literature and philosophy, several others attempt to convey a movement of relating that brings the two their most powerful expressions.

The strongest suggestion that poet and philosopher dwell peacefully in the same person is perhaps the announcement at the beginning of the apocryphal songbooks that Abel Martín and Juan de Mairena are, respectively, "poet and philosopher" (305) and "poet, philosopher, rhetorician, and inventor of a singing machine" (327). Within *Juan de Mairena*, of course, on the most intuitive level, we come across "original" poems and discussions of poets as well as lengthy discussions of philosophers of the stature of Kant, Hegel, Marx, Leibniz, Nietzsche, and Schopenhauer. Machado does not limit himself to description, as Alonso implies when he accuses the poet of seeking an encounter not with philosophy but with "the history of recent philosophy."[68] Although not at great length, Machado characterizes, questions, refines, and, in general, engages in a sort of philosophical dialogue. If this interweaving of poetry and philosophy resembles Nietzsche more than any other predecessor, it is still true that Nietzsche's investment in literature sometimes raises questions about his philosophical bona fides, even while he is widely considered more important to philosophy than to literature. Within *Juan de Mairena* some passages indicate a closer relation between poets and philosophers. Chapter 4 cites Hegel's description of philosophy as "the world seen inside out" (el mundo al revés) (S 93; E 9). For Hegel, incidentally, this provocative statement describes the necessary movement of philosophy from the minimal point of immediate certainty of the self to knowledge of the whole of beings, within which the self comes to realize itself completely as a subject of art, religion, and politics.[69] Mairena says, "Poetry, on the other hand [en cambio], is the inside-out of philosophy, the world seen, finally, right-side-out [del derecho]" (S 93; E 9 [revised]). Although this sounds like a statement of poetry's superiority, Mairena, citing his teacher Abel Martín, notes that it reveals the reciprocity of the two: "To see things right one must have first seen them inside out" (S 93; E 9 [revised]). The philosophy of Hegel, which attempts to gather all previous philosophies and sciences into itself, is a necessary condition for a poetry that would see the world as it is, neither backwards nor fragmented. Mairena "himself" adds to the Martín quote, "or vice versa" (S 93; E 9; the English translation does not preserve the distinction between Martín's words and Mairena's comments on them). He evokes then, a theme that will be dear to María Zambrano, the projection of a primordial, poetic experience of the whole of being from which philosophy took its own point of departure on its long trajectory to see the world in its own way. Philosophy's vision may be inside out but it is a vision of the whole, and, as such, a marvel comparable to poetry's. Chapter 22, as well, explains how poets and philosophers can learn from each other, something that only happens on the condition that they remain distinct as they relate to each other (S 191).

Machado's descriptions of Abel Martín and Juan de Mairena state "poet" first, and *Juan de Mairena* continues to express ways in which poetry deserves a privileged status. In chapter 22, philosophers might teach poets about skepticism, but the latter's skepticism is "deeper" (más hondo) (S 191). In chapter 30, *Juan de Mairena* insists that the "ground of our conscience" cannot be reason but something that belongs to the poet's "affirmation of absolute realities" (S 238; E 68). Chapter 31 describes reason's unjustified simplification of the world, "militating against the richness and variety of the world" (S 239; E 69 [revised]). Nonetheless, Machado also celebrates the possibilities of philosophy. We have seen the formulation of a "poetic thinking" or "poematic metaphysics"; chapter 12 also imagines that sufficiently clear vision could allow philosophers to draw up the "metaphysics for the poet that [Abel Martín] always dreamed of and for which there is such a palpable need" (S 131; E 26). Poets, in fact, suffer a lack in some of Mairena's meditations. In chapter 44, it is precisely the lack of confidence and security that gives rise to their work:

> insecurity, uncertainty, and misgivings are perhaps the only truths left us. We must hold fast to them all. . . . Insecurity is our mother; misgiving is our muse. If we turn to poets in the end, it is because, convinced of these things, we know we have good cause to sing . . . because we are well aware of the evils that we seek to dispel with our song. (S 322; E 103–4)

In a few sections in which Mairena characterizes the human being, he chooses as the essential characteristic the measure associated with philosophy rather than poetry: the human is the "animal that measures his time . . . that uses a watch" (S 345). He interprets Protagoras as saying, "Man is the measure that measures itself or aspires to measuring things by measuring itself, a measurer among incommensurables" (S 345). Where does the poet stand if the *zoon logon exon* turns into the *zoon metron exon*? Machado does not say in this passage, but, as in the earlier encounter with Hegel, we could posit an opposite that would be necessary for measure to come into its own. Poetry would be the measureless or merely unmeasured, the heterogeneous thing that contains and sets off the nature of homogenizing philosophy. Of course, this associates the poetic not with human life, or even animal life (*zoon*) but with life in general (*bios*). Like Ortega, Machado seems more interested in the human as an instance of life than as a specific kind of animal.

While he often casts suspicion on the achievements of the philosophical tradition, Machado is moved to preserve power, dignity, and distinction for philosophical thought through his reflections on philosophy and literature. The same person can certainly commit to one or the other, but each can only pursue its own activity as long as the other remains other. This is why, in Machado's fantasies of a poetological revolution, poetry and philosophy "exchange roles" and "confront each other face to face [frente a frente]" (S 263; E 78 [revised]). Short of that reversal, Machado says, "there are men who go from poetics to philosophy" (S 195). Machado is not interested in fusing poetry and philosophy but in finding in each a common stake in motion, change, *passing*.

The privileged figure of passage is not an approach to some particular destination but motion for its own sake, as it were, as the essence of life. For Machado, there is no more vital human creation than poetry or philosophy in their movement toward each other. In the final section of *Juan de Mairena*, where one might expect the book to come to rest, Machado gathers motifs in an effort to put a final spin on things and keep them going. Much of this brief section is devoted to quoting anonymous popular quatrains (compiled by the poet Antonio Machado y Ruiz's father and namesake, Antonio Machado y Álvarez) with rather brief commentary. All of them feature some sort of logical contradiction: "I would like to see you and not see you" (quisiera verte y no verte) (S 355); "yesterday I ached to see you / today I ache because I saw you" (penaba por verte . . . peno porque te vi); "I have an ache, such an ache / that I can almost say I don't ache" (tengo una pena, una pena / que casi puedo decir que no tengo la pena) (S 356). They are all love poems, recalling the importance of eroticism for the self-revelation of the heterogeneity of being. Yet here Mairena hardly says anything more than that these are examples of popular poetry, contrasted with "erudite" poems written by a distinguished educator. Instead, Mairena jumps into a "metaphysical" discussion about whether what we experience is real or illusion. We cannot decide, he says, but are brought into motion by the two polar opposites: "The disquieting thing [lo inquietante] lies not in our inability to pursue one or the other alternative, by some prodigious exercise of reason, but in our restless ambivalence between two contradictory beliefs [agitarse entre creencias contradictorias]" (S 538; E 118). By juxtaposing the poetic and philosophical discussions, Mairena suggests, without stating it directly, a common energy to the two distinct discourses. Through love and poetry one learns that life may confront us with paradoxes and that philosophy brings us before undecidable aporias.

The idea is not unique to Machado that the common experience here has something to do with life. We have seen in Unamuno and Ortega the way a notion of being alive and of a *bio*-logy come to account for philosophical and poetic activity. Machado continues this tradition with his emphasis on kinds of motion that remain in place: the "beating of the spirit" (palpitación del espíritu), like a pumping of the blood of being; a "vibration in the soul," and this "un-stillness" expressed in Spanish by "lo inquietante" (*quieto* can mean, like *quiet*, not just *silent* but also *motionless* or *still*). Finally, Machado refers to the vital state of indecision, literally, as "being agitated between contradictory beliefs" (S 538; E 118 [revised]). Here at the end of *Juan de Mairena*, he is referring to a perspective on the world as delusion or as reality. Throughout the book, *philosophy* names a belief in the world's existence, while the poet is struck by the transitoriness of all being, its failure to arrive at existence in its passage toward otherness. While signed first of all *Mairena*, this image provides the most general formula for Machado's writing life, including the dynamic it sets up with heteronyms: one vacillates between poetry and philosophy, giving each its turn without coming to rest in synthesis or fusion.

Literature, Philosophy, and the Machado Machine

The figure of paths opened in a trajectory of approach and withdrawal responds to Machado's personal concern with life, and this figure achieves what we associate with Romanticism: the inscription within the work of protocols of reading particular to the work. Accordingly, we would discern in Machado's multifaceted oeuvre an oscillation from the concrete and empirical toward the ideal and ideological, and back. Even brief pieces like the "Proverbios y cantares" could induce such movement in a minimal form, one as restrained as the way the image of a wake carved into the surface of the sea could be understood as an occasion to join and separate a poetic object of fascination with a philosophical notion. Friedrich Schlegel also presented an image of life as a vacillation between the extremes of poetry and philosophy for the sake of life. In the "Letter on Philosophy: To Dorothea," he extolled the written passage over spoken discourse, although in Schlegel's case it is for the aesthetic, sensual effect, how written language captures the border between the ideal and the real as the "twilight" (Dämmerung) of meaning. "Caminante" represents our lives as the trace of a passage across a surface, but not explicitly as writing nor as any sort of traversal from one shore to another. Movement is implicitly figured instead as the eventual disappearance of a wake, making the "happening" of human life both determinate and ephemeral.

In spite of appearances, Machado's connection to Heidegger seems incidental; it is too general and disconnected to help us think through the

Spanish poet's or the German thinker's unique characteristics. If anything, the evocation of Heidegger is emblematic of a writerly ambition to address the most general of philosophical issues as a part of a bid for poetic relevance. For Machado, as for many writers of fiction and poetry, philosophy poses a challenge to thinking that can only strengthen contemplation of subject matter like time and human existence. Machado did not really grant Heidegger the attention he might have; when he speaks of "Heidegger," he reports a set of propositions that do not delve deeply into the most original and unique initiatives of what even Heidegger considered an early, flawed approach to a thinking that would "overcome" metaphysics.[70] Sometimes a limited reading can push thinking into new territory; for Machado, Heidegger becomes a character in a thinking narrative that indeed attains something special. But this is detached from the question of *Dichten* and *Denken* as Heidegger develops it; for Machado, poetry and philosophy remain different in their approach to words, narrative, characters, and fiction, and the part of his work that this chapter analyzes bears witness to philosophical appropriation rather than dwelling on examples of poetic appropriations of philosophical theses and concepts.

One particular element in Machado's elaboration of "apocryphal" poets recalls Derrida's neologism "le poématique." Valéry represents an extreme possibility for philosophical activity within the realm of fiction, using fictionality as a resource for thought about time and mortal life. Such a gesture does not only provide a scenario for exploration of ideas without commitment to truth value, or for mere dramatization. As Plato worried in the *Republic*, because fiction is not limited by reality, it can produce fantastical figures like a centaur or chimera. It can also produce an immortal consciousness like the Parca, a living, speaking individual whose nonfinitude should, logically, deprive it of the very capacity for worry about anything, let alone death. Valéry's intermingling of philosophy and fiction stretches the possibility for thinking and offers an especially clear instance of one thing Machado meant to attempt with fictitious poets and philosophers, teachers and students, readers and auditors. As Derrida suggests in his comments on "that strange institution called literature," the possibility of invention—whether philosophical or literary—requires the interplay of an established tradition and the chance for an unexpected, anomalous event.

Earlier I passed by a reference to a poetry machine, *La máquina de trovar*, "invented" by Juan de Mairena and used to produce a volume of poetry. In Derrida, the quasi-concept of "le poématique" designates the operation of writing that would accept the appearance of the wholly other in a poem, an event that also, by producing a discourse characterized by iterability, also exposes the other to reappropriation by the same. "Le poématique," *poematics*, affirms both the institutional ideality of the literary work as untranslatable, unrepeatable singularity, and along with it, the necessity for that possible thing to be rendered impossible in its realization because it must incorporate also the mechanicity of the iterable mark. Machado's "singing machine" makes such a structure legible in its contours. To begin with, it is not only a fiction but a fiction of a fiction: the machine was invented by Mairena's invention, one of his own "apocryphal poets": "Mairena had imagined a poet who, in turn, had invented a device . . ." (*Poesías*, 339). The apocryphal's apocryphal, named *Jorge Meneses*, claims that his machine listens to the "surrounding lyric" (la lírica ambiente) and "translates" it into "its objective expression, completely deindividualized, in a sonnet, madrigal, *jácara* or *letrilla*" (341). Producing a poem without the intervention of a person, its work can be "recognized by all who hear it as their own, even though no one would have been able to compose them" (34142). The fictitious machine achieves the unification of poetry's two institutional demands: it is unique and universal. While it is a definitive expression of a moment in time, and thus possesses a "metaphysics" capable of rendering an account of any place and time, it offers up work that can be collected—as Mairena is said to do—in a volume signed, duplicated, and interpreted. Once the "atmosphere" (ambiente) has changed, however, the ideal fusion of opposites—the time and place and their "objective expression"—turns into the normal state of any poem, offering itself up to individual and collective work of interpretation.

For us, Machado's machine can be spoken of and described but not given or built. Its functioning even suggests that one could not tell the difference between its operation and a fraud. In a dialogue between Mairena and Meneses, the inventor describes the action of the "manipulator," who exercises choice and omission in the genesis of the verses, such that the evidence that the machine works without human intercession disappears (342–43). In this way, Machado suggests that the project of fusion of literature and philosophy functions as a complex and high-minded joke. Unlike so many other human figures in Machado's poetry, the operator of the poetry machine sits still. The concluding paragraph to this episode in Mairena's chronicle describes his prologue to the book of poems he presents as machine-made. This is not the poetry we really want, he says, but something to occupy us while we wait for the real thing. "*The Troubador Machine*, in short, can entertain the masses and initiate them in the expression of their own feelings, while the new poets arrive [mientras llegan], the singers of a new sentimentality" (344). The "new poets"—these future performers of another kind of poetry—must continue finding their paths across a space where they can move in one direction or another, but not come to rest.

Chapter 6

"Inconstant Clarity"

The Antagonism of Philosophy and Poetry in María Zambrano

Prologue: Beginning with Principles

"Philosophy, in telling its own history," says María Zambrano in *Confesión*, "disdainfully forgets its debt to other branches of knowledge born beyond and this side of it [otros saberes nacidos más allá y más acá de ella]."[1] Zambrano devoted her writing life to the diagnosis of this forgetting and to a recuperation of the other modes of knowing, which we could broadly describe as artistic and religious. For Zambrano, philosophy's culpability lies not only in its theoretical error but in a moral one, too, disparaging discourses or activities that do not meet its standards, even though, for Zambrano, they qualify as "knowing" and, moreover, reach farther than philosophy or, indeed, beneath or in back of the realm of philosophical knowledge. Zambrano also claims a unique mode of address so that advocacy for literary and religious speech might take place in a way that minimizes the reductive, even derisive character of philosophical discourse. Philosophical knowledge, after all, infuses all kinds of knowing, including theology and humanities scholarship, with its goals of clarity, conclusiveness, and accountability; if these qualities do not belong themselves to religious and artistic phenomena, the discourse that speaks of poetry or God is limited by the extent to which it betrays its defining ideals. This problem lies at the heart of the anxiety I described in chapter 1, as scholars attempt to reassure readers, and perhaps themselves, that they hear and intend to heed Zambrano. Ironically, then, what might appear as a flaw in another discourse can be cast as a matter of indifference, or even as a virtue. The "unsystematic and fragmentary" nature of her thinking, the "diffuse and scattered character," even "redundancy," add up to a "poetic-rational" principle. And, as we have seen, poetry gets combined with thought or reason in order to describe a methodology in which the relation of philosophy and literature is put into play.[2] While she does not unequivocally identify her position with poetry—indeed, she most often accepts the title of "philosopher"—Zambrano certainly means to avoid the many ways in which philosophy might distance itself from literature and religion. *El hombre y lo divino* (Man and the divine) begins by defining philosophy as the discourse that seeks answers to questions, while poetry responds to questions that have not been posed.[3] Only a few philosophers, Zambrano says, mentioning Nietzsche, Pascal, and Kierkegaard—all of whom are known for the fragmentary character of their writing or religious commitment—escape her indictment of philosophy, at least in this discussion. In them, "an inconstant clarity [una desigual claridad] provides, like an oil lamp, more evocative, more indecisive, nimble and tentative [indecisa, alada y vacilante] light than the uniform light of consciousness and 'pure' reason."[4] Convinced that this other enlightenment deserves a chance, Zambrano produced a defiantly imperfect discourse in which we encounter argumentative and stylistic faults: multiple repetitions of the same material, obscure symbols and metaphors, unsupported and even outlandish ideas, cascades of apposite phrases, obscure or nonexistent argumentative threads, and stylistic faux pas.[5] As we will see, an abrogation of philosophical formality is an attempt to institute a discourse not just beyond but this side of philosophy.

Considered in sequence with the three predecessors I have discussed, Zambrano's interrogation of the relation between literature and philosophy is the most direct and persistent. It is also the most ambitious, taking on not just a renewal of the feeling of life, as in Unamuno, or the completion of the philosophical project, as in Ortega and Machado, but the overcoming of a contemporary crisis of reason through the recuperation of nearly forgotten potentialities of human existence. Her treatment of the "ancient strife" also spans the history of philosophy—as in Barfield's and Mackey's panoramic accounts—and recurs from her first mentions of it in the 1930s to her final writings of the 1980s. For her, poetry and philosophy form part of a mythopoetic narrative in which they play out their roles by manifesting themselves in the lives of different writers and their works. She tells this story directly for the first time in *Pensamiento y poesía en la vida española* and *Poesía y filosofía*, two books composed almost simultaneously and published within a month of each other, such that Moreno Sanz comes to call them "twin books."[6] *Confession* and *La agonía de Europa* take up the same story between two antagonistic attitudes, this time casting philosophy as a denier of life against a religious impulse that embraces life, reality, and the divine. After brief mention in some essays in the forties, *El hombre y lo divino* offers the most extensive account, combining the previous versions into a story of "The Dispute between Philosophy and Poetry about the Gods."[7] The late text *Los bienaventurados* (The blessed ones) transforms it into the suppression of religion's visual proclivity by ancient philosophy.[8] In each case, it is worth noting that this narrative occupies the beginning of the book, setting the scene for the present moment, in which Zambrano inserts her proposals for a new thinking, and with it a new era. Zambrano scholars have not debated whether this motif evolved over the years, focusing instead on the shifting nature of her political engagement and the evolution of the role of the autobiographical in her work, specifically the extent to which the facts of exile and embodiment impacted her thinking.

There is a consensus that Zambrano meant to engage the time she was living in, which was characterized by unprecedented brutality. Nevertheless, as her comments on Machado's *La guerra* show, she addressed even the most pressing of real-life catastrophes by her unique intuitive and mythopoetic approach. In a short text from the 1960s, "La crisis de la palabra" (The crisis of the word) Zambrano acknowledges that contemporary thought has been concerned with the imbalance between scientific-technical capacities and thinking about what is uniquely human.[9] She agrees that modern practices of knowledge and mastery of nature have outstripped concern with the very lives of the people who produce and harness knowledge. We could assemble our own repertoire of catastrophes—regional, national, and planetary—and the way the notion of the human failed to provide decisive guidance, but Zambrano does not devote herself to this sort of speculation. In early books, written in the wake of the Second Republic's defeat to the Francoist rebellion and during the early political and military successes of Hitler and Mussolini, Zambrano's analyses of what she calls "the crisis of European rationalism" (the opening chapter of *Pensamiento y poesía en la vida española* [Thought and poetry in Spanish life]) and "Europe's agony" (in the book with that title, *La agonía de Europa*) call for, strangely enough, an account of the original sundering of philosophy and poetry in a distant past.[10] In "La crisis de la palabra," she will even say that "the most relevant phenomenon" in a time of genocide and intense, mechanized destruction is "the fate of the word."[11] None of the historical disasters need be mentioned; cultural and political initiatives—such as the ones she was directly involved in during the Second Republic, subsequent efforts like the United Nations, the Marshall Plan, decolonization, the Peace Corps, or the socialist experiments in China, Mexico, Cuba, and the Soviet Union—need not be evaluated in themselves because the fundamental question of the relationship between philosophy and poetry remains, for Zambrano, the most fundamental and urgent one. Zambrano considered the events she witnessed necessary consequences of the extreme suppression on the part of agents of rationality against those categorized as irrational. With rationality Zambrano associates knowledge, logic, method, and philosophy, although in her writing each of these terms also possesses a double, a version that would ostensibly escape the stigma of being an aggressive culprit in the crisis of modernity.

Zambrano's hope to contribute to an understanding of and response to the world's problems rests on describing and inflecting the critical relationship between the calculable and controllable, on the one hand, and the intuitive and ineffable, on the other. A mythopoetic description of philosophy and poetry occupies a key part in this project, which is to say, Zambrano does not primarily set out to provide a metaphilosophy or a theory of literature, but refers to these elements in an effort to account for modern life.[12] Her insistence on going behind or beneath the real problems to their sources might seem strange, but it rests on her convictions regarding the character of thought and life in general. She adopts Ortega's premises regarding the speech of the genuine philosopher, transforming them into a theory of writing, or rather, a vision of theory as writing. Ortega considers himself a philosopher genuinely attuned to life in the movement he calls "historical reason," bound to produce a discourse that expresses the true, underlying spatiotemporal unity of the cosmos as an element he calls *life* or the *bios*. Early in her career, Zambrano describes her own vision of writing as a kind of transcription from a secret intimacy of life. For example, in "Por qué se escribe" (Why one writes), she describes how spoken words, in the "spontaneity" and "immediacy" of their response to circumstances, break a particular moment away from the whole of life, fixing it in ephemeral words. By comparison, writing both detaches a present moment (as speech does) and works to undo the damage wrought by language. Rather than "life," Zambrano speaks of a silent realm of secrecy and self-identity, something only sensed ("presentido") and with which one can only have contact by waiting for it to appear on its own.[13] This appearance beyond our control has the potential for returning the rational thinker—through poetry or writing—to the source of the irrational or quasi-rational elements whose absence determines the crisis of modernity: soul, the divine, the poetic, human and ethnic communities, personhood, and so on. Zambrano goes on at some length about the necessity of relinquishing "vanity" so as to gain the "purifying" force that gives her or her writing such transcendent importance. To the end of her days, she will associate it, paradoxically, with a power to be passive, to wait for the arrival of the other of reason, all the while taking a sort of dictation, writing as "transcription," from which reason's tendency toward dictatorship is effectively resisted.[14]

If we want to call this dictation without dictatorship "poetic reason," we should acknowledge that the adjective does not just modify reason but appropriates it for poetry, mitigating its drive for control and mastery while leaving it its proper capacity for clarity, measure, and technical effectiveness. In any case, the relation between reason and poetry, between philosophy and literature, calls for a much more detailed analysis. Scholars often speak of unifying, fusing, and reconciling, as they speak of "poetic reason" without a clear, explicit account of the sometimes bewildering way in which Zambrano's writings relate its two components. Certainly, she sometimes speaks of "fusion," in *El hombre y lo divino*, for example.[15] But she also describes an originary unity in which "they remain without any possible differentiation, without consequently melting into each other [sin que se fundan]."[16] By dwelling at length on the relation of poetry and philosophy, I hope to address this peculiar configuration of the confrontation of two poles of human experience—undifferentiated without being fused—as Zambrano sees it, guided by an overall sense of her writing. "Mythopoesis" refers to her tendency to create a story (*mythos*) that claims to reach back to a primordial unity. In this case, philosophy and poetry find common ground in their relation to the world, and they separate into two different entities or essences. In one of her discussions of Unamuno she describes them "as not just two genres or forms of thought and creation with the word, but as two possibilities of being."[17] When she reiterates this story, she will depict the ways in which the philosophical-rational represses the poetic-religious-realistic, leading to the crisis of modern times. Zambrano thus represents the history of Europe, if not humanity, as a struggle between two antagonists, as a certain philosophy forces a certain poetry to find surreptitious means of survival. In contrast to most accounts of this motif, I don't view poetic reason as a solution rooted in reconciliation and reunification that might constitute or produce a "new anthropology," leaving all rationalism and philosophical humanism behind, above all one that would vanquish violence once and for all.[18] Instead, I will maintain that the unity does not eliminate the essential difference, which must retain the vital tension of crisis in order to avoid stagnation and death. Zambrano views the human as the site of necessary tensions between opposing forces, including the pull between a particularly human drive for mastery of its surroundings and a secret realm whose existence only manifests itself in ambiguous, precarious, and unpredictable ways.

The discourse that refers to this nonhuman otherness requires the writer to engage not just mythological but poetological strategies to devise ways of achieving this pointing inward and hearkening back. Zambrano's texts play with syntax and grammar and demand that we struggle with apparently incompatible predicates and propositions (for example, indifferentiation without fusion). Her characteristic style aims at remaining true to her own declared position as a transcriber of truth and at compelling belief in the thought figures she constructs in her mythopoetic narratives. She means to take responsibility for responding to what does not speak as itself and to formalize and proffer an account of history and being in which calculation and willfulness have all but obliterated what she is responding to and advocating for. Zambrano's writings confront us with a discourse that is simultaneously intraphilosophical and extraphilosophical, a borderline discourse in the sense that the line she traces lies inside both philosophy and poetry and, at the same time, lies within neither one. On the one hand, she speaks of philosophers, of philosophical problems and concepts, and she offers an account of a state of affairs by way of general statements. For example, in *Filosofía y poesía* she characterizes poetry as "encounter, gift" while "philosophy searches, an injunction [requerimiento] guided by a method."[19] In spite of her own misgivings about method, her work gives the impression of a willful search for insight. On the other hand, Zambrano claims to bear witness to a call and an encounter, to feel the warmth and palpitation of life, and to let mysteries remain unknowable even while pursuing a language that summons them by reference. She writes in a spontaneous manner, taking as points of departure the titles and headings that provide some sense of her guiding impulses, and meandering among a variety of modes, occasionally gathering her thoughts into a general formulation like those that are often used to characterize "poetic reason."[20] This locution, then, presents the unity of an order, with the two philosophemes of determinate meaning joined in such a way that they belong together and apart. Although they form a single expression and have the appearance of a single concept, their meanings pull them apart in opposite directions, toward life and toward the fixity of scientific meaning.[21]

Precedents and Departures: Genealogies of Poetry and Philosophy

In chapter 1, I elaborated on Zambrano's linkage of her work with the "poetic thinking" in Machado's Abel Martín and Juan de Mairena texts. Zambrano scholars have long recognized the extent to which her "poetic reason" continues "vital reason" and means to extend Ortega's notion to what even ratiovitalism might exclude.[22] Aranguren's idea of Zambrano as a "heretical" disciple seems apt: she attempts to outline the essential structure of a principle from which all things grow, something like Ortega's "life."[23] In *Pensamiento y poesía*, she even calls it "the intimate structure of life," from which history flows (25), and in *Confession* she refers to "life's need to express itself."[24] What distinguishes her is the insistence that life's self-expression produced the antagonism of poetry and philosophy, such that what is called for today is not a vital reason that might return life's precedence over rationality, but a poetic one that would remedy millennia of tyrannical reason through the force that poetry exerts upon reason. Roberta Johnson tells how Ortega remonstrated Zambrano for trying to go beyond something that she had not yet attained, vital reason.[25] For her, presumably, the realization of Ortega's ratiovitalism would have further alienated her from poetry.

Still, like Ortega, she understood her own life as an instance of Spanishness and her work as a further outgrowth of the particularity of a Spanish mode of life. In *Delirio y destino* (*Delirium and Destiny*), her most autobiographical work, she echoes Ortega's depiction of Spanish ontological privilege: "In few places on this planet does thought become life as quickly as in Spain, because it springs from life [brota de la vida]."[26] It thus suffices for Zambrano, like Ortega, to live in order to articulate the inner workings of the most fundamental element of the universe. In "A modo de autobiografía" (In the manner of an autobiography), she says,

> My true condition, that is, my vocation, has been being, not being something [ha sido la de ser, no la de ser algo], but thinking, seeing, watching, having a limitless patience that still remains so that I can live thinking, knowing that I cannot do otherwise [sino la de pensar, la de ver, la de mirar, la de tener la paciencia sin límites que aún me dura para vivir pensando, sabiendo que no puedo hacer otra cosa].[27]

Like Ortega, Zambrano considers herself an instance of the speaking, thinking life, an organ for the self-expression of the *bios*. Her speech, especially in the writings around the time of the Spanish Civil War, offered a sort of salvation through discourse, reuniting her audience to their roots, essences, and authentic selves. Throughout her life, Zambrano held fast to the idea of a crisis of Europe or of rationality in general, taking up the Ortegan program in a manner that differs in tone and in its incorporation of motifs from Machado and Unamuno. Her speech on receiving the 1988 Cervantes Prize acknowledges Unamuno's and Ortega's books on Don Quixote as the best ones to understand "Spanish being."[28] Even at the end of her writing life, in one of the essays on the poet Emilio Prados, which we will examine later, Zambrano credits Spanish life with achieving mystical union of life and death, which is, she suggests, the task of all poets and philosophers.[29]

In Unamuno, that conflict involves two human experiences: rational thought and individual desire, fear and hope. Zambrano would presumably trace Unamuno's conflict back to a more ancient and essential one between poetry and philosophy. However, in the performativity of her texts and recuperation of a sacred element for philosophy, Zambrano resembles no one as much as Unamuno. As in *The Tragic Sense of Life*, her impassioned reproach of philosophy aims at a recasting of philosophy, the forging of a different, less philosophical philosophy, aware of its history of tyranny and ready to make a place for Spanish literature and religiosity. Although Unamuno seems to consider that philosophy's attack on the soul, immortality, and God has a stimulating effect, Zambrano would like a meditation on the divine to occupy a place of equal prestige beside philosophy, if not an honored place within it. Like Unamuno, Zambrano remains convinced of a Spanish incapacity for systematic thought and believes this philosophical shortcoming allows an "intimate structure of life" to appear.[30] Unamuno and Zambrano both consider systematic thought an impediment to an intuition deeper and more original than philosophy; that is why she claims, in her 1986 preface to *Pensamiento y poesía en la vida española*, that the work is part of something "thought, more than thought, intuited, on a much greater scale" (pensado, más que pensado, intuido, con mucho mayor amplitud) (7). Zambrano seems to have learned from Unamuno that the history of philosophy was the story of rational suppression of Christian feeling and that modernity is defined by the cataclysmic victory of reason. However, while Unamuno seems to want us to embrace the confusion and dissolution of our age and their transformative power, Zambrano dreams of reconciliation in a discourse that uncannily undermines that dream with acknowledgments of an unresolvable tension.

As Zambrano repeats her story of philosophy and poetry over the course of her writing life, she also addresses the status of the story or her "method" in telling it. Before looking at two philosophical precedents for her genealogical procedure, let's consider one of her explanations. *Notas del método* (Notes on method) consists of a brief essay on method, followed by a series of fragments about philosophical themes, designated as "Notes" (Notas).[31] Although Moreno Sanz calls it a "synthesis of the whole philosophical problematic,"[32] the same could be said of many of Zambrano's publications since 1939, and the privilege of *Notas* might lie primarily in its being her last publication, written in 1988–89, after she received wide public acclaim and before her death in early 1991. As a late opportunity to write a direct and methodical exposition of her thought, *Notas de un método* is remarkable for centering on method while refusing, once again, to sum up her thinking in clear, unequivocal theses. She identifies method with philosophy and the procedure that it has always followed in an effort to reduce experience to rational terms (27). "Experience precedes all method," she says. "One could say that experience is 'a priori' and method 'a posteriori.' But this is only valid as an indication, since true experience cannot occur without the involvement of some sort of method" (18). Zambrano seeks to manifest "true experience," this side of philosophy's methodical procedure, and so she seeks a method that would be only quasi-philosophical, whose philosophical character would not exhaust its significance. Her priority is not rational exposition but documentation of human being before reason, even if this requires an intermingling with the adversary. She does not practice a principled, programmatic discourse, but aims at a "manifestation of a knowledge that would integrate fragmentary modes of knowing to which man, especially today, is subjected" (11). Like a conventional prologue, the essay on method offers guidance for reading the book, in this case justifying the meandering, disconnected manner of the "Notes." In any case, Zambrano says the word refers more to pitches in a melody than to comments or "annotations" (12).

Zambrano fails to acknowledge, then, the approach that *Notas de un método* shares with all her other texts, a strategy that she thematizes and carries out without always acknowledging it as her method. Method—like poetry, philosophy, confession, the divine, Europe, Spain, and so on—calls for a return to its origins, to its singular point of departure in the history that leads to the present moment. Here she says that "all human tasks" (todo humano quehacer) have their origins "in some essential aspect of the human being, their root and their ground" (19). Zambrano's procedure is to give an account of this origin and narrate its divergence from its essence. In *Pensamiento y poesía*, Zambrano speaks of the necessity of returning to "something previous and necessary to the posing of the problems of Spain," an "intimate structure" that appears as "its essential, fundamental history" (25). Zambrano articulates Spain's essence as a conflict between poetry and philosophy, one that also serves to articulate the crisis of European politics and thought and, furthermore, concerns humanity in general, if not the possibility of universality itself. Zambrano's "method"—if we can still call it that in spite of her misgivings—performs *logon didonai* both in the account of the origin and in the story of the departure from the origin. Zambrano never questions her presupposition of a pristine origin and essence for the individual, for a people, and for humanity as a whole. In addition, she appears to conform to the scholastic doctrine of essences, "per se prius est eo quod est per accidens," that which is in itself is prior to that which is contingent. She does not ask about the *per se* in itself, does not clarify the self-identity of originary elements. She seeks, as it were, the essential narrative behind the accidental historical crises without analyzing the possibility and essence, as it were, of those essences. In her 2004 introduction to *Pensamiento y poesía*, Mercedes Gómez Blesa calls the idea that "poetic cognition" will solve real crises "naïve."[33] We would also do well to note, at least, that arguments that Spaniards, Europeans, and humans need to return to an authentic or proper essence, sound anachronistic, both in popular and philosophical terms.

The exposition of origins has a venerable place in the history of Western thought, and perhaps we should not let Zambrano's essentialist vocabulary distract us from the dynamic potentials of her customary narrative procedure. Zambrano does not explicitly acknowledge two narratives of origins that resemble those she tells throughout her oeuvre. First, we should recall Rousseau's accounts of the emergence of social, economic, and linguistic communities throughout his work. Like Zambrano, Rousseau elaborates an imaginary scene of human encounters and emotions whose consequences continue in the cultural institutions to which they have given rise. The *Second Discourse on Inequality* includes a methodical aside that could serve for the *First Discourse* as well as the *Essay on the Origins of Language*. Rousseau acknowledges that there are no records of the transition from a state of nature to human society. Therefore, he proposes that we should "frame conjectures based solely on the nature of man and of the Beings that surround him."[34] The results are "hypothetical and conditional reasonings" (139), that is, an account of how the origins must have been, based on the manifest consequences of the structure of origination. The *First Discourse* devotes its first part to exploring the origins of inequality in classic Greek and Roman histories, but the second part turns to "the Sciences and Arts themselves" as instances of humans' departure from a state of nature. In the "Essay on the Origin of Languages," Rousseau infers a primordial poetry that characterized the peaceful, pristine state of natural man before the imposition of a philosophical or political authority: "At first men spoke only poetry; only much later did it occur to anyone to reason" (246). As language evolves, Rousseau says, it becomes more analytical, more "exact and clear," but it also loses its warmth and spontaneity and becomes "more sluggish, subdued, and cold" (253). Such a change affects "not its words but its genius," as poetic speech becomes something more like philosophy (253). For Rousseau, since the origin of language lay in emotion rather than practical needs, its origins should be imagined to occur in southern lands. Rousseau's description of the birth of language along with love at water wells suggests that he situates it not in areas of great natural abundance but those where humans had to gather to collect the adequate and easily available resources nature provided in exceptional places (see "Origin," 271–72). That is, Rousseau saw the origin of languages in an in-between climate like the Mediterranean.

Zambrano refers to Nietzsche as part of the crisis of rationality, discussing the concept of the overman and the death of God, but she does not acknowledge her debt to his genealogical method. In the first part of *Zur Genealogie der Moral* (*Genealogy of Morals*), he avails himself of his expertise in ancient Greek literature to discuss the emergence of a feeling of good and evil as a tool of the powerful. In the second part, however, he deduces what *must* have happened before history—"in the longest period of the human race, that of its prehistoric accomplishments"—in order to imagine the origin of guilt and conscience.[35] *Die Geburt der Tragödie* (*The Birth of Tragedy*) resembles Zambrano's essential histories not only in the narrative approach to a contemporary problem (for Nietzsche, the failure to appreciate Wagner's powerful artistic innovations), but also in its conclusions. As is well known, Nietzsche proposes that all art embodies a relationship between two opposing drives or "worlds" (Kunstwelten).[36] The Apollonian strives for imagery and light, providing pleasure through spatial equilibrium and graceful movement, and the Dionysian represents frenzy, ecstatic union in drunken revelry. The first sections of *The Birth* tell a history of Greek art and literature according to the relationship that obtains in between the Apollonian and Dionysian forces. Nietzsche believes it is necessary to explain art's origins in order to understand its materialization in the struggle between two antagonistic human impulses. Such an understanding will eventually rouse sympathy for Wagner's work, to which Nietzsche devotes the latter sections of *The Birth of Tragedy*. For Nietzsche, Wagner's philistine audience has lost a sense of art's fundamental structure, and with it, an ability to respond in a profoundly human way to music and spectacle that hearkens back to the origins of art.

In between the discussion of art's "duplicity" (Duplizität) (G 25; E 19 [revised]) and the interpretation of Wagner, Nietzsche tells a story that resembles Zambrano's later explanation of the relation between poetry and philosophy, describing how a philosophical attitude comes to dominate the creativity and productivity at the heart of human society: "Whereas in all truly productive men instinct is the creative-affirmative force [die schöpferisch-affirmative Kraft] and consciousness is the dissuader and critic, in the case of Socrates the instinct is the critic and consciousness the creator" (G 90; E 84 [revised]). "Aesthetic Socratism" operates by the dictum, "Everything must be understandable [verständig], in order to be beautiful" (G 85; E 79 [revised]). Socrates's victory drives Dionysius into a "mystery cult" that, Nietzsche says, eventually took over the world, and poetry is forced to subordinate itself to dialectic in order to survive (G 93; E 87). Nietzsche and Zambrano are both interested in hybrid phenomena, such as how, in Nietzsche's words, Plato's "creative gifts forced him to develop an art form deeply akin to the existing forms which he had repudiated," that is, the Socratic dialogue (G 93; E 87). Although Nietzsche remains in some ways the champion of art and life-affirming creative ecstasy, Zambrano devotes herself to inquiries into the restriction of poetry and Christian religiosity for the sake of their continued existence under the reign of philosophy, hoping, ostensibly, for a rehabilitation of the sacred and poetic. As in Nietzsche, Zambrano's narrative of poetry and philosophy personifies its antagonists, occasionally referring to specific poets and philosophers in a blend of interpretation and outright mythopoesis.

Zambrano's work has a recognizable procedure, in spite of the difficulty of finding and following a guiding thread in some individual texts. She presumes, first of all, an origin for the phenomena that pique her interest. Those phenomena are inevitably bound up with a contemporary crisis, which Zambrano understands as the consequences of a departure from the proper shape and dynamics present at the origin. She then elaborates a vision of the origin and indicates, occasionally, moments in which the original configurations show through the haze produced by human history's deviation from the origin. Those moments are often benevolent, such as Augustine's turning Greek consciousness back toward the sacred.[37] But she understands her contemporary moment as an apocalypse of sorts, especially full of indications of the origin, such that humanity can hardly go on so blind to its own detachment from its authentic roots. After assessing how she characterizes the modern crisis as a consequence of unresolved tension between literature and philosophy, we will see how Zambrano interprets some contemporary poetry in light of that relationship.

Reason in Crisis, in "Europe"

In 1923, Ortega claimed that *The Modern Theme* provided his definitive response to a crisis of humanity, one that required nothing less than a reorientation of thinking toward a "ratiovitalism" that would produce a "general biology." He considers himself a contemporary of Einstein in ushering in a new era of relativity.[38] In a footnote added to the 1933 edition, he comments on the ubiquity of the word "crisis," and brags that he had used it as early as 1921 and used the word in thoughts that he had "thought even earlier" than that.[39] In *Los intelectuales en el drama de España*, Zambrano devotes the first of two chapters on a "reformation of understanding"—"La reforma del entendimiento" and "La reforma del entendimiento español" ("The Reformation of Spanish Understanding"), both first published in 1937—to the motifs of *critique* and *crisis*, asserting that reason enters phases of self-examination in trying times.[40] What distinguishes her current moment, she says, echoing Ortega, is the initiation of a new phase of "constant criticism" that goes along with a new "consciousness of relativity."[41] The present crisis is not one among others; rather, it concerns, as the second "Reforma" essay explains, the essence of Spain, of Europe, and of humanity as a whole. Here she presents for the first time something like the conflict between philosophy and poetry, asserting that the novel, in particular, "presupposes a much greater human richness than philosophy."[42] According to Zambrano, in the first year of its Civil War, Spain felt the crisis of Europe more keenly than other nations because it lacked the advantages philosophy conferred. Echoing Comte's characterization of Spaniards, she claims that Spain is strong in poetic feeling but weak in philosophy, which helps all humans to find stability in the rich tumult of reality. But Spain will also, for Zambrano, provide the key for all of Europe to overcome the crisis with a "Spanish reformation" that will be valid for all of Europe, will be "deeper than [the reformation] brought about by Descartes and Galileo," and will inaugurate a new world in which reason's others have a renewed status.[43] It should come as no surprise that Zambrano felt deeply the unrest of her time, and even that she perceived it as possessing a certain logic within the development of reason. After looking at her historical context—one she shares until the late 1930s with her three predecessors—we will consider some of the parallels within the philosophical tradition.

The political and social unrest of the nineteenth and twentieth centuries and the unprecedented loss of life in their wars gave the distinct impression, even without the discourses of crisis, that rationality had failed, or even that it was itself destroying Europe. Zambrano says in *La agonía de Europa* that Europe is defined by the mastery of nature, a project that she sees as complete.[44] She is referring to the way in which the instrumental value of reason has resulted in a massive growth in the effectiveness of technology to control natural processes, including medicine and food production. For Zambrano, this manipulation of nature has not been accompanied by a commensurate easing of the burdens of living; in fact, technology has also improved means of manipulating public opinion through propaganda and the destructive powers wielded by the police and military. In the crisis of reason, instrumental rationality falls out of step with the fundamental values of human life that were assumed—since the Enlightenment, at least—to be rational human rights.

Zambrano does not speak very specifically or directly about any of the major crises she lived through. *Horizonte del liberalismo* and some chapters of *Los intelectuales* speak of the Restoration attempt at constitutional monarchy and the rise of fascism. In *Delirium and Destiny*, she tells of her experience of the euphoria surrounding the declaration of the Spanish Second Republic, in 1931. Before that, Miguel Primo de Rivera had relieved the country of the failed policies and indecisive bickering of alternating liberal and conservative parties, but at the price of a military dictatorship. For the first twenty-three years of the century, those national parties had agreed to share power by a system of taking turns in a dynamic designed to share blame for political failures and to avoid the series of coups that characterized nineteenth-century Spanish governance. It is little wonder, then, that what appeared to be rational solutions designed to achieve stability might have seemed mediocre and superficial. During the 1936 elections, the liberal majority in the republican legislature instituted universal suffrage, including women. One result was the increase in votes for the conservative party, as many women deferred to conservative clergy's calls to vote for a coalition of right-wing parties determined to dismantle the very reforms that helped the women gain power. In short, the rational ideal of gender equality contributed to the larger decay of the progressive politics that pursued it. In *Agonía*, Zambrano will extend this dynamic to Europe in general, claiming that "European thought got trapped in its own victories" (30) and describing how Europe's best accomplishments—painting, literature, philosophy, and now also democratic politics—were engaged in their own self-destruction (32).

The idea of a sense of crisis internal to reason—that reason gets itself into trouble all by itself—goes back as far as ancient Greece. We saw earlier how Aristotle and Descartes both warn that those with more philosophical training might be precisely the least capable of a reflection on metaphysical principles. At the beginning of his 1935 Vienna lecture, entitled "Philosophy and the Crisis of European Humanity," Edmund Husserl says that his theme is commonplace for his time, but certainly the sense that reason itself was losing its central significance for Europe and, consequently, for humanity as a whole, had intensified in the two centuries before Husserl, Ortega, and Zambrano wrote about *crisis*. In his *First Discourse on Inequality*, Rousseau declared outright the incompatibility of virtue with the arts and sciences, to which he attributes a common rational approach to the world (1). The following centuries display a series of different variations on this theme, as thinkers develop arguments and analyses of reason's failings, while struggling to distinguish their own discourses from an exclusively rational point of view. For example, Rousseau's appeal to his own unequivocal good will requires him to develop a theory of the duplicity of speech and writing, so as to blame the shortcomings of his writings on language, rather than anything proper to his own good heart.[45] After the industrial revolution, the feeling emerged of a world going to pieces. Kant's preface to the *Critique of Pure Reason* begins by narrating how "human reason" "precipitates itself into darkness and contradiction" by overstepping legitimate limits to its use.[46] In other words, the possession of some elements of rationality provides access to possibilities of evil and ignorance beyond what a merely irrational person might accomplish. Kant goes on to treat "antinomies of pure reason," demonstrating how reason can sometimes establish two contradictory arguments, a "thesis" and an "antithesis."[47] In his wake, Russian nihilists bluntly declared that reason destroys its own authority. If reason can lead to two mutually exclusive conclusions about anything, they seem to conclude, it can support incompatible propositions about everything. Fyodor Dostoyevsky's *Brothers Karamazov* represents this position in the character of Ivan, who maintains, in his "poem" of the Grand Inquisitor, that reason serves the interests of a cynical, power-hungry inquisitor, rather than support the generosity and kindness of Christ.[48] Ivan's despair and the anxieties of other characters are expressed in the nihilist maxim, "Everything is permitted."[49] This well-known statement is not true because no rationales are necessary to determine actions but, rather, because all rationales—including those that justify evil actions—can supposedly give an account of their foundation in reason. The negative *pathos* of Russian nihilism finds a positive counterpart in Nietzschean nihilism, since he considers its destructiveness a sign of strength and a resource for the impending "revaluation of all values."[50] For Nietzsche, it is reason itself that calls attention to the irrationality at its own foundations, motivating us to ponder the choices that allowed it to attain its particular form of power and prestige in Europe. In a similar way, Karl Marx diagnosed a crisis of reason in which "everything that is solid melts into air," foreseeing that the change in conditions of production brought about by industrialization would impact the rational political and economic discourses that sustained bourgeois society.[51]

Zambrano scholars agree upon the privileged status of Heidegger for Zambrano. Moreno Sanz says that Heidegger was her "quintessential 'philosopher,'" and Laura Llevadot Pascual, in a recent volume devoted the relationship between Zambrano and Heidegger, concurs with Moreno Sanz's judgment that "all of Zambrano's work . . . is literally a response to Heidegger's 'question' of Being."[52] However, her only direct commentary on Heidegger consists largely of a lengthy quotation from *Juan de Mairena*, and a study of her relationship to his work would require an elaboration of implicit connections based on "obvious" but not always literal references to him and the presence of his books in the library at the Fundación María Zambrano.[53] Husserl's "Crisis" essay provides a more direct point of contact and sets out a similar task in the name of a restoration of an original rationality, rather than a "new," "poetic" reason. In "Philosophy and the Crisis of European Humanity," or the Vienna lecture, Husserl acknowledges the widespread sense that Europe is undergoing a spiritual crisis. "The European nations are sick," he says.[54] While physicians may be able to cure bodily ailments using their knowledge of the mechanisms of nature, there as yet exists no widely accepted figure to address *spiritual* illness. Medicine treats physiological life with great success, but there is as yet little recognition that the "so-called humanistic disciplines" address a more comprehensive principle, "purposeful life accomplishing spiritual products" (270). German expresses "spiritual" and "human sciences" with the same root, *Geist*, which can refer to and has been translated as both *spirit* and *mind*. Husserl mentions Dilthey's effort to define the validity of the humanities or human sciences (*Geisteswissenschaften*) in a manner that would clearly distinguish them from the natural sciences (*Naturwissenschaften*), and decades later he laments the failure of that effort, saying that Dilthey and his followers were still "caught in objectivism" (296).[55] For Husserl, a successful differentiation of the two would require not just comparative analysis of two distinct kinds of science but the development of a theory of the *Umwelt*, or surrounding life-world, which he begins in his final, unfinished book, *The Crisis of the European Sciences and Transcendental Phenomenology: An Introduction to Phenomenological Philosophy*. The absence of such a theory has left natural scientists free to define the human sciences in a privative manner, according to Husserl; they view the human sciences as merely descriptive and historical, with no power to formulate laws about what should happen in the future (271). Ortega sought to remedy this weakness by proposing a framework in which a ratiovitalist doctrine—with a name that misleadingly suggests it is a natural science, "general *biology*"—could direct the future. For Husserl, the natural sciences have no right to establish norms and standards for the human sciences. The former fail to take into account how "purposeful life" differs from natural life and how encounters with "spiritual products" sustain human beings by generating meaning for life. The European "illness," Husserl says, results from this failure to effectively maintain the prestige of the humanities against the disparagement of natural sciences. While Husserl will address the value of philosophy in particular, he clearly advocates for the recognition and elevation of the humanities in a broad sense, including the arts and letters and the disciplines that study them.

For Husserl, the first step to overcoming the "crisis of the European sciences" involves providing a properly philosophical education, even *before* the philosophical project of a theory of the *Umwelt*. Philosophy—he says in a discussion that very much resembles the concerns of Unamuno, Machado, and Zambrano—has created the crisis by itself, by defining itself in a restrictive way during the modern age. The natural scientists' disdain for the humanities originates in their "one-sided rationalism," which is mistaken for "philosophical rationality as such" (292). Husserl calls their perspective "portentous naturalism" (273) and later "objectivism" (292). Contemporary philosophers fail to see that their practices of acquiring universally valid knowledge occur in a particular theoretical matrix that grounds those practices in intersubjective communication and a specific determination of their objects of study. Such a disciplinary world is, for Husserl, a particular region of the larger "surrounding life world" with which this phenomenon is concerned (295). The cultures of Europe experience crisis because the natural sciences have taught people to misjudge spiritual products like art and literature by the standards of the natural sciences. But, Husserl says, it would be more accurate to say that the human sciences, in general, or at least one of them, philosophy, has itself constructed the objective realm of phenomena in which the natural sciences operate. In this way, neither should the humanities be treated as a kind of deficient natural science, nor are human and natural sciences simply instances of a common conception of science. Rather, the human sciences, in their concern with the intellect or the spiritual (*das Geistliche*), has logical priority over the natural sciences. For Husserl, "nature is itself drawn into the spiritual sphere" through humanistic activity (298). That is, natural scientists must draw nature into the *Umwelt*—in a humanistic operation—in order to carry out their investigations. Strangely, this prior framing of a realm of inquiry into nature can be merely implicit, to the point of being ignored and even repudiated—retroactively, as it were—in the methodologies of the natural sciences, which can operate effectively without any need to pay attention to the conditions of their possibility.

Phenomenology, in its turn, belongs to the larger project of Europe, which Husserl goes to some lengths to describe in the Vienna lecture. He defines the idea of Europe as the origin and center of human efforts to achieve universal knowledge, telling of the origins of "the spiritual shape of Europe" in ancient Greece. On its appearance, Europe as an idea was a "new form of community" (278). Remaining valid today, it does not limit itself to an ethnic group or geographic region and projects itself into the future as part of its very constitution, since, Husserl says, it "renews itself through ideas" (278). Ideas take the form of "unconditioned truths" that are discovered and "reconstructed" throughout human history, remaining valid for those who choose to assume the universal human subjectivity he refers to as "Europe" (278–79). In short, Europe emerges through "free shaping of its existence, its historical life, through ideas of reason, through infinite tasks" (274). Its beginning involved a tearing away from a "natural primordial attitude" but retains a connection to it; the human is "first and always in the natural sphere" but adds to that a "universal critique of all life and all life-goals" (283). Husserl speculates that the origin of Europe might lie in play, or perhaps in interaction with neighboring human communities that provoke an inquiry into the possibility of shared knowledge and thoughts. That is to say, the "infinite task" of a search for universals in the midst of life results not from calculation of advantage but from a feeling; it is "the expression of a vital presentiment that arises through unprejudiced reflection" (275). Needless to say, philosophy is the discipline that, for Husserl, formulates the "critique" and bears its standard, but the source of its force and energy lies—as we have heard from Spanish writers—in a feeling of life.

I am not convinced that Zambrano's thought takes a precise enough shape to bear sustained comparison to Heidegger's radicalization of Husserl. The younger philosopher's initial project of an analytic of Dasein aims at outlining the existential possibilities implicit in the being that has Being as an issue for it. That would include something like philosophy, the specific possibility of inquiring into traditional ontological themes on the basis of the existential analytic, even before the latter has clarified the structure of Dasein. But *Being and Time* also describes a process of *Destruktion* carried out on the philosophical tradition. While one can debate the adequacy of Heidegger's manner of reading the texts of the tradition, it seems undeniable that Zambrano's approach to previous thinkers does not pay close attention to texts or intend to engage them as intimately as Heidegger does. *Being and Time* often reminds readers that it does not intend to provide a complete topography of Dasein, focusing instead only on those possibilities that account for and provide guidance for an incipient question of Being.[56] But even so, he certainly suggests that the analytic of Dasein ought to provide for a broader concept of the human than that offered by modern subjectivity. In the 1946 "Letter on Humanism," in comments on the earlier treatise, Heidegger states rather directly his suspicion that philosophical humanism may have underestimated the human.[57] In general, Zambrano would have said the same thing as Husserl and Heidegger: the "crisis" ought to lead to a broader concept of the human as a rational being. One name would be the "poetico-rational" being, the animal endowed not just with poetry and reason but with poetic reason, an ostensibly single mode of existence in which two antagonistic traits interact.

The "Ancient Quarrel," to Be Continued

In "The Reformation of Spanish Understanding," Zambrano contrasts a philosophical transformation of reality with the novel's presupposition of a worldly richness that it accepts without reservations. The two books she wrote almost simultaneously in her first year of residency abroad—right after the military defeat of the Spanish Republic in early 1939—begin to elaborate the narration of conflict between philosophy and poetry as the "essential story" that lies at the basis of the contemporary crisis in Spain and Europe. The ancillary texts of the *Obras completas* provide an account of the composition of what editor Moreno Sanz calls her "twin works": Zambrano wrote the first chapter of *Filosofía y poesía*, "Pensamiento y poesía" (Thought and poetry), first, in May 1939, at the urging of Octavio Paz. After that, she wrote the twenty-five chapters of *Pensamiento y poesía en la vida española* for a series of talks given in Mexico City in June and revised for publication in the following months.[58] While working at the Universidad Michoacana, Zambrano drafted four more chapters to *Filosofía y poesía* and turned them in to the publisher by early October. In a curious "Nota explicativa" (Explanatory note) included in the *Obras completas*, Zambrano places *Filosofía y poesía* at the center of her work, as "one of those centers that move one's vocation," and she adds that, "for this reason, it does not need to be rewritten, and even less does it need to be rethought."[59] While we could treat the books from 1939 as practically a single work, Zambrano will go on to repeat some prominent motifs throughout work of the 1940s and to expand on the narrative offered by the first chapter of *Filosofía y poesía* of the history of philosophy and poetry's divergence and relation. A survey of the development of this story should make it clear how Zambrano's texts do not advocate for a definitive fusion but an ongoing and multifaceted interaction. The "ancient quarrel" that Plato refers to goes back to the dawn of history, if not the dawn of thinking, and is to be continued; that is, the vital interests of humanity demand that they remain in relation to each other as others.

While Zambrano emphasizes that the conflict between philosophy and poetry occupies European history from ancient Greece to what she calls "today," it is remarkable how fascinated she remains with the origin of the divergence. *Pensamiento y poesía* provides a brief account of Greek thinking before turning to Spanish life and thinking, where, she says, that "divergence" retains its clearest form. The Spanish history of philosophy and poetry differs from the European one, she says, setting out in *Pensamiento y poesía* to explain "its fundamental instants, with its decisive changes" (48). That story also begins with ancient Greece but carries out its work in between the two extremes that emerged there. Echoing Nietzsche's *Birth of Tragedy*, she identifies philosophy as "methodical rational knowledge" and poetry as openness, "[offered] in an integral way without offering resistance to anything" (48). The history of the Spanish relation, Zambrano says, observes events in between these two extremes, where "Spanish culture rises up, with its poetic knowledge" (48).[60] In one of the most extensive definitions of "poetic reason," Zambrano identifies "poetic knowledge" with "poetic reason" in contrast to the truth of *aletheia*: poetic reason is "gracious and gratuitous revelation." The poetic operates by principles coming from the realm of religion—grace and revelation—whereas philosophical reason "conquers" (50). That being said, the same paragraph says that "poetic knowledge" "is achieved through an effort on the part of someone who meets an unknown presence half way" (50). While the mention of "conquest" suggests that Spaniards did indeed—in a uniquely consequential way—practice the dominant form of knowledge, this "half way" emphasizes that one can practice "poetic reason" only by virtue of dwelling in between, where one must move *actively* toward the "extreme" of poetic passivity. One can presumably confirm this structure in the instances she examines—Spanish stoicism, mysticism, and novel writing, Seneca, Jorge Manrique, and Benito Pérez Galdós—and learn from this tradition how to realize an alternative to European history. At least that is what Zambrano asserts in the introductory chapters of *Pensamiento y poesía*. "La crisis del racionalismo europeo" foresees a reconfiguring of European culture in which Spain leads from behind and poetry recuperates an honorable place alongside philosophy: a "new knowing" will be "poetic, philosophical, and historical" and will provide a "reconciliation, a new intimacy [entrañamiento]" (21). While *Filosofía y poesía* will go deeper into what it will take for the non-Spanish European to join in the "new knowing," later texts of the 1940s will make especially clear that "reconciliation" is not a simple synthesis.

Filosofía y poesía's introductory chapter, "Pensamiento y poesía" could be seen as a logical preliminary to the book *Pensamiento y poesía*, devoting two sections to the origins of this "divergence—which has many times been enmity" (*Pensamiento*, 16).[61] The dichotomy receives many characterizations throughout Zambrano's work. The first chapter of *Filosofía* has them divide in Plato into, on the one hand, "the methodical effort to capture something that we don't have and need to have," and, on the other hand, a "[loyalty] to primitive, ecstatic admiration" (16–17). Philosophy achieves clarity and security, and it offers knowledge of "something firm, something so true, compact, and independent that it is absolute, it needs no support and offers its support to all comers" (18). By contrast, "poetry pursued, of all things, the disdained multitude, the underappreciated heterogeneity, excluding nothing" (19). As suggested by Andrew Bush when he calls this story a "cosmogony," this curious story does not concern the disciplines or discourses that go by the conventional names *philosophy* and *poetry*.[62] In *El hombre y lo divino*, she will refer to them as "attitudes," but, in the beginning, they appear more like gods playing dramatic roles in a mythical episode. *Filosofía y poesía*'s first paragraph insists that "[poetry and thought] both want to have for themselves the soul where they will make their nest" (13). They pull individuals toward their own domain and attempt to exclude their adversary. Some lucky individuals, Zambrano says, can enjoy their "parallel developments" and others connect them (*trabarse*) "in a single expressive form," but the truth is, she says, "they clash" (se enfrentan) and their coexistence can ruin lives (13). Despite their separate drives for hegemony, Zambrano's later comments make it clear that philosophy cannot be dispensed with: it relieves us of the unbearable burden of life in the midst of constant change. Poetry retains a connection with origins and with others, but forfeits to philosophy even its basic ability to give an account of its own necessity, and this is what gives rise to the history to which Zambrano will dedicate the third and fourth chapters of *Filosofía y poesía*.

"Mística y poesía" and "Poesía y metafísica" extend the history of the conflict across the ages and provide a principle for the movement. After invoking again the *Republic*'s expulsion of poets, Zambrano attributes to Plato the establishment of philosophical domination of poetry, integrating poetry into a realm of rational action (59, 73). Although the narrative is not easy to follow because of Zambrano's lacunal and sometimes idiosyncratic interpretations, one can make out phases and figures that represent a "dramatic conflict" (14). She will repeat this history in *El hombre y lo divino*, attempting at one point to impose a clear structure of "stages" that does not get carried out as promised.[63] After Greece, philosophy and poetry become entangled in various medieval forms, finding "reconciliation" in mysticism and "unification, for the only time, perhaps," in *La Divina Commedia* (*El hombre*, 75). Leonardo Da Vinci represents a resurgence of the philosophical and begins the slow push to alienate God from European thought and the poetic from the conception of the human. *El hombre y lo divino* includes a representation of Descartes as the arrival of a concept of consciousness that exists in and of itself (163). From here, both texts describe "idealism" and "Romanticism," with mention of a long list of thinkers and poets to whom Zambrano attributes at times an overestimation of reason and at times a "new identification" of philosophy and poetry. Regarding systematic thought in general, she cannot seem to decide whether it is an apotheosis of the philosophical or, as in "Poema y sistema," an "intimate, essential, and living unity," a "unity that is identity."[64] From what happens next, I speculate that the ambiguity comes from the fact that philosophy brings about this union by defining poetry in terms of individual creation and initiative, rather than the passivity that is proper to it, to Zambrano's mind. Both versions of the story tell of a post-Hegelian emergence of a new "detachment" (*Filosofía*, 82). She associates the names of Baudelaire and Kierkegaard, Nietzsche and Valéry with a phase in which poetry produces its own theory and breaks philosophy's domination of it. Philosophy's response, in *El hombre* at least, is to look outside the human to the nonhuman, a process she also identifies with Marx (182). For reasons that I have mentioned, a close examination of these interpretations might have to neglect Zambrano's stated principle of reading for the essential; however, neither the short history in *Filosofía y poesía* nor the longer one in *El hombre y lo divino* seems to treat philosophers as anything more than representatives of a historical epoch. In that sense, however, she homogenizes the *corpora* in spite of her other, "poetic" principle of recognizing differences. In any event, Zambrano does indeed describe history as a dynamic interaction between two archetypes: "Each time that the reconciliation between two apparently irreconcilable principles is achieved . . . the struggle [rises up] anew" (*Filosofía*, 74). The history of philosophy and poetry—which conventional scholarship keeps apart—involves a cyclical movement of rapprochements and renewed antagonism.

Filosofía y poesía appears especially distant from political problems, except that the second chapter, "Poesía y ética," questions the genuineness of philosophical ethics, preferring the "charitable justice" of poetry to the calculations and self-reflective foundation of all rational thought (28). *Pensamiento y poesía*'s final chapter returns to Spanish particularity, asserting that it bears a "new hope," "expressed" or "revealed" in poetry (108). This concludes a series of meditations in which Spaniards and Spanish cultural products provide models for a "new culture" of poetic knowledge that hovers between philosophy and poetry (52). *Filosofía y poesía*'s final chapter dwells at length on philosophy's "reprehensible" deficiencies in knowledge and action, eventually contrasted with the humility, hopefulness, and receptivity of the "non-philosophers" (101–4). Recalling what Machado advises poets about reading Heidegger, Zambrano says the poetic nonphilosophers know better than to cross the threshold of the door to philosophy: "going towards Philosophy, to stop at the threshold [dintel] itself, without crossing it, because they have learned, at least, that once they cross it they will be lost forever [han sabido, eso sí, que una vez cruzado ya no tendría remedio posible]" (105). Poets remain bound to origins, reflecting on them and loving them like good children love their parents. This newly ethical stance echoes Machado also in the dynamic of philosophical approaches to poetry and vice versa, except that it appears that something like poetry presides over the relation, since "poetry is to flee and to search for, to receive a summons and get a fright, it is a departure and return, to be called only to run away, an anguish without limits and an all-embracing love" (107). *El hombre*'s reflection on origins and history gives a more prominent place to religion—the "revelation" carried out by poetic reason—in what she calls "the dispute of poetry with philosophy about the gods." Zambrano devotes four of its chapters to different practices that would rehabilitate what she believes excessive philosophy has squelched: the divine, piety, and the experience of love, death, and God. Like in her earlier books, Zambrano frames *El hombre* as an effort to combat the reduction of the human to merely philosophical terms—reduced to "a simple number, degraded under the category of quantity"—and places her hope for a "liberation" in the dissemination of the right origin story (23).

Although Zambrano often lets an animosity toward what she calls "philosophy" turn into an indictment, she acknowledges the vital function of scientific knowledge. If it is in a sense irreplaceable, she means to place it in a framework it does not control and maintain it in a relationship to what she considers more essential and more comprehensive with regard to humanity. "Poetry" turns out to be both one pole of this relation and the character of the relation itself. In addition to the confusion this produces, this is a mere reversal of the earlier problem—made apparent in Husserl, for example—in which philosophy both exists among the scientific disciplines and represents the discourse that frames those disciplines by providing them with guiding concepts. Advocacy for a "poetic" framework would benefit, it seems, from the cultivation of a practice of linguistic creation that may or may not directly engage the principles of knowledge and ethics. However, the offering of a poetic counterweight to philosophy's traditional priority itself produces, rather than merely thematizing, a polemical situation of relating. *Agonía de Europa* is perhaps where the character of this primordially conflictive relating stands out most clearly as performance in addition to theme.

While *Pensamiento y poesía en la vida española* asserts that Spaniards dwell in between philosophy and poetry, *Agonía* considers the Spanish condition a version of the more general European one, and the European is "conflict personified" (75). Here and in her next book, *Confession*, Zambrano shifts the terms of the antagonism to philosophy and *life*. In *Agonía*'s account, "European violence" prefers the stability and utility of its conceptual knowledge to the original complexity of the world. For Zambrano, "European man" gets split into the "life system" of his own devising and another aspect that suffers from the imposition of a restrictive "system" (74–75). Through Christianity, Europeans forge a life in between their constituent extremities, the philosopher and the religious person. Zambrano does not abandon her privileging of her own people or nation. For her, Augustine created the form of humanity as this in-between, creating a "new culture called Europe" in Africa (65), being himself "African, almost Spanish" (78–79). The first chapter reflects upon the contemporary crisis of this conception, not because of an excess of conflict, but because the conflict seems to nearly die out with the domination of one side, the philosophical. Europe seems, she says, to have given itself over to facts and deeds, and as a result of its very effectiveness at stabilizing reality and providing for itself, it falls into "decadence" (23). Not only that, but, as in Husserl's *Crisis*, the success of Europe's particular talent—scientific theory and knowledge—produces a "poison" that gets injected back into it (30). Zambrano frames her account of the historical struggle here, then, as the "[attempt] to find the essence of what we call Europe" and with it "the principle of a possible resurrection" (42). As Rodolphe Gasché argues, Zambrano envisions this "resurrection" not as a simple return from death to life but as an ongoing agonic struggle, a maintenance of life through the relation to the other.[65] When Zambrano refers to Europe as a ghost, it is not because a ghost is dead, but because ghosts dwell between life and death, neither living nor deceased. One knows ghosts, therefore, but not entirely. She calls Europe "a ghost that demands to be understood" and even "wants to be returned . . . to life" (44). But a return to life, or to come to fully know the specter, would result in its losing its essential character as a ghost.

By the same token, Zambrano regards the human as an unresolved and unresolvable tension between what she calls "philosophy" and "poetry," words that designate particular attitudes through which individuals and human communities can be understood. An excess of either "poetry" or "philosophy" causes problems; consequently, she projects a constant alertness and spontaneity, always ready to move back toward the opposite extreme. This is a unity without fusion, togetherness without synthesis, a reconciliation that does not relinquish vigilance, a space for both security and chance, method and revelation, thought and intuition. These are the things most often promised by the "poetic reason" attributed to Zambrano. But we would be justified in asking why Zambrano did not seem to privilege this term or even to state its principle in the form of a proposition. We can only speculate that a proposition errs on the side of the philosophical, and "poetic reason," in spite of its grammar, partakes more of the poetic than of what she considers "reason." It is not a reason purified of its abuses and transgressions; rather, the use of "poetic reason," like that of all reason, must assume its potential for harm at the same time that it lays claim to the proven benefits.

"Poetic Poetry": Zambrano and Her Contemporaries

Despite sometimes vilifying philosophy, Zambrano does not cease to call herself a philosopher.[66] As scholars commonly point out, her allegiance to poetry determines her adoption of the role of philosopher. We can expect that the relation played itself out in her life and writing, in addition to being thematized there, and we might suspect that her mention of an "unsuccessful professional career" caused by the "double pull" (doble tirón) mentioned in the first paragraph of *Filosofía y poesía* applies to her. After an exhausting stint of lecturing and teaching in Mexico, she managed to continue writing in spite of the economic precariousness of not holding an academic position. We might also suspect that her reference to "fortunate" individuals for whom literature and philosophy worked in tandem ("at the same time and in parallel fashion") or combined "in a single expressive form" remained a dream or goal, or even, as the canonical interpretation has it, a reality apparent to readers who are themselves "poetic" enough (*Filosofía*, 13). We would do well to ask, then, how the agonistic relationship depicted—albeit in an inconstant way—in the narrative of philosophy and poetry bears on her relationship to poetry and poets. While *La agonía de Europa* and other texts suggest that philosophy's conquest of poetry can never be complete or definitive, her theme of the "poetic poetry" of her generation implies the impossibility of a poetic victory over philosophy. She explicitly associates poetry with life and its origins, while philosophy has to do with the stabilization and maintenance of life. For Zambrano, a final fixing of their relation or the deactivation of one or the other would spell death.

This dynamic plays out in her meditations on the work of Emilio Prados. For the moment, I recall Zambrano's curious note in *Filosofía y poesía* stating that Prados "has made me see all of this that I am saying," where she speaks of the untenability of the poet's position, or rather, that of the "poet's poet" (el poeta del poeta) (107). Prados will represent the relationship between poetry and philosophy in action throughout his life. For

Prados, Zambrano's philosophy qualified her for the title of "the ideologue and principal representative of the Generation of 27."[67] Among commonplace characterizations of the group's members was an effort to distance themselves from Antonio Machado and his disdain for baroque's excessively "philosophical" character. Several of the members went on to teach Hispanic studies abroad, publishing, in addition to their poems, scholarly studies and anthologies of Spanish poetry. In spite of this engagement of literature and philosophy, the generation's scholarship maintained conventional forms and depended on traditional critical concepts. Prados's identification of Zambrano's thinking with the Generation of 27 is strange, then, for several reasons. Prados was an intimate friend of Zambrano, but he did not feel especially comfortable belonging to the Generation of 27, having asked to be left out of Gerardo Diego's 1932 anthology.[68] Though there are certainly similarities between Zambrano and the group, her belonging seems to rest more on simple synchrony than on her agreement with the group's unifying traits.[69] She did not write poems, nor was she present at the founding event, an homage to Luis de Góngora on the three hundredth anniversary of his death. She also did not share their sense of urgency to distance themselves from Antonio Machado for the sake of new literary directions, continuing to refer to Machado's accomplishments and to share his concerns. In addition, the poets of the Generation of 27 hardly needed an ideologue. Many of them wrote theoretical texts on poetry or poetics, such as Dámaso Alonso's *Poesía española: ensayo de métodos y límites estilísticos*, Pedro Salinas's *Reality and the Poet in Spanish Poetry*, and Jorge Guillén's *Language and Poetry* (the latter two published originally in English). Some points of contact could certainly be indicated: Federico García Lorca's interest in the ineffable *duende* as it is manifested in his poetry through a persistent interest in popular, intuitive arts such as flamenco music and dancing, bullfighting, and the blues; the interest in poets' relationships to reality, whether it is authentic perception of things or the elaboration of a reality more genuine than that of sensory perception; the reverence the poets showed for Golden Age precedents and other figures in a Spanish canon. Finally, Zambrano hardly embraced the role of ideologue for a generation in her own brief essay entitled "Acerca de la Generación del 27" (About the Generation of 27). In it we can continue to see the tense but fertile relation between philosophy and poetry that will play out in essays that speak more directly about poetry in general than about specific poets or poems.

In his "María Zambrano y la Generación del 27," James Valender observes that Zambrano wrote "Acerca de la Generación del 27" for an homage to the group of poets so categorized, published by *Ínsula* in 1977.[70] It begins with—and about half of it consists of—a critique of the Ortegan concept of *generation*. She soundly rejects one of Ortega's premises, the idea that generations are a natural, regular occurrence in cultural life, and she asserts, instead, that the changes that distinguish one group, style, or current from the next are irregular and vary in frequency and radicality. Of more interest for Zambrano than these regular groupings—the early twentieth century conventionally gets broken down into generations of '98, '14, '27, '36, the '50s—are *ruptures*.[71] For her, the Generation of '27 was not just a chronological grouping but a disruptive event. In short, in an homage predicated on the concept of generation, Zambrano suggests that the concept fails to address literary history's real meaning, even though its significance in literary history motivated this very homage.

The rest of "Acerca de la Generación del 27" concerns two commonplaces about the group, affirming, this time, an Ortegan notion about the specific generation. She mentions the rehabilitation of Góngora's reputation in the 1927 celebration, an intention that establishes that particular year as "the knife-edged summit of a historical moment" (160). In addition, she defines this reevaluation in terms that recall the idea of modernity, defined by Ortega y Gasset as "dehumanization." She describes the "knife-edged summit" as "an awakening and putting into gear not only of poetry itself—in Spain only?—in its makers, but also in the way that those who have need of it receive it, being poets in their own way" (160). Zambrano does not point it out, but she is repeating two characteristics of Ortega's seminal "La deshumanización del arte." First, the contemporary art that Ortega describes is "artistic art," it engages in a process of purification, eliminating the "human" aspects of art and maximizing the aesthetic elements.[72] All arts of a given period, including music and literature, he insists, will share the same essential traits, since "an identical inspiration, a single, self-same biological style pulsates [un mismo estilo biológico pulsa] in the several branches of art" (S 12; E 4 [revised]). In spite of her vision of generations as ruptures instead of a continuous, organic process, Zambrano agrees that the generation shares a single trait. She also agrees with Ortega's contention that the consumer of modern art and poetry must become an artist or poet, invent his or her own "unprecedented acts" (actos inéditos) to come to terms with these new objects of perception (S 27; E 20). For Zambrano, *poetry* takes over the new generation's poems, substituting its own nature for the human themes that predominated before. Readers must become poets, inventing new means to interact with these exceptional poetic creations.

At first glance, Zambrano seems to portray this generation as a moment of universalization, "dehumanization," and poetic modernity. She takes Góngora as a point of departure, but just as she did not mention Ortega in her characterization of the generation, she does not mention Alonso's well-known 1948 account of the homage to Góngora or Lorca's seminal essay on Góngora, "La imagen poética de don Luis de Góngora" ("The Poetic Image in Don Luis de Góngora").[73] While Lorca explains in detail the intensity of Góngora's work on metaphors, Zambrano's ruminations are much more abstract and detached from the texts. In her reading of poets, she frequently praises precisely their cultivation of solitude (the taking up of their own birth and death), such as she finds in Góngora's *Soledades*. Paradoxically, it is this taking up of their singularity that makes poets speak on behalf of all human beings. She writes, "It is about the liberation of poetry. About its appearing, poetry itself with its total presence: luminous and dark and a hidden fount that flows inexhaustibly through an unforeseeable channel into labyrinths that imprison by giving freedom" (161). In Góngora as well as in this generation-rupture, poetry can only be freed by becoming imprisoned; it clarifies by obscuring; it may have a channel through which it runs, but it constantly overflows this channel, disregarding the function of a riverbed, which is to indicate ahead of time where its eventual contents will flow. This spillage, waste, frustration, unpredictability is an essential part of what poetry is, what distinguishes poetry from philosophy.[74] With this in mind, Zambrano attributes this poetic character to precursors of the Generation of 27 in very formulaic ways, mere indications of how they need to be understood as frustrated projects: "Juan Ramón Jiménez 'sacrificed' "; Antonio Machado "with his thought"; and a list of poets from Romanticism to Unamuno who saw how "the shadow illuminates" (161). But, in general, Zambrano does not commit herself to reading the poets by interpreting their poems or expounding their thoughts. Rather, she limits herself to a proposition that is in itself paradoxical: the Generation of 27 distinguishes itself as the place where poetry as an archetype or principle puts itself to work and runs itself down to the ground. In this sense, Zambrano might be the "ideologue" of the generation only to the extent that she might be the "ideologue" of poetry in general. Or only to the extent that the Generation of 27 represents universal poetry, that it somehow transcends its moment and place to speak not on behalf of particular human beings or communities but for poetry as such, in a broader and more primordial sense than we are accustomed to giving it.

Accordingly, in the essays in *Algunos lugares de la poesía* (Some of poetry's places) devoted to individual writers, Zambrano considers poems to be points of access to poets, and poets as the privileged site of the manifestation of poetry. The poets are the "places of poetry" (lugares de la poesía) referred to in the title of a volume planned by Zambrano and only assembled posthumously by Ortega Muñoz.[75] For Zambrano, the concept of poetry is not deduced from the existence of poems; rather, poetry is *born*, and it is recognizable insofar as it bears the traces of its birth. *Algunos lugares* includes a brief, fragmentary text called "El nacimiento de la poesía" ("The birth of poetry"), in which the first generation of poets emerge from the rupture that begins human life. Zambrano's story, like Rousseau's account of the origin of language, begins with the human being breaking away from other creatures to become unique: "Poetry is born, like all transcendent action, from the rupture of an order, of an order previous to the separation of man as a singular creature, previous to his existence properly speaking" (69). For Zambrano, poetry coincides with the emergence of human existence proper, in the singularity of individuals. She refers, then, not to an existing thing, *poetry*, but to an activity, poetizing (*poetizar*), that plays the role of bringing the human being into his or her existence:

> But since man needed some time to feel himself existing, in this lapse, before man existed and after having been conceded the order that sheltered him, poetizing welled up in this creature, which had ceased to be a creature properly speaking, since the creature was already possessor of the word. (Mas como el hombre tardó en sentirse existir, en ese lapso, antes de que el hombre existiera y después de haber sido dejado el orden que lo albergaba, surgió el poetizar en esta criatura, que había dejado de serlo propiamente, ya dueña de la palabra.) (69)

Human existence happens in between the sheltering order she associates with philosophy and the miraculous, intangible sensation of being that she associates with poetry. The birth of poetry thus *almost* coincides with the birth of man as the *zoon logon exon*, the animal possessing rational discourse; it is hard to tell exactly whether word comes before *poetizing* or in what sense human beings existed before existing in a proper way, for themselves. The same kind of problem exists in Rousseau: the origin supplements an earlier "state," adding onto something already complete. This structure emerges in the *Origin of Languages* and elsewhere, to such an extent that one could identify this kind of logical knot as "properly" Rousseauvian.[76] In Zambrano's telling, the word provides stability to "man" even before he feels himself existing, and yet "he" only exists beyond the state of a "creature" when "he" "originates" in the coexistence of poetry and philosophy. Is there any other way to understand "word" than as an imitation of some prior thing? Zambrano insists, as does Rousseau, that language is not originally for communication; poetry was born, she says, "when the word, that is, was necessary in order to make and in order to establish, and to perform these necessary actions beyond communication, which one supposes was the originary function of the word" (cuando la palabra, pues, fue necesaria para hacer y para establecer, más allá de la comunicación que se supone sea el originario oficio de la palabra) (69). The words that "poetizing" introduces into the human being replace the original world with another, a second, less primordial "shelter" that is properly human: "The word's germ and its power of germination open together the time that is proper to man, his new shelter behind the lost orb" (el germen de la palabra y su poder de germinación abren al par el tiempo ya propio del hombre, su nuevo albergue tras del orbe perdido" (69). To poetry belongs temporalization and hence we owe to it the possibility of assuming our birth and death, our most temporal actions, in the most authentic of their possibilities. That is, to put it another way, if a human being's life is to be true to its original, essential make-up, it requires taking into account the poetic origins of our being-in-the-world. Authentic existence requires a return to poetry, which is a return to something we have, in a sense, never left and can never leave. For Zambrano, we have only allowed it to become corrupted with communication and other sources of security she associates—like Rousseau did—with philosophy and its "reason."

Another set of fragmentary notes included in *Algunos lugares* elaborates on this birth of poetry, which is the birth of the properly human being, following poetry from its origin in language per se to the modern crisis that requires a return toward poetry. Here we can see, again, poetry's status as original language, a language of the passions; and as we follow the history of poetry it again begins to take on the willfulness characteristic of a classical god or a person. "The first poetry that we are given to know" (La poesía primera que nos es dado conocer), she writes, "is language, and it seems to correspond to an age of the world in which the sacred was opening everything up" (es lenguaje y parece corresponder a una edad del mundo en que lo sagrado lo abría todo) (71). When poetry advances, with the epic, and when the sacred is replaced by the historical, poetry remains faithful to its origins, Zambrano says: "It will always maintain a certain fidelity to this, its first condition" (guardará siempre cierta fidelidad a esta su condición primera) (71). Poetry is clearly not simply writing in verse; in fact, in the beginning, it includes all language. For Zambrano, epic poetry confines the originary poetry to a particular form and is mistaken for that form, but it also gains independence: "Poetry gets its independence at the same time and on the identical occasion as when man takes it on" (la poesía cobra la independencia al mismo tiempo y con idéntica ocasión a como el hombre la toma) (73); poetry and the human being both get their freedom as particular beings from the sacred. Here is where their conflict with reason and philosophy emerge:

> With history, it gains independence and is born as poetry proper, finally detached from sacred language, since man has detached himself, too. BUT poetry, *preserving the memory of its origen*, situates itself in the time that is always a Golden Age. Poetry is born in this way as memory. And it will always conserve some memory, a memory opposed to reason. (Pero la poesía, *guardando memoria de su origen*, se sitúa en ese tiempo que es siempre una Edad de Oro. La poesía nace así como memoria. Y siempre conservará algo de memoria, de memoria opuesta a la razón.) (73 [Zambrano's italics, my emphasis added with all capitals])

This "but" I have highlighted in the middle of the passage suggests that, while poetry retains the connection with the sacred and with its origin, the human being in general *does not*. The passage continues:

> So when man decides to live his history is when the divergence between memory and reason appears; reason will create the conceptual form of thought, directed always to the future, to making possible the new form of life, to providing it with stability, balance. Memory, organ of nostalgia, always struggling to capture this other distinct time, privileged time compared to which the time that we live is only decadence. (Pues cuando el hombre se decide a vivir su historia es cuando se presenta claramente la divergencia entre memoria y razón; la razón creará la forma de pensar conceptual, dirigida siempre al porvenir, a hacer posible la nueva forma de vida, a proporcionarle firmeza, equilibrio. La memoria órgano de la nostalgia, siempre en lucha por captar este otro tiempo distinto, tiempo privilegiado del cual el que vivimos es sólo decadencia.) (73)

As we have seen, the beginning of *Filosofía y poesía* describes this conflict as a struggle between poetry and thinking for the soul of the human: "Each one of them wants for itself eternally the soul in which it builds its nest" (13). In practice, this struggle almost always results in the victory of philosophy over poetry, the relegation of poets to a kind of homelessness, or else the creation of a poetic existence lacking the security and balance that make home a shelter. In Emilio Prados she finds such a drama personified, and in his life and work she finds resources for another account of the fruitful altercation between poetry and philosophy.

"Counterpositioning": The Movement of "Poetic Reason" in Zambrano's Interpretation of Emilio Prados

Zambrano published two studies of Prados, and both treat the relationship of literature and philosophy in Prados; the second is, in fact, called "Pensamiento y poesía en Emilio Prados" (Thinking and poetry in Emilio Prados), while the first is "El poeta y la muerte" (The poet and death). As the latter title implies, Prados is treated synecdochally as a representative of poets in general; Prados is "the poet." Zambrano identifies three traits of "the poet," all of which her friend Prados exemplified. First, he is fascinated by things and thus seems removed from "reality," while he is, in fact, more attached to things than other people. Also, he experiences "continual birth" and a "true death," "living his death from a very young age."[77] None of this relates to his writing verse or his published writings. However, "El poeta y la muerte" ends with a dense passage that resembles Zambrano's account of the birth of poetry. It is meant to describe Prados's overcoming of silence thanks to philosophy. Not only does a poet remain a poet even when he is not writing poems, as Zambrano also says of Antonio Machado and Miguel Hernández.[78] His status as a poet pulls him toward silence, for to be a poet is to acquiesce to the gift of birth. Prados is "the abandoned one, in whom the one who has turned himself over to being-born has come to passively and freely remain [el abandonado en que viene a quedar pasiva y libremente el que se ha entregado al nacer], dispossessing himself first, it is true, turning himself over blindly to the light, the ultimate justice [desposeyéndose primero, eso sí, entregándose ciegamente a la luz, a la última justicia]" (195). Light, here, is not the light of reason but the light of being, that which is received in the "forest clearings" (claros del bosque) that Zambrano will also set against the pervasiveness of "rationality."[79] Prados, as poet, begins from silence: "Emilio's poetry was born from a grand silence, and, even when it was written down, he kept it quiet for a long time, and for long periods he went along in silence; he lost himself with the word" (La poesía de Emilio nacía de un gran silencio y, aun ya escrita, se la tenía callada mucho tiempo, y durante tiempos él mismo se iba en el silencio; se perdía con la palabra) (196). Just like the idea of "the abandoned one," this parallels Prados's personal life, his exile in Mexico and the solitude and isolation he expressed in letters to Zambrano.[80] But, in these two essays on the poet, the real protagonists are poetry and thought.

For Zambrano, thought did not save Prados; it just saved poetry, working as something of a midwife, helping in poetry's birth: "And from this depth, from this silence, his thinking saved poetry. The poem reached its realization by a tension of thinking. The demands of thinking helped poetry to be born" (El poema alcanzaba a realizarse por una tensión de pensamiento. La exigencia del pensamiento ayudaba a nacer a la poesía) (196–97). Now, apparently, *poetry* refers to actual written verse; the birth of poetry is the writing of poems, and the poetry needed to get written so that thinking could take place. Because thinking *had* to take place, thinking was *demanded*, the poems were born. It is in this sense that Zambrano says, evoking the title of her planned volume of essays on poetry, that "from poetry, more exactly, *from the place of poetry*, a philosophy was being made that might have proven consubstantial with it" (desde la poesía, más exactamente, desde el lugar de la poesía, se fue haciendo una filosofía consustancial con ella) (197 [emphasis added]). In contrast to the description as "consubstantial," Zambrano proposes the image of philosophy and poetry departing from a common origin with a common destination that they will never reach: "two paths that diverge from the same center and aim towards a horizon that is so wide and so distant that even though one could glimpse that they will form a circle, the two radiuses continue to look as if they were separated by a sort of unbridgeable gap" (196). Philosophy and poetry differ in their movement but share an origin and a destiny; one could be forgiven for thinking them absolute contraries. But if Zambrano does not agree with that view—which she attributes to millennia of philosophical thinking—she also does not propose the obliteration of the difference. Rather, she struggles to maintain her censure of philosophy while envisioning a new "philosophy" that lets its other remain different. The farthest Zambrano goes toward describing something like a genuine philosophy involves its function in the birthing of poetry. Clearly, this is not the philosophy that makes poetry cower in the shadows, but what she will sometimes call "poetic reason," a reason that "mediates," in a discursive sense, between antagonists whose tension structures human life. Here she says, "But, in truth, only Greek philosophy, and not in all of its moments, discovered this function, as an extreme mediator, of reason in its visible, patent mode" (Pero, en verdad, sólo la filosofía griega y no en todos sus momentos supo de esa función, extremadamente mediadora, de la razón en su modo visible, patente) (196). Philosophy, thinking, reason, all of these notions can be oppressive or liberating, and in Zambrano's discussions they more often accrue fault by overpowering poetry. But it would be an exaggeration to insist that thinking is subordinated to poetry here. One might wish she had found a better term for the element that keeps the space of altercation open. "Poetic reason" is neither poetic nor rational but a discourse exposed to their strife and committed to maintaining both difference and togetherness. Both philosophy and poetry act and need the action of the other. For Zambrano, Prados's particularity consist of the ability his case has of highlighting what must always be the case. Zambrano goes on to say that Prados "had to be a philosopher to be a poet, just as there are those who have to be poets in order to be philosophers" (197).

Zambrano does not speak, then, of a single figure that *fuses* poetry and thinking, but rather of two independent forces that make use of each other within the body of the writing poet. This is because each still has to remain itself; the difference has to be maintained:

> Poetry can not, without negating itself, depart in search of an idea of being, nor can it stabilize itself in the question about it; in a more naked struggle, it only uses reason to capture signs. (La poesía no puede, sin negarse a sí misma, partir a la búsqueda de una idea del ser, ni puede estabilizarse en la pregunta acerca de él; en una lucha más desnuda, sólo hace uso de la razón para captar sus signos.) (197)

In a way, this describes what Prados was involved in, but without saying it is what he *did*; in fact, the action is still performed by "poetry," acting in the person and in the name of Emilio Prados:

> It goes along, finding and offering a kind of alphabet . . . a kind of Odyssey around the interior of the soul . . . since, poetry, more than being transparent, accomplishes with its continual movement, which is reason, that the "things of being" should reach visibility

> and that their transparency should be felt as a presentiment. (Va encontrando y ofreciendo una especie de alfabeto. . . . Una especie de Odisea por el interior del alma . . . pues más que ser, ella, transparente, hace con su continuo moverse, que es razón, que las "cosas del ser" cobren la posible visibilidad y que se presienta su transparencia.) (197)

Poetry makes things visible without eliminating their invisibility; thanks to poetry, things can be both of this world and signs pointing to another dimension. Things are things and, simultaneously, indications of an otherness that dwells on a different level, "signs of being." In this passage we also see the meaning of *reason* that justifies calling the mediating or spatializing instance "poetic reason." The latter names "continuous movement," in which philosophy and poetry are free to approach and separate. What remains puzzling is how the same word should come to stand for movement and all the things it has traditionally meant, starting with the translation of *logos*, and including an etymological tie to *measure* and—in the principle of *ratio reddere*—the giving of an account that articulates foundations. At the same time, one could *imagine*, again, and perhaps perform, a gesture of thinking that departs from the grammatical relation of noun (*reason*) and adjective (*poetic*) to appropriate a meaning that puts poetry and reason on equal footing in a space—neither poetic nor rational—of open movement.

In "Pensamiento y poesía en Emilio Prados," Zambrano reminds us again of the details of poetry and philosophy in Prados's life. For him, it is a matter of his being found by poetry: "Poetry found him virginal, free of literary preferences and efforts" (La poesía le encontró virgen de aficiones y de intentos literarios), a sort of virgin birth.[81] She adds that he answered the call to be a poet by studying philosophy in Freiburg. She doesn't mention that this was the early 1920s, the final years of Heidegger's time as a colleague and protégé of Husserl in Freiburg. The duality that characterized him, then, was, on the one hand, an impulse to totality and, on the other hand, a fascination with particularity. From the moment of his commitment to poetry, she attributes to Prados the simultaneous assumption of

> a specific search for a totalizing order that philosophy discovers and proposes as objectivity, which threatens, certainly, to empty living beings of their obscure interior and sensible throbbing, and even their sensorial manifestation, something that was irrevocable for him as a poet of the immediate and the minimal [y con él

una específica búsqueda de un orden total que la filosofía descubre y propone como objetividad que amenaza, ciertamente, vaciar a los seres vivientes de su interior oscuro y de su palpitar sensible, y aun de su manifestación sensorial, cosa que le era irrenunciable como poeta de lo inmediato y de lo mínimo]. (201)

In other words, he was aware of the threat of philosophy and fled from it into immediacy and minimal things; he avoided the emptying out, the cutting off of living things from what is obscure and merely intuitive. This, for Zambrano, is where Prados's silence came from: "To perceive and shelter in the word this incessant movement of all things, he had to remain quiet; he had to steadily enter into quietude, without self-absorption" (para percibir y albergar en la palabra este incesante moverse de todas las cosas, tuvo que quedarse quieto, tuvo que ir adentrándose en la quietud, sin ensimismamiento) (201). He went in, without going into himself; or rather, going into himself, he went into things.

For Zambrano, this acquiescence proper to "the poet" would have yielded nothing but silence had Prados not *also* been gripped by philosophy. As she insists in "Pensamiento y poesía en Emilio Prados," Prados was "poet-philosopher, counterpositioning himself" (poeta-filósofo, contraponiéndose) (201). That is, he was at times one and at times the other, without the one losing sight of the other.[82] Even as a poet, Prados does not renounce philosophy or even attempt to tame it, or to reduce it to something less than what it is. In this, Zambrano contrasts him with Heidegger, for whom, she asserts, poetry is a mere refreshment, where the philosopher "goes to drink" after the serious business of philosophy is done (202). But Heidegger wrote philosophy, whereas, she writes, "in Prados's poetry the sensitivity towards the minimal and the concrete extends to the horizon that philosophy proposes to him" (202). Philosophy proposes the highest ambitions for poetry, which approaches them in the process of writing. In fact, poetry is doomed to failure, it is "consumed" and falls apart in this attempt. Prados's poetry is "this transcendence that is not achieved if it does not undo and consume" (ese transcender que no se logra si no deshace y consume) (202). As in Zambrano's treatments of poetry in general, the concrete case of Prados's poems enacts a scene of ruination.

The strength of Zambrano's analysis lies not in textual exegesis but in this creation of Prados as a poetic figure, as "the poet," as an archetype, an exemplar, of which other poets, it would seem, are at best alternative instances and at least an imperfect realization. "Pensamiento y poesía en

Emilio Prados" concludes with a gloss of a poem. Rather than an interpretation, Zambrano performs something akin to a rehearsal, a summary, or a kind of "riffing" on the poem. It is chosen, apparently, for its ability to evoke the difference between poetry and philosophy, its performance of this difference by a certain *lack*, which in the poem turns out to be an excess. The poem also appears *representative* for Zambrano; it takes on an issue that she says is constantly engaged in Prados's work, the issue of God, who, like philosophy, maintains an orientation toward totality and, like poetry, maintains an enigmatic presence within the intimacy of singular things. In response to a comment by Prados, Zambrano notes that the experience of God escapes conceptual thinking; when Prados talked of God, "it is easy to understand that he referred not to a concept but to a happening that sprouts by itself uncontainably" (203). She finds his experience encapsulated in the phrase, "And God always being born [Y Dios siempre naciendo]!" This phrase appears in the poem "Abril de Dios" (April of God) in *Río natural* (Natural river), and, she says, earlier as well. Zambrano says the poem *could* have been entitled "The Call" (La llamada) (203); it contains what she calls a "revelatory announcement," "something not learned nor found by the more or less logical discourse of the intellect" (algo no aprendido ni tampoco encontrado por el más o menos lógico discurrir del intelecto) (203). The poem is structured as a narrative meditation in which the poetic voice hears a call while on a walk and reflects on it; she says that this voice perhaps offers a new name, though this detail is not in "Abril de Dios." The poetic voice does note the call and wonders whether it comes from his surroundings or himself:

> Quien me llama soy yo:
> Viento entre los árboles.
> ¿El viento yo? No . . .
> **
> He who calls me is me myself:
> Wind among the trees.
> Me, the wind? No . . .[83]

The "new name" that Zambrano mentions so laconically might be the "poetic reason" that names a space of free, nonhierarchical encounter between poetry and philosophy, figured here as the movement of wind "among," or more literally, "between the trees." Trees are, after all, the source of an early meditation on matter (as *hyle*, in Aristotle), and a favorite topic for poets (for Machado, certainly). Here the poetic voice rejects the idea that he *is* the movement in between; but he does not immediately propose another way of positioning himself. The poem concludes with the strange coincidence of the speaker singing and bleeding through a wound that has appeared in his side, as on Christ's side while on the wooden cross. Zambrano notes, reasonably, that the song appears to coincide with the surging forth of blood from the wound, and that this song is the birth of the poet. She quotes, "My blood is a wound! / My freedom wells up: / I am born from my own side . . ." (¡Mi sangre es una herida! / Broto a mi libertad: / Nazco por mi costado . . .) (203). Noting that Prados does not finish this story with an explanation of the call, Zambrano stresses the lack of logical connection to the poem's final revelation: "And God / always being born" (203). Prados marks his difference from philosophy by this lack of logic, creating both the expectations of connection and their frustration. In a way that resembles Zambrano's writing, Prados integrates philosophical concepts and problems into a discourse that abstains from central philosophical conventions, speaking in a minor, perhaps forgotten element of philosophy while maintaining allegiance to the mysterious force of the poem.

This Side, the Nameless Clearing

For Zambrano, philosophy deliberately neglects the human debt to "modes of knowledge born beyond and this side of [philosophy]," but she intends to operate in another way. She attempts to give accounts of philosophy's commitment to itself alone and its effort to discredit religious practice, literary writing, and other acts of creation like painting and architecture. All these activities defy what are for Zambrano the quintessential philosophical traits: certainty, apodicticity, mastery, order, and so on. Zambrano seems to want to reawaken the most literal Platonic definition of the philosopher, the lover of wisdom, in order to maintain a place within philosophy while refusing to ascribe to all of its conventions.

Still, it remains obscure how "poetic reason" deserves to be considered her "great contribution" to philosophy. The signifiers imply an oxymoronic relationship, appearing exterior to philosophy and reasonable speech at the same time as the invocation of *reason* implies continuity with the philosophical tradition. By what authority—if not that of the simple ability to join noun and adjective, conferred by grammar—do we speak of a "poetic" reason? Language does not necessarily, after all, owe allegiance to philosophy;

it also serves other institutions, and at least one of them permits everything that can be said to be said. That "poetic reason" should be a method or a program, then, is certainly a possibility. But it seems to have the peculiarity, for a method or theoretical orientation, that its ability to articulate its foundations are limited by its own heterodoxy with respect to philosophical discourse. Bundgård's extensive discussion of it as a "hermeneutic method," for example, attempts to convince us of its revolutionary character but clearly chooses not to adopt it. The same is true for many other scholars, who, nevertheless, suggest that one ought to at least *believe in* "poetic reason" if one is to *speak of* it. If it does not allow itself, in a sense, to elaborate its principles, there can never be confidence that one is witnessing it or producing it, and, in addition, that uncertainty could remain indistinguishable from the lack of clarity and precision that might come from mere ignorance.

Still, one could interpret Zambrano's reticence with regard to "poetic reason" as a recognition that there is no such thing. Rather, the goals and aspirations expressed around "poetic reason" must be approached in ways that are always singular. The operation in relation to others described by Balibrea, Lough, and Sánchez Cuervo; "sentient," adaptable, interdisciplinary thinking, for Xon de Ros and Daniela Omlor; openness, tolerance for uncertainty and mystery, and other traits, may not be allowed to coalesce into what is conventionally expected of a theory or method: grounding concepts, argumentative procedures, standards of evidence and exposition, and so on.[84] If we take away the problematic designation of "poetic reason," Zambrano's (non)program for welcoming others while being other sounds like a revolutionary (non)position within Hispanic studies, the humanities, and philosophy. At the risk of being idiosyncratic or arbitrary, such a singular approach embraces the autobiographical, the accidents and inexplicable desires and inclinations of a writer. In this sense, it does not seem inaccurate to call "poetic reason" a "style," as Caballero Rodríguez does, but such a designation still defies philosophical convention in a way that Zambrano's connection to Ortega cannot remedy.[85]

As the space between philosophy and poetry, "poetic reason" does not seem to name anything available for use, either to produce knowledge or to bring about practical aims. Enquist Källgren comes to describe it as a "method or function by which fundamentally expressive beings . . . give form to being in historically contingent configurations," highlighting the ambiguity produced by the counterintuitive nature of its label.[86] Her definition goes on to incorporate the elements of the reason-poetry tension: "the way in which metaphysics is combined with ontology, potency with expressed form, being with particular beings."⁸⁷ Such a "way" may be opened or may already lie open for one to enter upon, or we might think of it somewhere between an opportunity and an action, a space of altercation coaxed open, with good fortune, in the movement of encounter between reason and poetry, or in discourse that intertwines similar elements: reason and fictional narrative, rationality and the real, knowledge and the divine, and so on. Prado's experience of philosophy provided him with an impetus to depart from the silence of a purely poetic attitude to speak poetically while moving in the direction of philosophy. Zambrano begins by imagining herself a philosopher, filled with knowledge of how an entire tradition has attempted to assure itself of existence. With the exception of a few gifted writers with "inconstant clarity," her philosophical predecessors sacrificed the poetic to certain, orderly thinking. But Zambrano lays claim to originality by her diagnosis of philosophical hegemony and her relentless advocacy for the "poetic," something she finds in all kinds of creative activity, including confessions and, at times, other marginal philosophers or the unappreciated margins of canonical figures, like Plato. Her approach to "the poetic" in her writing is what lends it its unique character and its polemical thrust.

Zambrano indeed resembles Machado, then, in ways she did not observe: she devotes herself to writing passages from philosophy toward poetry, and vice versa. Like Machado and Unamuno, poetry and philosophy are the quintessential human activities, accomplishing the highest spiritual function while struggling against any kind of descent into thoughtless, or ritualistic repetition. In spite of the echoes of Heidegger, the similarities are very general. When moved to address his work by name, she shows an insensitivity to his claims in relation to the philosophical tradition and his most ambitious initiatives, which have to do with reorienting philosophy toward greater openness and receptivity to new possibilities in human life. In "The Letter on Humanism," he expresses a hope that something like philosophy might "[guide] the essence of man to the point where it thoughtfully attends to that dimension of the truth of Being that thoroughly governs it," "to the honor of Being and for the benefit of Da-sein."⁸⁸ Such a task would require a preparatory attitude that combines the active and the passive, a "step back that lets thinking enter into a questioning that experiences."⁸⁹

For his part, Derrida often dwells, with attention and respect, upon the limits of Heidegger's openness. Among Derrida's concerns is the extent to which Heidegger fails to acknowledge the kinship of the "hearkening" of the thinker to a religious attitude. Zambrano's general demand that religion and art be taken more seriously as others to philosophy certainly parallel

Derrida's practice and expressed intentions. Her distinction between poems and poets, on the one hand, and "places of poetry" on the other, could be compared to Derrida's insistence on describing "some poetry" (du poème) or "the poematic" in "Che cos'é la poesia." My analysis of the relationship between poetry and philosophy could lead us to understand what Derrida describes, in general, as the intermingling of all things that are often too simply considered in opposition. Even the purest poem—or the most poetic style—bears within it the traces of rationality, knowledge, and mastery to which poetry or "the poetic," in its ideality, is opposed. Zambrano so often speaks as if one ought to engage in an act of purification, a restoration of the poetic or the divine, but the vein of her writing that I have surveyed acknowledges the different activities or experiences associated with literature and rationality, the legitimacy of both and the necessity of approximation and conflict without resolution. In that sense, "altercation" suggests that they relate to each other as others, *altera*, and impact each other without hope of eradicating the other, neither by destruction nor by fusion with the other.

In *Notas de un método*, Zambrano says, "Of poetic reason it is very difficult, almost impossible to speak. It is as if it made something die and be born at the same time; to be and not to be, silence and the word, without falling into martyrdom or delirium" (130). This may be true because "poetic reason" does not name anything in a conventional sense. Zambrano might have said that writing adapts itself better to "poetic reason" than speech. As Friedrich Schlegel suggests, writing evokes the unity of silence and expression. Like the "twilight" it could be the giving of light (*dar a luz*, birth) or its disappearance. Yet Zambrano's fullest statement arrives with the last phrase's opposition of "martyrdom" and "delirium." Too much "philosophy," and one sacrifices oneself to the impersonality of philosophical generality; too much poetry, and one's character becomes indistinguishable from madness. Instead, it is the space this side of each, where finite humans must write our lives.

Epilogue
Philosophy after Life

Before reflecting on the coherence of Unamuno, Ortega, Machado, and Zambrano's configurations of the relations of literature and philosophy, I would like to add a final, living writer to this sequence. Shortly after María Zambrano's rise to prominence and death, the novelist Javier Marías published two short articles elaborating a notion of "literary thinking" (pensamiento literario). "Volveremos" sets out to reassure the author of *Volverás a Región* (*Return to Region*), Juan Benet, that the nature of his work will maintain readers' interest.[1] (Benet suffered from late-stage cancer and would die the month after the publication of Marías's piece.) Marías first designates "literary thinking" as one of the forms that emerged after humans "began to think in writing [pensar por escrito]" (236). Marías recognizes that writing can bear thought in many different ways, and, like Machado, he contrasts a literary mode of thought with scientific and philosophical modes. Furthermore, Marías emphasizes that not all literature qualifies as "literary thought." A reader of this book might be surprised to find Marías announce to his Spanish readership that "many critics and novelists have renounced it—the former refusing to speak of it and the latter to practice it" (236). Juan Benet, by contrast, follows Shakespeare in cultivating "contradiction." Marías's example involves the creation of two separate and contrary perspectives in *Julius Caesar*, in equally rigorous and compelling lines spoken by Brutus and Mark Antony. That Marías has already examined this relation in an early book suggests that he, too, is a "literary thinker" in the sense he attributes to Benet.[2] The only precise definition of "literary thinking" arrives after Marías has quoted several passages from Benet, and it is almost entirely negative: "literary thinking" is not "subject to argument or demonstration"; it does not "depend on a guiding thread that has been reasoned out, nor does it need to show each of its steps" (237). Even the status of contradiction is formulated as the lifting of a prohibition that would presumably hold for all other types of thought (237). The list of quotes with which Marías closes are presented as "the deepest and most disturbing samples [muestras] of literary thinking in our language" (237). Thus Marías proposes that readers will return to Benet because the "literary thinking" we find there fails to resolve itself into clear conclusions, lacking the fullness of meaning expected from other modes of thought. What seems deficient from the point of view of practically all forms of thinking marks the success of "literary thinking."

In his later essay, "Contar el misterio" (Telling the mystery), Marías reflects on his last twenty-five years of writing and inscribes it in a practice he again calls "literary thinking." As in Unamuno, Ortega, Machado, and Zambrano, thinking becomes inseparable from life and from a practice of knowing that Marías places outside of traditional learned discourses like science and philosophy. Here he acknowledges having heard of "literary thinking" from his father, Julián Marías, who has had some things to tell us regarding Machado, Unamuno, and Ortega. Julián Marías did not publish a methodical analysis of "literary thinking," but we can imagine how his son might trust his scholar of a father's assurance that the notion itself is "ancient" without so much as acknowledging, still, the existence of a Spanish "literary thought" going by other, similar names.[3] In "Contar el misterio," Marías repeats the negative determinations from "Volveremos," along with the contrast with science and philosophy, adding that "literary thought" is different from "logical," "mathematical," and "even religious and political [thought]."[4] It is not about any topics in particular, and, especially, not "about literature or about literariness [lo literario]" (123). Struggling to speak in a positive way, Marías suggests that without "literary thinking" he would have *lived* less: "I know that when I write or tell stories and invent characters, I have discovered [sé que . . . he sabido] or recognized things or thought things that can only be discovered [sabido] or recognized or thought in writing [en la escritura]" (122). To recall the Spanish phrase from "Volveremos," "literary thinking" is emphatically thinking *by* writing, "por escrito"; idiomatically, Spanish uses this phrase interchangeably with "en la escritura" but *por* also suggests a traversal or causality: *by way of* writing or *through* writing. Without writing, Marías's life would be poorer, he says.

He arrives at greater precision at the end of "Contar el misterio," when he responds to the potential accusation that a writing lacking conventional modes of verification might be completely arbitrary. Marías describes the "privilege" of "literary thinking": "These sometimes enigmatic and gratuitous propositions speak, in their world of representations, and . . . often we recognize them as true" (123). Unlike the methodical discourses of knowledge, those of this "form of knowing" cross the divide between fiction and reality, imagination and objective knowledge. But the verification, authorization and experience do not follow the familiar, reliable channels. Instead, this kind of knowing relies on a flash of recognition. Marías tries to specify what it reveals, what gets acknowledged when a writer produces the event of recognition. The use of a lexical variable—like the x in a mathematical equation—suggests we are dealing with a possibility prior to reality: "literary thinking" is "a form of knowing that knows itself to be something that was unknown that was known" (una forma de saber que se sabe lo que no se sabía que se sabía) (123). Other translations are possible, but the key here is the revelation of a simultaneity of knowledge and ignorance in a kind of knowledge that highlights both what was covered (*lo que no se sabía*) and its dis-covery. While the temporality of consciousness or spoken discourse might not permit this simultaneity, the materiality of writing does. Concluding, he adds that "literary thinking" attempts "to give an account of [contar] what is only known and not known at the same time [lo solo sabido y a la vez ignorado]" (123). These unique things—the neutral pronoun *lo* leaving them as indeterminate as can be—are "recognized" but not grounded; what was unconsciously present is acknowledged as something that can always be present or absent, something that can pass in and out of consciousness, and that can alert us to the persistent and yet temporal limits of what we think we know.

The practice of narrative invention has enriched Marías's life, he says, and the resulting works offer the same to his readers: to endow them with a kind of knowledge that they can get in no other way. The crucial element is formulated as a paradoxical kind of knowledge, a knowledge of nonknowledge, knowing not just *what* one did not know but *that* one did not know it. Thinking literarily gives one a heightened sense of the ongoing and essential limits of knowledge. Whether Marías knows this or not, this "literary thinking"—though it may distinguish it from some philosophies— restates a classical conception of philosophy, the compulsion toward the broadest and most fundamental acts of knowing. As we saw in chapter 2, Socrates even says, as Marías does, that philosophy is not defined by the texts it produces or the subject matter it treats but by the general desire for truth. Yet, Marías's commitment to practicing an activity that confers a philosophical character on literature does not contribute to the restoration of the primacy of the mortal human individual, as in Unamuno, or to any of the other cultural and intellectual reformations envisioned by Ortega, Machado, or Zambrano. Marías does continue their association of literature with life and the somewhat vague insistence that philosophy is antagonistic to life. Readings from the Greeks, Romanticism, and Heidegger can show that this is a restrictive view of philosophy. I'll return to this point after noting a few other common threads that have developed in the four previous chapters devoted to Spanish literary thinkers.

My discussion of "poetic thinking" in Machado emphasizes the notion of a primordial heterogeneity to which a "poetic" orientation to the world might bear witness, and Zambrano's thinking, whether or not it goes by the name of "poetic reason," shares Machado's sense that the richness and diversity of reality has suffered from increasing rationalization. Unamuno, too, demonstrates concern that the predominant forms of reason perform an insidious process of reduction of the range of experience. Unamuno seems to set a precedent that will continue in Marías's writing, directing his disdain at critics who act as intermediaries between literary works and individuals as well as the contemporary writers whose work fails to get at an intimate experience this side of rationality's restrictive operations. Yet Unamuno struggles to find means to designate that which would escape the homogenization he decries, opting for a restless practice of alternating between different spheres of literature and philosophy in a process of approximation and remonstrance. An identity solid enough to lay claim to a proper name or eternal salvation might congeal in this passage between two distinct and relatively well-defined realms, but being oneself by becoming other requires the singularizing power of constant movement and vigilance.

In contrast to the other three, Ortega seems committed to giving an account of the unity of all humanity and all beings, in general, through the notion of "life." Otherness, for him, is primarily a transitional state as the thing at hand attains its place within the unity of bio-logy. This makes for a rich catalog of different historical moments and thinkers, poets, novelists, and artists that incarnate the temporal units of historical reason, yet are other to one another. And when it comes to the future, Ortega does not seem to abandon the Comtean aspiration to provide a rule for the others to come. Reading him alongside Unamuno, Machado, and Zambrano, then, we can perhaps observe the tension between a desire for an all-encompassing vision of the cosmos and a recognition of many heterogeneous, even internally contradictory points of view, of which his own might not be the blueprint but merely one perspective among others. Even though he assures his audiences that the truth he possesses might be shared in a communal revelation, the fragile and occasional conditions of exposition suggest to us—as Unamuno and Machado do in different ways—that time will ruin all claims to obtain the universal perspective of living reason. Rather than reaffirming Ortegan principles of ratiovital history, Javier Marías's "literary thinking" affirms the sense that, despite all future discoveries, there will never be an end to nonknowledge. Marías implies that life, in fact, is always partially in the dark, and if it weren't, we would have no reason to think through writing.

That being said, Ortega's attempt to cast all human activity in the terms of "life" provides the broadest characterization of what I have tried to formulate for these four, now five, Spanish writers. They all provide distinct techniques of revitalization by bringing literature and philosophy into relation. It is true that to say more about Javier Marías one would have to read the work in which "literary thinking" is performed in addition to the two essays that introduce the expression. Unamuno, Machado, Ortega, and Zambrano develop notions in ways that are more or less explicit and extensive, while at the same time—and again, to a greater or lesser degree—putting their protocols into practice. In Unamuno's case we have observed some incongruencies, and Machado and Ortega both suggest that the revolutionary practices of thinking that they envision will require a period of preparation and training to realize fully, assuming that that is, in fact, the objective. In Zambrano's case we find the affirmation that something like poetic reason offers itself as a model, a way of orienting an individual's life in general and in particular, including even the activity of a scholar committed to both poetry and, in some sense, reason. In a similar way, Plato, the early German Romantics, Heidegger, and Derrida, express, in one way or another, an interest in life, in living more intensely and more profoundly.

Let me observe, finally, the common motif among the Spaniards of reserve, of the need to hold oneself back from the threat of something like philosophy. For Ortega—perhaps the most philosopher of the four—this involves retaining his Mediterranean character in the face of the Germanic one, but to do so without receding completely into the immediacy of Mediterranean openness. Unamuno's extensive engagement with philosophers is often accompanied by disclaimers: he sometimes figures his readings as efforts to get at "the flesh and blood man"; sometimes attacks philosophical propositions that seem antithetical to his own point of view; and he often describes his reading as unorthodox and undisciplined, that of a kind of dilettante *in principle*. Machado and Zambrano explicitly issue a warning about becoming too immersed in philosophy, as if there lay, beyond the threshold that opens onto philosophical thought, a bed of quicksand in which readers would lose poetry and their lives. The literary-philosophical techniques thus provide a manner of resisting philosophy without relinquishing it, keeping one on this side, in life as a more genuinely human life than philosophy alone would allow. These techniques would supposedly indemnify the subject in the name of poetry, reality, religion, or singularity, all of which are sullied by a commitment to the universal that happens through philosophical discourse's method, rationality, or logic. All offer not only a theoretical but an ethical initiative, preserving a relation to self that promises a radically new relation to others. All four associate this new orientation toward the world—the things of the world and the people in it—with a figure of unresolved tension or perpetual movement that thwarts regression into rigid axioms of thought and behavior. One could even say, perhaps, that the existence of four or five different figures—even a tradition—discourages the formation of a single, homogeneous position, that of the "literary thinker," in favor of a loose set of concerns and aspirations. We have fairly elaborate concepts signed by Unamuno, Machado, Zambrano, and Marías, but this does not prohibit the same words, in different contexts, to mean different things. Indeed, readers who have written criticism about "poetic thought," "poetic reason," and "literary thought" have sometimes applied their own definitions of the constituent adjectives and nouns instead of working through the texts in which this terminology is elaborated.

It is worth asking, too, how appropriate it is to advise against too much philosophy. First of all, it is not at all obvious that one could go "full philosophy," what that would mean, or how one would do it. (The kind of unmitigated commitment to philosophy might just be an impression made by belonging to the canon, which none of the great philosophers are responsible for, on their own.) Clearly, different philosophers have different senses of the work and the life that characterize them, notions that involve other historically determinate issues, most importantly, the relationship between vocation and life. Machado, for one—through a certain posthumous Mairena—speaks of entering into "philosophy" at a moment when he discusses a philosophical work that, at least according to Julián Marías, he has not read. Surely one would not advise against reading philosophy, as if one feared a kind of medusa effect. The problem remains an ethical one, and one for which philosophy might already seem unqualified to answer. What *other* discourse would inquire into the rule that defines "too much philosophy"? The other candidates, perhaps, would include "the man in the street," as Machado wants to understand Heidegger's everyday Dasein. Yet, as Juan Valera and his contemporaries note, the common, "normal" point of view allows itself to be formalized into a set of values and rules that could be considered a kind of philosophy implicit to an ethnic collective. As one could glean from Kant, among others, being only *partially* philosophical, philosophical only up to some ill-defined point, might amount to not being philosophical at all, if it cannot account for the critical difference between one and the other. I hope it is clear that the four figures studied at length here set out to be relevant for philosophy, and the relationship between philosophy and its limits ought to count among the philosophical problems on which they shed some light. Although they could perhaps be said to intuit the internal borders and fractures of philosophy, they also call attention to its heterogeneous character, in particular philosophy's questioning of its commitment to rationality, logic, and totality, and of its relation to its others, such as literature.

In response to the provocations of Victor Delbos, *This Side of Philosophy* asserts not only that Spanish thinkers have weighed in on contemporary debates but that "having" Spanish might render their contributions and relevance more legible. Among these debates, after all, is the role of institutions such as idiom, canon, and national identity in the pursuit of philosophical inquiry. While all four writers studied here seem, on the surface, to point to the human individual as a "this side" of philosophy, such a view is complicated by Ortega's notion of an anthropocentric "life," along with their common concern with heterogeneity, which could be extended to a critique of the homogeneity of the human. These Spanish thinkers, living and dead, produce literary and philosophical texts as sites of relation between the two, and do so in ways that resonate with better known work of French, German, and Anglo-American writers. In particular, this sequence offers a coherent version of the "ancient dispute" in the form of the irreconcilability of invention and institution, between the need for, on the one hand, constant alteration of the laws that govern understanding and production and, on the other, the passing on of what has been understood and created. Poetry, the novel, or literature in general and philosophy are associated with two poles of this dispute; actual literary and philosophical works integrate both in the sense that they embody the tension and interaction. Because the texts at issue can be read as scenes of approximation and repulsion, the same texts also invite one to interpret them as sites of synthesis or fusion, two figures that give a privilege to homogeneity and harmony. Approaching them and describing them as spaces of dynamic encounter seems more in tune with a vitalist motif also found in these authors and in at least one vein of the traditional discussions of the relationship of literary creation and philosophical reflection.

Although "this side" seems sometimes to refer to the human, then, I think we can ultimately conclude that it evokes a more nebulous notion of *life*. Why would poetry or literature be associated with life? Teachers of literature have most likely heard students complain of "dissecting" texts, in the interest of a more open-ended and less analytical kind of appreciation that might, on the contrary, breathe life into them. Something about literary texts, at least in contemporary culture, gives the impression that they deserve to be treated with a kind of dignity and autonomy akin to individuals, with their idiosyncrasies and right to free thought. I also propose that the "right to say anything [tout dire]" that Derrida mentions associates literature with a kind of open totality. Literature is in principle open to all possibilities, to a totality beyond all powers of formalization or all thematic definition. In the same way, we associate "life" with the continual surpassing of limits, the appearance of new, unforeseen variants—even dangerous ones—as we remain aware of the richness and complexity of what already exists. While Ortega does not offer us a poetic or literary term like "literary thinking," the idea of ratio-vitalism and, later, general biology, envisions all kinds of human development on the model of artistic and literary innovation, to the extent that his program's completion is envisioned as a new, ebullient sort of language, with a new sort of dictionary and grammar.

Perhaps the activity of thinking that twentieth century intellectuals wanted to reform needed something more concrete than "life" to formulate a technique for revitalization, reaching, instead, for one of the activities that also seems to connect the human being with ineffable, inexplicable, infinite possibilities. If life requires that the possibilities of thinking be expanded, enlisting the power of literature might seem an obvious option. We can surely admit that even thinking is a restrictive notion—it is an activity of a particular sort that combines will, expression, knowledge, and discovery. In Javier Marías's formulations, let us note that "saber" often suggests not only "to know" but "to discover," in a real or implied past. Thinking puts knowledge to use and also seeks to know more, to discover, on the basis of its activity: the expressing, the will, too, having an effect on the activity and its outcome. The same should be said of *philosophy*, that, like thinking, like walking, or eating, it is inherently a more or less restrictive activity. That it is restrictive is not in itself a basis for censure. Indeed, philosophy's accusers—among them, in some ways and at some moments, Unamuno,

Ortega, Machado, and Zambrano—don't just decry *that* it limits but *what* it appears to exclude: intuition, religion, Spanish ethnicity, and so on. Two of them discuss an unusual Latin phrase that could speak for all of them: *primum vivere deinde philosophari*. It is strange because it is attributed to the English philosopher David Hume, to a so-called non-native speaker of Latin, although in this case one with a command of the idiom.[5] The infinitives are commonly read as imperatives—"first live, then philosophize"—and the epigram seems to say that we should only practice philosophy after we have lived, after life has provided us with guidelines that philosophy is not competent to give us on its own. This is more or less Unamuno's interpretation in *On the Tragic Sense of Life*: "[the philosopher] needs to live in order to be able to philosophize, and in fact he philosophizes in order to live."[6] Ortega, surprisingly, uses the epigram to introduce his vision of a post- or trans-philosophical perspective. In *The Idea of the Principle in Leibniz*, he associates *vivere* with a pre-philosophical orientation in life and *philosophari* with the long succession of philosophies that achieved progressive improvements over the centuries, culminating in positivism's understanding of the ego and all things of the world as "events."[7] For Ortega, Hobbes's epigram is not about individual agency, much less about how to assure that philosophy stands on firm ground, but an acknowledgment that something came before philosophy, "traditional beliefs" that are supposedly left behind, and that philosophy ought to give way to something new, "a totally new way of facing up to the Universe intellectually, a way which will be neither one of the precursors of philosophy nor a continuation of philosophy itself."[8] *Philosophari, deinde biologia generalis*, Ortega implies: not exactly a return to life but a renewed relation to a newly expanded notion of it.

And, again, other readings are possible, including one that seems consonant with the ethos of all four Spanish writers treated in this book, even those who have something different to say about Hobbes's epigram. Readers of Catullus will recall the repetition of *deinde* in carmen 5: "da mi basia mille, deinde centum / dein mille altera, dein segunda centum" (give me a thousand kisses, then a hundred / then another thousand, then a second hundred), and so on, for six *dein(de)*s in all, until the kissers lose track of the exact number.[9] "Deinde" is not necessarily a definitive movement beyond, like *ergo*; philosophy does not necessarily leave life behind for another world of rigid concepts and laws. Rather, one could imagine a series, "vivere primum, deinde philosophari, deinde vivere, deinde philosophari. . . ." The point would not be to suggest a simple alternative but the difference and nonexteriority of life and philosophy, which one addresses through the passage from one to the other. It is ultimately not self-evident that life comes before philosophy, even if we try to imagine a distant past before "thinking in writing." That philosophy comes after some stretch of living seems more obvious, to be sure. But, as Unamuno, Ortega, Machado, and Zambrano say, each in very different ways, philosophy remains always in relation to life as it differentiates, distances, and returns, in the same way that we will return to the texts and their magnetic power.

Javier Marías's first discussion of "literary thinking" follows Benet in disregard for Spanish writers, claiming that "Spanish literature has not been especially prodigal when it comes to literary thinking" (236). For Marías, Benet promises to add a Spanish name to the list of great literary thinkers: Diderot, Conrad, Kafka, and Proust. In his article about "literary thinking," Santiago Bertrán provides a long list of Spanish writers to whom Julián Marías's applies this term, among them Unamuno and Machado.[10] Nonetheless, Javier's father would have been familiar with a sequence of writers into which "literary thinking" would fit, if only for the lexical similarity to the obvious parallels "poetic thinking" and "poetic reason." Javier's oversight belongs to a more widespread cultural tendency that still affects the academy and publishing, if not the—somewhat harder to measure—worlds of everyday, nonspecialist readers. Javier Marías also betrays a narrow conception of philosophy, one in which it is believed to be as easily defined as the other kinds of thought—"logical," "political," "religious," and so on—and that is essentially incapable of discovery through writing, with its right and ability to include contraries. We might reserve such a possibility for literature, for certain types of literature. But we might also be prepared to consider other philosophies that, together with resources often considered literary, not only come after life but go after life, pursuing ever greater openness to future possibilities of thought and action.

Notes

Chapter 1

1. Alain Guy, *La Philosophie espagnole* (Paris: Presses Universitaires de France, 1995), 3. Guy's 1995 book builds on his anthology *Les Philosophes espagnols d'hier et aujourd'hui* (Paris: Privat, 1956) and condenses his longer *Histoire de la philosophie espagnole* (Toulouse: Publications de l'Université de Toulouse-Le Mirail, 1985). The 1956 book also introduces its topic with Delbos's provocative statement about the uselessness of Spanish for philosophers (9).

2. Ivo Höllhuber, *Geschichte der Philosophie im spanischen Kulturbereich* (Munich: Reinhardt, 1967), 9.

3. Höllhuber, *Geschichte der Philosophie im spanischen Kulturbereich*, 9–10.

4. Juan Valera, "De la filosofía española," in *Obras completas*, ed. Luis Araujo Costa, vol. 2 (Madrid: Aguilar, 1961), 1560.

5. Paolino Garagorri, *La filosofía española en el siglo XX: Unamuno, Ortega, Zubiri (Dos precursores, Clarín y Ganivet, y cuatro continuadores)* (Madrid: Alianza, 1985), 11.

6. Garagorri, *La filosofía española en el siglo XX*, 11–13.

7. Fernando Moroy, prologue to *Pensadores españoles universales*, ed. Nuria Ramos and Sergio Casquet (Madrid: LID, 2014), 7.

8. Moroy, prologue, 8. *Pensadores españoles universales* stands out for its journalistic, rather than scholarly character, which limits its usefulness for this study to an indicator of the way academic commonplaces find their way into popular conceptions of intellectual history. In a brief introduction, its authors express a hope that this collection of Spanish thinkers might contribute solutions to contemporary problems, especially those concerned with international business (14), and contribute to a growing "recognition for universal Spanish thought" (15). A similar project was carried out by the Francoist ideologue González Fernández de la Mora, who, in the late 1960s, produced a series of six volumes of profiles of Spanish philosophers entitled *Pensamiento español* (Madrid: Ediciones Rialp, 1964–69) in addition to

a smaller selection, *Filósofos españoles del siglo XX* (Barcelona: Planeta, 1987). He expresses an intention to apply his "neutral and straightforward national consciousness" to promoting "our five great twentieth century thinkers" and combatting what he regards as a Spanish tendency of thinking that everything foreign is good and everything native is bad (13).

    9. Guy, *Les Philosophes*, 23.

    10. Guy, *Les Philosophes*, 11.

    11. John R. Welch, preface to *Other Voices: Readings in Spanish* (Notre Dame, IN: University of Notre Dame Press, 2010), ix.

    12. A. R. Caponigri, *Contemporary Spanish Philosophy: An Anthology* (Notre Dame, IN: University of Notre Dame Press, 1967), vii–x.

    13. Since a vigorous academic debate concerns the definition of "Spanish" and the homogeneity of fields of literature and philosophy, I would like to insist that these notions deserve to be as inclusive and impartial as possible. My use of the qualifier "Spanish" throughout is meant to be conventional, not to acquiesce to traditional notions of Spanishness as an essence or a simple unity. It would be worth scrutinizing the value of "Spanish" for the authors on whom I focus, all of whom, as will be seen, frequently speak in the name of a national or cultural unity that they call "Spain" and to which they attribute historical continuity as well as a diversity that embraces, at least, the Iberian peninsula's non-Castillian-speaking minorities and, at most, native Spanish speakers such as Latin Americans plus one-time inhabitants of the Iberian peninsula who did not write in Spanish, such as Seneca, Averroes, or George Santayana. It does not seem to me adequate to rely, as José Gaos does in his *Antología del pensamiento de lengua española en la edad contemporánea* (Mexico: Editorial Séneca, 1945), on language as an organizing principle of thought (10), since one could also question the "unity" of the Spanish language.

    14. Georg Wilhelm Friedrich Hegel, *Introduction to the Lectures on the History of Philosophy*, trans. T. M. Knox and A. V. Miller (Oxford: Clarendon, 1985), 17.

    15. Hegel, *Introduction to the Lectures on the History of Philosophy*, 25.

    16. Rodolphe Gasché, *Europe, or the Infinite Task: A Study of a Philosophical Concept* (Stanford, CA: Stanford University Press, 2009), 6. Subsequent references to this book will appear parenthetically in the text.

    17. José Luis Abellán, "Spain, Philosophy in," in *Routledge Encyclopedia of Philosophy*, ed. Edward Craig, vol. 9 (London: Routledge, 1998), 70–77.

    18. Manuel Garrido, "Spanish Philosophy," in *Cambridge History of Philosophy, 1870–1945*, ed. Thomas Baldwin (Cambridge: Cambridge University Press, 2003), 469–76.

    19. Susana Nuccetelli, "How to Solve the Invisibility Problem for Spanish and Latin American Philosophy," *Teorema* 31, no. 1 (2012): 137. Nuccetelli's title borrows from Eduardo García-Ramírez's 2011 article, "On the Invisibility Problem of Latin American Philosophy," *American Philosophical Association Newsletter* 10, no. 2 (2011): 12–17. Nuccetelli observes that the Spain-focused sections of *El legado filosófico* include literary figures like Unamuno and Machado, while the

Latin American sections omit mention of "non-academic philosophy" pursued by writers like Octavio Paz or Carlos Fuentes (132). In his recommendations for a "therapy" that would address Latin American invisibility, García Ramírez agrees with other scholars that the inclusion of these types of writers would bring "freshness" and perhaps even an improved "self-image" to the community of "Latin American philosophers" (15–16).

20. José Luis Abellán, *Historia crítica del pensamiento español*, vol. 1 (Madrid: Espasa-Calpe, 1988), 14. Further references to this volume will appear parenthetically in the text.

21. Auguste Comte, *Cours de philosophie positive*, in *Auguste Comte and Positivism: The Essential Writings*, ed. Gertrud Lenzer (Chicago: University of Chicago Press, 1983), 72–73. Further references will appear in the text.

22. Julián Marías, *Historia de la filosofía* (Madrid: Revista de Occidente, 1966), 431–55, and *History of Philosophy*, trans. Stanley Appelbaum and Clarence C. Strowbridge (New York: Dover, 1967), 444–68. Marías frames his history with the claim that philosophy's definition may finally be fixed here at the end of its development, allowing one to discern its touchstones. "God has allowed us to close this history, as is just, with Spanish names," he says, closing with the hope that the world will no longer consider Spain to be "outside" its historical development, but, on the contrary, take a commanding role (*Historia*, 455; *History*, 468).

23. José Luis Abellán, "Pensamiento español: una categoría historiográfica," *ÉNDOXA: Series Filosóficas*, no. 12 (2000): 306. Subsequent references to this piece appear in the text.

24. Manuel Garrido et al., eds., *El legado filosófico español e hispanoamericano del siglo XX*, (Madrid: Cátedra, 2009), 1081.

25. Garrido et al., *El legado filosófico*, 667–71. The defense of Ortega's historical framework justifies the choice of a national and regional framework for the roughly 150 pages (out of a total of over 1,200) devoted to Latin America. Nuccetelli's generally approving review, "How to Solve the Invisibility Problem," remarks upon the omission of many countries (132). It is also worth noting the generally disparaging tone regarding the theoretical developments in the humanities in the 1980s and 1990s (668–69). Among those developments, the postcolonial current would have something to say about the relative status of Latin America to Spain in this history of what sometimes are called "Ibero-American" traditions.

26. See Garrido et al., *El legado filosófico*, 7.

27. To cite a recent example of this characterization, which will recur in the scholarship cited throughout this book, Nuccetelli notes that "non-academic philosophy" is "a distinctively Hispanic hybrid genre" that makes up a significant part of the "history of ideas in Spain and Latin America." Nuccetelli, "How to Solve the Invisibility Problem," 129.

28. Ricardo Gullón's provocative "La invención del 98," in *La invención del 98 y otros ensayos* (Madrid: Gredos, 1969), emphasizes the "generation's" tendency to present the patriotism or even provincialism of early twentieth-century Spanish

writing to the exclusion of its cosmopolitan aspects (10). Roberta Johnson suggests that the generational category has worked to exclude women from accounts of the period by drawing attention to literary experimentation and neglecting the more traditionally realist novels written by women. See "Narrative in Culture, 1868–1936," in *The Cambridge Companion to Modern Spanish Culture*, ed. David T. Gies (Cambridge: Cambridge University Press, 2005), 130. By contrast, one of the preeminent scholars of Spanish intellectual history devoted much of his career to exploring the potential of the concept of the Generation of 98 for clarifying the literary and journalistic texts of the era. See E. Inman Fox, *La crisis intelectual del 98* (Madrid: Cuadernos para el Diálogo, 1976). The contributors of the 1997 volume edited by Manuel Aznar Soler, *En el 98* (Madrid: Fundación Duques de Soria, 1997), propose that the term be eliminated from academic and journalistic discourse. While their arguments are compelling, such a change in the practice of teaching and scholarship will need to struggle against a massive accumulation of critical and educational materials that treat the concept of the Generation of 98 as if it were beyond question. For the time being, it seems necessary to continue to mention the concept in order to call attention to its persistent, pernicious effects, including sexist and provincialist distortions of the literature of early twentieth-century Spain.

29. In *Poesía y filosofía en Juan Ramón Jiménez* (Córdoba: Monte de Piedad; Caja de Ahorros, 1987), María Luisa Amigo Fernandez expounds on the worldview of the poet, as expressed in his poems. I single out Matute's singular examinations of the innocence of childhood, Lorca's narratives of passion, and Jiménez's notion of a "pure" poetry as representatives of points of view that merely appear at the opposite extreme from philosophical complexity and sophistication. See Jonathan Mayhew's interesting assessment of the question, "Was Lorca a Poetic Thinker?," *Romance Quarterly* 58, no. 4 (2011): 276–88.

30. Quoted in David T. Gies, "The Funes Effect," in *The Cambridge History of Spanish Literature*, ed. David T. Gies (Cambridge: Cambridge University Press, 2004), 5.

31. Nicolás Fernández-Medina's *Life Embodied: The Promise of Vital Force in Spanish Modernity* (Montreal: McGill-Queen's University Press, 2018) explicitly argues against the "critical myopia" that continues to present the anachronistic picture of a deficiency in natural and human sciences in eighteenth- and nineteenth-century Spain (xxviii–xxix). He provides a detailed picture of a vibrant scientific and philosophical scene and a useful bibliography of other studies that contribute to the rectification of the common preconception, to which the central figures in my study, without exception, were often in thrall.

32. Valera, "De la filosofía española," 1559. Subsequent references appear in the text.

33. Juan Valera and and Ramón de Campoamor, *La metafísica y la poesía: polémica* (Madrid: Sáenz de Jubera, 1891), 11.

34. Ramón de Campoamor, *El personalismo: apuntes para una filosofía* (Madrid: M. Rivadeneyra, 1855), 1.

35. Guy, *Les Philosophes espagnoles*, 22. In *Encounters with Bergson(ism) in Spain: Reconciling Philosophy, Literature, Film and Urban Spaces* (Chapel Hill: University of North Carolina Press, 2010), Benjamin Fraser has shown the particular resonance that Bergson and Bergsonism had in twentieth-century Spain, in the effort they exerted to produce "a new way of thinking," one "more closely attuned to the movement of life" (19). As the subtitle of his book indicates, he counts himself among the scholars for whom the relationship of literature and philosophy in the cultural life of Spain deserves to be seen as a reconciliation rather than a conflict. Nevertheless, in elaborating the Bergsonian concept of "composite" or "dissolution," Fraser provides a possible model for the opposition literature/philosophy, a dyad whose elements are not identical but cannot be separated from each other (80).

36. Marcelino Menéndez Pelayo, *La ciencia española*, 3 vols. (Santander: Aldus, 1953).

37. Manuel de la Revilla Moreno, "Filosofía española," in Menéndez Pelayo, *La ciencia española*, 1:193.

38. Julián Marías, "Machado y Heidegger," *Suplemento de Ínsula* 94 (1953): 1.

39. Marcelino Menéndez Pelayo, *La filosofía española*, ed. Constantino Lascaris Comneno (Madrid: Rialp, 1955), 50.

40. Menéndez Pelayo, *La filosofía española*, 54

41. Menéndez Pelayo, *La filosofía española*, 319.

42. In "La matemáticas sutiles o los límites del saber en *La vida es sueño*," *Bulletin of Spanish Studies* 88, no. 4 (2011), Brian Brewer offers detailed analyses of such of Calderón's contemporaries as Domingo de Soto, Andrés González, Bartolomé Alonso de la Calle, Lope de Deza, Pedro de Valencia, and Martín González de Cellorigo, in order to show that Calderón's literary thought took place in an intellectual atmosphere in which—contrary to the common assumption—more conventionally philosophical work was also being done.

43. Menéndez Pelayo, *La filosofía española*, 309.

44. Victor Navarro Brotóns and William Eamon, eds., *Más allá de la Leyenda Negra: España y la Revolución científica/Beyond the Black Legend: Spain and the Scientific Revolution*, ed. (Valencia: Instituto de Historia de la Ciencia y Documentación López Piñero, 2007), 27. Subsequent references to this book appear in the text.

45. Laureano Robles, "Don Marcelino, visto por Unamuno," *Cuadernos Cátedra Miguel de Unamuno* 45, no. 1 (2008): 108. Subsequent references to this article and the Unamuno manuscript it contains appear in the text.

46. Miguel de Unamuno, "Sobre la filosofía española," in *Ensayos*, vol. 1 (Madrid: Aguilar, 1966), 557. Subsequent references to this volume appear in the text.

47. Miguel de Unamuno, *Epistolario americano (1890–1836)* (Salamanca: Ediciones Universidad de Salamanca, 1996), 249.

48. Most recently, Luis Álvarez Castro, in *Los espejos del yo: existencialismo y metaficción en la narrativa de Miguel de Unamuno* (Salamanca: Ediciones Universidad de Salamanca, 2015), quotes this passage in order to describe the "concept of *nimbus* (*nimbo*)" that precedes the division between genres and out of which genuine literary writing emerges (134). That Álvarez Castro believes Unamuno realized this ideal in his work is suggested by his characterization of the oeuvre as "fusion [fusión] of the theoretical and the creative" (21) in the introduction to his reconstruction of Unamuno's ideas about literary creation. Luis Jiménez Moreno, in the portrait of Unamuno featured in his panoramic study *Práctica del saber en filósofos españoles: Gracián, Unamuno, Ortega y Gasset, E. d'Ors, Tierno Galván* (Barcelona: Anthropos, 1991), refers to a "union of poetry and philosophy" (28).

49. Unamuno, *Epistolario americano*, 249.

50. Miguel de Unamuno, *Vida de don Quijote y Sancho Panza* (Madrid: Cátedra, 2015), 245, and *Our Lord Don Quixote: The Life of Don Quixote and Sancho and Related Essays*, trans. Anthony Kerrigan (Princeton, NJ: Princeton University Press, 1976), 96 (revised).

51. Unamuno, *Vida*, 245, and *Our Lord*, 96 (revised).

52. Miguel de Unamuno, "Sobre la erudición y la crítica," in *Obras completas*, vol. 1 (Madrid: Eslicer, 1966), 1271.

53. Miguel de Unamuno, *Niebla* (Madrid: Cátedra, 1987), 251, and *Mist: Novela/Nivola*, trans. Anthony Kerrigan (Princeton, NJ: Princeton University Press, 1976), 188. Subsequent references to these editions of the novel will appear in the text, with an "S" preceding the page number of this Spanish edition and an "E" indicating the English translation.

54. S. Marc Cohen, "Aristotle's Metaphysics," in *Stanford Encyclopedia of Philosophy*, edited by Edward N. Zalta. Accessed July 19, 2022, https://plato.stanford.edu/entries/aristotle-metaphysics/.

55. References to the *Metaphysics* may be consulted by line number at the open-source Perseus website. The English is taken from the translation available there: Aristotle, *Metaphysics*, in *Aristotle in 23 Volumes*, vols.17, 18, trans. Hugh Tredennick (Cambridge, MA: Harvard University Press; London: Heinemann, 1933, 1989).

56. I rely on Richard Hope's translation of Aristotle's *Metaphysics* (Ann Arbor: University of Michigan Press, 1956) for the rendering of "archikōtatē" as "the most controlling" (7).

57. Martin Heidegger, *Fundamental Concepts of Metaphysics: World, Finitude, Solitude*, trans. William McNeill and Nicholas Walker (Bloomington: Indiana University Press, 1995), 26, 34.

58. Heidegger, *Fundamental Concepts*, 39.

59. Heidegger, *Fundamental Concepts*, 51. In her account of Spanish philosophy in German universities, "La presencia explícita de filosofía española en universidades alemanas" [The explicit presence of Spanish philosophy in German universities], in *Nuevos estudios sobre histora del pensamiento español: actas de las V*

Jornadas de Hispanismo Filosófico (Madrid: Fundación Ignacio Larramendi; Associación de Hispanismo Filosófico, 2005), Nicole Holzenthal describes the "enormous presence" of Spanish thinkers in seventeenth-century Germany (595). The most influential was Suárez, who also has the distinction of being the theme of nearly a quarter of all philosophy dissertations (34 of 121) devoted to Spanish philosophy between 1885 and 1985 (590).

60. Most recently, María Rodríguez García, in *Filosofía y novela: De la generación del 98 a José Ortega y Gasset* (Seville: Athenaica, 2018), characterizes modern philosophy since Descartes as an effort to rationalize life by reducing the significance of the irrational share of human nature, which she refers to as, "in short, the world of life" (15). See also Katrine Helene Andersen, "Miguel de Unamuno: una filosofía novelada," in *Unamuno eterno* (Barcelona: Anthropos, 2015), for whom this scene and those discussed in chapter 3 constitute Unamuno's substitution for the Cartesian subject of a subject that would be "affective" and "creative" (350).

61. René Descartes, *Principles of Philosophy*, trans. John Cottingham, in *The Philosophical Writings of Descartes*, vol. 1 (Cambridge: University Press, 1985), 179, 184. Subsequent references to this volume appear in the text.

62. René Descartes, *Discourse on the Method*, trans. Robert Stoothoff, in *The Philosophical Writings of Descartes*, vol. 1 (Cambridge: University Press, 1985), 120. Subsequent references to this work appear in the text.

63. Jacques Derrida, "Cogito and the History of Madness," in *Writing and Difference*, trans. Alan Bass (Chicago: University of Chicago Press, 1978), 58.

64. In its attention to the internal tensions and contradictions that characterize the oeuvres of Descartes and Montaigne, Hassan Mehely's *Writing Cogito* (Albany: State University of New York Press, 1997) provides a detailed and insightful counterpoint to the tendency of both philosophical and literary studies to enforce a "homogeneous and uniform" image of canonical figures. His readings combat the conventional representation of Descartes as simply the founding figure of a rationalism that must be overcome by a more personal, affective style of thinking.

65. See Roberta Johnson, *Crossfire: Philosophy and the Novel in Spain, 1900–1934* (Lexington: University of Kentucky Press, 1993), 2. Ortega y Gasset's claim that nineteenth-century Spanish philosophy was in thrall to positivism must be seen in the light of his own historicist convictions regarding philosophy and his own self-characterization as the overcoming of positivism through its "radical broadening" into his own "absolute positivism." See *¿Qué es filosofía?*, in *Obras completas*, vol. 7 (Madrid: Revista de Occidente, 1966), 285–86, 352, and *What Is Philosophy?*, trans. Mildred Adams (New York: Norton, 1964), 28, 125. Speaking of positivism's early influence on Unamuno, Abellán clarifies that the philosophical current that struggled for predominance with scholasticism in Spanish universities of the nineteenth century was a Krausist version of positivism. See "El impacto positivista en el pensamiento de Unamuno," in *Pensamiento y literatura en España en el siglo XIX*, ed. Yvan Lissorges (Mirail, France: Presses Universitaires de Mirail, 1996), 248–50.

66. This is the approach of Francisco José Martín in Garrido et al., *El legado filosófico* (ch. 3, "El genio filosófico de la literatura"), and his panoramic *La tradición velada: Ortega y el pensamiento humanista* (Madrid: Biblioteca Nueva, 1999), where Ortega himself provides the operative concepts for Martin's analysis of "el hombre-Ortega" (40).

67. Juan José Lanz, "José Ortega y Gasset, filosofía y literatura," *Revista de Occidente* 300 (2006): 24.

68. Lanz, "José Ortega y Gasset," 25.

69. José Luis Molinuevo, "Literatura y filosofía en Ortega y Gasset," *Revista de Occidente* 132 (1992): 69.

70. Julián Marías, introduction to José Ortega y Gasset, *Meditaciones del Quijote* (Madrid: Cátedra, 2010), 20.

71. Pedro Cerezo Galán, *La voluntad de aventura: aproximamiento al pensamiento de Ortega* (Madrid: Ariel, 1984), 338.

72. Martín, *La tradición velada*, 52n4.

73. See the discussion of "this century, our father" (este siglo, nuestro padre), in José Ortega y Gasset, *Meditaciones del Quijote* (Madrid: Alianza, 1987), 118, and *Meditations on Quixote*, trans. Evelyn Rugg and Diego Marín (New York: Norton, 1961), 40. Subsequent references to these two editions will appear with a "S" to indicate the Spanish and an "E" to indicate the English.

74. In his prologue to Adolfo Bioy Casares's *La invención de Morel* (New York: Penguin, 1996), Borges contests Ortega's prediction of the death of the novel. For an analysis of this encounter, see Stephen Gingerich, "Prefatory Conventions and Invention: Rereading Borges's Prologue to *La invención de Morel*," *Revista de Estudios Hispánicos* 52, no. 3 (2018): 983–1005.

75. Jordi Gracia, *José Ortega y Gasset* (Madrid: Taurus, 2014), 11–14.

76. Gracia, *José Ortega y Gasset*, 12.

77. José Ferrater Mora, "Ortega y Gasset: An Outline of his Philosophy," in *Three Spanish Philosophers*, ed. J. M. Terricabras (Albany: State University of New York Press, 2003), 130, 142n5. Ferrater Mora recognizes that the biographical approach prescribed by Ortega involves the exegete in a "vicious circle" before proceeding with his analysis (131).

78. Cerezo, *La voluntad*, 184.

79. Marías, introduction, 17. For the argument that "Adán" ought to be regarded as the first exposition of his philosophy, see Pedro Blas González, "Biographical Life and Ratio-vitalism in the Thought of Ortega y Gasset," *Philosophy Today* 46, no. 4 (2002): 406–16.

80. Regarding the age of readers, see Ortega y Gasset, *Meditations*: "I would like to propose . . . to readers who are younger than me, the only ones whom I can address personally" (S 14; E 34). Regarding national identity: "[these ideas] would like to awaken in fraternal souls other human thoughts . . . [in] a broad collaboration about national themes" (S 20; E 40).

81. See Javier Crespo Sánchez's provocative "Ortega, el fin de la filosofía y la tarea del pensamiento," *Revista de Estudios Orteguianos*, 14–15 (2007), in which the author explains that Ortega's is "not a new philosophy but something new and different that confronts philosophy" (188) and for this reason recommends writing "philosophy" in parentheses when interpreting Ortega (202). Crespo Sánchez also counts among the scholars who takes an interest in the "tensions within the Ortegan corpus" (183).

82. E. Inman Fox sums up the scholarly discussion about this peculiarity of the *Meditations* after a new edition revealed the larger project Ortega originally intended to create. See "Revelaciones textuales sobre las *Meditaciones* de Ortega," *Insula* 35, no. 455 (1984): 4–5. Fox eventually published the anthology *Meditaciones sobre la literatura y el arte: la manera española de ver las cosas* (Madrid: Clásicos Castalia, 1987) as a corrective to viewing the *Meditations* as incomplete, whether essentially or accidentally.

83. Nicolás Fernández-Medina defines the genre of the "Proverbios" in his excellent study of the many ways they anticipate Machado's later experiments with the relation between literature and philosophy, in *The Poetics of Otherness in Antonio Machado's "Proverbios y cantares"* (Cardiff: University of Wales Press, 2011). While this relation is not exactly the focus of his book, no one shows better than Fernández-Medina how multifarious it is, such that his book itself offers reasons to disagree with his conclusion that literature and philosophy are "complementary halves" of a single inquiry (17).

84. See Dámaso Alonso, "Fanales de Antonio Machado," in *Cuatro poetas españoles* (Madrid: Gredos, 1962). Miguel García-Posada points out in "Antonio Machado y la modernidad: una revisión," *Cuadernos Hispanoamericanos*, no. 691 (2008), that a literary history from 1997 refers to Machado after *Fields of Castile* as "almost an ex-poet" (66n3).

85. See Antonio Machado, *Poesías completas* (Madrid: Espasa-Calpe, 1983), 305–26, and two sections of poems attributed to Abel Martín, 344–45, 348–54.

86. See Machado, *Poesías completas*, 327–44.

87. Antonio Machado, *Juan de Mairena*, ed. Antonio Fernández Ferrer (Madrid: Cátedra, 2003), and the abridged English version, *Juan de Mairena*, ed. and trans. Ben Belitt (Berkeley: University of California Press, 1963). Although not indicated in its title, the English excerpts the Spanish original according to principles of selection that are not explicit. The Cátedra edition of *Juan de Mairena* includes the work proper in volume 1 and provides a second volume that compiles magazine pieces signed "Mairena," which Machado did not publish in book form during his lifetime. When not otherwise indicated, references to *Juan de Mairena* are to the first volume of this edition. Future references to these editions appear in the text, with an "S" indicating the Spanish and an "E" the English translation. When a passage is omitted in Belitt's volume, I still use the "S" to indicate the omission from "E."

88. José Martínez Hernández, *Antonio Machado, un pensador poético* (Murcia: Ediciones Almuzara, 2019), introduction, loc. 65, kindle.

89. See Pedro Cerezo Galán, *Palabra en el tiempo: poesía y filosofía en Antonio Machado* (Madrid: Gredos, 1975), 19.

90. José María Valverde, introduction to *Nuevas canciones y de un cancionero apócrifo*, by Antonio Machado (Madrid: Castalia, 1975), 7, and Eustaquio Barjau, *Antonio Machado: teoría y práctica del apócrifo* (Barcelona: Ariel, 1975), 23.

91. Fernández-Medina, *The Poetics of Otherness*, 14.

92. Xon de Ros's *The Poetry of Antonio Machado: Changing the Landscape* (Oxford: Oxford University Press, 2015) treats gender in the first chapter, discusses a shift away from the Romantic notion of nature to "multiple perspectives and movement" in chapter 2 (80), and analyzes translations in chapter 4, all with reference to Juan de Mairena as well as concrete poems.

93. Machado, *Poesías completas*, 337.

94. In addition to the critics already mentioned for their characterization of the difference between poetry and philosophy in Machado, Mario Socrate's study *Il linguaggio filosofico della poesia di Antonio Machado* (Padua: Marsilio, 1972) deserves recognition as a book-length study of this problem, taking into account both philosophical and literary predecessors and an extensive analysis of Machado's oeuvre. Socrate concludes that poetry and philosophy must be kept apart, in a tense oppositionality generated by their each being "grounded" upon the other (3).

95. María Zambrano, "*La guerra* de Antonio Machado," in *Obras completas*, ed. Jesús Moreno Sanz, vol. 1 (Barcelona: Galaxia Gutenberg, 2015), 185–94. Future references to this work appear in the text.

96. Goretti Ramírez, *María Zambrano, crítica literaria* (Madrid: Devenir Ensayo, 2004), 154, and Ana Bundgård, *Más allá de la filosofía: sobre el pensamiento filosófico-místico de María Zambrano* (Madrid: Editorial Trotta, 2000), 179ff. Future references to these two books appear in the text.

97. Guy, *Les Philosophes,* 208–11.

98. José Luis L. Aranguren, "Los sueños de María Zambrano," *Revista de Occidente* 12 (1966): 207–12.

99. See Juan Fernando Ortega Muñoz, *Introducción al pensamiento de María Zambrano* (México: Fondo de Cultura Económica, 1994), 20–23.

100. For a list of recipients and other information, see "Miguel de Cervantes Prize," Wikipedia, last modified September 22, 2021, 03:32, https://en.wikipedia.org/wiki/Miguel_de_Cervantes_Prize.

101. Zambrano, *Obras completas*, vols. 1–4, 6, with planned vols. 5, 7, 8. See Jesús Moreno Sanz, "*Obras completas* de María Zambrano," *Revista de Filosofía* 46, no. 1 (2021): 229–38. The scholarly value of this critical edition is limited by the overwhelming volume and sometimes idiosyncratic content of editorial material, and by the limited availability of volumes, some of which are out of print. For this

reason, I use commonly available trade editions for references to Zambrano's major works, while occasionally referring to the edition's ancillary materials.

102. Beatriz Caballero Rodríguez, review of *The Cultural Legacy of María Zambrano*, ed. Xon de Ros and Daniela Omlor, *Modern Language Review* 15, no. 1 (2020): 195.

103. Francis Lough, "María Zambrano: Philosophy, Literature, and Democracy," in *The Cultural Legacy of María Zambrano*, eds. Xon de Ros and Daniela Omlor (Cambridge: Legenda, 2017), 186. The introduction to "María Zambrano amongst the Philosophers," ed. Mari Paz Balibrea, Francis Lough, Antolín Sánchez Cuervo, special issue of *History of European Ideas* 44, no. 7 (2018), calls "poetic reason" Zambrano's "great contribution to philosophy" (838).

104. Lough, "María Zambrano," 186.

105. Janet Pérez, "*La razón de la sinrazón:* Unamuno, Machado, and Ortega in the Thought of María Zambrano," *Hispania* 82, no. 1 (1999): 57–59.

106. Pérez describes Ortega's "clarity" in "*La razón,*" 58, and Bundgård speaks of Ortega's maintenance of an "argumentative, propositional discourse" in *Más allá*, 229–32.

107. Xon de Ros and Daniela Omlor, introduction to *The Cultural Legacy of María Zambrano*, 2–3, 11. Ortega Muñoz also attributes Zambrano's "sensitivity" to being a woman, in *Introducción al pensamiento*, 11. One of two entries devoted to her in Garrido et al., *El legado filosófico español e hispanoamericano del siglo XX*—written by Juana Sánchez-Gey Venegas and included in the section "La reflexión sobre la mujer" (The reflexión on woman)—notes that Zambrano did not write *about* women but "thinks as a woman" (1090).

108. Jesús Moreno Sanz, introduction to Zambrano, *Obras completas*, 1:xxxviii.

109. Ros and Omlor, introduction, 5.

110. José Luis Abellán, *María Zambrano: una pensadora de nuestro tiempo* [A thinker of our time] (Barcelona: Anthropos, 2006), 11; Mercedes Gómez Blesa, "Unamuno-Zambrano: un pensamiento poético," prologue to María Zambrano, *Unamuno*, ed. Mercedes Gómez Blesa (Madrid: Debate, 2004), 13.

111. Jesús Moreno Sanz, *El logos oscuro: tragedia, mística y filosofía en María Zambrano*, vol. 1 (Madrid: Verbum, 2008), 22.

112. María Zambrano, "Ortega y Gasset, filósofo español," in *España, sueño y verdad* (Barcelona: Edhasa, 2002), 115–16.

113. Teresa Rocha Barco, ed., *María Zambrano: la razón poética o la filosofía* (Madrid: Tecnos, 1997); Carmen Revilla, ed., *Claves de la razón poética* (Madrid: Trotta, 1998); Jesús Moreno Sanz, ed., *María Zambrano, 1904–1991: de la razón cívica a la razón poética* (Madrid: Publicaciones de la Residencia de Estudiantes; Vélez-Málaga: Fundación María Zambrano, 2004); Beatriz Caballero Rodríguez, *María Zambrano: A Life of Poetic Reason and Political Commitment* (Cardiff: University of Wales Press, 2017); Karolina Enquist Källgren, *María Zambrano's Ontology of Exile: Expressive Subjectivity* (Cham, Switzerland: Palgrave, 2019), 5.

114. See Bundgård, *Más allá*, 14, and Enquist Källgren, *María Zambrano's Ontology*, 14.

115. José Ángel Valente, "El sueño creador," in *Las palabras de la tribu* (Barcelona: Tusquets, 1994), 10. This article originally appeared as "María Zambrano y 'El sueño creador,'" in the journal *Insula*, in 1967.

116. José Ignacio Eguizábal's "Filosofía y poesía," in Moreno Sanz, *María Zambrano, 1904–1991*, 379, and Moreno Sanz, introduction to Zambrano, *Obras completas*, 1:xxxvii.

117. Pedro Chacón and Mariano Rodríguez, "Anejo a *Filosofía y poesía*," in Zambrano, *Obras completas*, 1:978–91.

118. Francisco LaRubia-Prado, "Filosofía y poesía: María Zambrano y la retórica de la reconciliación," *Hispanic Review* 65, no. 2 (1997): 202.

119. LaRubia-Prado, "Filosofía y poesía," 205.

120. Tatjana Gajić, *Paradoxes of Stasis: Literature, Politics, and Thought in Francoist Spain* (Lincoln: University of Nebraska Press, 2019), 173.

121. Gajić, *Paradoxes*, 178.

122. See Gajić, *Paradoxes*, 183, where she asserts that Zambrano offers a "glimpse" of "the possibility of history freed from the crime of a civil war and from exile as a form of punishment that preserves the trace of that crime in history."

123. Jesús Moreno Sanz, "La razón no polémica en María Zambrano: lugares elementales y palabras con cuerpo," in Rocha Barco, *María Zambrano: la razón poética o la filosofía*, 142.

124. Zambrano, "A los poetas chilenos de 'madre España,'" in *Obras completas*, 1:378.

125. Such a reconfiguration seems to be behind the assertion made in the title of Teresa Rocha Barco's anthology, *María Zambrano: la razón poética o la filosofía*. Although her own introduction also asserts that "without a doubt, for María Zambrano . . . poetic reason is the same as philosophy" (12), she does not elaborate on how that might be the case or how poetic reason is also an alternative to traditional philosophy.

126. Pío Baroja, *Camino de perfección/The Road to Perfection*, trans. Walter Borenstein (Oxford: Oxbow, 2008), 17–18.

Chapter 2

1. Hans Feger, ed., *Handbuch Literatur und Philosophie* (Stuttgart: Metzler, 2012), v.

2. Barry Stocker, introduction to *The Palgrave Handbook of Philosophy and Literature*, ed. Barry Stocker and Michael Mack (London: Palgrave Macmillan, 2018), 1. The slightly earlier anthology published by Palgrave, Andrea Selleri and Philip Gaydon, eds., *Literary Studies and the Philosophy of Literature* (Cham, Switzerland:

Palgrave Macmillan; Springer, 2016), also seeks to take note of polemics while providing a "platform for open discussion about the mutual usefulness of the two disciplines" (introduction, 2).

3. Louis Mackey, *The Ancient Quarrel Continued: The Troubled Marriage of Philosophy and Literature* (Lanham, MD: University Press of America, 2002), vi.

4. Raymond Barfield, *The Ancient Quarrel between Philosophy and Poetry* (Cambridge: Cambridge University Press, 2011), 1.

5. Barfield, *The Ancient Quarrel*, 1. See Hans Blumenberg, *The Laughter of the Thracian Woman: A Protohistory of Theory*, trans. Spencer Hawkins (New York: Bloomsbury, 2015).

6. Anthony J. Cascardi, *The Cambridge Introduction to Literature and Philosophy* (Cambridge: Cambridge University Press, 2014), 3. Subsequent references to this book will appear in the text.

7. Anthony J. Cascardi, introduction to *Literature and the Question of Philosophy*, ed. Anthony J. Cascardi (Baltimore: Johns Hopkins University Press, 1987), xii.

8. Anthony J. Cascardi, "Between Philosophy and Literature: Ortega's *Meditations on Quixote*," in *José Ortega y Gasset: Proceedings of the Espectador universal International Interdisciplinary Conference*, ed. Nora de Marval-McNair (New York: Greenwood, 1987), 17.

9. Mark Edmundson, *Literature against Philosophy, Plato to Derrida: A Defence of Poetry* (Cambridge: Cambridge University Press, 1995), 1–2. Subsequent references appear in the text.

10. See Cascardi, *Cambridge Introduction*, on idea and form (1) and reason and feelings (95), and Mackey, *The Ancient Quarrel*, on conceptual and figural "textuality" (v). On the relation between generality and particularity, see Andrew Benjamin, *Philosophy's Literature* (Manchester: Clinamen, 2001), vii–viii.

11. See Martha Nussbaum, *Love's Knowledge: Essays on Philosophy and Literature* (New York: Oxford University Press, 1990), 3, and Cascardi, "Between Philosophy and Literature," 16.

12. Patrick Hayes and Jan Wilm, eds., *Beyond the Ancient Quarrel: Philosophy, Literature, and J. M. Coetze* (New York: Oxford University Press, 2017). See the introduction, "Ancient Quarrels, Modern Contexts," in which the editors describe the contemporary institutional frameworks of literary studies and philosophy and their capacity for cooperation in the study of the challenging work of J. M. Coetze (1–15). The editors of the *Palgrave Handbook of Philosophy and Literature* and *Literary Studies and the Philosophy of Literature* also base their argument for untroubled interaction on the institutional understanding of literature, either as literary studies or using literary studies as the institutional proxy for the voice of literature and literary writers. In his *Literature and Philosophy: A Guide to Contemporary Debates* (London: Palgrave Macmillan, 2006), David Rudrum also represents the relation as if it were a matter of professional collegiality: "the often stormy relations between literature and philosophy" call for "the reciprocally informative relations between

literature and philosophy" (5). He thus seems undecided whether strife is necessary or accidental, contrasting their "entente cordial" in writers like Sartre and de Beauvoir with the "much bleaker" vision of Bataille and Blanchot (9) before expressing a preference for a "bridging of the divide" (11).

13. Cascardi, *The Cambridge Introduction*, 187.

14. Mackey, *The Ancient Quarrel*, vi. Benjamin, in *Philosophy's Literature*, maintains that literature has always constituted a "challenge" to philosophy, one in which it is forced to define itself in relation to "a conception of the Absolute" (vii–viii). As we will see later, Rodolphe Gasché takes issue with the suggestion that literature is philosophy's only or primary other.

15. Stocker, *The Palgrave Handbook*, 1.

16. Marsha Collins, "Romance," *The Palgrave Handbook of Philosophy and Literature*, edited by Barry Stocker and Michael Mack (London: Palgrave Macmillan, 2019), 263–92, and Isabel Jaén Portillo, "Fictions of Human Development: The Renaissance," in Stocker and Mack, *The Palgrave Handbook*, 315–38.

17. For a historically focused account of the development of Hispanic studies away from a focus on Peninsular classics, see Sebastiaan Faber, "Fantasmas hispanistas y otros retos transatlánticos," in *Cultura y cambio social en América Latina*, ed. Mabel Moraña (Madrid: Iberoamericana, 2008), 315–40.

18. See Cascardi, *Cambridge Introduction*, 6, for the locution "philosophical twin," not attributed to Unamuno; 3, for the reference to Borges; 18, 182 for Ortega.

19. See Gilles Deleuze and Félix Guattarri, *What Is Philosophy?*, trans. Hugh Tomlinson and Graham Burchell (New York: Columbia University Press, 1994). They regard philosophy, art (including literature), and science as distinct practices: "It is thought that philosophy is given a great deal by being turned into the art of reflection but actually it loses everything," they say, calling the collapse of the difference of art and philosophy a "bad joke" (7). For Deleuze and Guattarri, universals must be explained in philosophy, they cannot simply be explored or dramatized. They recognize only three contemporary philosophical traditions—German, French, and English—and maintain that Italian and Spanish philosophy were prevented from taking shape "in the capitalist era" by the strength of theology (102–3). Subsequent references to this book appear in the text.

20. See Richard Rorty, introduction to *Philosophy in History: Essays on the Historiography of Philosophy*, ed. Richard Rorty, J. B. Schneewind, and Quentin Skinner (Cambridge: Cambridge University Press, 1984), 1–8, and Jorge Gracia, *Philosophy and Its History: Issues in Philosophical Historiography* (Albany: State University of New York Press, 1992), xv–xvii.

21. That literary scholars merely report on ideas rather than engage them (as philosophers do) in a search for truth, is clearly Feger's concern in the introduction of his *Handbuch Literatur und Philosophie* (1). Nevertheless, one can find discussions of major figures in Spanish thought that subject them to questions of rigor and rightness. As we will see later, Pedro Ribas takes Unamuno to task for his idiosyncratic

and opportunistic, sometimes simply erroneous, readings of canonical philosophical texts. Michael Candelaria, *The Revolt of Unreason: Miguel de Unamuno and Antonio Caso on the Crisis of Modernity*, ed. Stella Villarmea (Amsterdam: Rodopi, 2012), likewise points out the shortcomings of Unamuno's philosophical interpretations, and Jan E. Evans, *Unamuno and Kierkegaard: Paths to Selfhood in Fiction* (Lanham, MD: Lexington Books, 2005), asserts that Unamuno does not develop an understanding of Kierkegaard in accordance with the latter's own self-understanding, especially the key notion of "reintroducing Christianity to Christendom" (5).

22. Gerardo Bolado, "Luces y sombras de la última historiografía filosófica en España," in *Nuevos estudios sobre historia del pensamiento español: actas de las V Jornadas de Hispanismo Filosófico* (Madrid: Fundación Ignacio Larramendi; Asociación de Hispanismo Filosófico, 2005), 601–2. Subsequent references to this article will appear in the text.

23. In *Unamuno: el vasco universal* (Madrid: Endymion, 2015), Pedro Ribas describes the resistance he encountered in the early seventies when he proposed a dissertation on Unamuno for a doctorate in philosophy. Guy describes his pioneering introduction of Spanish philosophy into his philosophy department in France in the 1970s (*Histoire de la philosophie espagnole*, 2–3). Holzenthal, in "La presencia explícita de filosofía española en universidades alemanas," describes the relative absence of Spanish philosophy within German universities, including an account of the problems encountered when courses are indeed offered (585–87).

24. Raymond Williams, *Keywords: A Vocabulary of Culture and Society* (New York: Oxford University Press, 1976), 197.

25. References are to the edition of Plato available on the Perseus archive. Quotes in English come from the more recent translation in the *Complete Works*, ed. John M. Cooper (Indianapolis: Hackett, 1997), with page numbers after the reference to the Greek text.

26. For Julia Sushytska, Plato's invention of the "quarrel" included its being speciously assigned an "ancient" status by Socrates. See "On the Non-rivalry Between Poetry and Philosophy: Plato's *Republic* Reconsidered," *Mosaic* 45, no. 1 (2012): 55–70. For Sushytska, classical scholars mistakenly assume that Plato takes the side of philosophy against literature; instead, she argues, this invention was intended to establish a relationship of "consort" between the two (60), characterized as "difference between and co-belonging of mythical and logical thinking" (56).

27. See Jacques Derrida, "Plato's Pharmacy," in *Dissemination*, trans. Barbara Johnson (Chicago: University of Chicago Press, 1972), for an analysis of this ambivalence, particularly in *Phaedrus*. In short, Plato describes writing as a part of the system that something with all the essential traits of writing institutes. This "general writing" is "the prior medium in which differentiation in general is produced," such as the common difference between spoken and written speech (126). That is, writing becomes, in *Phaedrus*, both the principle (the truth written on the soul) and a regrettable consequence of the principle (writing differs from spoken language).

28. Alison Denham, the editor of *Plato on Art and Beauty* (New York: Palgrave, 2012), acknowledges this interpretation, while maintaining that "the tendency to focus exclusively on [Book 10 of the *Republic*] has encouraged too reductive and simplified accounts of Plato's attitude to the visual arts" (xxi), which would presumably be true too for his view of literature.

29. In what follows, I quote in English from Richard Hope's translation of Aristotle's *Metaphysics* (Ann Arbor: University of Michigan Press, 1960), rather than the Perseus website's English text.

30. Barfield, *The Ancient Quarrel*, 33.

31. Williams, *Keywords*, 150. Subsequent references to this book appear in the text.

32. Madame de Staël, *De la littérature considérée dans ses rapports avec les institutions sociales* (Paris: InfoMédia Communication, 1998), 16, and *Madame de Staël on Politics, Literature and National Character*, trans. Ed Morroe Berger (London: Sidgwick and Jackson, 1964), 113 (revised). Apart from her decision to consider all thinking writing "literature," de Staël expressed a common dismissal of Spanish literature and philosophy. In general, she says, the literary failures of the Spanish—in spite of the Iberian Peninsula being a beautiful setting in which Northern and Southern peoples mixed—force her to evaluate them based on "the few, scattered efforts that we can still gather" (*De la littérature*, 164). Furthermore, "not a single element of philosophy was able to develop in Spain" (165).

33. See Jacques Barzun's "To the Rescue of Romanticism," *American Scholar* 9, no. 2 (1940): 147–58, for this characterization of the debate on nomenclature. Barzun's defense of romanticism notes, along the way, the separation of a loose, vague, colloquial use of the term from a precise, historically grounded one, which, for him constitutes an identifiable "attitude" that appeared in the work of Montaigne, Shakespeare, and Pascal, and came to dominate a "generation" he brackets between the years 1770 and 1850.

34. The selections in Welch's *Other Voices* provide a clear demonstration that Muslim and Jewish thinkers, Averröes and Maimonides, devoted much of their writing to reconciling religious doctrine to the Greek philosophy they admired.

35. I do not argue that early German Romanticism represents the whole or the essence of the historical phenomenon known as *romanticism*. I use a capital letter to mark my reference to early German Romanticism, and the lower case to refer to the larger cultural phenomenon.

36. See Dagmar Mirbach, "Dichtung als *representatio*: G. W. Leibniz und A. G. Baumgarten," in Feger, *Handbuch Literatur und Philosophie*, 13, and Andreas Michel and Assenka Oksiloff, "Romantic Crossovers: Philosophy as Art and Art as Philosophy," in *Theory as Practice: A Critical Anthology of Early German Romantic Writings*, ed. and trans. Jochen Schulte-Sasse et al. (Minneapolis: University of Minnesota Press, 1997), 157.

37. See Feger, introduction to *Handbuch Literatur und Philosophie*, 4, and Michel and Oksiloff, "Romantic Crossovers," 159.

38. See Immanuel Kant, *Critique of Judgement*, trans. J. H. Bernard (New York: Hafner, 1952), par. 46, "Beautiful Art Is the Art of Genius," where Kant explains that works of art must be examples of beauty without possessing explicit rules for its production: "[the genius] cannot describe or indicate scientifically how it brings about its products, but it gives the rule just as nature does" (150–51).

39. F. W. J. Schelling, *System of Transcendental Idealism*, trans. Peter Heath (Charlottesville: University of Virginia Press, 1993), 219–32.

40. Novalis, *Fichte Studies*, in *Theory as Practice: A Critical Anthology of Early German Romantic Writings*, ed. and trans. Jochen Schulte-Sasse et al. (Minneapolis: University of Minnesota Press, 1997), 96. See also Feger, "Die Poetische Vernunft in der Frühromantik," in *Handbuch Literatur und Philosophie*, 76.

41. Michel and Oksiloff, "Romantic Crossovers," 169.

42. Michel and Oksiloff, "Romantic Crossovers," 169.

43. Michel and Oksiloff, "Romantic Crossovers," 169.

44. Walter Benjamin, "The Concept of Criticism in German Romanticism," in *Selected Writings*, eds. Marcus Bullock and Michael W. Jennings, vol. 1 (Cambridge, MA: Belknap Press of Harvard University Press, 1996), 160.

45. Philippe Lacoue-Labarthe and Jean-Luc Nancy, *The Literary Absolute: The Theory of Literature in German Romanticism*, trans. Philip Barnard and Cheryl Lester (Albany: State University of New York Press, 1988), 30. Subsequent references to this book appear in the text.

46. Feger, "Die poetische Vernunft in der Frühromantik," 67–86.

47. A. O. Lovejoy, "On the Meaning of 'Romantic' in Early German Romanticism," *Modern Language Notes* 31, no. 7 (1916): 395.

48. Friedrich Schlegel, "On Philosophy: To Dorothea," in *Theory as Practice: A Critical Anthology of Early German Romantic Writings*, ed. and trans. Jochen Schulte-Sasse et al. (Minneapolis: University of Minnesota Press, 1997), 437. Further references to this work appear in the text. Reference will be made to the German text, "Über die Philosophie: an Dorothea," in Schlegel, *Schriften zur Kritischen Philosophie*, ed. Andreas Arndt and Jure Zovko (Hamburg: Meiner, 2007), identifying the editions with an "E" for English and a "G" for German.

49. Andreas Arndt and Jure Zovko, introduction to Schlegel, *Schriften*, iv.

50. Kant, *Critique of Judgement*, 160, and *Kritik der Urteilskraft* (Leipzig: Meiner, 2006), 316.

51. Lisa C. Roetzel, "Feminizing Philosophy," in *Theory as Practice: A Critical Anthology of Early German Romantic Writings*, edited and translated by Jochen Schulte-Sasse et al., Minneapolis: University of Minnesota Press, 1997), 378, and Dorothea Veit-Schlegel, "Selected Diaries and Letters," in *Theory as Practice*, 441.

52. Roetzel, "Feminizing," 369.

53. Both "Comments on Karl Jaspers' *Psychology of Worldviews*" and "Wilhelm Dilthey's Research and the Struggle for Historical Worldview" may be found in Martin Heidegger, *Supplements: From the Earliest Essays to "Being and Time" and Beyond*, ed. John Van Buren (Albany: State University of New York Press, 2002). Heidegger expresses agreement with Jaspers and Dilthey's common task of "orienting our Dasein to the immediate reality of life" and the need for "enriching, fostering and intensifying life" (81). While skeptical of Jasper's "psychological" approach, he concurs with the goal of "[rendering our understanding] more receptive and more versatile, i.e. more perceptive regarding nuances, dimensions and levels of our psychical being [seelisches Leben]" (72).

54. Thomas Sheehan, "Reading a Life," in *Cambridge Companion to Heidegger*, ed. Charles B. Guignon (Cambridge: Cambridge University Press, 1991), 79.

55. Sheehan, "Reading," 79.

56. Sheehan describes the impact of *Being and Time* in "Heidegger's Early Years," in *Heidegger, the Man and the Thinker*, ed. Thomas Sheehan (New Brunswick, NJ: Transaction, 2010), 15. Heidegger's unfinished lecture series *Introduction to Philosophy: Thinking and Poetizing*, trans. Phillip Jacques Braunstein (Bloomington: University of Indiana Press, 2017), introduces Hölderlin and Nietzsche in these terms, "der denkende Dichter" and "der dichtende Denker."

57. Machado, *Juan de Mairena*, vol. 2 (Madrid: Cátedra, 2003), 89–94.

58. In *¿Qué es filosofía?*, Ortega defines philosophy as "an integral system of intellectual attitudes in which the desire for absolute knowledge is organized methodically" (310) and praises Heidegger for carrying this project out in *Being and Time*'s "analysis of life" (416). English translation is from *What Is Philosophy?* 63, 218.

59. Heidegger, *Being and Time*, trans. John Macquarrie and Edward Robinson (New York: Harper Collins, 1962), 19–22.

60. Krzysztof Ziarek, *Inflected Language: Toward a Hermeneutic of Nearness: Heidegger, Levinas, Celan, Stevens* (New York: State University of New York Press, 1994), 24. Further references will be in the text.

61. Sheehan, "Heidegger's Early Years," 9.

62. Heidegger, *Introduction to Philosophy*, 42–43.

63. Timothy Clark takes issue with Hofstadter's translation of the title "Aus der Erfahrung des Denkens" in "Can Place Think?," *Cultural Politics* 4, no. 1 (2008), arguing that "The Thinker as Poet" is inappropriate for its elision of the difference between poetry and thinking. While I agree, the conflation depends on the meaning of "as," which does not necessarily ascribe a single identity to thinker and poet. The title suggests that the text is a product of thinking, that something akin to verse flows from thinking ("from the experience of thinking"), but the preposition *aus* also might be read as a marker of the exteriority of the ostensibly poetic text from thinking ("out of the experience of thinking"). Further references to Heidegger, "The Thinker as Poet," *Poetry, Language, Thought* (New York: Harper and Row, 1971), and "Aus der Erfahrung," *Gesamtausgabe*, vol. 13 (Frankfurt:

Vittorio Klostermann, 1976), in English and German will be indicated in the text, distinguished by an "E" and a "G."

64. In "Can Place Think?," Clark explains that the scenery described corresponds to Todtnauberg and that this "experimental text" (107) was written to commemorate the twenty-fifth year after Heidegger and his wife Elfride had their cabin built (111).

65. See, for example, the "Erbetene Vorbemerkung zu einer Dichterlesung auf Bühlerhöhe am 24. Februar 1951," in *Gesamtausgabe*, vol. 16, *Reden und andere Zeugnisse eines Lebensweges 1910–1976* (Frankfurt: Vittorio Klostermann, 2000), where Heidegger warns that "*Dichtung* does not mean the same as *Poesie*" (470) and proposes "extracting poetry from the notion of the writer" (das Dichten aus dem Schriftstellertum zu befreien) in which it has been "banished" (471).

66. See Gasché, *Europe*, 155.

67. Clark, "Can Place Think?" 116.

68. Martin Heidegger, *Introduction to Metaphysics*, trans. Gregory Fried and Richard Polt, 2nd ed. (New Haven, CT: Yale University Press, 2014), 166.

69. Heidegger, *Introduction to Metaphysics*, 166.

70. Ziarek, *Inflected Language*, describes "another, poetic thinking" (18) and proposes it as a label for Heidegger's thinking after the abandonment of the project of "fundamental ontology" (23). Clearly, it would also pertain to his own activity in interpreting thinking poets Wallace Stevens and Paul Celan, although without constituting a method or concrete protocols of reading. Ziarek's reticence on the impact of this "other" thinking might be compared to Jennifer Gosetti-Ferencei's contention in *Heidegger, Hölderlin, and the Subject of Poetic Language* (New York: Fordham University Press, 2009) that the reconstitution of a "poetic subject" can provide a "palliative resource" for failed postmodern theories of subjectivity (xiii).

71. This consensus accounts for Claudio César Calabrese's emphatic tone when he states his intention to "make clear [Heidegger's] perspective on the relation poetry-philosophy" in his commentary to his translation of the book *Aus der Erfahrung des Denkens (Desde la experiencia del pensar)* (Buenos Aires: Vórtice, 2014), which includes the short text in verse called "Aus der Erfahrung des Denkens." In short, he rightly says that Heidegger "does not make [poetry and thinking] identical, does not deny their specific traits" (22).

72. Heidegger, *Introduction to Philosophy*, 2. Further references to this book appear in the text.

73. For a list of these moments and a valuable series of assessments of Derrida's "identification" with this quasi-Hispanic figure, see Erin Graff Zivin, ed., *The Marrano Specter: Derrida and Hispanism* (New York: Fordham University Press, 2018), especially the editor's introduction, 2–8.

74. See Heidegger, *Being and Time*, ch. 7, especially 49–55, on different conceptions of the *phenomenon*, and 58–61, where Heidegger relates *phenomenology* as

a methodological principle to what is of necessity "covered up," being, its "subject matter."

75. J. Hillis Miller, "Derrida and Literature," in *Jacques Derrida and the Humanities*, ed. Tom Cohen (Cambridge: Cambridge University Press, 2001), 63.

76. Jacques Derrida, *Of Grammatology*, trans. Gayatri Chakravorty Spivak (Baltimore: Johns Hopkins University Press, 1976), 160.

77. Derrida, *Of Grammatology*, 160.

78. Rodolphe Gasché, *The Tain of the Mirror: Derrida and the Philosophy of Reflection*, (Cambridge, MA: Harvard University Press, 1986), ch. 8, especially 142–54.

79. Jacques Derrida, "Signature, Event, Context," in *Limited, Inc.*, trans. Samuel Weber and Jeffrey Mehlman (Evanston, IL: Northwestern University Press, 1988), 17.

80. Derrida, "Signature, Event, Context," 16.

81. Miller, "Derrida and Literature," 60.

82. For example, in Jacques Derrida, Maurizio Ferraris, *A Taste for the Secret*, trans. Giacomo Donis, ed. Giacomo Donis and David Webb (Cambridge, UK: Polity, 2001).

83. See Miller, "Derrida and Literature," 64.

84. J. Hillis Miller, "Sovereignty Death Literature Unconditionality Democracy University," in *Deconstructing Derrida: Tasks for the New Humanities* (New York: Palgrave Macmillan, 2005), 35.

85. Jacques Derrida and Derek Attridge, "This Strange Institution Called Literature," trans. Geoffrey Bennington and Rachel Bowlby, in *Acts of Literature*, ed. Derek Attridge (New York: Routledge, 1991), 34.

86. Rodolphe Gasché, "A Relation Called 'Literary,'" in *Of Minimal Things: Studies on the Notion of Relation* (Stanford, CA: University Press, 1999), 287. Subsequent references appear parenthetically in the text.

87. Gasché, *The Tain of the Mirror*, 318.

88. Jacques Derrida, "Che cos'è la poesia?," in *The Derrida Reader: Between the Blinds*, ed. Peggy Kamuf (New York: Columbia University Press, 1991), 223. Further references appear in the text.

89. See *Athäneum* fragment 52: "A fragment should be like a little work of art, complete in itself and separated from the rest of the universe like a hedgehog." Friedrich Schlegel, *Philosophical Fragments*, trans. Peter Firchow (Minneapolis: University of Minnesota Press, 1991), 137.

90. For a comparison of some aspects of Heidegger's thinking of the relation of thinking and poetry to María Zambrano's—done in the context of an analysis of Juan Benet's curious volume, *DEL POZO Y DEL NUMA (un ensayo y una leyenda)*—see Stephen Gingerich, "Returning to the Originary Enmity of Philosophy and Literature: Juan Benet's *DEL POZO Y DEL NUMA (Un ensayo y una leyenda)*," *Revista de Estudios Hispánicos* 38, no. 2 (2004): 321–23. In later chapters I will mention several other critical works relating Unamuno, Ortega, Machado, and Zambrano to Heidegger.

Chapter 3

1. José Ortega y Gasset and Miguel de Unamuno, *Epistolario completo Ortega-Unamuno*, ed. Laureano Robles (Madrid: El Arquero, 1987), 90. In the introduction to his translation of Unamuno's *Tratado de amor de dios, Treatise on Love of God* (Urbana: University of Illinois Press, 2007), Nelson Orringer offers an account of Ortega and Unamuno's correspondence between 1905 and 1908, arguing convincingly that the *Treatise* was intended for Ortega to read, as part of a deepening dialogue between the two ambitious intellectuals (xxiv), while *The Tragic Sense of Life* was a reaction to hurtful remarks made by the younger Ortega in the course of that correspondence (xxxiv–xxxvi).

2. Orringer, translator's introduction to *Treatise on Love of God*, xi–xii.

3. Ortega and Unamuno, *Epistolario*, 90.

4. In Spanish, the "h" usually has no sound, making the only difference between *Unamuno* and *un humano* the position of two vowels. Unamuno announced, in *Cómo se hace una novela* (*How to Make a Novel*), in *Manual de Quijotismo; Cómo se hace una novela; Epistolario Miguel de Unamuno/Jean Cassou* (Salamanca: Ediciones Universidad de Salamanca, 2005), 187, that a longer name for him, incorporating his mother's surname and the Basque village where she was born (Larraza), could be "Unamuno Jugo de La Raza," that is, in Anthony Kerrigan's translation, "marrow of the race." See his translator's introduction to *The Tragic Sense of Life in Men and Nations* (Princeton, NJ: Princeton University Press, 1977), ix. Rachel Schmidt, *Forms of Modernity: Don Quijote and Modern Theories of the Novel* (Toronto: Toronto University Press, 2011), in her commentary on this passage, follows the conventional wisdom in drawing the connection from Unamuno to Spain (169). Unamuno depicts himself as, literally, an exemplary member of the so-called "human race." Unamuno's famous remark "me duele España" also plays on near homophony, that of his country's name in Spanish and one of his favorite words for the concrete human, *entrañas* (innards or guts).

5. Veit-Schlegel, "Selected Diaries and Letters," 441.

6. Luis Alvarez Castro, *La palabra y el ser en la teoría literaria de Unamuno* (Salamanca: Ediciones Universidad de Salamanca, 2005), and *Los espejos del yo: existencialismo y metaficción en la narrativa de Unamuno* (Salamanca: Ediciones Universidad de Salamanca, 2015).

7. Álvarez Castro, *La palabra*, 21.

8. Álvarez Castro, *La palabra*, 40.

9. Pedro Ribas, *Para leer a Unamuno* (Madrid: Alianza, 2002), 104.

10. Ribas, *Para leer*, 112.

11. Álvarez Castro, *La palabra*, 21, and *Espejos*, 17.

12. Carlos Blanco Aguinaga, *El Unamuno contemplativo* (Mexico: Colegio de México, 1959), 10. Subsequent references to this book will appear in the text.

13. Álvarez Castro expresses weariness with the "agonic Unamuno" in the form of what he calls "paradojismo" in Unamuno criticism (*La palabra*, 21), and

he renders a version of Blanco Aguinaga's theme as a "concept of the nimbus" (*La palabra*, 133–36).

14. Ribas, *Unamuno*, 40. In *The Revolt of Unreason*, Candelaria detects a quest for peace and resolution, speaking of a "saving skepticism as the way out of the agony of Christianity," although his chosen quote from Unamuno suggests there is, in fact, no "way out": "These two powers [reason and faith] can never conclude peace and we must live by their war" (73).

15. Unamuno, "Escritor ovíparo," in *Obras completas*, vol. 8 (Madrid: Eslicer, 1966), 208–9.

16. Unamuno, "A lo que salga," in *Obras completas*, vol. 1 (Madrid: Eslicer, 1966), 1194–1204. References to this edition of the essay appear in the text.

17. See, for example, Robert Spires, "From Augusto Pérez to Alejandro Gómez to Us: Unamuno's Existential Web," *Revista de Estudios Hispánicos* 20, no. 2 (1986), and Paul R. Olson, *The Great Chiasmus: Word and Flesh in the Novels of Unamuno* (Lafayette, IN: Purdue University Press, 2003). The references are so commonplace that Álvarez Castro complains of the triteness of this reference, in *La palabra*, 26. Gayana Jurkevich, in "Unamuno's Gestational Fallacy: 'Niebla' and 'Escribir a lo que salga,'" *Anales de la literatura española contemporánea* 15, no. 1/3 (1990), complains that the difference between oviparous and viviparous writing has been miscast by critics (65–81). None of these scholars has dwelt at length on Unamuno's claim that writing produces and embodies life, even Nicolás Fernández-Medina, who devotes a chapter to Unamuno in *Life Embodied*, his book on "vital force." In her severe reading of Unamuno—*Miguel de Unamuno: The Contrary Self* (London: Tamesis, 1976)—Frances Wyers rightly takes her peers to task for endorsing this claim and considering it a major contribution to Western civilization.

18. Peter Fenves, *"Chatter": Language and History in Kierkegaard* (Stanford, CA: Stanford University Press, 1993), xii.

19. For the theme of "intrahistoria," whereby the communal identity of a people confers an extended past and future life to the individual, see Unamuno's *En torno al casticismo* (Madrid: Biblioteca Nueva, 1996). Ribas comments on the relation of "intrahistoria" and the concept of *Volksgeist* in *Para leer*, 127, and "Unamuno lector de Hegel," *Revista de Occidente* 96 (1989): 120.

20. In "*Del sentimiento trágico de la vida* a *Niebla*: algunas líneas de relación e interpretación simbólica," in *Unamuno eterno*, ed. J. A. Garrido Ardila (Barcelona: Anthropos, 2015), Sergio Arlandis considers that the two books' simultaneous composition ought to provide some clues to their interpretation (93). His article provides some indications of structural similarities, including "numerical outlines" (99). As a prelude to his own analysis of *Niebla* as metafiction—a concept he describes as "fusion of theory, criticism, and literary creation" (43)—Álvarez Castro credits the novelist Eugenio de Nora with first positing the close relationship between the treatise and the novel in his 1958 essay "La novela agónica de Miguel de Unamuno" (*Espejos*, 17).

21. See Mario Valdés, introduction to *Niebla*, by Miguel de Unamuno (Madrid: Cátedra, 1987), 49.

22. See Roberta Johnson, "El problema del conocimiento en Unamuno y la composición de *Niebla*," in *Actas del IX Congreso de la Asociación Internacional de Hispanistas, 18–23 agosto 1986, Berlin*, vol. 2 (Frankfurt: Vervuert, 1989), 306.

23. Valdés, introduction, 55.

24. Johnson, "El problema," 306.

25. Unamuno, *Del sentimiento trágico de la vida en los hombres y en los pueblos* (Madrid: Austral, 1966), 14, and *The Tragic Sense of Life in Men and Nations*, trans. Anthony Kerrigan (Princeton, NJ: Princeton University Press, 1972), 10. Subsequent references to these volumes will appear in the text, with an "S" and an "E" to indicate Spanish and English editions.

26. Jan Evans, *Unamuno and Kierkegaard*, rightly relates this statement of purpose to Kierkegaard's most direct effort to reflect on his writing career, *The Point of View for My Work as an Author*, while assessing the putting into practice of a "maieutic ideal" in *Concluding Unscientific Postscript*. Unlike the previous books on Kierkegaard and Unamuno, Evans stresses the extent to which these two authors intend to not only convey ideas but force the reader into an unresolvable struggle between incompatible spheres of existence.

27. Alison Sinclair, "Definition as the Enemy of Self-Definition: A Commentary on the Role of Language in Unamuno's *Niebla*," in *Words of Power: Essays in Honour of Alison Fairlie*, eds. Dorothy Gave Coleman and Gillian Jondorf (Glasgow: University of Glasgow Publications in French Langauge and Literature, 1987), 188.

28. Álvarez Castro, *La palabra*, 22.

29. Miguel de Unamuno, *Niebla*, 102, and *Mist: Novela/ Nivola*, 8 (revised). References to these editions of the novel appear in the text, with an "S" preceding the page number of the Spanish edition and an "E" indicating the English.

30. See Valdés, introduction, 55.

31. Compare Miguel de Unamuno, *Fog*, trans. Elena Barcia (Evanston, IL: Northwestern University Press, 2017). Alberto Manguel's introduction to this edition does not address the relative merits of this new translation compared to the older, better-established choice of "mist."

32. Colette Rabaté and Jean Claude Rabaté, *Miguel de Unamuno: Biografía* (Madrid: Taurus, 2009).

33. Jean Cassou, "Retrato de Unamuno por Jean Cassou," in Miguel de Unamuno, *Manual de Quijotismo; Cómo se hace una novela; Epistolario Miguel de Unamuno/Jean Cassou* (Salamanca: Ediciones Universidad de Salamanca, 2005), 164.

34. Ortega and Unamuno, *Epistolario*, 110. Subsequent references to this letter appear parenthetically in the text.

35. In *Unamuno*, Ribas devotes chapter 3, "His Vision of Germany," to documenting Unamuno's knowledge of German language and culture, and confirming the overall negative image of Germans expressed in this letter (57–73). It is worth

noting that, while there were exceptional Germans whom he never included within his dismissal of Germans as "lourds" (62), his general opinion began to change during the years of his exile (1924–30), when he became aware of the interest his work had aroused among German readers (74–81).

36. Immanuel Kant, *Critique of Pure Reason*, trans. Norman Kemp Smith (New York: Modern Library, 1958), 9. Subsequent references to this book appear in the text.

37. See Immanuel Kant, *Religion within the Limits of Reason Alone*, trans. Theodore M. Greene and Hoyt H. Hudson (New York: Harper Torchbooks, 1960). Kant insists that religion and reason cannot be absolute others. Like reason, the mystery of religion confers a kind of knowledge, which must conform to a priori laws worked out by pure reason (129). The "limits" are drawn between universal knowledge, which may become a maxim for practical action, and the idiosyncratic knowledge of religious revelation, which may not. Contrary to what Unamuno often says, eternal life is rational and should serve as the basis for action, which is not to say that faith relieves believers of anxiety (117).

38. See Johan Gottfried Herder, *Against Pure Reason: Writings on Religion, Language, and History*, ed. and trans. Marcia Bunge (Minneapolis: Fortress, 1993). Herder's "Ideas Toward a Philosophy of History" begins with an attack on philosophers "who have exalted human reason to a pure power that is autonomous and independent of the senses and organs" (49). In place of pure reason, Herder proposes that language functions as "the principal instrument of our thought," and thus proposes a different rationality belonging to different and strictly demarcated national identities (49).

39. Zambrano, "Presencia de Don Miguel," in *Unamuno*, ed. Mercedes Gómez Blesa (Madrid: Debolsillo, 2004), 202.

40. Salvador de Madarriaga, "Unamuno Re-read," in Unamuno, *Tragic Sense of Life*, trans. Anthony Kerrigan, xxxi.

41. François Meyer, *L'Ontologie de Miguel de Unamuno* (Paris: Presses Universitaires de France, 1955), viii–ix.

42. Meyer, *L'Ontologie*, x.

43. Meyer, *L'Ontologie*, xi.

44. Ribas, *Para leer*, 10–11. Subsequent references to this book appear parenthetically in the text.

45. Meyer, *L'Ontologie*, 111.

46. Candelaria concludes that Unamuno errs in his interpretation of Kant (*Revolt*, 31–32).

47. G. W. F. Hegel, *Phenomenologie des Geistes* (Frankfurt: Suhrkamp, 1986), 162, and *Phenomenology of Spirit*, trans. A. V. Miller (Oxford: Oxford University Press, 1977), 125. Subsequent references will be given in the text with a "G" to indicate the German original and an "E" to indicate the English translation.

48. Meyer, *L'Ontologie*, ch. 1, and Georges Bataille, *Inner Experience*, trans. Leslie Anne Boldt (Albany: State University of New York Press, 1988), xxxiii.

49. See Ribas, "Unamuno lector de Hegel," 112.

50. Madarriaga, "Unamuno Re-read," xxix.

51. Julián Marías, "La 'meditatio mortis' tema de nuestro tiempo," in "Homenaje a Miguel de Unamuno en el primer centenario de su muerte," special issue of *Revista de Occidente* 7, no. 19 (1964): 50.

52. Mario J. Valdés, *Death in the Literature of Unamuno* (Urbana: University of Illinois Press, 1966), 4.

53. Dezsö Csejtei, *Muerte e inmortalidad en la obra filosófica y literaria de Miguel de Unamuno* (Salamanca: Ediciones Universidad, 2009), 25.

54. Ferrater Mora, *Three Spanish Philosophers*, 3.

55. Garagorri, *La filosofía española en el siglo XX*, 19.

56. Miguel Cruz Hernández, "La misión socrática de don Miguel de Unamuno," *Cuadernos de la Cátedra Miguel de Unamuno* 3 (1952): 44.

57. Cruz Hernández, "La misión socrática," 47.

58. Unamuno's devotion to the prologue is especially apparent in Eva Álvarez Ramos's analysis, in "El prólogo literario en el siglo XX y la retórica clásica," *Ogigia: Revista Electrónica de Estudios Hispánicos*, no. 1 (2007): 61–73. For Álvarez Ramos, Unamuno serves as the guiding example for characterizing the genre within European literature in general.

59. Anthony Kerrigan's 1972 translation corrects *Del sentimiento*'s idiosyncrasy by assigning a chapter number to this epilogical text, deleting the title "Conclusión" and converting the subtitle into the title, both in the table of contents (v) and the text proper (322). The earlier translation by J. E. Crawford Flitch preserves the outline of the Spanish first edition. See Miguel de Unamuno, *The Tragic Sense of Life in Men and in Peoples*, trans. J. E. Crawford Flitch (London: Macmillan, 1921). In his illuminating and exhaustively researched study and translation of *Treatise on Love of God*, Orringer omits the label "Conclusion" when he refers to this text, but he also affirms its paratextual function, calling it "polemical" and "not strictly necessary to the work" (xxxv–xxxvi). In his Spanish edition of *Del sentimiento* and *Tratado* (Madrid: Tecnos, 2005), Orringer compromises between the earlier English editions, maintaining the title "Conclusión" but adding a chapter number.

60. Orringer's expositions in the introductions to his Spanish edition of *Tratado de amor de dios* and to his English translation, *Treatise on the Love of God*, are especially schematic and persuasive summaries of the basic ideas.

61. Candelaria, *Revolt*, 21.

62. Orringer, translator's introduction, xxx–xxxvi, and introduction to *Del sentimiento*, 57–69.

63. Martin Heidegger, *Fundamental Concepts of Metaphysics*, 42.

64. Immanuel Kant, *Critique of Practical Reason*, trans. Lewis White Beck (New York: Macmillan, 1956), 126ff.

65. Maurice Blanchot, "Literature and the Right to Death," in *The Work of Fire*, trans. Charlotte Mandell (Stanford, CA: Stanford University Press, 1995), 336. In "The Felicities of Paradox," in *Of Minimal Things: Studies on the Notion of Relation* (Stanford, CA: Stanford University Press, 1999), Rodolphe Gasché explores the parallels between Blanchot's paradoxical characterization of literature and the tension that emerges in the chapters of the *Phenomenology* devoted to individuality and freedom, which is to say, the section on the unhappy consciousness that we have examined in relation to Unamuno. See especially 314–30.

66. In *Hegel: The Restlessness of the Negative* trans. Jason Smith and Steven Miller) Minneapolis: University of Minnesota Press, 2002), Jean-Luc Nancy calls attention not only to this surprising and unconventional aspect of Hegel in the *Phenomenology* and other work.

67. In *Unamuno*, Ribas outlines the master-slave dialectic and argues that Unamuno never understood the fundamental methodological notion of *Aufhebung*, which maintains all previous movements of spirit in its subsequent development, making the centrality of death in the section on self-consciousness a ubiquitous feature of the Hegelian system (124–35).

68. Cruz Hernández, "La misión socrática," 42.

69. Cruz Hernández, "La misión socrática," 42.

70. Thomas Sheehan, in his introduction to *Heidegger, the Man and the Thinker*, describes the this-sidedness of Being as "a pre-ontological principle undiscovered and undiscoverable by metaphysics" (ix).

71. Heidegger, *Being and Time*, 27. Subsequent references appear in the text.

72. Heidegger also elaborates on this point in chapter 6, on the history of ontology, and chapter 10, distinguishing the analytic of Dasein from psychology, anthropology, and biology.

73. See Heidegger, *Being and Time*, chs. 54–60. More precisely, the structure of resoluteness in Dasein corresponds to the possible decision to attend to the call of conscience, in which an *other* calls out, "Guilty!" (326ff.). Attention to this strange manifestation of otherness within Dasein—although it calls from outside—might prevent the miscasting of Heidegger's existential analytic as "solipsistic" in an interpretation such as Csejtei's in *Muerte e inmortalidad* (22).

74. Thomas R. Franz, "*Niebla*: Infinite Authors/Infinite Fictions," *Occasional Papers in Language, Literature and Linguistics*, series A, no. 33 (1987): 1.

75. Evans, *Unamuno and Kierkegaard*, 5.

76. Valdés, *Death*, 2.

77. Brian Cope, "The Hellenic Origins of Unamuno's Skepticism and *Niebla*'s Skeptical Parody of Cartesianism," *Hispanic Review* 77, no. 4 (2009): 471–93.

78. Cope, "The Hellenic Origins," 482.

79. See Valdés, introduction, 49. Johnson's 1989 article "El problema del conocimiento" provides a detailed account of how this description applies to the incomplete novel, chapters 1–8 (305).

80. In "A lo que salga" Unamuno tells the anecdote of a young reader of novels who cried out "Filler! . . . Filler!" (¡Paja! . . .¡Paja!) when she came across passages that lacked dialogue (1200).

81. In his edition of *Niebla* (Newark, DE: Cervantes, 2007), Francisco Aragón Guiller overstates the case of the *nivola* when he calls it an "entirely new literary genre" (30n10).

82. Gérard Genette, *Paratexts: Thresholds of Interpretation*, trans. Lane E. Lewin (Cambridge: Cambridge University Press, 1997), 1. Subsequent references to this book appear parenthetically in the text.

83. In "From Augusto Pérez to Alejandro Gómez to Us" and his longer analysis of *Fog* in *Beyond the Metafictional Mode: Directions in the Modern Spanish Novel* (Lexington: University Press of Kentucky, 1984), Robert Spires focuses on how Unamuno turns himself and the reader into "linguistic entities" (*Beyond*, 37) and creates for characters "the illusion of autonomy" ("From Augusto," 39). Notably, Unamuno places more emphasis on the life of the character, his flesh and blood and mortality, than he does on that other venerable philosophical characteristic of human life, freedom.

84. In *Rhetoric of Fiction* (Chicago: University of Chicago Press, 1983), Wayne C. Booth introduces the concept of "implied author" in a chapter on the assumed "objectivity" of authors, stressing that only the "implied author" engendered by the work of fiction, and not the "real" author, must be "objective" (67). A typology of authors appended to the second edition of *Rhetoric* includes a "flesh-and-blood author" who has several choices about the attitude of the narrator he will create (428–29).

85. Unamuno, "Entrevista con Augusto Pérez," in *Niebla* (Madrid: Cátedra, 1987), 74.

86. Descartes, *Discourse*, 127.

87. José Ortega y Gasset, "En la muerte de Unamuno," in *Miguel de Unamuno*, ed. Antonio Sánchez Barbudo (Madrid: Taurus, 1974), 19.

88. Ortega y Gasset, "En la muerte," 21.

89. Jorge Luis Borges, "Inmortalidad de Unamuno," in *Jorge Luis Borges in Sur (1931–1980)* (Buenos Aires: Emecé, 1999), 144, and "Presencia de Miguel de Unamuno," in *Textos cautivos: Ensayos y reseñas de "El Hogar,"* ed. Enrique Sacerio-Garí (Barcelona: Tusquets, 1986), 82. Subsequent references to these brief essays will appear in the text.

90. See *Online Etymological Dictionary*, s.v. "discuss," accessed June 29, 2021, https://www.etymonline.com/search?q=discuss, and *Diccionario de la lengua española*, s.v. "discutir," Real Academia Española, accessed June 29, 2021, https://dle.rae.es/discutir?m=form.

91. Miguel de Unamuno, *Tres novelas ejemplares y un prólogo* (Madrid: Alianza, 1987), and *Three Exemplary Novels*, trans. Angel Flores (New York: Grove, 1987).

92. Miguel de Unamuno, *Manual de Quijotismo; Cómo se hace una novela; Epistolario Miguel de Unamuno/Jean Cassou*, and *How to Make a Novel*, in *Novela/*

Nivola, vol. 6 of *Selected Works*, trans. Anthony Kerrigan (Princeton, NJ: Princeton University Press, 1976).

93. Miguel de Unamuno, *San Manuel Bueno, mártir* (Madrid: Cátedra, 2003), and *Saint Manuel Bueno, Martyr*, trans. Paul Burns and Salvador Ortiz-Carboneres (Oxford: Oxbow, 2009).

Chapter 4

1. José Ortega y Gasset, "Adán en el Paraíso," in *La deshumanización del arte y otros ensayos de estética* (Madrid: Alianza; Revista de Occidente, 2000), 90. Subsequent references to this work appear parenthetically in the text.

2. José Ortega y Gasset, "Ni vitalismo ni racionalismo," in *Obras completas*, vol. 3 (Madrid: Revista de Occidente, 1966), 270.

3. Ortega, "Ni vitalismo," 270.

4. José Ortega y Gasset, *La idea del principio en Leibniz*, in *Obras Completas*, 8:292n1, and *The Idea of the Principle in Leibniz and the Evolution of Deductive Theory*, trans. Mildred Adams (New York: Norton, 1971), 304n6 (slightly revised).

5. José Ortega y Gasset, "Prólogo para alemanes," in *Obras completas*, 8:8, and "Preface for Germans," *Phenomenology and Art*, trans. Phillip Silver (New York: Norton, 1975), 21.

6. Ortega y Gasset, "Prólogo," 8, and "Preface," 21 (revised).

7. See Nelson Orringer, "Sobre las cuatro etapas de Ortega," *Los Ensayistas* 3, no. 5, (1978): 26, and Cerezo Galán, *La voluntad de aventura*, 39. Peter Gordon Mann's connection of Ortega with Simmel—in "Saving Europe in Spain: José Ortega y Gasset's *Meditaciones de Quijote* and the Politics of Self, Nation, and Europe," *Journal of European Studies* 49, no. 2 (2019)—provides a detailed explanation of Simmel's investment in the term "life."

8. In *The Idea of the Principle in Leibniz* Ortega accuses Heidegger of arbitrarily assigning the name "Being" to what can be properly called "life." After confessing his befuddlement at the necessity of asking the question of Being, he gives a historical overview intended to show that "the meaning of Being" is a function of *life*'s unfolding (*La idea*, 271–79; *The Idea*, 277–87). Ortega's comments do not acknowledge that *Being and Time*'s first page warned about the lack of perplexity regarding Being, since one typically assumes one knows what "being" means (Heidegger, *Being and Time*, 1).

9. See "Dos grandes metáforas," in *Obras completas*, 2:387–400. For Ortega, there is no such thing as literal, "direct thought" (387). The metaphor is "an essential means of intellection," through which life reaches consciousness (390).

10. Ortega, "Prólogo," 16, and "Preface," 19 (revised). For a discussion of Ortega's association of idiom with a "Spanish secret," see Stephen D.

Gingerich, "Ortega: Secrecy and the World," *CR: The New Centennial Review* 3 (2014): 49–74.

11. Lanz, "José Ortega y Gasset," 25.
12. Hegel, *Phenomenology*, 58–59.
13. Hegel, *Phenomenology*, 58.
14. Hegel, *Phenomenology*, 107.
15. For a later, and slightly more detailed account of this history, one may consult Ortega's *Historia como sistema* ("History as a System"), section 6, where he asserts the necessity of breaking with the concept of being, typical of the "old-fashioned Greeks [calenda griega]," in favor of an up-to-date concept of "human life" as the "radical reality." See *Historia como sistema* (Madrid: Revista de Occidente, 1970), 28–35, and *History as System and Other Essays toward a Philosophy of History*, trans. Helene Weyl (New York: Norton, 1961), 187–99.
16. Jorge García-Gómez, introduction to Antonio Rodríguez Huéscar, *José Ortega y Gasset's Metaphysical Innovation: A Critique and Overcoming of Idealism*, trans. Jorge García-Gómez (Albany: State University of New York Press, 1995), xiii.
17. See book 1 of *Metaphysics*, 984b–993a.
18. In addition to the previous references to Lanz and Molinuevo, see Valeriano Bozal's discussion of *La deshumanización del arte* and his gloss of Silver's work in his prologue to *La deshumanización del arte* (Madrid: Espasa-Calpe, 1987). Bozal sums up, "Reality is the reality of a painting" (14). He explains Silver's position that the event of "immediate relation of the 'I' with things" happens in the "artistic image" (24).
19. Javier San Martín praises Ortega for his elaboration of this "culture before reflection" in the *Meditations*. See *Fenomenología y cultura en Ortega* (Madrid: Tecnos, 1998), 12.
20. In "Reason, Practice and the Promise of a New Spain: Ortega's 'Vieja y nueva política' and *Meditaciones del Quijote*," *Bulletin of Hispanic Studies* 77 (2000), Tatiana Gajić asks by what right Ortega creates the terms for his own reception. She may not provide an answer to this question, but we should not be surprised that he cultivates an audience that grants him authority to do so, in part because of their desire for what he is offering them: a Spanish philosopher ready to match wits with the French, German, and English canon.
21. Ortega y Gasset, *¿Qué es filosofía?*, 279, and *What Is Philosophy*, 18. Further references appear in the text, with the Spanish indicated by an "S" and the English by an "E."
22. See Victor Ouimette's offer of an introduction that would allow Ortega's work to be "read and . . . savored" and, ultimately, "completed" by the reader, in *José Ortega y Gasset* (Boston: Twayne, 1982), 9.
23. See Ouimette, *José Ortega y Gasset*, 28–30, and Jordi Gracia, *José Ortega y Gasset* (Madrid: Taurus, 2014), 12. Ouimette also mentions Ortega's depression

in the 1940s, when he toured incessantly, trying to overcome the sensation that his star was fading (35).

24. Ortega y Gasset, "Goethe desde adentro," in *Obras completas*, 4:381–541, and "In Search of Goethe from Within," in *The Dehumanization of Art and Other Writings on Art and Culture*, trans. Willard Trask (Garden City: Doubleday, 1956), 121–60.

25. As Mann explains, readers of the *Meditations* were meant not only to reread *Don Quixote* in a new way, but to approach life with a new, "heroic" attunement. "Saving Europe," 108–42.

26. See Basil Cleveland, "The Concept of Reading in Ortega's *Meditations on Quijote*," *CLIO* 34, no. 1–2 (2004–5): 83–98. Cleveland especially emphasizes the "constant tension between these two possibilities" (92) and speculates that Ortega's rhetorical invitation to heroic and amorous action serves to draw readers into an unattractive situation of dwelling within a "double movement" in which failure is a real possibility (94–95).

27. See Orringer, "Sobre las cuatro etapas de Ortega," 21.

28. José Ortega y Gasset, *El tema de nuestro tiempo*, in *Obras completas*, 3:143, and *The Modern Theme*, trans. James Cleugh (New York: Harper and Row, 1961), where Ortega's "doctrina" is rendered a "theory" (9). Subsequent references appear in the text, with the Spanish identified by "S" and this English translation by "E."

29. Perhaps it is not too indiscrete, here in the margins, to pass on an indicator of which organ might guide Ortega's thinking. Octavio Paz tells of a conversation with Ortega in 1951 in which the sixty-seven year old tells Paz, "Thinking is an erection, and I still think." See Octavio Paz, "José Ortega y Gasset: el cómo y el para qué/2: Tres omisiones," *El País*, October 23, 1980, https://elpais.com/diario/1980/10/24/opinion/341190008_850215.html, and "José Ortega y Gasset, the Why and the Wherefore," *On Poets and Others*, trans. Michael Schmidt (New York: Seaver, 1986), 150.

30. Astrid Wagner, José María Ariso, the editors of *Rationality Reconsidered: Ortega y Gasset and Wittgenstein on Knowledge, Belief and Practice* (Berlin: de Gruyter 2016), sum up Ortega's claims and endorse them: "Traditional culture must become biological culture, whilst pure reason must cede its sovereignty to form a new reason called vital reason" (2).

31. See Ortega y Gasset, *Historia como sistema*; *History as System and Other Essays*; "En torno a Galileo," in *Obras completas*, 5:9–164; and *Man and Crisis*, trans. Mildred Adams (New York: Norton, 1958).

32. See Manuel Garrido et al., *El legado filosófico español e hispanoamericano del siglo XX*, ch. 8, "Ortega, o la aurora de la filosofía visto como deporte," coordinated by Orringer; and Antonio Gutiérrez-Pozo, *La aurora de la razón vital: fenomenología y vitalismo en el origen de la filosofía de Ortega y Gasset* (Madrid: Mileto Ediciones, 2003).

33. In "Preface for Germans," he explains that he has considered it expedient to publish Freud in his *Revista de Occidente* but insists that his interest in Freud's work has been "evanescent" to the point of disappearance. "Prólogo," 33; "Preface," 42.

34. Ortega y Gasset, "Goethe desde adentro," 401, and "In Search of Goethe," 131.

35. Ortega y Gasset, "Prólogo," 52, and "Preface," 67 (revised).

36. Ortega y Gasset, "Prólogo," 52, and "Preface," 67 (revised).

37. Orringer, "Sobre las cuatro etapas de Ortega," 21.

38. For Orringer and Garrido, the essential character of late Ortega is defined by the idea of "philosophy as sport." See Manuel Garrido, et al., *El legado filosófico español e hispanoamericano del siglo XX*, ch. 8, "Ortega, o la aurora del filosofar como deporte."

39. Bruno Bosteels, "Hegel in America," in *Hegel and the Infinite: Religion, Politics and Dialectic*, ed. Slavoj Žižek et al. (New York: Columbia University Press, 2011), 67–70.

40. Jacques Derrida, "*Ousia* and *Grammé*: Note on a Note from *Being and Time*," in *Margins of Philosophy*, trans. Alan Bass (Chicago: University of Chicago Press, 1982), 31–67. Subsequent references to this essay appear in the text.

41. Unamuno quotes this twice, in the first and fourth chapters of his treatise. In English, "Living comes first, then philosophizing." See Miguel de Unamuno, *Del sentimiento trágico*, 30, 91, and *The Tragic Sense of Life*, 91, 127.

42. Octavio Paz, "José Ortega y Gasset: el cómo y el para qué/1," *El País*, October 22, 1980, elpais.com; "José Ortega y Gasset: el cómo y el por qué/2"; and "José Ortega y Gasset: The Why and the Wherefore," 139–51. Since the original publication has no page numbers, page numbers, subsequently given in the text, are to the English translation only.

43. Jesús M. Díaz Álvarez and Jorge Brioso, "Esperar lo inesperado. Algunas reflexiones sobre la contingencia a partir de la obra de Antonio Rodríguez Huéscar y José Ortega y Gasset," *Bajo Palabra: Revista de Filosofía* 2, no. 11 (2015): 127–30.

44. Díaz Álvarez and Brioso, "Esperar lo inesperado," 129.

45. For a brief overview of Ortega's misogynistic representation of women as the weaker sex, see Ángeles J. Perona and Ramón del Castillo Santos, "El pensamiento español y representaciones de género," in *Sociología de las mujeres españolas*, ed. María Antonia García de León, Marisa García de Cortázar, and Félix Ortega (Madrid: Editorial Complutense, 1996), 342–44. Regarding a certain "agism," consider Ortega's contention that Husserl was too old to adequately comprehend the younger thinker's "objection to phenomenology": "When I became acquainted with the admirable Husserl . . . his age and his infirmities did not permit him to take up difficult themes from his own output" *La idea*, 273n2; *The Idea*, 280n3.

46. See Garrido et al., *El legado filosófico*, 669.

47. See Garrido et al., *El legado filosófico*, ch. 42, "Filosofía y género en España: de su irrupción en el siglo XX a su fortalecimiento en el siglo XXI."

48. See José Luis Abellán, "Pensamiento español: una categoría historiográfica," 310–11.

Chapter 5

1. Antonio Machado, *Poesías completas* (Madrid: Espasa-Calpe, 1983), 227. While this translation is my own, this poem can also be found in English in Machado, *Border of a Dream: Selected Poems of Antonio Machado*, trans. Willis Barnstone (Port Townsend, WA: Copper Canyon Press, 2004), 285, *Times Alone: Selected Poems of Antonio Machado*, trans. Robert Bly (Middletown, CT: Wesleyan University Press, 1983), 118, and Alice McVan, *Antonio Machado* (New York: Hispanic Society of America, 1959), 167.

2. See Francisco Caudet's traversal of Machado's work with attention to the "space/time axes," in *En el inestable circuito del tiempo: Antonio Machado: de "Soledades" a "Juan de Mairena"* (Madrid: Cátedra: 2009), 9.

3. Machado, *Poesías*, 335. The "apocryphal songbooks" may be consulted in any standard edition of Machado's *Poesías completas* in sections numbered 167 and 168. References to this edition appear parenthetically in the text.

4. See Kant, *Critique of Pure Reason*, 82, and Aristotle, *On the Soul*, trans. W. S. Hett (London: W. Heinemann; Cambridge, MA: Harvard University Press, 1957), part 3, 35ff.

5. See Antonio Sánchez Barbudo, *El pensamiento de Antonio Machado* (Madrid: Guadarrama, 1974), 7–8, Cerezo Galán, *Palabra en el tiempo*, 11, and Valverde, introduction to Machado's *Nuevas canciones*, 9.

6. Selections from *Soledades* are available in several anthologies, but there is no complete translation in a single volume. Robert Bly felicitously calls his edition of poems from this volume only *Times Alone: Twelve Poems from Soledades* (Port Townsend, WA: Graywolf Press, 1983), and I will continue to refer to it, as Bly's subtitle does, by the Spanish name.

7. Antonio Machado, *Poesías*, 68. Subsequent references are indicated parenthetically in the text.

8. See Fernando Pessoa, *A Little Larger Than the Entire Universe: Selected Poems*, ed. and trans. Richard Zenith (New York: Penguin, 2006), especially the excerpted "Biographical Sketch" by Pessoa in which he defines "heteronymic works" as being "by the author outside his own person, [by] a full-fledged individual created by [the author]" (3).

9. José Luis Abellán, "El filósofo 'Antonio Machado,'" in *Antonio Machado hacia Europa*, ed. Pablo Luis Ávila (Madrid: Visor, 1993), 172, and Patrick Duran-

tou, "Poesía y filosofía de Antonio Machado," *Antonio Machado hacia Europa*, ed. Pablo Luis Ávila (Madrid: Visor, 1993), 202.

10. Sánchez Barbudo, *El pensamiento de Antonio Machado*, 7–8.

11. Pedro Cerezo Galán, "Lo apócrifo machadiano: 'un ensayo de esfuerzos fragmentarios,'" in *Antonio Machado hoy (1939–1989)*, ed. Paul Aubert (Madrid: Casa de Velázquez, 1994), 186.

12. Jorge Guillén, "El apócrifo Antonio Machado," in *Estudios sobre Antonio Machado*, ed. José Ángeles (Barcelona: Ariel, 1977), 221.

13. Aurora de Albornoz, *La presencia de Unamuno en Machado* (Madrid: Gredos, 1968), 320–23.

14. Biruté Ciplijauskaité, "*Ser* y *estar* en la palabra: Machado, Heidegger y la deconstrucción," in *Divergencias y unidad: perspectivas sobre la Generación del 98 y Antonio Machado*, ed. John P. Gabriele (Madrid: Orígenes, 1990), 232, 228–29.

15. Steven Hutchinson, "El movimiento en la obra de Antonio Machado," in *Divergencias y unidad: perspectivas sobre la Generación del 98 y Antonio Machado*, ed. John P. Gabriele (Madrid: Orígenes, 1990), 253.

16. Rafael Gutiérrez Girardot, "Lírica y filosofía en Antonio Machado," in *Antonio Machado hoy (1939–1989)*, ed. Paul Aubert (Madrid: Casa de Velázquez, 1994), 131.

17. Julián Marías, "Antonio Machado y el pensamiento," *Antonio Machado hacia Europa*, ed. Pablo Luis Ávila (Madrid: Visor, 1993), 151–54.

18. Guillermo de Torre, "Teorías literarias de Antonio Machado," in *Antonio Machado*, ed. Ricardo Gullón and Allen W. Phillips (Madrid: Taurus, 1973), 229.

19. Barjau, *Antonio Machado*, 60.

20. Barjau, *Antonio Machado*, 55, 22.

21. Fernández Ferrer, introduction to *Juan de Mairena*, 11.

22. Fernández Ferrer, introduction, 28.

23. Fernández Ferrer, introduction, 33.

24. Cerezo Galán's analysis of Machado in his second book on the poet wavers between the attribution of unity and the recognition of an unresolvable tension between literature and philosophy. He speaks of a "rhapsodic" relationship of self to other and self to self, characterized by incompleteness. When it comes to describing Antonio Machado, he reverts to the idea of a single "soul" in which heterogeneous poet-philosopher figures resound. See *Antonio Machado en los apócrifos: una filosofía de poeta* (Almería: Editorial Universidad, 2012), 119–22.

25. Machado, "Poética," *Poesías*, 71.

26. Machado, "Poética," *Poesías*, 71.

27. Belitt's translation of *Juan de Mairena* includes this poem in an appendix (135).

28. Hegel, *Phenomenologie des Geistes*, 111, and *Phenomenology of Spirit*, 81.

29. Hegel, *Phenomenologie*, 132, and *Phenomenology*, 100.

30. Bergson, *Time and Free Will: An Essay on the Immediate Data of Consciousness*, trans. F. L. Pogson (New York: Harper and Row, 1960), ix, 137–39.

31. Bergson, *Time and Free Will*, 233–40.

32. See Cerezo, *Palabra en el tiempo*, 119, and Sánchez Barbudo's attribution of identification of the theme of heterogeneity to Bergson, in *El pensamiento*, 21. For a more recent examination of Machado's debt to Bergson, see Robert Havard, *From Romanticism to Surrealism: Seven Spanish Poets* (Cardiff: University of Wales Press, 1988), ch. 3.

33. Oreste Macrí, introduction to *Poesía y prosa*, by Antonio Machado, ed. Oreste Macrí, vol. 1, *Introducción* (Madrid: Espasa-Calpe; Fundación Antonio Machado, 1989), 74. Subsequent references to this work appear parenthetically in the text.

34. Philip W. Silver has made a similar argument in *Ortega as Phenomenologist: The Genesis of "Meditations on Quixote"* (New York: Columbia University Press, 1978), reconstructing an origin of the *Meditations* and the whole of Ortega's work in the absence of a *"central* text" (5).

35. For a readable and well-documented account of the continuity between Husserl's early and late work, especially with regard to the effort to provide ultimate grounds for objective knowledge in the reduction of the transcendental subject, see John Cogan, "Phenomenological Reduction," *Internet Encyclopedia of Philosophy*, accessed July 5, 2020, https://iep.utm.edu/phen-red/.

36. Jacques Derrida, *Speech and Phenomena and Other Essays on Husserl's Theory of Signs*, trans. David Allison and Newton Garver (Evanston, IL: Northwestern University Press, 1974), 5. Subsequent references to this work appear parenthetically in the text.

37. See Husserl's assertion in the *Logical Investigations* that a team of researchers could attain a "scientific philosophy," making the necessary "discoveries" over the course of "a generation of research-workers" with "resolute cooperation." *Logical Investigations*, trans. J. N. Findlay, vol. 1 (London: Routledge and Kegan Paul, 1982), 256.

38. Leonard Lawlor, in the introduction for his new translation of the Derrida work as *Voice and Phenomenon* (Evanston, IL: Northwestern University Press, 2011), argues convincingly for this motif ("the deconstruction of phenomenology as metaphysics of presence") as one of the three distinguishing "features" of Derrida's thought (xi–xii).

39. Derrida, *Speech and Phenomena*, 31. For example, "Husserl . . . will ceaselessly strive to keep signification outside the self-presence of transcendental life"; "Husserl believes in the existence of a pre-expressive and prelinguistic stratum of sense, which the reduction must sometimes disclose by excluding the stratum of language."

40. In *Speech and Phenomena*, Derrida explains that *différance* precedes consciousness or presence, making it possible while at the same time "fissuring" and "retarding" it (88).

41. Antonio Machado, *Escritos dispersos (1893–1936)*, ed. Jordi Doménech (Barcelona: Octahedro, 2009) 313. Subsequent references will appear parenthetically in the text.

42. Jordi Doménech's introduction to Machado, *Escritos dispersos (1893–1936)*, 314n3.

43. The *Poesías completas* include a "Cancionero apócrifo" of "Doce poetas que pudieron existir" ("12 Poets Who Could Have Existed"), including one with the name of "Antonio Machado," whose biographical data clearly distinguishes him from his homonymous creator (404).

44. J. L. Austin, *How to Do Things with Words* (Cambridge, MA: Harvard University Press, 1962), 60–61.

45. Pablo del Barco, in the prologue to his edition of *Juan de Mairena* (Madrid: Alianza, 1995), offers three convenient categories, although one can easily see they are intermingled: "on the human condition," "on philosophy," and "on poetics" (17).

46. See the first lines of their respective songbooks in the *Poesías completas*, 305, 327. The moment of Mairena's death is also mentioned in *Juan de Mairena* (S 157; E 36)

47. For a recent, comprehensive exposition of this essentially Romantic facet of Machado's work, see Caudet, *En el inestable circuito del tiempo*. For Caudet, Machado's multifaceted discourse integrates fragments from many perspectives in a process of "assemblage" that is intended to capture "the ultimate meaning of parcels of reality" and convey that meaning to the reader (10).

48. Jochen Mecke, "La 'alterización' del arte: estética y filosofía apócrifas en Antonio Machado," in *Hoy es siempre todavía. Curso internacional sobre Antonio Machado, Córdoba 7–11 de noviembre de 2005*, ed. Jordi Doménech (Sevilla: Renacimiento/Ayuntamiento de Córdoba, 2006), 547. Fernández-Medina's *Poetics of Otherness* closes with a discussion of Machado's kinship to Levinas (169–73).

49. I refer to the premise of *Madness and Civilization*—indicated more clearly in the French title, *Folie et déraison*—of contesting the simplistic opposition of madness and reason. See Michel Foucault, *Madness and Civilization* (New York: Routledge, 2001).

50. Antonio Machado, *Los complementarios*, in *Poesía y prosa*, vol. 3, *Prosas completas (1893–1936)*, eds. Oreste Macrí and Gaetano Chiappini (Madrid: Espasa-Calpe; Fundación Antonio Machado, 1989), 1320, 1341, and 1322, respectively.

51. Machado, *Los complementarios*, 1367.

52. The phrase is Julián Marías's, in "Machado y Heidegger," 2. In "Antonio Machado y la modernidad," García Posada refers specifically to the precedent of Mr. Teste (73), as does Valverde in his introduction to *Juan de Mairena* (22).

53. Clavería provides the most extensive account of the relationship of Machado to Valéry, focussing on what was originally a lecture given in 1939. See Carlos Clavería, "Notas sobre la poética de Antonio Machado," *Hispania* 28, no. 2 (1945): 174–80.

54. Paul Valéry, *An Anthology*, ed. and trans. James R. Lawler (Princeton, NJ: Princeton University Press, 1977), 3.

55. Valéry, *Anthology*, 140–42.

56. Valéry, *Anthology*, 142.

57. Machado, *Los complementarios*, 1367. "Reflexiones" appeared in two versions, only the first of which contains the reference to Valéry and "Romain" (*sic*), as in the version in *Los complementarios*. The first published version may be consulted in *Cuadernos Hispanoamericanos*, no. 45 (1953): 279–91, while the second, published first in 1925, appears in Machado, *Poesía y prosa*, vol. III, *Prosas completas (1893–1936)*, 1649–662.

58. See "La Jeune Parque/ The Young Fate," in Valéry, *Anthology*, 198–235.

59. Valéry, *Anthology*, 205.

60. Valéry, *Anthology*, 210–11.

61. Bergson, *Time and Free Will*, 235–40.

62. Valéry, *Anthology*, 200.

63. Machado devotes a part of the "Cancionero apócrifo: Abel Martín" to the self-reflection that would serve as the basis of a "poet's metaphysics" (318–21). This forms the basis for Nancy Newton's interpretation of poetic knowledge as a kind of negative power, in "Structures of Cognition: Antonio Machado and the Via Negativa," *MLN* 90, no. 2 (1975): 231–51.

64. Machado, *Juan de Mairena*, S 238. The English translation includes the quatrain and much of the commentary that prepares for it but omits comments that frame the poem, which are key for understanding the connection to Valéry and the relationship between poetry and thought: "For the poet it is only necessary *to see and to blind, a seeing that sees itself,* pure evidence, which is being itself, and a creative act, necessarily negative, which is nothingness itself." Directly after the quatrain, Mairena speaks to his students, concluding, "Take note of these verses, even if it is only for their rhetorical value, as a model for an emphatic expression of thought. And let us leave for another day the task of going deeper into the poetics of my teacher" (E 68).

65. Marías, "Machado y Heidegger," 2.

66. See Heidegger, "Comments on Karl Jaspers' *Psychology of Worldviews*," 71–104.

67. See Heidegger, *Being and Time*, 41–49.

68. Dámaso Alonso, "Fanales de Antonio Machado," 176.

69. Hegel, *Phenomenologie*, 29–30, and *Phenomenology*, 14–5.

70. In "The Letter on Humanism," Heidegger comments on the shortcomings of *Being and Time* and attempts to combat the misinterpretations of his thought as an "existentialist," anthropological doctrine. See "The Letter on Humanism," *Basic Writings*, ed. David Farrell Krell (New York: Harper Collins, 1993), 213–66. Heidegger also comments briefly on simplistic dismissals of his thinking (such as, if it questions "rationality," it must be "irrationalist") and characterizes his goal of "overcoming": "Thinking does not overcome metaphysics by climbing still higher,

surmounting it, transcending it somehow or other; thinking overcomes metaphysics by climbing back down into the nearness of the nearest" (254).

Chapter 6

1. María Zambrano, *La confesión: género literario* (Madrid: Ediciones Siruela, 1995), 13, and *Confession*, in *Two Confessions*, by María Zambrano and Rosa Chacel, trans. Noël Valis and Carol Maier (Albany: State University of New York Press, 2015), 14 (revised).

2. See Janet Pérez, "*Circunstancia*, Reason, and Metaphysics: Context and Unity in the Thought of María Zambrano," in *Spanish Women Writers and the Essay*, ed. Kathleen M. Glenn and Mercedes Mazquiarán de Rodríguez (Columbia: University of Missouri Press, 1998), 145, and Bundgård, *Más allá de la filosofía*, 12. Bundgård speaks of "thematic redundancies" of Zambrano's texts in "La creación al modo humano o el rostro de la nada: María Zambrano y Nietzsche," 467.

3. Zambrano, *El hombre y lo divino* (Mexico City: FCE, 2001), 68.

4. Zambrano, *El hombre*, 176.

5. Caballero Rodríguez singles out Zambrano's tendency to start sentences with "y" (and) and to make up words, hypothesizing that her intention is to "destabilize" the reader (*María Zambrano*, 155). Bundgård's "La creación al modo humano o el rostro de la nada" acknowledges the difficulty of making sense of her texts (469), a task that her book and many essays have excelled in. The following analyses quote extensively enough to exemplify most of these idiosyncrasies. Since many of my translations retain an awkwardness from the original, I have included abundant quotations of the Spanish. While much of Zambrano's work is available in major European languages, *Delirium and Destiny* and *Confession* are the only English translations of entire books.

6. Moreno Sanz, introduction to María Zambrano, *Obras completas*, vol. 1, ed. Jesús Moreno Sanz et al., x–xxxviii (Barcelona: Galaxia Gutenberg, 2015), xxxii.

7. Zambrano, *El hombre*, 66–77.

8. Zambrano, *Los bienaventurados* (Madrid: Siruela, 2004), 11–16.

9. Zambrano, "La crisis de la palabra," in *Algunos lugares de la poesía*, ed. Juan Fernando Ortega Muñoz (Madrid: Trotta, 2007), 75.

10. Zambrano, *Pensamiento y poesía en la vida española* (Madrid: Endymion, 1996), 11–19, and *La agonía de Europa* (Madrid: Trotta, 2000). An English version of first chapter of the latter book may be found in an issue of *History of European Ideas* devoted to articles on Zambrano and a series of translations: "The Agony of Europe," trans. Jennifer Arnold, *History of European Ideas* 44, no. 7 (2018): 952–59.

11. Zambrano, "La crisis de la palabra," 75.

12. "Metaphilosophy" is the term proposed by Bundgård, "La creación," 473. Janet Pérez speaks of "metarationality" in her article about "poetic reason," "*Circunstancia*, Reason, and Metaphysics," 150. As I hope to have shown in chapter

2, philosophy already includes, in the moment of its first articulations, the reflection on itself, a sort of gaze back from beyond its specifically theoretical or ethical modes. This vein of Spanish writing seems committed to questioning philosophy's conditions of possibility in a mode that is not exhaustively determined ahead of time by philosophy, and hence to correspond neither to "meta" as beyond nor to "philosophy" or "rationality."

13. "Por qué se escribe" in Zambrano, *Hacia un saber sobre el alma* (Buenos Aires: Losada, 2005), 27–36.

14. Ortega Muñoz, in *Introducción al pensamiento*, speaks of the power of "poetic reason" to overcome the "dictatorship of reason" (24).

15. Zambrano, *El hombre*, 70.

16. Zambrano, "Cuba secreta," in *"La cuba secreta" y otros ensayos*, ed. Jorge Luis Arcos (Madrid: Endymion, 1996), 109.

17. Zambrano, "La religión poética de Unamuno," in *España, sueño y verdad* (Barcelona: Edhasa, 2002), 175.

18. This is one of the ways Balibrea, Lough, and Sánchez Cuervo characterize Zambrano's thought in "María Zambrano amongst the philosophers," 828. In this, they follow Pérez's description of an "anthropology" that would guide the *anthropos* to "vital plenitude and excellence" and Pedro Cerezo Galán's means of describing her thought is as a "pneumatic anthropology." See Pérez, "*Circunstancia*, Reason, and Metaphysics," 165, and Cerezo Galán "El alma y la palabra," in *Filosofía y literatura en María Zambrano*, ed. Pedro Cerezo Galán (Seville: Fundación José Manuel Lara, 2005), 15.

19. María Zambrano, *Filosofía y poesía* (Mexico City: FCE, 1996), 13. Subsequent references will appear parenthetically in the text.

20. José Luis L. Aranguren likens Zambrano's style to children's play, commending her for establishing a new style of philosophy while regretting that, in her wandering, she often seems "to know too well" exactly where her feet will take her. See Aranguren, "Filosofía y poesía," in *El pensamiento de María Zambrano: papeles de Almagro* (Madrid: Zero, 1983), 116.

21. In the beginning of *Creación por la metáfora: introducción a la razón poética* (Barcelona: Anthropos, 1992), Chantal Maillard offers an apt description of Zambrano feeling the pull of both philosophy and poetry, with the genesis of the work constituted by the attempt to hold herself in the space created by that play of opposing forces (10). "Doble tirón" is the expression Zambrano uses in the first lines of *Filosofía y poesía* (13).

22. Abellán, in "María Zambrano, la 'razón poética' en marcha," in *Filosofía española en América (1936–1966)* (Madrid: Ediciones Guadarrama; Seminarios y Ediciones, 1967), 169–89, and Aranguren, in "Los sueños de María Zambrano," approach her as a follower of Ortega. More recently, Sergio Sevilla asserts that Zambrano frees "vital reason" from its limitations in Ortega's writing, opening

reason to its others, primarily poetry. See "La razón poética: mirada, melodía y metáfora: María Zambrano y la hermenéutica," in *María Zambrano: la razón poética o la filosofía*, 87–108.

23. Aranguren, "Filosofía y poesía," 114.

24. Zambrano, *La confesión*, 25, and *Confession*, 20.

25. Roberta Johnson, "What María Zambrano Discovered in the New World," in *María Zambrano: Between the Caribbean and the Mediterranean*, ed. Madeline Cámara and Luis Ortega (Newark, DE: Juan de la Cuesta, 2015), 26. This story is also told by Balibrea, Lough, and Sánchez Cuervo in *María Zambrano amongst the Philosophers*, 835.

26. Zambrano, *Delirio y destino: los veinte años de una española* (Madrid: Editorial Centro de Estudios Ramón Areces, 1998), 60, and *Delirium and Destiny: A Spaniard in Her Twenties*, trans. Carol Maier (Albany: State University of New York Press, 1999), 29.

27. Zambrano, "A modo de autobiografía," *Anthropos* 70–71 (1986): 70.

28. Zambrano, "Miguel de Cervantes," in *Algunos lugares*, 115.

29. Zambrano, "Pensamiento y poesía en Emilio Prados," in *Algunos lugares*, 202.

30. Zambrano, *Pensamiento y poesía*, 25. Further references appear parenthetically in the text.

31. Zambrano, *Notas de un método* (Madrid: Mondadori, 1989), 47, 93. Subsequent references appear in the text.

32. "Presentado, 'Notas de un método,' último libro de María Zambrano," *El País*, May 16, 1989, elpais.com.

33. Mercedes Gómez Blesa, introduction to *Pensamiento y poesía en la vida española*, by María Zambrano, ed. Mercedes Gomez Blesa (Madrid: Biblioteca Nueva, 2004), 44.

34. Jean-Jacques Rousseau, *The First and Second Discourses Together with the Replies to Critics and Essay on the Origin of Languages*, ed. and trans. Victor Gourevitch (New York: Harper and Row, 1986), 140. Subsequent references to Rousseau's work appear parenthetically in the text.

35. Friedrich Nietzsche, *Zur Genealogie der Moral, Sämtliche Werke*, vol. 5 (Berlin: de Gruyter, 1988), 293, and *The Birth of Tragedy and The Genealogy of Morals*, trans. Francis Golffing (New York: Doubleday Anchor, 1956), 190 (revised).

36. Friedrich Nietzsche, *Die Geburt der Tragödie aus dem Geiste der Musik, Sämtliche Werke*, vol. 1 (Berlin: de Gruyter, 1988), 26, and *The Birth of Tragedy and The Genealogy of Morals*, 19. Subsequent references appear in the text with a "G" to indicate the German original and an "E" to refer to this English translation.

37. Zambrano's most detailed and provocative readings involve figures who seem to collaborate with "philosophy" while preserving "poetry" or "the divine":

Plato, Seneca, Augustine, Nietzsche, and so on. For commentary on Augustine, see *Confesión*, 39–72, *Confession*, 28–45, and *La agonía de Europa*, 50–57.

38. See Ortega, *El tema de nuestro tiempo*, 200n1, where he says he considers Einstein's theory a "magnificent confirmation" of the philosophy of "perspectivism" that he had formulated "irrefutably" in an unspecified 1916 journal article.

39. Ortega y Gasset, *El tema de nuestro tiempo*, 186.

40. Zambrano, "La reforma del entendimiento" and "La reforma del entendimiento español," in *Los intelectuales en el drama de España*, *Obras completas*, 1:195–201; 205–20. The latter appeared as "The Reformation of Spanish Understanding," trans. Francis Lough, *History of European Ideas* 44, no. 7 (2018): 943–51.

41. Zambrano, "La reforma del entendimiento," 201.

42. Zambrano, "La reforma del entendimiento español," 213, and "The Reformation," 947.

43. Zambrano, "La reforma del entendimiento español," 220, and "The Reformation," 950.

44. Zambrano, *La agonía*, 27.

45. This is one of the implications of Derrida's reading of Rousseau in *Of Grammatology* when he shows that, in spite of Rousseau's "praise of living speech," all language is characterized by the structures of "supplementarity" that Rousseau denounces in writing (241–45).

46. Kant, *Critique of Pure Reason*, 7.

47. Kant, *Critique of Pure Reason*, 384–421.

48. Fyodor Dostoyevsky, *Brothers Karamazov*, trans. Richard Pevear and Larissa Volokhonsky (New York: Farrar, Straus and Giroux, 1990), 245–62.

49. See Dostoyevsky, *Brothers*, 69, 82, 263, 593.

50. See, for example, *Nachgelassene Fragmente, 1887–1889*, *Sämtliche Werke*, vol. 12 (Berlin: Walter de Gruyter, 1988): "In the hands of the strongest, every type of pessimism and nihilism [becomes] merely a hammer and tool with which a new pair of wings can be fashioned" (101).

51. Karl Marx and Friedrich Engels, *The Communist Manifesto*, in *Marx-Engels Reader*, ed. Robert C. Tucker (New York: Norton, 1978), 476.

52. See Moreno Sanz, *El logos oscuro*, 1:20, and Laura Llevadot Pascual, introduction to *Aurora: papeles del "Seminario María Zambrano," Número Especial Zambrano-Heidegger*, no. 12 (2011): quoted 27–28.

53. The Zambrano essay is "Antonio Machado y Unamuno, precursores de Heidegger," in *Algunos lugares*, 135–36. Sebastián Fenoy devotes part of his "Breve informe bibliográfico sobre la presencia de Martin Heidegger en la obra de María Zambrano," *Aurora*, no. 11 (2010), to listing moments in the publications in which reference to Heidegger is "obvious" (palmaria) (152). Caballero Rodríguez's comparisons, in *María Zambrano*, identify Heidegger with a humanistic, "existentialist" anthropology. See especially chapters 5 (97–100) and 6 (135–37).

54. Edmund Husserl, "Philosophy and the Crisis of European Humanity," in *The Crisis of the European Sciences and Transcendental Phenomenology: An Introduction to Phenomenological Philosophy*, trans. David Carr (Evanston, IL: Northwestern University Press, 1970), 269–99. Subsequent references will appear in the text.

55. When Husserl writes in the Vienna lecture that "an objective theory of the soul . . . has never existed and will never exist" (297), this is not because there is no soul, but because the soul is of a character that objectivism cannot grasp. He specifies the soul as something outside the realm of the natural sciences, "the soul in its own essential sense, which is, after all, the ego that acts and suffers" (296). Zambrano's *Hacia un saber sobre el alma* seeks to "discover" the soul "apart from what the intellect has said about that part of it that falls under its jurisdiction" (26). Her dismissal of Husserl's philosophy as "strict science" (*Algunos lugares*, 13) suggests she was unaware of the extent to which their interests and ambitions overlapped.

56. Among Zambrano's misprisions: in a note to *El hombre y el destino* she reproaches Heidegger for saying that the tradition forgot "the question of 'being' ": "But, in reality, 'being' has not been the question, but the answer that philosophy found, and all ontology has begun with it" (162).

57. Heidegger, "The Letter on Humanism": "Humanism is opposed because it does not set the *humanitas* high enough" (233–34).

58. See Moreno Sanz, introduction to María Zambrano, *Obras completas*, 1:xxxi, and Mercedes Gómez Blesa's "Anejo a *Pensamiento y poesía en la vida española*," in *Obras completas*, 1:915–35.

59. Zambrano, *Obras completas*, 1:682.

60. For an account of how Zambrano's thought participates in a tradition of Spanish exceptionalism based, paradoxically, on the idea that Spain's realism and attention to death render it more universal than other world cultures, see Stephen Gingerich, "Europe's Frenzy: European and Spanish Universality in María Zambrano," *CR: The New Centennial Review* 8, no. 3 (2008): 189–214.

61. I assume there is an erratum in the passage from which I take this quote: "Y con esto, parece que hayamos tocado el punto más íntimo y delicado de la divergencia—que muchas veces ha sido enemistad—entre filosofía y filosofía, entendiendo por filosofía esta del racionalismo tradicional: la diferencia frente al hecho del humano fracaso" (Zambrano, *Pensamiento*, 16). After a discussion of failure, Zambrano discusses *poetry's* relationship to failure, implying that it was meant to be one of the two elements in the "divergence." Although one of the purposes of the copiously annotated *Obras completas* was the establishment of a critical edition and, with it, the documentation of variants, the text of *Pensamiento y poesía* in vol. 1 simply corrects the relevant passage to "entre filosofía y pensamiento" without providing explanation or documentation (*Obras completas*, 1:566).

62. Andrew Bush, "María Zambrano and the Survival of Antigone," *Diacritics* 34, nos. 3–4 (2004): 98.

63. See Zambrano, *El hombre y lo divino*, 73, where she identifies four "essential stages in the dispute between philosophy and poetry," the last of which is the Platonic denunciation. She soon drops this schema of epochs that one could easily line up to observe the course of history, even though she refers conventionally to the Middle Ages and Renaissance, Romanticism, and modernity. Subsequent references to this edition appear parenthetically in the text.

64. Zambrano, "Poema y sistema," in *Hacia un saber sobre el alma*, 47.

65. Rodolphe Gasché, "Of a Ghost and Its Resurrection: María Zambrano on the Agony of Europe," *Research in Phenomenology* 50 (2020): 351–69.

66. In his introduction to *María Zambrano: palabras para el mundo*, ed. Madeline Cámara and Luis Pablo Ortega (Newark, DE: Juan de la Cuesta, 2011), Ortega Muñoz explains that she prefers the masculine noun "filósofo" to "filósofa" because, in her words, "la filosofía no tiene género" (9).

67. See Antonio Souvrión Rodriguez, introduction to *María Zambrano y la "Edad de Plata" de la cultura española: actas III Congreso Internacional sobre la Vida y Obra de María Zambrano* (Vélez-Málaga: Fundación María Zambrano, 2004), 6, where he cites this statement from an unpublished letter to Zambrano found in the archives of the Fundación María Zambrano.

68. See Gerardo Diego, "Prólogo (1934)," in *Antología de Gerardo Diego: poesía española contemporánea*, ed. Andrés Soria Olmedo (Madrid: Taurus, 1991), 81.

69. A RTVE documentary, "Las sinsombrero" (Women without hats) places Zambrano among the "women of 1927," as if the category were merely a matter of chronology. Episode 1 of *Imprescindibles*, RTVE, 2014, streaming video, https://www.rtve.es/play/videos/las-sinsombrero/.

70. James Valender, "María Zambrano y la Generación del 27," in *María Zambrano, 1904–1991*, ed. Jesús Moreno Sanz (Madrid: Publicaciones de la Residencia de Estudiantes; Vélez-Málaga: Fundación María Zambrano, 2004), 271.

71. See Zambrano, "Acerca de la generación del 27," in *Algunos lugares*, 159–60. Subsequent references to this essay appear in the text.

72. José Ortega y Gasset, "La deshumanización del arte," in *La deshumanización del arte y otros ensayos de estética* (Madrid: Alianza; Revista de Occidente, 2000), 15–19, and "The Dehumanization of Art," in *The Dehumanization of Art and Other Writings*, trans. Willard Trask (Garden City, NY: Doubleday, 1956), 8–11. Subsequent references to this work will appear parenthetically, with an "S" to indicate the Spanish original and an "E" to indicate the English translation.

73. See Alonso, "Una generación (1920–1936)," in *Poetas españoles contemporáneos*, 3rd ed. (Madrid: Gredos, 1965), 155–77; Federico García Lorca, "La imagen poética de don Luis de Góngora," in *Obras completas*, ed. Miguel García-Posada, vol. 3 (Barcelona: Galaxia Gutenberg; Círculo de Lectores, 1996), 53–77, and "The Poetic Image of Don Luis de Góngora," in *Deep Song and Other Prose*, ed. and trans. Christopher Maurer (New York: New Directions, 1980), 59–85.

74. See Andrew Bush's insightful analysis of ruins in "María Zambrano," 91–95.

75. See Ortega Muñoz, "La presente edición," in Zambrano, *Algunos lugares*, 31–44.

76. In *Of Grammatology*, Derrida identifies Rousseau and a "'Rousseauist' moment" with the denunciation of non-self-presence together with an inability to locate self-presence (16–17).

77. Zambrano, "El poeta y la muerte," in *Algunos lugares*, 193. Subsequent references to this essay appear in the text.

78. See Zambrano, *Algunos lugares*, 138, 182.

79. See the first piece in *Claros del bosque*, in *Obras completas*, vol. 4, part 1, in which Zambrano describes the titular notion—"clearings in the forest"—in terms that align it with poetry and the sacred: one doesn't access it by willful searching, by questioning or method, yet one sometimes finds oneself within it (77–83).

80. See Valender, "María Zambrano y la Generación del 27," 271–93, and Francisco Chica's publication of their correspondence, "Un cielo sin reposo: Emilio Prados y María Zambrano, correspondencia," *Homenaje a María Zambrano* (Mexico: Colegio de Mexico, Centro de Estudios Lingüísticos, 1998), 199–259.

81. Zambrano, "Pensamiento y poesía en Emilio Prados," in *Algunos lugares*, 207. Subsequent references to this essay appear in the text.

82. "Contra-poner" could be related to the structure of "Aus-einander-setzung," developed by Heidegger in his writings of the thirties and forties, including the Hölderlin commentaries found in Zambrano's library. See Sebastián Fenoy, "Breve informe bibliográfico sobre la presencia de Martin Heidegger en la obra de María Zambrano," 153. "Aus-einander-setzung" names a process of holding apart and in-relation in such a way that differences and similarities both stand out. See Rodolphe Gasché, "Toward an Ethics of *Auseinandersetzung*," in *The Honor of Thinking* (Stanford, CA: Stanford University Press, 2007), 103–20.

83. Emilio Prados, "Abril de Dios," in *Antología comentada de la Generación del 27* (Madrid: Espasa-Calpe, 1998), 498.

84. Balibrea, Lough, and Sánchez Cuervo, in *María Zambrano*, propose the figure of "the exile," as the practitioner of "poetic reason": "a personification of a radical and interpellating alterity which questions the logic from which he has been dismissed" (840). See Ros and Omlor's description of "poetic reason" in their introduction to *The Cultural Legacy of María Zambrano*, ed. Xon de Ros and Daniela Omlor (Cambridge, UK: Legenda, 2017), 4–11.

85. Caballero Rodríguez, *María Zambrano*, 157. As a "style," the effects of "poetic reason" begin with "self-development," and only later does it impact the broader sphere of politics.

86. Enquist Källgren, *María Zambrano's Ontology of Exile*, 18.

87. Enquist Källgren, *María Zambrano's Ontology of Exile*, 18–19.

88. Heidegger, "The Letter," 233.
89. Heidegger, "The Letter," 246.

Epilogue

1. Javier Marías, "Volveremos," in *Literatura y fantasma* (Madrid: Alfaguara, 2001). Subsequent references to this edition of the essay appear parenthetically in the text. The original publication can be found online, *El País*, December 22, 1991, elpais.com.

2. See Javier Marías, "Fragmento y enigma y espantoso azar," in *Literatura y fantasma*. This essay first appeared as part of his novel *Monarca del tiempo* (Madrid: Alfaguara, 1978), where he presented it alongside three short stories and a short drama. Heike Scharm's *El tiempo y el ser en Javier Marías* (Amsterdam: Rodopi, 2013) is framed by the idea that Marías's work ought to be viewed as "literary thinking," an activity she views as "a hybrid space in which the best of two terrains [the literary and the philosophical] are fused," producing a new "poetic philosophy" that is "a harmonic symbiosis between literature and philosophy, between form and content, between language and thought" (14). She acknowledges that the philosophical characterization of Javier Marías's work as Heideggerian has occupied a few scholars before her (14).

3. Santiago Bertrán, in "La visión responsable de Javier Marías: una narrativa entre el pensamiento literario de Julián Marías y la literatura como reconocimiento de Marcel Proust," *Artes del Ensayo: Revista Internacional Sobre el Ensayo Hispánico*, no. 3 (2019): 215–44, regrets the lack of precision in earlier interpretations of Javier Marías's "literary thinking," but his own lengthy exegesis concentrates almost exclusively on *Julián* Marías's work. Bertrán says repeatedly that the son's idea can "only" (solo) be understood as an adoption of his father's ideas, as elaborated in an unpublished 1980s lecture course in the Instituto de España archives, which is itself based on Ortegan principles (217–22). This makes for an interesting case, but the fact remains that Javier Marías has provided rather little to go on. In his gloss, Bertrán neglects to mention the paradoxical nature of "thinking through writing" and relegates the assertion that Spaniards do not practice it or discuss it to a footnote (223n11).

4. Javier Marías, "Contar el misterio," in *Literatura y fantasma*, 118–23. Subsequent references appear in the text.

5. Unamuno refers to it as an "old Latin adage" (*Del sentimiento trágico*, 30; *On the Tragic Sense*, 34). To document the attribution to Hobbes, Wikipedia in French cites Renzo Tozi, *Dictionnaire des sentences latines et grecques* (Paris: Jérôme Millon, 2010), 1453. See "Primum vivere deinde philosophari," Wikipédia, last modified April 14, 2020, 22:20, https://fr.wikipedia.org/wiki/Primum_vivere_deinde_philosophari.

6. Unamuno, *Del sentimiento trágico*, 30, and *On the Tragic Sense*, 34. Later on his quotation of the epigram serves as a pretext for his revision of it, rendering it nearly unrecognizable, and of dubious Latin grammaticality: "primum supervivereo superesse" (S 91; E 127).

7. Ortega y Gasset, *La idea*, 268, and *The Idea*, 273.

8. Ortega y Gasset, *La idea*, 268, 270, *The Idea*, 273, 275 (revised).

9. C. Valerius Catullus, "Carmina (Catullus)/5," Wikisource, last modified January 31, 2018, 19:21, https://la.wikisource.org/wiki/Carmina_(Catullus)/5.

10. Bertrán, "La visión responsable," 223n11.

Bibliography

Abellán, José Luis. "El filósofo 'Antonio Machado.'" In *Antonio Machado hacia Europa*, edited by Pablo Luis Ávila, 172–77. Madrid: Visor, 1993.

———. "El impacto positivista en el pensamiento de Unamuno." In *Pensamiento y literatura en España en el siglo XIX*, edited by Yvan Lissorges, 248–50. Mirail, France: Presses Universitaires de Mirail, 1996.

———. *Historia crítica del pensamiento español*. 5 vols. Madrid: Espasa-Calpe, 1988.

———. *Historia del pensamiento español de Séneca a nuestros días*. Madrid: Espasa Calpe, 1996.

———. "María Zambrano, la 'razón poética' en marcha." In *Filosofía española en América (1936–1966)*, 169–89. Madrid: Ediciones Guadarrama; Seminarios y Ediciones, 1967.

———. *María Zambrano: una pensadora de nuestro tiempo*. Madrid: Anthropos, 2006.

———. *Ortega y Gasset en la filosofía española: ensayos de apreciación*. Madrid: Tecnos, 1966.

———. "Pensamiento español: una categoría historiográfica." *ÉNDOXA: Series Filosóficas*, no. 12 (2000): 305–11.

———. "Spain, Philosophy in." In *Routledge Encyclopedia of Philosophy*, edited by Edward Craig, 9:70–77. London: Routledge, 1998.

Albornoz, Aurora de. *La presencia de Unamuno en Machado*. Madrid: Gredos, 1968.

Alonso, Dámaso. "Fanales de Antonio Machado." In *Cuatro poetas españoles*, 137–85. Madrid: Gredos, 1962.

———. "Una generación poética (1920–1936)." In *Poetas españoles contemporaneos*, 3rd ed., 155–77. Madrid: Gredos, 1965.

Álvarez Castro, Luis. *La palabra y el ser en la teoría literaria de Unamuno*. Salamanca: Ediciones Universidad de Salamanca, 2005.

———. *Los espejos del yo: existencialismo y metaficción en la narrativa de Miguel de Unamuno*. Salamanca: Ediciones Universidad de Salamanca, 2015.

Álvarez Ramos, Eva. "El prólogo literario en el siglo XX y la retórica clásica: de las *partes orationis* a los tópicos más comunes." *Ogigia: Revista electrónica de estudios hispánicos*, no. 1 (2007): 61–73.

Amigo Fernandez, María Luisa. *Poesía y filosofía en Juan Ramón Jiménez.* Córdoba: Monte de Piedad; Caja de Ahorros, 1987.

Andersen, Katrine Helene. "Miguel de Unamuno: una filosofía novelada." In *Unamuno eterno*, edited by J. A. Garrido Ardila, 330–52. Barcelona: Anthropos, 2015.

Aranguren, José Luis L. "Filosofía y poesía." In *El pensamiento de María Zambrano: papeles de Almagro*, 111–21. Madrid: Zero, 1983.

———. "Los sueños de María Zambrano." *Revista de Occidente* 12 (1966): 207–12.

Aristotle. *Metaphysics.* Translated by Richard Hope. Ann Arbor: University of Michigan Press, 1956.

———. *Metaphysics.* In *Aristotle in 23* Volumes, vols.17, 18, translated by Hugh Tredennick. Cambridge, MA: Harvard University Press; London: Heinemann, 1933, 1989. http://www.perseus.tufts.edu/hopper/text?doc=Perseus:text:1999.01.0052.

———. *On the Soul.* Translated by W. S. Hett. London: Heinemann; Cambridge, MA: Harvard University Press, 1957.

Arlandis, Sergio. "*Del sentimiento trágico de la vida* a *Niebla*: algunas líneas de relación e interpretación simbólica." In *Unamuno eterno*, edited by J. A. Garrido Ardila, 92–125. Barcelona: Anthropos, 2015.

Arndt, Andreas, and Jure Zovko. Introduction to *Schriften zur Kritischen Philosophie*, by Friedrich von Schlegel, iii–ix. Edited by Andreas Arndt and Jure Zovko. Hamburg: Meiner, 2007.

Austin, J. L. *How to Do Things with Words.* Cambridge, MA: Harvard University Press, 1962.

Aznar Soler, Manuel, ed. *En el 98.* Madrid: Fundación Duques de Soria, 1997.

Balibrea, Mari Paz, Francis Lough, and Antolín Sánchez Cuervo. Introduction to "María Zambrano amongst the Philosophers." Special issue of *History of European Ideas* 44, no. 7 (2018): 827–42.

Barco, Pablo del. Prologue to *Juan de Mairena*, by Antonio Machado, 9–32. Madrid: Alianza, 1995.

Barfield, Raymond. *The Ancient Quarrel between Philosophy and Poetry.* Cambridge: Cambridge University Press, 2011.

Barjau, Eustaquio. *Antonio Machado: teoría y práctica del apócrifo.* Barcelona: Ariel, 1975.

Baroja, Pío. *Camino de perfección/The Road to Perfection.* Translated by Walter Borenstein. Oxford: Oxbow, 2008.

Barzun, Jacques. "To the Rescue of Romanticism." *American Scholar* 9, no. 2 (1940): 147–58.

Bataille, Georges. *Inner Experience.* Translated by Leslie Anne Boldt. Albany: State University of New York Press, 1988.

Benjamin, Andrew. *Philosophy's Literature.* Manchester: Clinamen, 2001.

Benjamin, Walter. "The Concept of Criticism in German Romanticism." In *Selected Writings*, edited by Marcus Bullock and Michael W. Jennings, 116–200. Cambridge, MA: Belknap Press of Harvard University Press, 2002.

Bergson, Henri. *Time and Free Will: An Essay on the Immediate Data of Consciousness.* Translated by F. L. Pogson. New York: Harper and Row, 1960.
Bertrán, Santiago. "La visión responsable de Javier Marías: una narrativa entre el pensamiento literario de Julián Marías y la literatura como reconocimiento de Marcel Proust." *Artes del Ensayo: Revista Internacional Sobre el Ensayo Hispánico,* no. 3 (2019): 215–44.
Blanchot, Maurice. "Literature and the Right to Death." In *The Work of Fire,* translated by Charlotte Mandell, 300–344. Stanford, CA: Stanford University Press, 1995.
Blanco Aguinaga, Carlos. *El Unamuno contemplativo.* Mexico: Colegio de México, 1959.
Blumenberg, Hans. *The Laughter of the Thracian Woman: A Protohistory of Theory.* Translated by Spencer Hawkins. New York: Bloomsbury, 2015.
Bolado, Gerardo. "Luces y sombras de la última historiografía filosófica en España." In *Nuevos estudios sobre histora del pensamiento español: actas de las V Jornadas de Hispanismo Filosófico,* 601–20. Madrid: Fundación Ignacio Larramendi; Associación de Hispanismo Filosófico, 2005.
Booth, Wayne C. *Rhetoric of Fiction.* Chicago: University of Chicago Press, 1983.
Borges, Jorge Luis. "Inmortalidad de Unamuno." In *Jorge Luis Borges en Sur, 1931–1980,* 143–44. Buenos Aires: Emecé, 1999.
———. "Presencia de Miguel de Unamuno." In *Textos cautivos: Ensayos y reseñas de "El Hogar,"* edited by Enrique Sacerio-Garí, 79–82. Barcelona: Tusquets, 1986.
———. Prologue to *La invención de Morel,* by Adolfo Bioy Casares, v–vii. New York: Penguin, 1996.
Bosteels, Bruno. "Hegel in America." In *Hegel and the Infinite: Politics and Dialectic,* edited by Slavoj Žižek et al., 67–90. New York: Columbia University Press, 2011.
Bozal, Valeriano. Prologue to José Ortega y Gasset, *La deshumanización del arte,* 13–37. Madrid: Espasa-Calpe, 1987.
Brewer, Brian. "La matemáticas sutiles o los límites del saber en *La vida es sueño.*" *Bulletin of Spanish Studies* 88, no. 4 (2011): 487–521.
Bundgård, Ana. "El binomio España-Europa en el pensamiento de Zambrano, Ferrater Mora y Ortega y Gasset." In *Claves de la razón poética: María Zambrano, un pensamiento en el orden del tiempo,* edited by Carmen Revilla, 43–54. Madrid: Editorial Trotta, 1998.
———. "La creación al modo humano o el rostro de la nada: María Zambrano y Nietzsche." In Moreno Sanz, *María Zambrano, 1904–1991,* 467–82.
———. *Más allá de la filosofía: sobre el pensamiento filosófico-místico de María Zambrano.* Madrid: Editorial Trotta, 2000.
Bush, Andrew. "María Zambrano and the Survival of Antigone." *Diacritics* 34, nos. 3–4 (2004): 90–111.

Caballero Rodríguez, Beatriz. *Maria Zambrano: A Life of Poetic Reason and Political Commitment*. Cardiff: University of Wales Press, 2017.

———. Review of *The Cultural Legacy of María Zambrano*, edited by Xon de Ros and Daniela Omlor. *Modern Language Review* 15, no. 1 (2020): 195–96.

Campoamor, Ramón de. *El personalismo: apuntes para una filosofía*. Madrid: M. Rivadeneyra, 1855.

Candelaria, Michael. *The Revolt of Unreason: Miguel de Unamuno and Antonio Caso on the Crisis of Modernity*. Edited by Stella Villarmea. Amsterdam: Rodopi, 2012.

Caponigri, A. R. *Contemporary Spanish Philosophy: An Anthology*. Notre Dame, IN: University of Notre Dame Press, 1967.

Cascardi, Anthony J. "Between Philosophy and Literature: Ortega's *Meditations on Quixote*." In *José Ortega y Gasset: Proceedings of the Espectador universal International Interdisciplinary Conference*, edited by Nora de Marval-McNair, 15–50. New York: Greenwood, 1987.

———. *The Cambridge Introduction to Literature and Philosophy*. Cambridge: Cambridge University Press, 2014.

———. Introduction to *Literature and the Question of Philosophy*. Edited by Anthony J. Cascardi, x–xv. Baltimore: Johns Hopkins University Press, 1987.

Cassou, Jean. "Retrato de Unamuno por Jean Cassou." In *Manual de Quijotismo; Cómo se hace una novela; Epistolario Miguel de Unamuno/Jean Cassou*, by Miguel de Unamuno, 161–67. Salamanca: Ediciones Universidad de Salamanca, 2005.

Catullus, C. Valerius. "Carmina (Catullus)/5." Wikisource, last modified January 31, 2018, 19:21. https://la.wikisource.org/wiki/Carmina_(Catullus)/5.

Caudet, Francisco. *En el inestable circuito del tiempo: Antonio Machado: de "Soledades" a "Juan de Mairena."* Madrid: Cátedra: 2009.

Cerezo Galán, Pedro. *Antonio Machado en los apócrifos: una filosofía de poeta*. Almería: Editorial Universidad, 2012.

———. "El alma y la palabra: bases para una antropología pneumática en María Zambrano." In *Filosofía y literatura en María Zambrano*, edited by Pedro Cerezo Galán, 15–51. Seville: Fundación José Manuel Lara, 2005.

———. *La voluntad de aventura: aproximamiento al pensamiento de Ortega*. Madrid: Ariel, 1984.

———. *Las máscaras de lo trágico: filosofía y tragedia en Miguel de Unamuno*. Madrid: Trotta, 1996.

———. "Lo apócrifo machadiano: 'un ensayo de esfuerzos fragmentarios.' " In *Antonio Machado hoy (1939–1989)*, edited by Paul Aubert, 185–207. Madrid: Casa de Velázquez, 1994.

———. *Palabra en el tiempo: poesía y filosofía en Antonio Machado*. Madrid: Gredos, 1975.

Chacón, Pedro, and Mariano Rodríguez. "Anejo a *Filosofía y poesía*." In *Obras completas*, by María Zambrano, 1:978–91. Edited by Jesús Moreno Sanz. Barcelona: Galaxia Gutenberg, 2015.

Chica, Francisco. "Un cielo sin reposo: Emilio Prados y María Zambrano, correspondencia." In *Homenaje a María Zambrano*, 199–259. Mexico: Colegio de Mexico, Centro de Estudios Lingüísticos, 1998.

Ciplijauskaité, Biruté. "*Ser y estar* en la palabra: Machado, Heidegger y la deconstrucción." In *Divergencias y unidad: perspectivas sobre la Generación del 98 y Antonio Machado*, edited by John P. Gabriele, 227–44. Madrid: Orígenes, 1990.

Clark, Timothy. "Can Place Think?" *Cultural Politics* 4, no. 1 (2008): 100–22.

Clavería, Carlos. "Notas sobre la poética de Antonio Machado." *Hispania* 28, no. 2 (1945): 166–83.

Cleveland, Basil. "The Concept of Reading in Ortega's *Meditations on Quijote*." *CLIO* 34, no. 1–2 (2004–5): 83–98.

Cogan, John. "Phenomenological Reduction." *Internet Encyclopedia of Philosophy*. Accessed July 5, 2020. https://iep.utm.edu/phen-red/.

Cohen, S. Marc. "Aristotle's Metaphysics." In *Stanford Encyclopedia of Philosophy*, edited by Edward N. Zalta. Accessed July 19, 2022. https://plato.stanford.edu/entries/aristotle-metaphysics/.

Collins, Marsha. "Romance." In Stocker and Mack, *The Palgrave Handbook of Philosophy and Literature*, 263–92.

Comte, Auguste. *Cours de philosophie positive*. In *Auguste Comte and Positivism: The Essential Writings*, edited by Gertrud Lenzer, 71–306. Chicago: University of Chicago Press, 1983.

Cope, Brian. "The Helenic Origins of Unamuno's Skepticism and *Niebla*'s Skeptical Parody of Cartesianism." *Hispanic Review* 77, no. 4 (2009): 471–93.

Crespo Sánchez, Javier. "Ortega, el fin de la filosofía y la tarea del pensamiento." *Revista de Estudios Orteguianos* 14–15 (2007): 183–202.

Cruz Hernández, Miguel. "La misión socrática de don Miguel de Unamuno." *Cuadernos de la Cátedra Miguel de Unamuno* 3 (1952): 41–53.

Csejtei, Dezsö. *Muerte e inmortalidad en la obra filosófica y literaria de Miguel de Unamuno*. Salamanca: Ediciones Universidad, 2009.

Deleuze, Gilles, and Félix Guattari. *What Is Philosophy?* Translated by Hugh Tomlinson and Graham Burchell. New York: Columbia University Press, 1994.

Denham, A. E., ed. *Plato on Art and Beauty*. New York: Palgrave Macmillan, 2012.

Derrida, Jacques. "Che cos'è la poesia?" In *The Derrida Reader: Between the Blinds*, edited by Peggy Kamuf, 222–37. New York: Columbia University Press, 1991.

———. "Cogito and the History of Madness." In *Writing and Difference*, translated by Alan Bass, 31–63. Chicago: University of Chicago Press, 1978.

———. *Of Grammatology*. Translated by Gayatri Chakravorty Spivak. Baltimore: Johns Hopkins University Press, 1976.

———. "*Ousia* and *Grammé*: Note on a Note from *Being and Time*." In *Margins of Philosophy*, translated Alan Bass, 31–67. Chicago: University of Chicago Press, 1982.

———. "Plato's Pharmacy." In *Dissemination*, translated by Barbara Johnson, 63–171. Chicago: University of Chicago Press, 1972.

———. "Signature, Event, Context." In *Limited, Inc.*, translated by Samuel Weber and Jeffrey Mehlman, 1–24. Evanston, IL: Northwestern University Press, 1988.

———. *Speech and Phenomena and Other Essays on Husserl's Theory of Signs*. Translated by David Allison and Newton Garver. Evanston, IL: Northwestern University Press, 1974.

Derrida, Jacques, and Derek Attridge. "'This Strange Institution Called Literature': An Interview with Jacques Derrida." Translated by Geoffrey Bennington and Rachel Bowlby. In *Acts of Literature*, edited by Derek Attridge, 33–75. New York: Routledge, 1991.

Derrida, Jacques, and Maurizio Ferraris. *A Taste for the Secret*. Translated by Giacomo Donis. Edited by Giacomo Donis and David Webb. Cambridge, UK: Polity, 2001.

Descartes, René. *Discourse on the Method*. Translated by Robert Stoothoff. In *The Philosophical Writings of Descartes*, 1:111–51. Cambridge: Cambridge University Press, 1985.

———. *Principles of Philosophy*. Translated by John Cottingham. In *The Philosophical Writings of Descartes*, 1:177–291. Cambridge: Cambridge University Press, 1985.

Díaz Álvarez, Jesús M., and Jorge Brioso. "Esperar lo inesperado: algunas reflexiones sobre la contingencia a partir de la obra de Antonio Rodríguez Huéscar y José Ortega y Gasset." *Bajo Palabra: Revista de Filosofía* 2, no. 11 (2015): 127–30.

Diccionario de la lengua española, s.v. "Discutir." Real Academia Española. Accessed June 29, 2021. https://dle.rae.es/discutir?m=form.

Diego, Gerardo. "Prólogo (1934)." In *Antología de Gerardo Diego: poesía española contemporánea*, edited by Andrés Soria Olmedo, 81–85. Madrid: Taurus, 1991.

Dostoyevsky, Fyodor. *The Brothers Karamazov*. Translated by Richard Pevear and Larissa Volokhonsky. New York: Farrar, Straus and Giroux, 1990.

Durantou, Patrick. "Poesía y filosofía de Antonio Machado." In *Antonio Machado hacia Europa*, edited by Pablo Luis Ávila, 202–9. Madrid: Visor, 1993.

Edmundson, Mark. *Literature against Philosophy, Plato to Derrida: A Defence of Poetry*. Cambridge: Cambridge University Press, 1995.

Eguizábal, José Ignacio. "Poesía y filosofía." In Moreno Sanz, *María Zambrano, 1904–1991*, 375–83.

Enquist Källgren, Karolina. *María Zambrano's Ontology of Exile: Expressive Subjectivity*. Cham, Switzerland: Palgrave, 2019.

Evans, Jan E. *Unamuno and Kierkegaard: Paths to Selfhood in Fiction*. Lanham, MD: Lexington Books, 2005.

Faber, Sebastiaan. "Fantasmas hispanistas y otros retos transatlánticos." In *Cultura y cambio social en América Latina*, edited by Mabel Moraña, 315–40. Madrid: Iberoamericana, 2008.

Feger, Hans, ed. "Die poetische Vernunft in der Frühromantik." In *Handbuch Literatur und Philosophie*, 67–86.
———. *Handbuch Literatur und Philosophie*. Stuttgart: Metzler, 2012.
Fenoy, Sebastián. "Breve informe bibliográfico sobre la presencia de Martin Heidegger en la obra de María Zambrano." *Aurora*, no. 11 (2010): 152–53.
Fenves, Peter. *"Chatter": Language and History in Kierkegaard*. Stanford, CA: Stanford University Press, 1993.
Fernández de la Mora, Gonzalo. *Filósofos españoles del siglo XX*. Barcelona: Planeta, 1987.
———. *Pensamiento español*. 6 vols. Madrid: Ediciones Rialp, 1964–69.
Fernández Ferrer, Antonio. Introduction to *Juan de Mairena*, by Antonio Machado, 1:9–52. Edited by Antonio Fernández Ferrer. Madrid: Cátedra, 2003.
Fernández-Medina, Nicolás. *Life Embodied: The Promise of Vital Force in Spanish Modernity*. Montreal: McGill-Queen's University Press, 2018.
———. *The Poetics of Otherness in Antonio Machado's "Proverbios y cantares."* Cardiff: University of Wales Press, 2011.
Ferrater Mora, José. "Ortega y Gasset: An Outline of His Philosophy." In *Three Spanish Philosophers*, edited by J. M. Terricabras, 123–208. Albany: State University of New York Press, 2003.
———. *Three Spanish Philosophers: Unamuno, Ortega, and Ferrater Mora*. Edited by J. M. Terricabras. Albany: State University of New York Press, 2003.
Fox, E. Inman. *La crisis intelectual del 98*. Madrid: Cuadernos para el Diálogo, 1976.
———. "Revelaciones textuales sobre las *Meditaciones* de Ortega." *Insula* 35, no. 455 (1984): 4–5.
Foucault, Michel. *Madness and Civilization*. New York: Routledge, 2001.
Franz, Thomas R. "*Niebla*: Infinite Authors/Infinite Fictions." *Occasional Papers in Language, Literature and Linguistics*, series A, no. 33 (1987): 1–12.
Fraser, Benjamin. *Encounters with Bergson(ism) in Spain: Reconciling Philosophy, Literature, Film and Urban Spaces*. Chapel Hill: University of North Carolina Press, 2010.
Gajić, Tatjana. *Paradoxes of Stasis: Literature, Politics, and Thought in Francoist Spain*. Lincoln: University of Nebraska Press, 2019.
———. "Reason, Practice and the Promise of a New Spain: Ortega's 'Vieja y nueva política' and *Meditaciones del Quijote*." *Bulletin of Hispanic Studies* 77 (2000): 193–215.
Gaos, José. *Antología del pensamiento de lengua española en la edad contemporánea*. Mexico: Editorial Séneca, 1945.
Garagorri, Paolino. *La filosofía española en el siglo XX: Unamuno, Ortega, Zubiri (Dos precursores, Clarín y Ganivet, y cuatro continuadores)*. Madrid: Alianza, 1985.
García-Gómez, Jorge. Introduction to Antonio Rodríguez Huéscar, *José Ortega y Gasset's Metaphysical Innovation: A Critique and Overcoming of Idealism*.

Translated by Jorge García-Gómez, vii–xiii. Albany: State University of New York Press, 1995.
García Lorca, Federico. "La imagen poética de don Luis de Góngora." In *Obras completas*, edited Miguel García-Posada, 3:53–77. Barcelona: Galaxia Gutenberg; Círculo de Lectores, 1996.
———. "The Poetic Image of Don Luis de Góngora." In *Deep Song and Other Prose*, edited and translated by Christopher Maurer, 59–85. New York: New Directions, 1980.
García Posada, Miguel. "Antonio Machado y la modernidad: una revisión." *Cuadernos Hispanoamericanos*, no. 691 (2008): 65–84.
García-Ramírez, Eduardo. "On the Invisibility Problem of Latin American Philosophy." *American Philosophical Association Newsletter* 10, no. 2 (2011): 12–17.
Garrido, Manuel. "Spanish Philosophy." In *Cambridge History of Philosophy, 1870–1945*, edited by Thomas Baldwin, 469–76. Cambridge: Cambridge University Press, 2003.
Garrido, Manuel, Nelson R. Orringer, Luis M. Valdés, Margarita M. Valdés, eds. *El legado filosófico español e hispanoamericano del siglo XX*. Madrid: Cátedra, 2009.
Gasché, Rodolphe. *Europe, or the Infinite Task: A Study of a Philosophical Concept*. Stanford, CA: Stanford University Press, 2009.
———. "The Felicities of Paradox." In *Of Minimal Things: Studies on the Notion of Relation*, 309–43. Stanford, CA: Stanford University Press, 1999.
———. "Of a Ghost and Its Resurrection: María Zambrano on the Agony of Europe." *Research in Phenomenology* 50 (2020): 351–69.
———. "A Relation Called 'Literary.'" In *Of Minimal Things: Studies on the Notion of Relation*, 285–308. Stanford, CA: Stanford University Press, 1999.
———. *The Tain of the Mirror: Derrida and the Philosophy of Reflection*. Cambridge, MA: Harvard University Press, 1986.
———. "Toward an Ethics of *Auseinandersetzung*." In *The Honor of Thinking*, 103–20. Stanford, CA: Stanford University Press, 2007.
Genette, Gérard. *Paratexts: Thresholds of Interpretation*. Translated by Lane E. Lewin. Cambridge: Cambridge University Press, 1997.
Gentic, Tania. "Rethinking the Cartesian Subject in Latin America and Spain: Decolonial Theory and María Zambrano's philosophy." *Journal of Spanish Cultural Studies* 16, no. 4 (2015): 415–35.
Gies, David T. "The Funes Effect." In *The Cambridge History of Spanish Literature*, edited by David T. Gies, 3–12. Cambridge: Cambridge University Press, 2004.
Gingerich, Stephen. "Europe's Frenzy: European and Spanish Universality in María Zambrano." *CR: The New Centennial Review* 8, no. 3 (2008): 189–214.
———. "Ortega: Secrecy and the World." *CR: The New Centennial Review* 14, no. 3 (2014): 49–74.
———. "Prefatory Conventions and Invention: Rereading Borges's Prologue to *La invención de Morel*." *Revista de Estudios Hispánicos* 52, no. 3 (2018): 983–1005.

———. "Returning to the Originary Enmity of Philosophy and Literature: Juan Benet's *DEL POZO Y DEL NUMA (Un ensayo y una leyenda)*." *Revista de Estudios Hispánicos* 38, no. 2 (2004): 321–23.
Gómez Blesa, Mercedes. "Anejo a *Pensamiento y poesía en la vida española*." In *Obras completas*, by María Zambrano, 1:915–35. Edited by Jesús Moreno Sanz, Barcelona: Galaxia Gutenberg, 2015.
———. Introduction to *Pensamiento y poesía en la vida española*, by María Zambrano, 9–76. Edited by Mercedes Gomez Blesa. Madrid: Biblioteca Nueva, 2004.
———. "Unamuno-Zambrano: un pensamiento poético." Prologue to *Unamuno*, by María Zambrano, 9–26. Edited by Mercedes Gómez Blesa,. Madrid: Debate, 2004.
González, Pedro Blas. "Biographical Life and Ratio-vitalism in the Thought of Ortega y Gasset." *Philosophy Today* 46, no. 4 (2002): 406–16.
Gosetti-Ferencei, Jennifer. *Heidegger, Hölderlin, and the Subject of Poetic Language*. New York: Fordham University Press, 2009.
Gracia, Jordi. *José Ortega y Gasset*. Madrid: Taurus, 2014.
Gracia, Jorge. *Philosophy and Its History: Issues in Philosophical Historiography*. Albany: State University of New York Press, 1992.
Graff Zivin, Erin, ed. *The Marrano Specter: Derrida and Hispanism*. New York: Fordham University Press, 2018.
Guillén, Jorge. "El apócrifo Antonio Machado." In *Estudios sobre Antonio Machado*, edited by José Ángeles, 218–30. Barcelona: Ariel, 1977.
Gullón, Ricardo. "La invención del 98." In *La invención del 98 y otros ensayos*, 7–19. Madrid: Gredos, 1969.
Gutiérrez Girardot, Rafael. "Lírica y filosofía en Antonio Machado." In *Antonio Machado hoy (1939–1989)*, edited by Paul Aubert, 117–32. Madrid: Casa de Velázquez, 1994.
———. *Poesía y prosa en Antonio Machado*. Madrid: Guadarrama, 1969.
Gutiérrez-Pozo, Antonio. *La aurora de la razón vital: fenomenología y vitalismo en el origen de la filosofía de Ortega y Gasset*. Madrid: Mileto Ediciones, 2003.
Guy, Alain. *Histoire de la philosophie espagnole*. Toulouse: Publications de l'Université de Toulouse-Le Mirail, 1985.
———. *La Philosophie espagnole*. Paris: Presses Universitaires de France, 1995.
———. *Les Philosophes espagnols d'hier et d'aujourd'hui*. Paris: Privat, 1956.
Havard, Robert. *From Romanticism to Surrealism: Seven Spanish Poets*. Cardiff: University of Wales Press, 1988.
Hayes, Patrick, and Jan Wilm, eds. *Beyond the Ancient Quarrel: Philosophy, Literature, and J. M. Coetze*. New York: Oxford University Press, 2017.
Hegel, Georg Wilhelm Friedrich. *Introduction to the Lectures on the History of Philosophy*. Translated by T. M. Knox and A. V. Miller. Oxford: Clarendon, 1985.
———. *Phenomenologie des Geistes*. Frankfurt: Suhrkamp, 1986.

———. *Phenomenology of Spirit*. Translated by A. V. Miller. Oxford: Oxford University Press, 1977.
———. *The Philosophy of History*. Translated by J. Sebree. New York: Dover, 1956.
Heidegger, Martin. "Aus der Erfahrung des Denkens." In *Gesamtausgabe*, vol. 13, *Aus der Erfahrung des Denkens 1910–1976*, 75–86. Frankfurt: Vittorio Klostermann, 1976.
———. *Aus der Erfahrung des Denkens (Desde la experiencia del pensar)*. Translated by Claudio César. Buenos Aires: Vórtice, 2014.
———. *Being and Time*. Translated by John Macquarrie and Edward Robinson. New York: Harper Collins, 1962.
———. "Comments on Karl Jaspers' *Psychology of Worldviews*." In *Supplements*, 71–104.
———. "Erbetene Vorbemerkung zu einer Dichterlesung auf Bühlerhöhe am 24. Februar 1951." In *Gesamtausgabe*, vol. 16, *Reden und andere Zeugnisse eines Lebensweges 1910–1976*, 470–72. Frankfurt: Vittorio Klostermann, 2000.
———. *Fundamental Concepts of Metaphysics: World, Finitude, Solitude*. Translated by William McNeill and Nicholas Walker. Bloomington: Indiana University Press, 1995.
———. *Introduction to Metaphysics*. Translated by Gregory Fried and Richard Polt. 2nd ed. New Haven, CT: Yale University Press, 2014.
———. *Introduction to Philosophy: Thinking and Poetizing*. Translated by Phillip Jacques Braunstein. Bloomington: Indiana University Press, 2011.
———. "The Letter on Humanism." In *Basic Writings*, edited and translated by David Farrell Krell, 213–66. New York: Harper Collins, 1993.
———. *Supplements: From the Earliest Essays to "Being and Time" and Beyond*. Edited by John Van Buren. Albany: State University of New York Press, 2002.
———. "The Thinker as Poet." In *Poetry, Language, Thought*, translated by Albert Hofstadter, 3–14. New York: Harper and Row, 1971.
Herder, Johan Gottfried. *Against Pure Reason: Writings on Religion, Language, and History*. Translated and edited by Marcia Bunge. Minneapolis: Fortress, 1993.
Höllhuber, Ivo. *Geschichte der Philosophie im spanischen Kulturbereich*. Munich: Reinhardt, 1967.
Holzenthal, Nicole. "La presencia explícita de filosofía española en universidades alemanas." In *Nuevos estudios sobre histora del pensamiento español: actas de las V Jornadas de Hispanismo Filosófico*, 385–600. Madrid: Fundación Ignacio Larramendi; Associación de Hispanismo Filosófico, 2005.
Husserl, Edmund. *The Crisis of the European Sciences and Transcendental Phenomenology: An Introduction to Phenomenological Philosophy*. Translated by David Carr. Evanston, IL: Northwestern University Press, 1970.
———. *Logical Investigations*. Translated by J. N. Findlay. 2 vols. London: Routledge and Kegan Paul, 1970.
———. "Philosophy and the Crisis of European Humanity." In *The Crisis of the European Sciences and Transcendental Phenomenology: An Introduction to Phe-*

nomenological Philosophy, translated by David Carr, 269–99. Evanston, IL: Northwestern University Press, 1970.

Hutchinson, Steven. "El movimiento en la obra de Antonio Machado." In *Divergencias y unidad: perspectivas sobre la Generación del 98 y Antonio Machado*, edited by John P. Gabriele, 245–54. Madrid: Orígenes, 1990.

Jaén Portillo, Isabel. "Fictions of Human Development: The Renaissance." In Stocker and Mack, *The Palgrave Handbook of Philosophy and Literature*, 315–38.

Jiménez Moreno, Luis. *Práctica del saber en filósofos españoles: Gracián, Unamuno, Ortega y Gasset, E. d'Ors, Tierno Galván*. Barcelona: Anthropos, 1991.

Johnson, Roberta. *Crossfire: Philosophy and the Novel in Spain, 1900–1934*. Lexington: University of Kentucky Press, 1993.

———. "El problema del conocimiento en Unamuno y la composición de *Niebla*." In *Actas del IX Congreso de la Asociación Internacional de Hispanistas, 18–23 agosto 1986, Berlín*, 2:303–7. Frankfurt: Vervuert, 1989.

———. "Narrative in Culture, 1868–1936." In *The Cambridge Companion to Modern Spanish Culture*, edited by David T. Gies, 123–33. Cambridge: Cambridge University Press, 2005.

———. "What María Zambrano Discovered in the New World." In *Maria Zambrano: Between the Caribbean and the Mediterranean*, edited by Madeline Cámara and Luis Ortega, 23–32. Newark, DE: Juan de la Cuesta, 2015.

Jurkevich, Gayana. "Unamuno's Gestational Fallacy: 'Niebla' and 'Escribir a lo que salga.'" *Anales de la literatura española contemporánea* 15, no. 1/3, (1990): 65–81.

Kant, Immanuel. *Critique of Judgement*. Translated by J. H. Bernard. New York: Hafner, 1952.

———. *Critique of Practical Reason*. Translated by Lewis White Beck. New York: Macmillan, 1956.

———. *Critique of Pure Reason*. Translated by Norman Kemp Smith. New York: Modern Library, 1958.

———. *Kritik der reinen Vernunft*. Leipzig: Felix Meiner, 1919.

———. *Kritik der Urteilskraft*. Leipzig: Meiner, 2006.

———. *Religion within the Limits of Reason Alone*. Translated by Theodore M. Greene and Hoyt H. Hudson. New York: Harper Torchbooks, 1960.

Kauffman, Lane. "Género y praxis en *Juan de Mairena*." In *Divergencias y unidad: perspectivas sobre la Generación del 98 y Antonio Machado*, edited by John P. Gabriele, 269–81. Madrid: Orígenes, 1990.

Lacoue-Labarthe, Philippe, and Jean-Luc Nancy. *The Literary Absolute: The Theory of Literature in German Romanticism*. Translated by Philip Barnard and Cheryl Lester. Albany: State University of New York Press, 1988.

Lanz, Juan José. "José Ortega y Gasset, filosofía y literatura." *Revista de Occidente* 300 (2006): 23–48.

Larubia-Prado, Francisco. *Alegorías de la voluntad: pensamiento orgánico, retórica y deconstrucción en la obra de Miguel de Unamuno*. Madrid: Libertarias; Prodhufi, 1996.

———. "Filosofía y poesía: María Zambrano y la retórica de la reconciliación." *Hispanic Review* 65, no. 2 (1997): 199–216.
———. "*Niebla* de Miguel Unamuno: ironía y deconstrucción." In *El hispanismo en los Estados Unidos: discursos críticos/prácticas textuales*, edited by José María del Pino and Francisco la Rubia Prado, 111–32. Madrid: Visor, 1999.
"Las sinsombrero." Episode 1 of *Imprescindibles*. RTVE, 2014. Streaming video. https://www.rtve.es/play/videos/las-sinsombrero/.
Lawlor, Leonard. Translator's introduction to *Voice and Phenomenon*, by Jacques Derrida, xi–xxxiv. Evanston, IL: Northwestern University Press, 2011.
Llevadot Pascual, Laura. Introduction to *Aurora: papeles del Seminario María Zambrano*, *Número Especial Zambrano-Heidegger*, no. 12 (2011): 27–28.
Lough, Francis. "Maria Zambrano: Philosophy, Literature, and Democracy." In *The Cultural Legacy of Maria Zambrano*, edited by Xon de Ros and Daniela Omlor, 185–99. Cambridge: Legenda, 2017.
Lovejoy, A. O. "On the Meaning of 'Romantic' in Early German Romanticism." *Modern Language Notes* 31, no. 7 (1916): 385–96.
Machado, Antonio. *Border of a Dream: Selected Poems of Antonio Machado*. Translated by Willis Barnstone. Port Townsend, WA: Copper Canyon Press, 2004.
———. *Escritos dispersos (1893–1936)*. Edited by Jordi Doménech. Barcelona: Octahedro, 2009.
———. *Juan de Mairena*. Edited by Antonio Fernández Ferrer. 2 vols. Madrid: Cátedra, 2003.
———. *Juan de Mairena*. Edited and translated by Ben Belitt. Berkeley: University of California Press, 1963.
———. *Los complementarios*. In *Poesía y prosa*, vol. 3, *Prosas completas (1893–1936)*, edited by Oreste Macrí and Gaetano Chiappini, 1149–1375. Madrid: Espasa-Calpe; Fundación Antonio Machado, 1989.
———. *Poesías completas*. Madrid: Espasa-Calpe, 1983.
———. "Reflexiones sobre la lírica." *Cuadernos Hispanoamericanos* 45 (1953): 279–91.
———. "Reflexiones sobre la lírica." In *Poesía y prosa*, vol. 3, *Prosas completas (1893–1936)*, edited by Oreste Macrí and Gaetano Chiappini, 1649–62. Madrid: Espasa-Calpe; Fundación Antonio Machado, 1989.
———. *Times Alone: Selected Poems of Antonio Machado*. Translated by Robert Bly. Middletown, CT: Wesleyan University Press, 1983.
———. *Times Alone: Twelve Poems from Soledades*. Translated by Robert Bly. Port Townsend, WA: Graywolf Press, 1983.
Mackey, Louis. *The Ancient Quarrel Continued: The Troubled Marriage of Philosophy and Literature*. Lanham, MD: University Press of America, 2002.
Macrí, Oreste. Introduction to *Poesía y prosa*, by Antonio Machado. Edited by Oreste Macrí. Vol. 1, *Introducción*. Madrid: Espasa-Calpe; Fundación Antonio Machado, 1989.

Madarriaga, Santiago de. "Unamuno Re-read." In *Tragic Sense of Life in Men and Nations*, by Miguel de Unamuno, xix–xlvi. Translated by Anthony Kerrigan. Princeton, NJ: Princeton University Press, 1972.

Maillard, Chantal. *Creación por la metáfora: introducción a la razón poética*. Barcelona: Anthropos, 1992.

Mann, Peter Gordon. "Saving Europe in Spain: José Ortega y Gasset's *Meditations on Quixote* and the Politics of Self, Nation, and Europe." *Journal of European Studies* 49, no. 2 (2019): 108–42.

Marías, Javier. "Contar el misterio." In *Literatura y fantasma*, 117–23. Madrid: Alfaguara, 2001.

———. "Fragmento y enigma y espantoso azar." In *Literatura y fantasma*, 437–64. Madrid: Alfaguara, 2001.

———. *Monarca del tiempo*. Madrid: Alfaguara, 1978.

———. "Volveremos." In *Literatura y fantasma*, 236–38. Madrid: Alfaguara, 2001.

Marías, Julián. "Antonio Machado y el pensamiento." In *Antonio Machado hacia Europa*, edited Pablo Luis Ávila, 151–58. Madrid: Visor, 1993.

———. *Historia de la filosofía*. Madrid: Revista de Occidente, 1966.

———. *History of Philosophy*. Translated by Stanley Appelbaum and Clarence C. Strowbridge. New York: Dover, 1967.

———. Introduction to José Ortega y Gasset, *Meditaciones del Quijote*, 15–36. Madrid: Catedra 2010.

———. "La 'meditatio mortis' tema de nuestro tiempo." In "Homenaje a Miguel de Unamuno en el primer centenario de su muerte," special issue of *Revista de Occidente* 7, no. 19 (1964): 41–50.

———. "Los géneros literarios en filosofía." In *Ensayos de teoría*, 7–42. Madrid: Revista de Occidente, 1966.

———. "Machado y Heidegger." *Suplemento de Ínsula* 94 (1953): 1–2.

Martín, Francisco José. "El genio filosófico de la literatura." In Garrido et al., *El legado filosófico español e hispanoamericano del siglo XX*, 96–104. Madrid: Cátedra, 2009.

———. *La tradición velada: Ortega y el pensamiento humanista*. Madrid: Biblioteca Nueva, 1999.

Martínez Hernández, José. *Antonio Machado, un pensador poético*. Murcia: Almuzara, 2019. Kindle.

Marx, Karl, and Friedrich Engels. *The Communist Manifesto*. In *Marx-Engels Reader*, edited by Robert C. Tucker, 469–500. New York: Norton, 1978.

Mayhew, Jonathan. "Was Lorca a Poetic Thinker?" *Romance Quarterly* 58, no. 4 (2011): 276–88.

McVan, Alice. *Antonio Machado*. New York: Hispanic Society of America, 1959.

Mecke, Jochen. "La 'alterización' del arte: estética y filosofía apócrifas en Antonio Machado." In *Hoy es siempre todavía: Curso internacional sobre Antonio Machado*,

Córdoba 7–11 de noviembre de 2005, edited by Jordi Doménech, 526–58. Sevilla: Renacimiento/Ayuntamiento de Córdoba, 2006.

Mehely, Hassan. *Writing Cogito*. Albany: State University of New York Press, 1997.

Menéndez Pelayo, Marcelino. *La ciencia española*. 3 vols. Santander: Aldus, 1953.

———. *La filosofía española*. Edited by Constantino Lascaris Comneno. Madrid: Rialp, 1955.

Meyer, François. *L'Ontologie de Miguel de Unamuno*. Paris: Presses Universitaires de France, 1955.

Michel, Andreas, and Assenka Oksiloff. "Romantic Crossovers: Philosophy as Art and Art as Philosophy." In *Theory as Practice: A Critical Anthology of Early German Romantic Writings*, edited and translated by Jochen Schulte-Sasse et al., 157–79. Minneapolis: University of Minnesota Press, 1997.

"Miguel de Cervantes Prize." Wikipedia. Last modified September 22, 2021, 03:32. https://en.wikipedia.org/wiki/Miguel_de_Cervantes_Prize.

Miller, J. Hillis. "Derrida and Literature." In *Jacques Derrida and the Humanities*, edited by Tom Cohen, 58–81. Cambridge: Cambridge University Press, 2001.

———. "Sovereignty Death Literature Unconditionality Democracy University." In *Deconstructing Derrida: Tasks for the New Humanities*, 233–45. New York: Palgrave Macmillan, 2005.

Mirbach, Dagmar. "Dichtung als *representatio*: G. W. Leibniz und A. G. Baumgarten." In Feger, *Handbuch Literatur und Philosophie*, 10–20.

Molinuevo, José Luis. "Literatura y filosofía en Ortega y Gasset." *Revista de Occidente* 132 (1992): 69–74.

Moreno Sanz, Jesús. *El logos oscuro: tragedia, mística y filosofía en María Zambrano*. Vol. 1. Madrid: Verbum, 2008.

———. *Encuentro sin fin: con el camino del pensar de María Zambrano, y otros encuentros*. Madrid: Endymion, 1996.

———. Introduction to *Obras completas*, by María Zambrano. Vol. 1. Edited Jesús Moreno Sanz et al., x–xxxviii. Barcelona: Galaxia Gutenberg, 2015.

———. "La razón no polémica en María Zambrano: lugares elementales y palabras con cuerpo." In *María Zambrano: la razón poética o la filosofía*, edited by Teresa Rocha Barco, 137–49. Madrid: Tecnos, 1997.

———, ed. *María Zambrano, 1904–1991: de la razón cívica a la razón poética*. Madrid: Publicaciones de la Residencia de Estudiantes; Vélez-Málaga: Fundación María Zambrano, 2004.

———. "*Obras completas* de María Zambrano." *Revista de Filosofía* 46, no. 1 (2021): 229–38.

Moroy, Fernando. Prologue to *Pensadores españoles universales*. Edited by Nuria Ramos and Sergio Casquet, 7–12. Madrid: LID, 2014.

Nancy, Jean-Luc. *Hegel: The Restlessness of the Negative*. Translated by Jason Smith and Steven Miller. Minneapolis: University of Minnesota Press, 2002.

Navarro Brotóns, Victor, and William Eamon, eds. *Más allá de la Leyenda Negra: España y la Revolución científica/Beyond the Black Legend: Spain and the Scientific Revolution*. Valencia: Instituto de Historia de la Ciencia y Documentación López Piñero, 2007.

Newton, Nancy. "Structures of Cognition: Antonio Machado and the Via Negativa." *MLN* 90, no. 2 (1975): 231–51.

Nietzsche, Friedrich. *The Birth of Tragedy and The Genealogy of Morals*. Translated Francis Golffing. New York: Doubleday Anchor, 1956.

———. *Die Geburt der Tragödie aus dem Geiste der Musik*. In *Sämtliche Werke*, 1:7–157. Berlin: de Gruyter, 1988.

———. *Nachgelassene Fragmente, 1887–1889*. *Sämtliche Werke*, vol. 13. Berlin: de Gruyter, 1988.

———. *Zur Genealogie der Moral*. In *Sämtliche Werke*, 5:245–412. Berlin: de Gruyter, 1988.

Novalis. *Fichte Studies*. In *Theory as Practice: A Critical Anthology of Early German Romantic Writings*, edited and translated by Jochen Schulte-Sasse et al., 90–111. Minneapolis: University Minnesota Press, 1997.

Nuccetelli, Susana. "How to Solve the Invisibility Problem for Spanish and Latin American Philosophy." *Teorema* 31, no. 1 (2012): 129–38.

Nussbaum, Martha. *Love's Knowledge: Essays on Philosophy and Literature*. New York: Oxford University Press, 1990.

Olson, Paul R. *The Great Chiasmus: Word and Flesh in the Novels of Unamuno*. Lafayette, IN: Purdue University Press, 2003.

Online Etymological Dictionary, s.v. "Discuss." Accessed June 29, 2021. https://www.etymonline.com/search?q=discuss.

Orringer, Nelson. Introduction to Miguel de Unamuno, *Del sentimiento trágico de la vida en los hombres y los pueblos y Tratado de amor de dios*. Edited Nelson Orringer, 13–92. Madrid: Tecnos, 2005.

———. "Sobre las cuatro etapas de Ortega." *Los Ensayistas* 3, no. 5 (1978): 19–31.

———. Translator's introduction to *Treatise on Love of God*. Edited and translated by Nelson Orringer, xi–xxxviii. Urbana: University of Illinois Press, 2007.

Ortega Muñoz, Juan Fernando. *Introducción al pensamiento de María Zambrano*. México: Fondo de Cultura Económica, 1994.

———. Introduction to *Maria Zambrano: palabras para el mundo*. Edited Madeline Cámara and Luis Pablo Ortega, 9–15. Newark, DE: Juan de la Cuesta, 2011.

Ortega y Gasset, José. "Adán en el Paraíso." In *La deshumanización del arte y otros ensayos de estética*, 67–90. Madrid: Alianza; Revista de Occidente, 2000.

———. "The Dehumanization of Art." In *The Dehumanization of Art and Other Writings on Art and Culture*, translated by Willard Trask, 1–50. Garden City, NY: Doubleday, 1956.

———. "Dos grandes metáforas." In *Obras completas*, 2:387–400. Madrid: Revista de Occidente, 1966.

———. *El tema de nuestro tiempo.* In *Obras completas*, 3:143–203. Madrid: Revista de Occidente, 1966.

———. "En la muerte de Unamuno." In *Miguel de Unamuno*, edited Antonio Sánchez Barbudo, 20–21. Madrid: Taurus, 1974.

———. "En torno a Galileo." In *Obras completas*, 5:9–164. Madrid: Revista de Occidente, 1966.

———. "Goethe desde adentro." In *Obras completas*, 4:381–541. Madrid: Revista de Occidente, 1966.

———. *The Idea of the Principle in Leibniz and the Evolution of Deductive Theory.* Translated by Mildred Adams. New York: Norton, 1971.

———. "In Search of Goethe from the Within." In *The Dehumanization of Art and Other Writings on Art and Culture*, translated by Willard Trask, 121–60. Garden City, NY: Doubleday, 1956.

———. *Historia como sistema.* Madrid: Revista de Occidente, 1970.

———. *History as System and Other Essays toward a Philosophy of History.* Translated by Helene Weyl. New York: Norton, 1961.

———. "La deshumanización del arte." In *La deshumanización del arte y otros ensayos de estética*, 11–54. Madrid: Alianza; Revista de Occidente, 2000.

———. *La idea del principio en Leibniz.* In *Obras completas*, 8:61–356. Madrid: Revista de Occidente, 1966.

———. *Man and Crisis.* Translated by Mildred Adams. New York: Norton, 1958.

———. *Meditaciones del Quijote.* In *Obras completas*, 1:309–400. Madrid: Revista de Occidente, 1966.

———. *Meditaciones del Quijote.* Madrid: Alianza, 1987.

———. *Meditaciones del Quijote.* Edited by Julián Marías. Madrid: Cátedra, 2010.

———. *Meditaciones sobre la literatura y el arte: (la manera española de ver las cosas).* Edited by E. Inman Fox. Madrid: Clásicos Castalia, 1987.

———. *Meditations on Quixote.* Translated by Evelyn Rugg and Diego Marín. New York: Norton, 1961.

———. *The Modern Theme.* Translated by James Cleugh. New York: Harper and Row, 1961.

———. "Ni vitalismo ni racionalismo." In *Obras completas*, 3:270–80. Madrid: Revista de Occidente, 1966.

———. "Preface for Germans." In *Phenomenology and Art*, translated by Phillip Silver, 17–76. New York: Norton, 1975.

———. "Prólogo para alemanes." In *Obras completas*, 8:13–58. Madrid: Revista de Occidente, 1966.

———. *¿Qué es filosofía?* In *Obras completas*, 7:273–437. Madrid: Revista de Occidente, 1966.

———. *What Is Philosophy?* Translated by Mildred Adams. New York: Norton, 1964.
Ortega y Gasset, José, and Miguel de Unamuno. *Epistolario completo Ortega-Unamuno*. Edited by Laureano Robles Carcedo. Madrid: El Arquero, 1987.
Ouimette, Victor. *José Ortega y Gasset*. Boston: Twayne, 1982.
Paz, Octavio. "José Ortega y Gasset: el cómo y el para qué/1." *El País*, October 22, 1980. Accessed July 1, 2021. elpais.com.
———. "José Ortega y Gasset: el cómo y el para qué/2: Tres omisiones." *El País*, October 23, 1980. https://elpais.com/diario/1980/10/24/opinion/341190008_850215.html.
———. "José Ortega y Gasset, the Why and the Wherefore." In *On Poets and Others*, translated by Michael Schmidt, 139–51. New York: Seaver, 1986.
Pérez, Janet. "*Circunstancia*, Reason, and Metaphysics: Context and Unity in the Thought of María Zambrano." In *Spanish Women Writers and the Essay*, edited by Kathleen M. Glenn and Mercedes Mazquiarán de Rodríguez, 144–71. Columbia: University of Missouri Press, 1998.
———. "*La razón de la sinrazón*: Unamuno, Machado, and Ortega in the Thought of María Zambrano." *Hispania* 82, no. 1 (1999): 56–67.
Perona, Ángeles J., and Ramón del Castillo Santos. "El pensamiento español y representaciones de género." In *Sociología de las mujeres españolas*, edited by María Antonia García de León, Marisa García de Cortázar, and Félix Ortega, 325–49. Madrid: Editorial Complutense, 1996.
Pessoa, Fernando. *A Little Larger Than the Entire Universe: Selected Poems*. Edited and translated by Richard Zenith. New York: Penguin, 2006.
Plato. *Complete Works*. Edited by John M. Cooper. Indianapolis: Hackett, 1997.
———. *Phaedo*. Perseus Digital Library. http://www.perseus.tufts.edu/hopper/text.jsp?doc=Perseus:text:1999.01.0170:text=Phaedo.
———. *Phaedrus*. Perseus Digital Library. http://www.perseus.tufts.edu/hopper/text?doc=Perseus%3atext%3a1999.01.0174%3atext%3dPhaedrus.
———. *Republic*. Perseus Digital Library. http://www.perseus.tufts.edu/hopper/text?doc=Perseus:text:1999.01.0167.
———. *Theaetetus*. Perseus Digital Library. http://www.perseus.tufts.edu/hopper/text.jsp?doc=Perseus:text:1999.01.0171:text=Theaet.
Prados, Emilio. "Abril de Dios." In *Antología comentada de la Generación del 27*, 498–99. Madrid: Espasa-Calpe, 1998.
"Presentado, 'Notas de un método' último libro de María Zambrano." *El País*, May 16, 1989. elpais.com.
"Primum vivere deinde philosophari." Wikipédia. Last modified April 14, 2020, 22:20. https://fr.wikipedia.org/wiki/Primum_vivere_deinde_philosophari.
Rabaté, Colette, and Jean Claude Rabaté. *Miguel de Unamuno: biografía*. Madrid: Taurus, 2009.
Ramírez, Goretti. *María Zambrano, crítica literaria*. Madrid: Devenir Ensayo, 2004.

Revilla, Carmen, ed. *Claves de la razón poética*. Madrid: Trotta, 1998.
Revilla Moreno, Manuel de la. "Filosofía española." In Menéndez Pelayo, *La ciencia española*, 1:192–98.
Ribas, Pedro. *Para leer a Unamuno*. Madrid: Alianza, 2002.
———. "Unamuno lector de Hegel." *Revista de Occidente* 96 (1989): 108–25.
———. *Unamuno: el vasco universal*. Madrid: Endymion, 2015.
Robles, Laureano. "Don Marcelino, visto por Unamuno." *Cuadernos Cátedra Miguel de Unamuno* 45, no. 1 (2008): 91–130.
Rocha Barco, Teresa, ed. *María Zambrano: la razón poética o la filosofía*. Madrid: Tecnos, 1997.
Rodríguez García, María. *Filosofía y novela: de la generación del 98 a José Ortega y Gasset*. Seville: Athenaica, 2018.
Roetzel, Lisa C. "Feminizing Philosophy." In *Theory as Practice: A Critical Anthology of Early German Romantic Writings*, edited and translated by Jochen Schulte-Sasse et al., 361–81. Minneapolis: University of Minnesota Press, 1997.
Rorty, Richard. Introduction to *Philosophy in History: Essays on the Historiography of Philosophy*. Edited Richard Rorty, J. B. Schneewind, and Quentin Skinner, 1–8. Cambridge: Cambridge University Press, 1984.
Ros, Xon de. *The Poetry of Antonio Machado: Changing the Landscape*. Oxford: Oxford University Press, 2015.
Ros, Xon de, and Daniela Omlor. Introduction to *The Cultural Legacy of Maria Zambrano*. Edited by Xon de Ros and Daniela Omlor, 1–11. Cambridge, UK: Legenda, 2017.
Rousseau, Jean-Jacques. *The First and Second Discourses Together with the Replies to Critics and Essay on the Origin of Languages*. Edited and translated by Victor Gourevitch. New York: Harper and Row, 1986.
Rudrum, David. *Literature and Philosophy: A Guide to Contemporary Debates*. London: Palgrave Macmillan, 2006.
Sánchez Barbudo, Antonio. *El pensamiento de Antonio Machado*. Madrid: Guadarrama, 1974.
San Martín, Javier. *Fenomenología y cultura en Ortega*. Madrid: Tecnos, 1998.
Scharm, Heike. *El tiempo y el ser en Javier Marías*. Amsterdam: Rodopi, 2013.
Schelling, F. W. J. *System of Transcendental Idealism*. Translated by Peter Heath. Charlottesville: University of Virginia Press, 1993.
Schlegel, Friedrich. *Dialogue on Poetry and Literary Aphorisms*. Translated by Ernst Behler and Roman Struc. University Park: Pennsylvania State University Press, 1968.
———. "Gespräch über die Poesie." In *"Athenäums"—Fragmente und andere Schriften*, 165–224. Stuttgart: Reklam, 1978.
———. "On Philosophy: To Dorothea." Translated by Lisa C. Roetzel. In *Theory as Practice: A Critical Anthology of Early German Romantic Writings*, edited and translated by Jochen Schulte-Sasse et al., 419–39. Minneapolis: University of Minnesota Press, 1997.

———. *Philosophical Fragments*. Translated by Peter Firchow. Minneapolis: University of Minnesota Press, 1991.

———. "Über die Philosophie: an Dorothea." In *Schriften zur Kritischen Philosophie*, edited by Andreas Arndt and Jure Zovko, 71–95. Hamburg: Meiner, 2007.

Schmidt, Rachel. *Forms of Modernity: Don Quixote and Modern Theories of the Novel*. Toronto: University of Toronto Press, 2011.

Selleri, Andrea, and Philip Gaydon. *Literary Studies and the Philosophy of Literature*. Cham, Switzerland: Palgrave Macmillan; Springer, 2016.

Sevilla, Sergio. "La razón poética: mirada, melodía y metáfora: María Zambrano y la hermenéutica." In *María Zambrano: la razón poética o la filosofía*, edited by Teresa Rocha Barco, 87–108. Madrid: Tecnos, 1997.

Sheehan, Thomas. Introduction to *Heidegger, the Man and the Thinker*. Edited by Thomas Sheehan, vii–xx. New Brunswick, NJ: Transaction, 2010.

———. "Reading a Life." In *Cambridge Companion to Heidegger*, edited by Charles B. Guignon, 70–96. Cambridge: Cambridge University Press, 1991.

Silver, Philip W. *Ortega as Phenomenologist: The Genesis of "Meditations on Quixote."* New York: Columbia University Press, 1978.

Sinclair, Alison. "Definition as the Enemy of Self-Definition: A Commentary on the Role of Language in Unamuno's *Niebla*." In *Words of Power: Essays in Honour of Alison Fairlie*, edited by Dorothy Gave Coleman and Gillian Jondorf, 187–225. Glasgow: University of Glasgow Publications in French Language and Literature, 1987.

Socrate, Mario. *Il linguaggio filosofico della poesia di Antonio Machado*. Padua: Marsilio, 1972.

Souvrión Rodríguez, Antonio. Introduction to *María Zambrano y la "Edad de Plata" de la cultura española: actas III Congreso Internacional sobre la Vida y Obra de María Zambrano*, 5–6. Vélez-Málaga: Fundación María Zambrano, 2004.

Spires, Robert. *Beyond the Metafictional Mode: Directions in the Modern Spanish Novel*. Lexington: University Press of Kentucky, 1984.

———. "From Augusto Pérez to Alejandro Gómez to Us: Unamuno's Existential Web." *Revista de Estudios Hispánicos* 20, no. 2 (1986): 39–49.

Staël, Madame de. *De la littérature considérée dans ses rapports avec les institutions sociales*. Paris: InfoMédia Communication, 1998.

———. *Madame de Staël on Politics, Literature and National Character*. Translated by Ed Morroe Berger. London: Sidgwick and Jackson, 1964.

Stocker, Barry. Introduction to Stocker and Mack, *The Palgrave Handbook of Philosophy and Literature*, 1–37

Stocker, Barry, and Michael Mack, eds. *The Palgrave Handbook of Philosophy and Literature*. London: Palgrave Macmillan, 2018.

Sushytska, Julia. "On the Non-rivalry between Poetry and Philosophy: Plato's *Republic* Reconsidered." *Mosaic* 45, no. 1 (2012): 55–70.

Torre, Guillermo de. "Teorías literarias de Antonio Machado." In *Antonio Machado*, edited by Ricardo Gullón and Allen W. Phillips, 227–42. Madrid: Taurus, 1973.

Unamuno, Miguel. "A lo que salga." In *Obras completas*, edited by Manuel García Blanco, 1:1194–1204. Madrid: Eslicer, 1966.

———. *Amor y pedagogía*. Madrid: Espasa-Calpe, 1968.

———. *Cómo se hace una novela*. In *Manual de Quijotismo; Cómo se hace una novela; Epistolario Miguel de Unamuno/Jean Cassou*. Salamanca: Ediciones Universidad de Salamanca, 2005.

———. *Del sentimiento trágico de la vida en los hombres y en los pueblos*. Madrid: Austral, 1966.

———. *Del sentimiento trágico de la vida en los hombres y en los pueblos y Tratado del amor de Dios*. Edited by Nelson Orringer. Madrid: Tecnos, 2005.

———. *En torno al casticismo*. Madrid: Biblioteca Nueva, 1996.

———. *Epistolario americano (1890–1836)*. Salamanca: Ediciones Universidad de Salamanca, 1996.

———. "Escritor ovíparo." In *Obras completas*, edited by Manuel García Blanco, 8:208–9. Madrid: Eslicer, 1966.

———. *Fog*. Translated by Elena Barcia. Evanston, IL: Northwestern University Press, 2017.

———. *How to Make a Novel*. In *Novela/Nivola*, vol. 6 of *Selected Works*, translated by Anthony Kerrigan. Princeton, NJ: Princeton University Press, 1976.

———. *Love and Pedagogy*. Translated by Michael Van de Berg. Amsterdam: Peter Lang, 1996.

———. *Manual de Quijotismo; Cómo se hace una novela; Epistolario Miguel de Unamuno/Jean Cassou*. Salamanca: Ediciones Universidad, 2005.

———. *Mist: Novela/Nivola*. Translated by Anthony Kerrigan. Princeton, NJ: Princeton University Press, 1976.

———. "My Religion." In *Perplexities and Paradoxes*. Translated by Stuart Gross, 1–9. Westport, Connecticut: Greenwood, 1945.

———. *Niebla*. Madrid: Cátedra, 1987.

———. *Niebla*. Edited by Francisco Aragón Guiller. Newark, DE: Cervantes, 2007.

———. *Our Lord Don Quixote: The Life of Don Quixote and Sancho and Related Essays*. Translated by Anthony Kerrigan. Princeton, NJ: Princeton University Press, 1976.

———. *Saint Manuel Bueno, Martyr*. Translated by Paul Burns and Salvador Ortiz-Carboneres. Oxford: Oxbow, 2009.

———. *San Manuel Bueno, mártir*. Madrid: Cátedra, 2003.

———. "Sobre la erudición y la crítica." In *Obras completas*, edited by Manuel García Blanco, 1:1264–78. Madrid: Eslicer, 1966.

———. "Sobre la filosofía española." In *Ensayos*, 1:555–69. Madrid: Aguilar, 1966.

———. *Three exemplary novels*. Translated by Angel Flores. New York: Grove, 1987.

———. *The Tragic Sense of Life in Men and in Peoples*. Translated by J. E. Crawford Flitch. New York: Dover, 1954.

———. *The Tragic Sense of Life in Men and Nations*. Translated by Anthony Kerrigan. Princeton, NJ: Princeton University Press, 1972.
———. *Tres novelas ejemplares y un prólogo*. Madrid: Alianza, 1987.
———. *Vida de don Quijote y Sancho Panza*. Madrid: Cátedra, 2015.
Valdés, Mario J. *Death in the Literature of Unamuno*. Urbana: University of Illinois Press, 1966.
———. Introduction to *Niebla*, by Miguel de Unamuno, 9–58. Edited by Mario J. Valdés. Madrid: Cátedra, 1987.
Valender, James. "María Zambrano y la Generación del 27." In Moreno Sanz, *María Zambrano, 1904–1991*, 271–93.
Valente, José Ángel. "El sueño creador." In *Las palabras de la tribu*, 193–200. Barcelona: Tusquets, 1994.
Valera, Juan. "De la filosofía." In *Obras completas*, edited by Luis Araujo Costa, 2:1559–1688. Madrid: Aguilar, 1961.
Valera, Juan, and Ramón de Campoamor. *La metafísica y la poesía: polémica*. Madrid: Sáenz de Jubera, 1891.
Valéry, Paul. *An Anthology*. Edited and translated by James R. Lawler. Princeton, NJ: Princeton University Press, 1977.
Valverde, José María. Introduction to *Nuevas canciones y de un cancionero apócrifo*, by Antonio Machado, 7–74. Edited by José María Valverde. Madrid: Castalia, 1975.
Veit-Schlegel, Dorothea. "Selected Diaries and Letters." In *Theory as Practice: A Critical Anthology of Early German Romantic Writings*, edited and translated by Jochen Schulte-Sasse et al., 440–43. Minneapolis: University of Minnesota Press, 1997.
Wagner, Astrid, and José María Ariso, eds. *Rationality Reconsidered: Ortega y Gasset and Wittgenstein on Knowledge, Belief and Practice*. Berlin: de Gruyter, 2016.
Welch, John R., ed. *Other Voices: Readings in Spanish Philosophy*. Notre Dame, IN: University of Notre Dame Press, 2010.
Williams, Raymond. *Keywords: A Vocabulary of Culture and Society*. New York: Oxford University Press, 1976.
Wyers, Frances. *Miguel de Unamuno: The Contrary Self*. London: Tamesis, 1976.
Zambrano, María. "A los poetas chilenos de 'madre España.'" In *Obras completas*, 1:338–78. Barcelona: Galaxia Gutenberg, 2015.
———. "A modo de autobiografía." *Anthropos* 70–71 (1986): 69–73.
———. "Acerca de la generación del 27." In *Algunos lugares de la poesía*, 159–62.
———. "The Agony of Europe." Translated by Jennifer Arnold. *History of European Ideas* 44, no. 7 (2018): 952–59.
———. *Algunos lugares de la poesía*. Edited by Juan Fernando Ortega Muñoz. Madrid: Trotta, 2007.

———. "Antonio Machado y Unamuno, precursores de Heidegger." In *Algunos lugares de la poesía*, 156–57.
———. *Claros del bosque*. In *Obras completas*, vol. 4, part 1. Barcelona: Galaxia Gutenberg, 2018.
———. *Confession*. In *Two Confessions*, by María Zambrano and Rosa Chacel, 13–64. Translated by Noël Valis and Carol Maier. Albany: State University of New York Press, 2015.
———. *Delirio y destino: los veinte años de una española*. Madrid: Editorial Centro de Estudios Ramón Areces, 1998.
———. *Delirium and Destiny: A Spaniard in Her Twenties*. Translated by Carol Maier. Albany: State University of New York Press, 1999.
———. *El hombre y lo divino*. Mexico City: FCE, 2001.
———. "El poeta y la muerte." In *Algunos lugares de la poesía*, 191–97.
———. *Filosofía y poesía*. Mexico City: FCE, 1996.
———. *Hacia un saber sobre el alma*. Buenos Aires: Losada, 2005.
———. *La agonía de Europa*. Madrid: Trotta, 2000.
———. *La confesión: género literario*. Madrid: Ediciones Siruela, 1995.
———. "La crisis de la palabra." In *Algunos lugares de la poesía*, 75–76.
———. "La Cuba secreta." In *"La Cuba secreta" y otros ensayos*, edited Jorge Luis Arcos, 107–11. Madrid: Endymion, 1996.
———. "*La guerra* de Antonio Machado." In *Obras completas*, edited by Jesús Moreno Sanz, 1:185–94. Barcelona: Galaxia Gutenberg, 2015.
———. "La reforma del entendimiento." In *Obras completas*, 1: 195–201. Barcelona: Galaxia Gutenberg, 2015.
———. "La reforma del entendimiento español." In *Obras completas*, 1: 205–20. Barcelona: Galaxia Gutenberg, 2015.
———. "La religión poética de Unamuno." In *España, sueño y verdad*, 157–98. Barcelona: Edhasa, 2002.
———. *Los bienaventurados*. Madrid: Siruela, 2004.
———. "Miguel de Cervantes." In *Algunos lugares de la poesía*, 115–22.
———. *Notas de un método*. Madrid: Mondadori, 1989.
———. "Ortega y Gasset, filósofo español." In *España, sueño y verdad*, 113–56. Barcelona: Edhasa, 2002.
———. *Obras completas*, edited Jesús Moreno Sanz, et al. 6 vols. Barcelona: Galaxia Gutenberg, 2010–21.
———. "Pensamiento y poesía en Emilio Prados." In *Algunos lugares de la poesía*, edited by Juan Fernando Ortega Muñoz, 198–204. Madrid: Trotta, 2007.
———. *Pensamiento y poesía en la vida española*. Madrid: Endymion, 1996.
———. "Poema y sistema." In *Hacia un saber sobre el alma*, 43–48. Buenos Aires: Losada, 2005.
———. "Presencia de Don Miguel." In *Unamuno*, edited by Mercedes Gómez Blesa, 199–203. Madrid: Debolsillo, 2004.

———. "The Reformation of Spanish Understanding." Translated by Francis Lough. *History of European Ideas* 44, no. 7 (2018): 943–51.

Ziarek, Krzysztof. *Inflected Language: Toward a Hermeneutic of Nearness: Heidegger, Levinas, Celan, Stevens.* New York: State University of New York Press, 1994.

Index

Abellán, José Luis, xi, 7, 8–13, 16, 28, 41, 43, 58, 164, 172, 268n17, 273n65
affect. *See* feeling
Albornoz, Aurora de, 172
Alonso, Dámaso, 36, 207
Álvarez Castro, Luis, 93–94, 100, 272n48, 288n17
Andersen, Katrine Helen, 273n60
Aragón Guiller, Francisco, 293n81
Aranguren, José Luis L., 41, 221, 304n20
Aristotle, 18, 23, 24–29, 64–66, 76, 87, 104, 124, 139, 142, 148, 161–62, 169, 185, 229, 252
Arlandis, Sergio, 288n20
Augustine, 85, 227, 239
Austin, J. L. 82, 188

Balibrea, Mari Paz, 254, 277n103, 304n18, 305n25, 309n84
Barco, Pablo del, 301n45
Barfield, Raymond, 54, 55, 57, 64
Barjau, Eustaquio, 173–74
Baroja, Pío, 49–51
Barzun, Jacques, 67, 282n33
Benet, Juan, 257–58, 266, 286n90
Benjamin, Andrew, 280n14
Benjamin, Walter, 69

Bergson, Henri, 17, 178, 201–5, 271
Bertrán, Santiago, 266, 310n3
Blanchot, Maurice, 117–18
Blanco Aguinaga, Carlos, 94
body, the, 26, 48, 92, 95, 103, 116, 127, 138–40, 141, 148, 153, 164, 296n29
Bolado, Gerardo, 58–59
Booth, Wayne C., 130–31, 293n84
Borges, Jorge Luis, 31, 133–35, 191, 274n74
Bosteels, Bruno, 159
Bozal, Valeriano, 143, 295n18
Brewer, Brian, 271n42
Brioso, Jorge, 163
Bundgård, Ana, xi, 41, 43, 44, 45, 46, 254, 277n106, 303n2, 303n5, 303n12
Bush, Andrew, 235, 309n74

Caballero Rodríguez, Beatriz, 45, 254, 303n5, 306n53, 309n85
Calderón de la Barca, Pedro, 18, 21, 182, 271n42
Candelaria, Michael, 111, 281n21, 288n14, 290n46
Caponigri, A.R., 2
Cascardi, Anthony, 54–55, 57, 58
Catullus, 265

Caudet, Francisco, 298n2, 301n47
Cerezo Galán, Pedro, xi, 31, 32, 140, 150, 163, 172, 178, 304n18
Ciplijauskaité, Biruté, 173
Clark, Timothy, 79, 81, 284n63, 285n64
Clavería, Carlos, 200, 301n53
Cleveland, Basil, 296n26
Csejtei, Dezsö, 109, 292n73
Cogan, John, 300n35
Comte, Auguste, 9–12, 28–29, 137, 140, 164, 227, 260
Cope, Brian, 124–5, 131
Crespo Sánchez, Javier, 275n81
Cruz Hernández, Miguel, 109, 119
Csejtei, Dezsö, 109, 292n73

death, iv, 62, 86–87, 94–96, 98, 103, 108–110, 115–19, 122–25, 131–35, 148, 155, 163, 168, 220, 239–40, 247, 307n60
Deleuze, Gilles, 57, 280n19
Denham, Alison, 282n28
Derrida, Jacques, xii, 6, 27, 59, 80–87, 88, 95, 161–62, 164–65, 184–86, 211–12, 255–56, 261, 264, 281–82n27, 286n73, 300n38, 300n40, 306n45
Descartes, René, 5, 26–29, 59, 104, 132, 185, 229, 236
Díaz Álvarez, Jesús M., 163
divine, the. *See* religion
Doménech, Jordi, 187
Dostoyevsky, Fiodor, 230
Durantou, Patrick, 172

Edmundson, Mark, 55
Eguizábal, José Ignacio, 45
emotion. *See* feeling
Enquist Källgren, Karolina, 45, 254
Europe: concept of, 5–7, 114, 222, 227–33; as cultural identity, 10, 18, 19, 34–35, 37–38, 47, 49, 67, 110, 133, 152, 219, 224, 235, 238–39
Evans, Jan E. 124, 281n21, 289n26

Faber, Sebastiaan, 280n17
feeling, 10–11, 34, 49, 65–66, 68, 87, 92–94, 100–105, 113–17, 121–25, 145–46, 155, 156, 169–72, 191, 222, 225, 233, 244
Feger, Hans, 53, 57, 70, 780n21
Fenoy, Sebastián, 306n53
Fenves, Peter, 97
Fernández Ferrer, Antonio, 38, 173, 174
Fernández-Medina, Nicolás, 38, 196, 270n31, 275n83, 288n17, 301n48
Ferrater Mora, José, 31, 109, 274n77
Fichte, Johann Gottlieb, 68
Foucault, Michel, 196, 301n49
Fox, E. Inman, 270n28, 275n82
Franz, Thomas, 124
Fraser, Benjamin, 271n35

Gajić, Tatjana, 46, 295n20
Gaos, José, 268n13
Garagorri, Paulino, 1–2, 109
García-Gómez, Jorge, 141
García-Posada, Miguel, 275n84, 301n52
García Lorca, Federico, 241, 243, 270n29
Garrido, Manuel, xi, 7, 164, 269n25, 297n38
Gasché, Rodolphe, 5–6, 75, 82, 84–85, 289, 280n14, 292n65
generation, concept of, 7, 13, 30, 32, 153, 164, 242–43
Generation of 27, 241–43
Generation of 98, 14–15, 269–70n28
Genette, Gérard, 129–30, 187, 190
Germany: cultural identity of, 2, 10–13, 34–35, 91, 103–4, 137–38,

142–45, 289–90n35; Spanish philosophy in, 273n60, 281n23
Giménez Caballero, Ernesto, 186–88
Gómez Blesa, Mercedes, 44, 224
Gosetti-Ferencei, Jennifer, 285n70
Gracia, Jordi, 31, 146
Gracia, Jorge, 58
Graff Zivin, Erin, 285n73
Guattari, Félix, 57, 280n19
Guillén, Jorge, 172, 241
Gullón, Ricardo, 269n28
Gutiérrez Girardot, Rafael, 173
Guy, Alain, 1–2, 41, 58, 267n1

Hegel, Georg Wilhelm Friedrich, 4–7, 12, 50, 68, 107–8, 116–19, 123, 135, 141–42, 159, 162, 169, 178, 185, 207–8
Heidegger, Martin, xii, 9, 12, 25, 59, 74–80, 81, 84, 88, 116, 119–23, 125, 142, 146, 163, 164, 172, 198–206, 210–11, 230, 233, 250–51, 255, 260, 261, 284n53m, 284n56, 294n8, 302n70, 309n82
Herder, Johann Gottfried, 106, 290n38
heteronymity, 37, 186–91, 298n8
Hofstadter, Albert, 77, 284n63
Husserl, Edmund, 5, 184–85, 229–33, 238, 239, 300n35
Hutchinson, Steven, 173

immediacy, 11, 68, 74, 96, 117–18, 141, 143, 179–80, 185, 207, 218, 250–51, 261, 284n53, 295n18

Jewish thought, 16, 282n34
Johnson, Roberta, xi, 98–99, 131, 221, 270n28, 292n79
Jurkevich, Gayana, 288n17

Kant, Immanuel, 5, 17, 50, 59, 62, 68–69, 71, 99, 103–8, 116, 139, 152, 169, 185, 229, 263, 283n38, 290n37
Kerrigan, Anthony, 101, 287n4, 291n59
Kierkegaard, Søren, 5, 50, 97, 191, 216, 237, 281n21, 289n26

Lacoue-Labarthe, Philippe, 70Lanz, Juan José, 30–1, 141, 143
Larubia-Prado, Francisco, xi, 46
Lawlor, Leonard, 300n38
Levinas, Emmanuel, 196, 301n48
life, xi–xii, 23, 29–32, 36–37, 42–4, 50, 65–66, 71–76, 87, 91–104, 111–19, 127–35, 137–65, 169–78, 187, 193–95, 205, 208–10, 216–222, 230–33, 245–46, 257–58
Llevadot Pascual, Laura, 230
Lorca, Federico García. *See* García Lorca, Federico
Lough, Francis, 43, 254, 277n103, 304n18, 305n25, 309n84

Machado, Antonio, 14, 33, 36–40, 46–48, 167–213, 260–66; Derrida and, 184–86, 211–12; Heidegger and, 76, 193, 198–206, 210–11; poetic thought and, 39, 41, 169, 176, 181, 193, 196–99, 208, 260; Romanticism and, 210
Mackey, Louis, 53–54, 56, 57
Macrí, Oreste, 183–84
Madarriaga, Salvador, 106, 109
Maillard, Chantal, 304n21
Mann, Peter Gordon, 294n7
Manrique, Jorge, 168, 182
Marías, Javier, 257–62, 264, 266
Marías, Julián, 9, 13, 17, 31, 109, 173, 202–3, 262, 269n22
Marx, Karl, 75, 230, 237
Mecke, Jochen, 196
Mehely, Hassan, 273n64

Menéndez Pelayo, Marcelino, 8–9, 17–20, 34, 50, 181
Meyer, François, 106–7, 108
Miller, J. Hillis, 81–83, 129
Molinuevo, José Luis, 30–31
Moreno Sanz, Jesús, 42, 43, 44, 45, 46, 217, 223, 230
Muslim thought, 16, 268n13, 282n34

Nancy, Jean-Luc, 70, 292n66
Newton, Nancy, 302n64
nihilism, 229–30
Nietzsche, Friedrich, xiv, 5, 12, 50, 57, 75, 76, 77, 79, 80, 191, 207, 216, 225–26, 230, 234, 237
Novalis, 68, 69
Nuccetelli, Susana, 7, 268n19, 269n25

Omlor, Daniela, 254
organs, bodily. *See* body
Orringer, Nelson, 91, 111–12, 114, 150, 158, 287n1, 291n59, 297n38
Ortega Muñoz, Juan Fernando, 42, 227n107, 304n14, 308n66
Ortega y Gasset, José, 1–2, 9–13, 18, 29–36, 133–34, 137–65, 242, 260–61; correspondence with Unamuno, 91–92, 103, 112, 115, 116, 119, 287n1, 296n 29, 297n45; Heidegger and, 76, 142, 146, 163, 164, 294n8; historical reason and, 30–31, 164, 218, 260; ratiovitalism and, 141, 154–57, 163–64, 221, 227, 231, 264–65, 274n80; relationship with Zambrano, 221
Ouimette, Victor, 146, 295n22, 295–96n23

paratexts, 129–30
Paz, Octavio, 162–65, 234
Pelayo, Marcelino Menéndez. *See* Menéndez Pelayo, Marcelino

Pérez, Janet, xi, 43, 277n106, 303n12
Pessoa, Fernando, 171, 298n8
philosophy: definition of, 4–10, 57, 59–65, 104–5, 108, 121–22, 158–62; Spanish, x–xi, 1–3, 7–10, 12, 16–21, 114–15, 272–73n59, 273n65, 280n19, 281n23
Plato, 5, 76, 87, 95, 139, 151, 154, 211, 226, 234, 235, 236, 253, 261, 281n26, 281n27, 282n28; "ancient quarrel," 53–56, 59–66, 151, 234
positivism, 9–11, 28–9, 67, 108, 164, 273n65
prologues, conventions of, ix, xv, 129, 291n58
pseudonymity, 186–91

Ramírez, Goretti, 41, 43–4
reason: historical . . . vital . . . poetic, *see* poetic reason
religion, 48, 71–72, 99, 105, 117, 163, 154, 217, 222, 235, 238, 290n37
Revilla, Manuel de la, 17
Ribas, Pedro, 94, 106–7, 108, 117, 280n21, 281n23, 289n35, 292n67
Roetzl, Lisa, 71, 72
romanticism, 55, 59, 66–68, 100, 236, 282n33; early German, 68–74, 84, 86–88, 94, 99, 135, 210, 260
Ros, Xon de, 38, 254, 276n92
Rousseau, Jean-Jacques, xiv, 81, 224–25, 229, 244–45, 306n45, 309n76
Rudrum, David, 279n12

San Martín, Javier, 31, 147, 295n19
Sánchez Barbudo, Antonio, xi, 172, 174, 178, 300n32
Sánchez Cuervo, Antolín, 254, 277n103, 304n18, 305n25, 309n84
Scharm, Heike, 310n2
Schelling, Friedrich, 68

Schlegel, Friedrich, 69–73, 210, 256
sensation. *See* feeling
Sheehan, Thomas, 75, 76–77
Silver, Philip W., 143, 300n34
Sinclair, Alison, 100
Sushytska, Julia, 281n26
Socrate, Mario, 276n94
Spain: cultural identity of, ix–x, 1–3, 7–28, 33–35, 47, 49–51, 57, 114, 137, 144, 146, 221–24, 227–28, 237, 268n13, 269n22
Spires, Robert, 293n83
spontaneity, 16, 22, 42–43, 62, 71, 96, 110–14, 128, 135, 144–46, 151–53, 156, 192, 218, 220, 225, 239
Staël, Madame de, 66, 282n32
Suárez, Francisco, 25, 273n59

textuality, 60–63, 71, 73–74, 95–98, 135, 171, 192, 218–19, 229, 256, 258–59, 281n27, 306n45
Torre, Guillermo de, 173

Unamuno, Miguel de, 5, 14–18, 33, 37, 47, 50, 87, 91–135, 146, 160, 162, 164, 169, 188; 222–23, 260–62 265–66; correspondence with Ortega, 91–92, 103, 112, 115, 116, 119, 287n1, 296n 29, 297n45; Descartes and, 26–29, 132; Heidegger and, 116, 119–23; Kant and, 103–8, 116; Romanticism and, 99–100, 135

Valdés, Mario, 98, 109, 124–25
Valender, James, 241
Valente, José Ángel, 45
Valera, Juan, 1, 16–21, 263
Valéry, Paul, 199–203, 211, 301n53
Veit-Schlegel, Dorothea, 68, 71, 92
vitality. *See* life

Welch, John, 2, 282n34
Williams, Raymond, 59, 66
writing. *See* textuality
Wyers, Frances, 288n17

Zambrano, María, 14, 40–49, 207, 215–256; Derrida and, 255–6; Heidegger and, 230, 233, 251, 255; poetic reason and 40–49, 219–220, 221, 235, 239–40, 249–52, 253–54, 256, 278n125; Unamuno and, 106, 222
Ziarek, Krzysztof, 76–77, 79, 80–81, 285n70

www.ingramcontent.com/pod-product-compliance
Lightning Source LLC
Chambersburg PA
CBHW031431230426

43668CB00007B/493